I0625680

2007 (58th) Edition

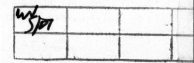

STANLEY GIBBONS LTD

By Appointment to H.M. the Queen
Stanley Gibbons Ltd, London Philatelists.

London and Ringwood

COLLECT BRITISH STAMPS

The 2007 edition

From the famous Penny Black of 1840 to the absorbing issues of today, the stamps of Great Britain are highly popular with collectors. *Collect British Stamps* has been our message since very early days – but particularly since the First Edition of this checklist in September 1967. This 58th edition includes all the recent issues. Prices have been carefully revised to reflect today's market. Total sales of *Collect British Stamps* are now over 3·8 million copies.

Collect British Stamps appears in the autumn of each year. A more detailed Great Britain catalogue, the *Concise,* is published each spring. The *Great Britain Concise* incorporates many additional listings covering watermark varieties, phosphor omitted errors, missing colour errors, stamp booklets and special commemorative First Day Cover postmarks. It is ideally suited for the collector who wishes to discover more about GB stamps.

Listings in this edition of *Collect British Stamps* include all 2006 issues which have appeared up to the publication date.

Scope. *Collect British Stamps* comprises:

- All stamps with different watermark (*wmk*) or perforation (*perf*).
- Visible plate numbers on the Victorian issues.
- Graphite-lined and phosphor issues, including variations in the numbers of phosphor bands.
- First Day Covers for Definitives from 1936, Regionals and all Special Issues.
- Presentation, Gift and Souvenir Packs.
- Post Office Yearbooks.
- Regional issues and War Occupation stamps of Guernsey and Jersey.
- Postage Due and Official Stamps.
- Post Office Picture Cards (PHQ cards).
- Commemorative gutter pairs and 'Traffic Light' gutter pairs listed as mint sets.
- Royal Mail Postage Labels priced as sets and on P.O. First Day Cover.

Stamps of the independent postal administrations of Guernsey, Isle of Man and Jersey are contained in *Collect Channel Islands and Isle of Man Stamps.*

Layout. Stamps are set out chronologically by date of issue. In the catalogue lists the first numeral is the Stanley Gibbons catalogue number; the black (boldface) numeral alongside is the type number referring to the respective illustration. A blank in this column implies that the number immediately above is repeated. The denomination and colour of the stamp are then shown. Before February 1971 British currency was:

£1 = 20s   One pound = twenty shillings *and*
1s = 12d   One shilling = twelve pence.

Upon decimalisation this became:

£1 = 100p   One pound = one hundred (new) pence.

The catalogue list then shows two price columns. The left-hand is for unused stamps and the right-hand for used. Corresponding small boxes are provided in which collectors may wish to check off the items in their collection.

Our method of indicating prices is:
Numerals for pence, e.g. 10 denotes 10p (10 pence). Numerals for pounds and pence, e.g. 4·25 denotes £4·25 (4 pounds and 25 pence). For £100 and above, prices are in whole pounds and so include the £ sign and omit the zeros for pence.

Colour illustrations. The colour illustrations of stamps are intended as a guide only; they may differ in shade from the originals.

Size of illustrations. To comply with Post Office regulations stamp illustrations are three-quarters linear side. Separate illustrations of surcharges, overprints and watermarks are actual size.

Prices. Prices quoted in this catalogue are our selling prices at the time the book went to press. They are for stamps in fine condition; in issues where condition varies we may ask more for the superb and less for the sub-standard. The unused prices for stamps of Queen Victoria to King George V are for lightly hinged examples. Unused prices for King Edward VIII to Queen Elizabeth II are for unmounted mint (though when not available unmounted, mounted stamps are often supplied at a lower price). Prices for used stamps refer to fine postally used copies. All prices are subject to change without prior notice and we give no guarantee to supply all stamps priced, since it is not possible to keep every catalogued item in stock. Individual low value stamps sold at 399, Strand are liable to an additional handling charge. Commemorative issues may only be available in complete sets.

In the price columns:

† = Does not exist.

(—) or blank = Exists, or may exist, but price cannot be quoted.

* = Not normally issued (the so-called 'Abnormals' of 1862–80).

Perforations. The 'perforation' is the number of holes in a length of 2 cm, as measured by the Gibbons *Instanta* gauge. The stamp is viewed against a dark background with the transparent gauge put on top of it. Perforations are quoted to the nearest half. Stamps without perforation are termed 'imperforate'.

From 1992 certain stamps occur with a large elliptical (oval) hole inserted in each line of vertical perforations. The £10 definitive, No. 1658, is unique in having two such holes in the horizontal perforations.

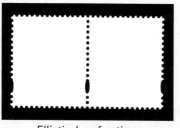

Elliptical perforations

Se-tenant combinations. *Se-tenant* means 'joined together'. Some sets include stamps of different design arranged *se-tenant* as blocks or strips and these are often collected unsevered as issued. Where such combinations exist the stamps are priced both mint and used, as singles or complete sets. The set price refers to the unsevered combination plus singles of any other values in the set.

First day covers. Prices for first day covers are for complete sets used on plain covers (Nos. 430/8, 453/60, 462/78b, 485/90, and 503/12) or on special covers (Nos. 461, 479/84, 491/502 and 513 onwards), the stamps of which are cancelled with ordinary operational postmarks (1924–1962) or by the *standard* 'First Day of Issue' postmarks (1963 onwards). The British Post Office did not provide 'First Day' treatment for every definitive issued after 1963. Where the stamps in a set were issued on different days, prices are for a cover from each day.

Presentation Packs. Special packs comprising slip-in cards with printed information inside a protective covering, were introduced for the 1964 Shakespeare issue. Collectors packs, containing commemoratives from the preceding twelve months, were issued from 1967. Some packs with text in German from 1968–69 exist as does a Japanese version of the pack for Nos. 916/17. Yearbooks, hardbound and illustrated in colour within a slip cover, joined the product range in 1984.

PHQ cards. Since 1973 the Post Office has produced a series of picture cards, which can be sent through the post as postcards. Each card shows an enlarged colour reproduction of a current British stamp, either of one or more values from a set or of all values. Cards are priced here in fine mint condition for sets complete as issued. The Post Office gives each card a 'PHQ' serial number, hence the term. The cards are usually on sale shortly before the date of issue of the stamps, but there is no officially designated 'first day'.

Used prices are for cards franked with the stamp depicted, on the obverse or reverse; the stamp being cancelled with an official postmark for first day of issue.

For 1973–76 issues cards with stamps on the obverse are worth about 25% more than the prices quoted.

Gutter pairs. Almost all modern Great Britain commemoratives are produced in sheets containing two panes of stamps separated by a blank horizontal or vertical margin known as a gutter. This feature first made its appearance on some supplies of the 1972 Royal Silver Wedding 3p, and marked the introduction of Harrison & Sons' new 'Jumelle' stamp-printing press. There are advantages for both the printer and the Post Office in such a lay-out which has now been used for almost all com-memorative issues since 1974.

The term 'gutter pair' is used for a pair of stamps separated by part of the blank gutter margin.

We do not list gutter pairs for self-adhesive stamps since, although the production format is the same, the stamps are separated by die-cutting.

Traffic light gutter pair

Catalogue numbers used. This checklist uses the same catalogue numbers as other current Stanley Gibbons catalogues.

Latest issue date for stamps recorded in this edition is 30 November 2006.

Gutter pair

Most printers include some form of colour check device on the sheet margins, in addition to the cylinder or plate numbers. Harrison & Sons used round 'dabs' or spots of colour, resembling traffic lights. For the period from the 1972 Royal Silver Wedding until the end of 1979 these colour dabs appeared in the gutter margin. Gutter pairs show-ing these 'traffic lights' are worth considerably more than the normal version.

From the 2004 Entente Cordiale set, Walsall reintroduced traffic lights in the gutters of certain sets. Where these extend over more than one sec-tion of gutter margin on any stamp they are priced as blocks rather than pairs.

STANLEY GIBBONS LTD

Head Office: 399 Strand, London WC2R OLX.
Auction Room and Specialist Stamp Departments–
Open Monday–Friday 9.30 a.m. to 5 p.m.
Shop – Open Monday to Friday 9 a.m. to 5.30 p.m.
and Saturday 9.30 a.m. to 5.30 p.m.
Telephone 0207-836 8444 for all departments
E-mail: enquiries@stanleygibbons.co.uk
Website: www.stanleygibbons.com

Stanley Gibbons Publications:
Parkside, Christchurch Road, Ringwood, Hants BH24 3SH. Telephone: 01425 472363
Publications Mail Order, FREEPHONE: 0800 611622
E-mail: info@stanleygibbons.co.uk

ISBN: 0-85259-637-5
© Stanley Gibbons Ltd 2006

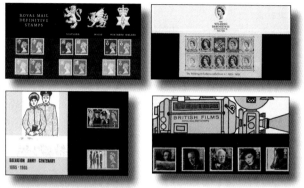

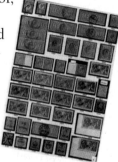

Commemorative Design Index

This index gives an easy reference to the inscriptions and designs of the Special Stamps 1953 to November 2006. Where a complete set shares an inscription or type of design, then only the catalogue number of the first stamp is given in addition to separate entries for stamps depicting popular thematic subjects. Paintings, inventions, etc., are indexed under the name of the artist or inventor, where this is shown on the stamp.

2. DECIMAL CURRENCY 1971–2004

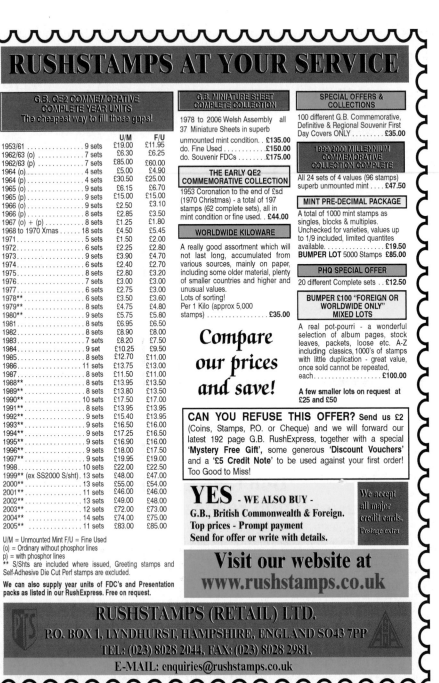

QUEEN VICTORIA

1837 (20 June)–1901 (22 Jan.)

IDENTIFICATION. In this checklist Victorian stamps are classified firstly according to which printing method was used –line-engraving, embossing or surface-printing.

Corner letters. Numerous stamps also have letters in all four, or just the lower corners. These were an anti-forgery device and the letters differ from stamp to stamp. If present in all four corners the upper pair are the reverse of the lower. Note the importance of these corner letters in the way the checklist is arranged.

Watermarks. Further classification depends on watermarks: these are illustrated in normal position, with stamps priced accordingly.

1854–57 (*i*) *Wmk Small Crown Type* **2** *Perf* 16

17	**1b**	1d red-brown	. . . . .	£275	20·00	☐	☐
19	**3**	2d blue	. . . .	£2750	85·00	☐	☐

(*ii*) *Wmk Small Crown Type* **2** *Perf* 14

24	**1b**	1d red-brown	. . . . .	£450	45·00	☐	☐
23	**3**	2d blue	. . . .	£5000	£200	☐	☐

(*iii*) *Wmk Large Crown Type* **4** *Perf* 16

26	**1b**	1d red	. . . .	£800	80·00	☐	☐
27	**3**	2d blue	. . . .	£6500	£350	☐	☐

(*iv*) *Wmk Large Crown Type* **4** *Perf* 14

40	**1b**	1d red	. . . .	40·00	9·00	☐	☐
34	**3**	2d blue	. . . .	£1900	50·00	☐	☐

7

1 Line-engraved Issues

1

1a

1b

5

8

6

3 White lines added above and below head

2 Small Crown watermark

4 Large Crown watermark

9 Watermark extending over three stamps

Letters in lower corners

1840 *Wmk Small Crown Type* **2** *Imperforate*

Cat No.	Type		Unused	Used		
2	**1**	1d black	£6000	£275	☐	☐
5	**1a**	2d blue	£15000	£650	☐	☐

1841

8	**1b**	1d red-brown	£400	15·00	☐	☐
14	**3**	2d blue	£3000	75·00	☐	☐

Letters in all four corners

Plate numbers. Stamps included a 'plate number' in their design and this affects valuation. The cheapest plates are priced here; see complete list of plate numbers overleaf.

1858–70 (*i*) *Wmk Type* **9** *Perf* 14

48	**7**	½d red	90·00	15·00	☐	☐

(*ii*) *Wmk Large Crown Type* **4** *Perf* 14

43	**5**	1d red	15·00	2·00	☐	☐
52	**8**	1½d red	£375	50·00	☐	☐
45	**6**	2d blue	£300	10·00	☐	☐

PLATE NUMBERS
on stamps of 1858–70 having letters in all four corners

Positions of Plate Numbers

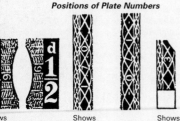

Shows Plate 9 ($\frac{1}{2}$d)

Shows Plate 170 (1d, 2d)

Shows Plate 3 (1$\frac{1}{2}$d)

HALFPENNY VALUE (S.G. 48)

Plate	Un.	Used			Plate	Un.	Used		
1	£225	70·00	☐ ☐		11	£110	15·00	☐ ☐
3	£150	35·00	☐ ☐		12	£100	15·00	☐ ☐
4	£130	25·00	☐ ☐		13	£100	15·00	☐ ☐
5	90·00	15·00	☐ ☐		14	£100	15·00	☐ ☐
6	£100	15·00	☐ ☐		15	£150	35·00	☐ ☐
8	£250	95·00	☐ ☐		19	£175	50·00	☐ ☐
9	£4500	£700	☐ ☐		20	£250	70·00	☐ ☐
10	£110	15·00	☐ ☐					

Plates 2, 7, 16, 17 and 18 were not completed, while Plates 21 and 22 though made were not used. Plate 9 was a reserve plate, not greatly used.

PENNY VALUE (S.G. 43)

Plate	Un.	Used			Plate	Un.	Used				Plate	Un.	Used			Plate	Un.	Used		
71	35·00	3·00	☐ ☐		112	70·00	2·25	☐ ☐			154	50·00	2·00	☐ ☐		190	50·00	6·00	☐ ☐
72	40·00	4·00	☐ ☐		113	50·00	12·00	☐ ☐			155	50·00	2·25	☐ ☐		191	30·00	7·00	☐ ☐
73	40·00	3·00	☐ ☐		114	£250	12·00	☐ ☐			156	45·00	2·00	☐ ☐		192	50·00	2·00	☐ ☐
74	40·00	2·00	☐ ☐		115	90·00	2·25	☐ ☐			157	50·00	2·00	☐ ☐		193	30·00	2·00	☐ ☐
76	35·00	2·00	☐ ☐		116	75·00	9·00	☐ ☐			158	30·00	2·00	☐ ☐		194	50·00	8·00	☐ ☐
77	(—)	£120000	☐ ☐		117	45·00	2·00	☐ ☐			159	30·00	2·00	☐ ☐		195	50·00	8·00	☐ ☐
78	90·00	2·00	☐ ☐		118	50·00	2·00	☐ ☐			160	30·00	2·00	☐ ☐		196	50·00	5·00	☐ ☐
79	30·00	2·00	☐ ☐		119	45·00	2·00	☐ ☐			161	60·00	7·00	☐ ☐		197	55·00	9·00	☐ ☐
80	45·00	2·00	☐ ☐		120	15·00	2·00	☐ ☐			162	50·00	7·00	☐ ☐		198	40·00	6·00	☐ ☐
81	45·00	2·20	☐ ☐		121	40·00	9·50	☐ ☐			163	50·00	3·00	☐ ☐		199	55·00	6·00	☐ ☐
82	90·00	4·00	☐ ☐		122	15·00	2·00	☐ ☐			164	50·00	3·00	☐ ☐		200	60·00	2·00	☐ ☐
83	£110	7·00	☐ ☐		123	40·00	2·00	☐ ☐			165	45·00	2·00	☐ ☐		201	30·00	5·00	☐ ☐
84	60·00	2·25	☐ ☐		124	28·00	2·00	☐ ☐			166	45·00	6·00	☐ ☐		202	60·00	8·00	☐ ☐
85	40·00	2·25	☐ ☐		125	40·00	2·00	☐ ☐			167	45·00	2·00	☐ ☐		203	30·00	16·00	☐ ☐
86	50·00	4·00	☐ ☐		127	55·00	2·25	☐ ☐			168	50·00	8·00	☐ ☐		204	55·00	2·25	☐ ☐
87	30·00	2·00	☐ ☐		129	40·00	8·00	☐ ☐			169	60·00	7·00	☐ ☐		205	55·00	3·00	☐ ☐
88	£130	8·00	☐ ☐		130	55·00	2·25	☐ ☐			170	35·00	2·00	☐ ☐		206	55·00	9·00	☐ ☐
89	40·00	2·00	☐ ☐		131	65·00	16·00	☐ ☐			171	15·00	2·00	☐ ☐		207	60·00	9·00	☐ ☐
90	40·00	2·00	☐ ☐		132	£130	22·00	☐ ☐			172	30·00	2·00	☐ ☐		208	55·00	16·00	☐ ☐
91	55·00	6·00	☐ ☐		133	£110	9·00	☐ ☐			173	70·00	9·00	☐ ☐		209	50·00	9·00	☐ ☐
92	35·00	2·00	☐ ☐		134	15·00	2·00	☐ ☐			174	30·00	2·00	☐ ☐		210	65·00	12·00	☐ ☐
93	50·00	2·00	☐ ☐		135	95·00	26·00	☐ ☐			175	60·00	3·50	☐ ☐		211	70·00	20·00	☐ ☐
94	45·00	5·00	☐ ☐		136	90·00	20·00	☐ ☐			176	60·00	2·25	☐ ☐		212	60·00	11·00	☐ ☐
95	40·00	2·00	☐ ☐		137	28·00	2·25	☐ ☐			177	40·00	2·00	☐ ☐		213	60·00	11·00	☐ ☐
96	45·00	2·00	☐ ☐		138	18·00	2·00	☐ ☐			178	60·00	3·50	☐ ☐		214	65·00	18·00	☐ ☐
97	40·00	3·50	☐ ☐		139	60·00	16·00	☐ ☐			179	50·00	2·25	☐ ☐		215	65·00	18·00	☐ ☐
98	50·00	6·00	☐ ☐		140	18·00	2·00	☐ ☐			180	60·00	5·00	☐ ☐		216	70·00	18·00	☐ ☐
99	55·00	5·00	☐ ☐		141	£110	9·00	☐ ☐			181	45·00	2·00	☐ ☐		217	70·00	7·00	☐ ☐
100	60·00	2·25	☐ ☐		142	70·00	24·00	☐ ☐			182	90·00	5·00	☐ ☐		218	65·00	8·00	☐ ☐
101	60·00	9·00	☐ ☐		143	60·00	15·00	☐ ☐			183	55·00	3·00	☐ ☐		219	90·00	70·00	☐ ☐
102	45·00	2·00	☐ ☐		144	95·00	20·00	☐ ☐			184	30·00	2·25	☐ ☐		220	40·00	7·00	☐ ☐
103	50·00	3·50	☐ ☐		145	30·00	2·25	☐ ☐			185	50·00	3·00	☐ ☐		221	70·00	16·00	☐ ☐
104	75·00	5·00	☐ ☐		146	40·00	6·00	☐ ☐			186	65·00	2·25	☐ ☐		222	80·00	40·00	☐ ☐
105	90·00	7·00	☐ ☐		147	50·00	3·00	☐ ☐			187	50·00	2·00	☐ ☐		223	90·00	60·00	☐ ☐
106	55·00	2·00	☐ ☐		148	40·00	3·00	☐ ☐			188	70·00	10·00	☐ ☐		224	£125	50·00	☐ ☐
107	60·00	7·00	☐ ☐		149	40·00	6·00	☐ ☐			189	70·00	7·00	☐ ☐		225	£2200	£650	☐ ☐
108	80·00	2·25	☐ ☐		150	15·00	2·00	☐ ☐✓											
109	85·00	3·50	☐ ☐		151	60·00	9·00	☐ ☐											
110	60·00	9·00	☐ ☐		152	60·00	5·50	☐ ☐											
111	50·00	2·25	☐ ☐		153	£100	9·00	☐ ☐											

Plates 69, 70, 75, 77, 126 and 128 were prepared but rejected. No stamps therefore exist, except for a very few from Plate 77 which somehow reached the public. Plate 177 stamps, by accident or design, are sometimes passed off as the rare Plate 77.

THREE-HALFPENNY VALUE (S.G. 52)

Plate	Un.	Used			Plate	Un.	Used		
(1)	£550	70·00	☐ ☐		3	£375	50·00	☐ ☐

Plate 1 did *not* have the plate number in the design. Plate 2 was not completed and no stamps exist.

TWOPENNY VALUE (S.G. 45)

Plate	Un.	Used			Plate	Un.	Used		
7	£1200	45·00	☐ ☐		13	£325	20·00	☐ ☐
8	£1000	32·00	☐ ☐		14	£425	25·00	☐ ☐
9	£300	10·00	☐ ☐		15	£400	25·00	☐ ☐
12	£1800	£120	☐ ☐					

Plates 10 and 11 were prepared but rejected.

2 Embossed Issues

Prices are for stamps cut square and with average to fine embossing. Stamps with exceptionally clear embossing are worth more.

12   11   10

13

1847–54 *Wmk* **13** *(6d), no wmk (others)* *Imperforate*

59	12	6d lilac	£6500	£800 ☐ ☐
57	11	10d brown	£5500	£1000 ☐ ☐
54	10	1s green	£8250	£750 ☐ ☐

3 Surface-printed Issues

IDENTIFICATION. Check first whether the design includes corner letters or not, as mentioned for 'Line-engraved Issues'. The checklist is divided up according to whether any letters are small or large, also whether they are white (uncoloured) or printed in the colour of the stamp. Further identification then depends on watermark.

PERFORATION. Except for Nos. 126/9 all the following issues of Queen Victoria are perf 14.

14

15 Small Garter   16 Medium Garter   17 Large Garter

18   19   20 Emblems

No corner letters

1855–57 *(i) Wmk Small Garter Type* **15**

62	14	4d red	£5000	£375 ☐ ☐

(ii) Wmk Medium Garter Type **16**

64	14	4d red	£4500	£350 ☐ ☐

(iii) Wmk Large Garter Type **17**

66a	14	4d red	£1100	£100 ☐ ☐

(iv) Wmk Emblems Type **20**

70	18	6d lilac	£900	95·00 ☐ ☐
72	19	1s green	£1250	£260 ☐ ☐

Plate numbers. Stamps Nos. 90/163 should be checked for the 'plate numbers' indicated, as this affects valuation (the cheapest plates are priced here). The mark *'Pl.'* shows that several numbers exist, priced in separate list overleaf.

Plate numbers are the small numerals appearing in duplicate in some part of the frame design or adjacent to the lower corner letters (in the 5s value a single numeral above the lower inscription).

21   22   23

24   25

Small white corner letters

1862–64 *Wmk Emblems Type* **20**, *except* 4d (*Large Garter Type* **17**)

76	21	3d red	£1500	£250 ☐ ☐
80	22	4d red	£1100	90·00 ☐ ☐
84	23	6d lilac	£1400	90·00 ☐ ☐
87	24	9d bistre	£2750	£350 ☐ ☐
90	25	1s green *Pl.*	£1700	£175 ☐ ☐

3

26 **27** **28** (hyphen in SIX-PENCE) **32** **33** Spray of Rose **34**

29 **30** **31**

Large white corner letters

1865–67 *Wmk Emblems Type* **20** *except* 4d (*Large Garter Type* **17**)

			Un	Used		
92	26	3d red (Plate 4)	£1350	£180	□	□
94	27	4d vermilion *Pl.*	£450	55·00	□	□
97	28	6d lilac *Pl.*	£725	80·00	□	□
98	29	9d straw *Pl.*	£2200	£500	□	□
99	30	10d brown (Plate 1) . . .	†	£25000		□
101	31	1s green (Plate 4)	£1450	£170	□	□

1867–80 *Wmk Spray of Rose Type* **33**

			Un	Used		
103	26	3d red *Pl.*	£450	55·00	□	□
105	28	6d lilac (with hyphen) (Plate 6)	£1100	80·00	□	□
109		6d mauve (without hyphen) *Pl.*	£500	80·00	□	□
110	29	9d straw (Plate 4)	£1700	£275	□	□
112	30	10d brown *Pl.*	£2300	£300	□	□
117	31	1s green *Pl.*	£650	35·00	□	□
119	32	2s blue *Pl.*	£2750	£175	□	□
121		2s brown (Plate 1) . . .	£15000	£2800	□	□

1872–73 *Wmk Spray of Rose Type* **33**

			Un	Used		
122b	34	6d brown *Pl.*	£550	50·00	□	□
125		6d grey (Plate 12)	£1400	£200	□	□

PLATE NUMBERS
on stamps of 1862–83

Cat No. / Plate No. / Un / Used

Small White Corner Letters (1862–64)

			Un	Used		
90	1s green	2	£1700	£175	□	□
		3	£20000		□	□

Plate 2 is actually numbered as '1' and Plate 3 as '2' on the stamps.

Large White Corner Letters (1865–83)

			Un	Used		
103	3d red	4	£825	£190	□	□
		5	£450	55·00	□	□
		6	£475	55·00	□	□
		7	£550	60·00	□	□
		8	£525	55·00	□	□
		9	£525	60·00	□	□
		10	£650	£110	□	□
94	4d verm	7	£500	£100	□	□
		8	£500	60·00	□	□
		9	£500	60·00	□	□
		10	£550	£110	□	□
		11	£500	60·00	□	□
		12	£475	55·00	□	□
		13	£500	55·00	□	□
		14	£550	85·00	□	□
97	6d lilac	5	£725	80·00	□	□
		6	£2200	£150	□	□
109	6d mauve	8	£500	£110	□	□
		9	£500	80·00	□	□
		10	*	£22000	□	□
122b	6d brown	11	£600	85·00	□	□
123	6d buff	12	£2000	£250	□	□
98	9d straw	4	£2200	£500	□	□
		5	£15000		□	□

			Un	Used		
112	10d brown	1	£2300	£300	□	□
		2	£22000	£8500	□	□
117	1s green	4	£825	50·00	□	□
		5	£650	35·00	□	□
		6	£1000	35·00	□	□
		7	£1000	60·00	□	□
119	2s blue	1	£2200	£175	□	□
		3	*	£7000	□	□
126	5s red	1	£5000	£600	□	□
		2	£7500	£950	□	□

Large Coloured Corner Letters (1873–83)

			Un	Used		
139	2½d mauve	1	£500	80·00	□	□
		2	£500	80·00	□	□
		3	£775	£120	□	□
141	2½d mauve	3	£925	£100	□	□
		4	£425	50·00	□	□
		5	£425	50·00	□	□
		6	£425	50·00	□	□
		7	£425	50·00	□	□
		8	£425	50·00	□	□
		9	£425	50·00	□	□
		10	£475	65·00	□	□
		11	£425	50·00	□	□
		12	£425	50·00	□	□
		13	£425	50·00	□	□
		14	£425	50·00	□	□
		15	£425	50·00	□	□
		16	£425	50·00	□	□
		17	£1250	£240	□	□
142	2½d blue	17	£375	55·00	□	□
		18	£400	40·00	□	□
		19	£375	40·00	□	□
		20	£375	40·00	□	□

			Un	Used		
157	2½d blue	21	£350	35·00	□	□
		22	£350	35·00	□	□
		23	£350	28·00	□	□
143	3d red	11	£350	45·00	□	□
		12	£400	45·00	□	□
		14	£425	45·00	□	□
		15	£350	45·00	□	□
		16	£350	45·00	□	□
		17	£400	45·00	□	□
		18	£400	45·00	□	□
		19	£350	45·00	□	□
		20	£480	85·00	□	□
158	3d red	20	£350	£130	□	□
		21	£400	80·00	□	□
152	4d verm	15	£1750	£425	□	□
		16	*	£22000	□	□
153	4d green	15	£1000	£275	□	□
		16	£900	£250	□	□
		17	*	£15000	□	□
160	4d brown	17	£350	60·00	□	□
		18	£350	60·00	□	□
147	6d grey	13	£400	60·00	□	□
		14	£400	60·00	□	□
		15	£400	60·00	□	□
		16	£400	60·00	□	□
		17	£675	£140	□	□
161	6d grey	17	£400	65·00	□	□
		18	£350	65·00	□	□
150	1s green	8	£575	£120	□	□
		9	£575	£120	□	□
		10	£575	£140	□	□
		11	£575	£120	□	□
		12	£500	£100	□	□
		13	£500	£100	□	□
		14	*	£22000	□	□
163	1s brown	13	£625	£140	□	□
		14	£500	£140	□	□

35

36

37

38

39 Maltese Cross

40 Large Anchor

1867–83 (*i*) *Wmk Maltese Cross Type* **39** *Perf* 15½ × 15

126	**35**	5s red *Pl.*	£5000	£600	□	□
128	**36**	10s grey (Plate 1)	£38000	£2500	□	□
129	**37**	£1 brown (Plate 1) . . .	£50000	£3750	□	□

(*ii*) *Wmk Large Anchor Type* **40** *Perf* 14

134	**35**	5s red (Plate 4)	£14000	£2700	□	□
135	**36**	10s grey (Plate 1)	£60000	£3500	□	□
132	**37**	£1 brown (Plate 1) . . .	£80000	£8000	□	□
137	**38**	£5 orange (Plate 1) . . .	£9000	£4000	□	□

41

42

43

44

45

46

47 Small Anchor

48 Orb

Large coloured corner letters

1873–80 (*i*) *Wmk Small Anchor Type* **47**

139	**41**	2½d mauve *Pl.*	£500	80·00	□	□

(*ii*) *Wmk Orb Type* **48**

141	**41**	2½d mauve *Pl.*	£425	50·00	□	□
142		2½d blue *Pl.*	£375	40·00	□	□

(*iii*) *Wmk Spray of Rose Type* **33**

143	**42**	3d red *Pl.*	£350	45·00	□	□
145	**43**	6d pale buff (Plate 13) .	* £15000		□	□
147		6d grey *Pl.*	£400	60·00	□	□
150	**44**	1s green *Pl.*	£500	£100	□	□
151		1s brown (Plate 13) . . .	£3250	£575	□	□

(*iv*) *Wmk Large Garter Type* **17**

152	**45**	4d vermilion *Pl.*	£1750	£425	□	□
153		4d green *Pl.*	£900	£250	□	□
154		4d brown (Plate 17) . . .	£1500	£450	□	□
156	**46**	8d orange (Plate 1) . . .	£1100	£300	□	□

49 Imperial Crown

(50) Surcharges in red (51)

1880–83 *Wmk Imperial Crown Type* **49**

157	**41**	2½d blue *Pl.*	£350	28·00	□	□
158	**42**	3d red *Pl.*	£400	80·00	□	□
159		3d on 3d lilac (surch Type 50)	£450	£130	□	□
160	**45**	4d brown *Pl.*	£350	60·00	□	□
161	**43**	6d grey *Pl.*	£350	65·00	□	□
162		6d on 6d lilac (surch Type 51)	£500	£130	□	□
163	**44**	1s brown *Pl.*	£500	£140	□	□

52

53

54

55

56

1880–81 *Wmk Imperial Crown Type* **49**

164	52	½d green	45·00	10·00	☐	☐
166	53	1d brown	22·00	10·00	☐	☐
167	54	1½d brown	£175	45·00	☐	☐
168	55	2d red	£225	90·00	☐	☐
169	56	5d indigo	£625	£110	☐	☐

57

Die I

Die II

1881 *Wmk Imperial Crown Type* **49**

(*a*) 14 dots in each corner, Die I

| 171 | 57 | 1d lilac | £200 | 30·00 | ☐ | ☐ |

(*b*) 16 dots in each corner, Die II

| 174 | 57 | 1d mauve | 2·50 | 1·50 | ☐ | ☐ |

58

59

60

Coloured letters in the corners

1883–84 *Wmk Anchor Type* **40**

178	58	2s 6d lilac	£450	£140	☐	☐
181	59	5s red	£775	£200	☐	☐
183	60	10s blue	£1700	£475	☐	☐

61

1884 *Wmk 3 Imperial Crowns Type* **49**

| 185 | 61 | £1 brown | £22000 | £2200 | ☐ | ☐ |

1888 *Wmk 3 Orbs Type* **48**

| 186 | 61 | £1 brown | £50000 | £3500 | ☐ | ☐ |

1891 *Wmk 3 Imperial Crowns Type* **49**

| 212 | 61 | £1 green | £3000 | £650 | ☐ | ☐ |

62

63

64

65

66

1883–84 *Wmk Imperial Crown Type* **49** (*sideways on horiz designs*)

187	52	½d blue	20·00	7·00	☐	☐
188	62	1½d lilac	95·00	38·00	☐	☐
189	63	2d lilac	£175	70·00	☐	☐
190	64	2½d lilac	75·00	12·00	☐	☐
191	65	3d lilac	£190	85·00	☐	☐
192	66	4d dull green	£425	£175	☐	☐
193	62	5d dull green	£425	£175	☐	☐
194	63	6d dull green	£450	£200	☐	☐
195	64	9d dull green	£875	£375	☐	☐
196	65	1s dull green	£950	£200	☐	☐

The above prices are for stamps in the true dull green colour. Stamps which have been soaked, causing the colour to run are virtually worthless.

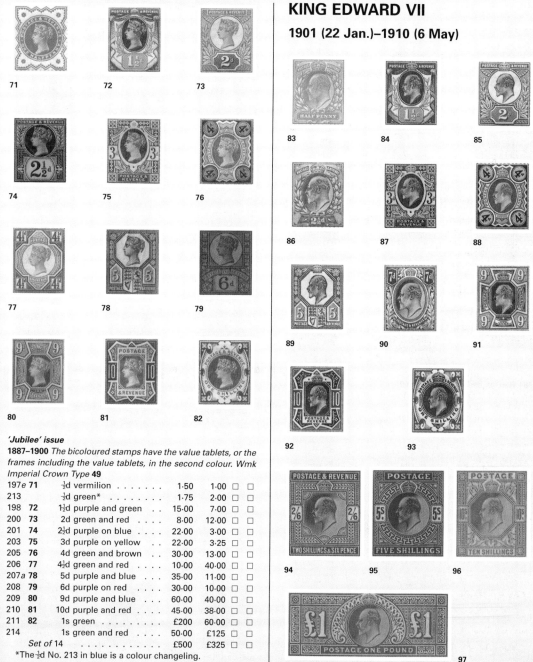

KING EDWARD VII

1901 (22 Jan.)–1910 (6 May)

'Jubilee' issue

1887–1900 *The bicoloured stamps have the value tablets, or the frames including the value tablets, in the second colour. Wmk Imperial Crown Type* **49**

197e	**71**	½d vermilion	1·50	1·00	☐	☐
213		½d green*	1·75	2·00	☐	☐
198	**72**	1½d purple and green . .	15·00	7·00	☐	☐
200	**73**	2d green and red	8·00	12·00	☐	☐
201	**74**	2½d purple on blue . . .	22·00	3·00	☐	☐
203	**75**	3d purple on yellow . .	22·00	3·25	☐	☐
205	**76**	4d green and brown . .	30·00	13·00	☐	☐
206	**77**	4½d green and red . . .	10·00	40·00	☐	☐
207a	**78**	5d purple and blue . . .	35·00	11·00	☐	☐
208	**79**	6d purple on red	30·00	10·00	☐	☐
209	**80**	9d purple and blue . . .	60·00	40·00	☐	☐
210	**81**	10d purple and red	45·00	38·00	☐	☐
211	**82**	1s green	£200	60·00	☐	☐
214		1s green and red	50·00	£125	☐	☐
	Set of 14	. . . .	£500	£325	☐	☐

*The ½d No. 213 in blue is a colour changeling.

7

1902–13 *Wmks Imperial Crown Type* **49** (½d to 1s), *Anchor Type* **40** (2s 6d to 10s), *Three Crowns Type* **49** (£1) (a) *Perf* 14

215	83	½d blue-green	2·00	1·50	□	□
217		½d yellow-green	2·00	1·50	□	□
219		1d red	2·00	1·50	□	□
221	84	1½d purple and green . .	35·00	18·00	□	□
291	85	2d green and red	25·00	20·00	□	□
231	86	2½d blue	20·00	10·00	□	□
234	87	3d purple on yellow	35·00	15·00	□	□
238	88	4d green and brown . .	40·00	18·00	□	□
240		4d orange	20·00	15·00	□	□
294	89	5d purple and blue . . .	30·00	20·00	□	□
297	83	6d purple	30·00	20·00	□	□
249	90	7d grey	10·00	18·00	□	□
307	91	9d purple and blue . . .	60·00	60·00	□	□
311	92	10d purple and red	70·00	60·00	□	□
314	93	1s green and red	55·00	35·00	□	□
260	94	2s 6d purple	£220	£140	□	□
318	95	5s red	£350	£180	□	□
265	96	10s blue	£650	£450	□	□
266	97	£1 green	£1600	£650	□	□
		Set of 15 (*to* 1s)	£400	£275	□	□

(b) *Perf* 15 × 14

279	83	½d green	40·00	45·00	□	□
281		1d red	15·00	15·00	□	□
283	86	2½d blue	22·00	15·00	□	□
285	87	3d purple on yellow . .	45·00	15·00	□	□
286	88	4d orange	30·00	15·00	□	□
		Set of 5	£130	90·00	□	□

KING GEORGE V

1910 (6 May)–1936 (20 Jan.)

PERFORATION. All the following issues are Perf 15 × 14 except vertical commemorative stamps which are 14 × 15, unless otherwise stated.

98 (Hair dark)   **99** (Lion unshaded)   **100**

1911–12 *Wmk Imperial Crown Type* **49**

322	98	½d green	4·00	4·00	□	□
327	99	1d red	4·50	2·50	□	□

1912 *Wmk Royal Cypher* ('Simple') *Type* **100**

335	98	½d green	40·00	40·00	□	□
336	99	1d red	30·00	30·00	□	□

101 (Hair light)   **102** (Lion shaded)   **103**

1912 *Wmk Imperial Crown Type* **49**

339	101	½d green	8·00	4·00	□	□
341	102	1d red	5·00	2·00	□	□

1912 *Wmk Royal Cypher* ('Simple') *Type* **100**

344	101	½d green	7·00	3·00	□	□
345	102	1d red	8·00	4·50	□	□

1912 *Wmk Royal Cypher* ('Multiple') *Type* **103**

346	101	½d green	12·00	8·00	□	□
350	102	1d red	18·00	10·00	□	□

104   **105**   **106**

107

108

111

1912–24 *Wmk Royal Cypher Type* **100**

351	105	½d green	1·00	1·00	□	□
357	104	1d red	1·00	1·00	□	□
362	105	1½d brown	4·00	1·50	□	□
368	106	2d orange	4·00	3·00	□	□
371	104	2½d blue	12·00	4·00	□	□
375	106	3d violet	5·00	3·00	□	□
379		4d grey-green	15·00	2·00	□	□
381	107	5d brown	15·00	5·00	□	□
385		6d purple	15·00	7·00	□	□
		a. Perf 14	90·00	£110	□	□
387		7d olive-green	20·00	10·00	□	□
390		8d black on yellow	32·00	11·00	□	□
392	108	9d black	15·00	6·00	□	□
393*a*		9d olive-green	£110	30·00	□	□
394		10d blue	22·00	20·00	□	□
395		1s brown	20·00	4·00	□	□
	Set of 15		£250	95·00	□	□

1913 *Wmk Royal Cypher* (*'Multiple'*) *Type* **103**

397	105	½d green	£150	£180	□	□
398	104	1d red	£225	£225	□	□

See also Nos. 418/29.

109

110

T 109. Background around portrait consists of horizontal lines

1913–18 *Wmk Single Cypher Type* **110** *Perf* 11 × 12

413*a*	109	2s 6d brown	£100	65·00	□	□
416		5s red	£250	£110	□	□
417		10s blue	£375	£160	□	□
403		£1 green	£2200	£1200	□	□
	Set of 4		£2250	£1200	□	□

See also Nos. 450/2.

1924–26 *Wmk Block Cypher Type* **111**

418	105	½d green	1·00	1·00	□	□
419	104	1d red	1·00	1·00	□	□
420	105	1½d brown	1·00	1·00	□	□
421	106	2d orange	2·50	2·50	□	□
422	104	2½d blue	5·00	3·00	□	□
423	106	3d violet	10·00	2·50	□	□
424		4d grey-green	12·00	2·50	□	□
425	107	5d brown	20·00	3·00	□	□
426*a*		6d purple	3·00	1·50	□	□
427	108	9d olive-green	12·00	3·50	□	□
428		10d blue	40·00	40·00	□	□
429		1s brown	22·00	3·00	□	□
	Set of 12		£110	60·00	□	□

112

112a

British Empire Exhibition

1924–25 *Wmk* **111** *Perf* 14 (*a*) 23.4.24. *Dated '1924'*

430	112	1d red	10·00	11·00	□	□
431	112a	1½d brown	15·00	15·00	□	□
	First Day Cover			£400		□

(*b*) 9.5.25. *Dated '1925'*

432	112	1d red	15·00	30·00	□	□
433	112a	1½d brown	40·00	70·00	□	□
	First Day Cover			£1500		□

113

114   115

116 St George and the Dragon

117

Ninth Universal Postal Union Congress
1929 (10 MAY) (a) Wmk **111**

434	113	½d green	2·25	2·25	☐	☐
435	114	1d red	2·25	2·25	☐	☐
436		1½d brown	2·25	1·75	☐	☐
437	115	2½d blue	10·00	10·00	☐	☐

(b) Wmk **117** Perf 12

438	116	£1 black	£750	£550	☐	☐
434/7 Set of 4	. . . .	15·00	14·50	☐	☐
434/7 First Day Cover (4 vals.)		£550	☐
434/8 First Day Cover (5 vals.)		£7500	☐

118

119

120

121

122

1934–36 Wmk **111**

439	118	½d green	50	50	☐	☐
440	119	1d red	50	50	☐	☐
441	118	1½d brown	50	50	☐	☐
442	120	2d orange	75	75	☐	☐
443	119	2½d blue	1·50	1·25	☐	☐
444	120	3d violet	1·50	1·25	☐	☐
445		4d grey-green	2·00	1·25	☐	☐
446	121	5d brown	6·50	2·75	☐	☐
447	122	9d olive-green	12·00	2·25	☐	☐
448		10d blue	15·00	10·00	☐	☐
449		1s brown	15·00	1·25	☐	☐
	Set of 11	. . . .	50·00	20·00	☐	☐

T 109 (re-engraved). Background around portrait consists of horizontal and diagonal lines
1934 Wmk **110** Perf 11 × 12

450	109	2s 6d brown	70·00	40·00	☐	☐
451		5s red	£160	85·00	☐	☐
452		10s blue	£340	80·00	☐	☐
	Set of 3	. . . .	£525	£190	☐	☐

123

123a

123b

123c

Silver Jubilee
1935 (7 MAY) Wmk **111**

453	123	½d green	1·00	1·00	☐	☐
454	123a	1d red	1·50	2·00	☐	☐
455	123b	1½d brown	1·00	1·00	☐	☐
456	123c	2½d blue	5·00	6·00	☐	☐
	Set of 4	. . . .	8·00	9·25	☐	☐
	First Day Cover		£600	☐

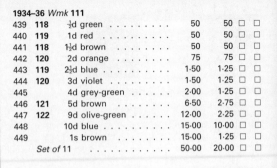

KING EDWARD VIII

1936 (20 Jan.–10 Dec.)

124

125

1936 *Wmk* **125**

457	**124**	½d green	30	30	☐	☐
458		1d red	60	50	☐	☐
459		1½d brown	30	30	☐	☐
460		2½d blue	30	85	☐	☐
	Set of 4	. . . .	1·25	1·75	☐	☐

First Day Covers

1 Sept. 1936	Nos. 457, 459/60	£150	☐
14 Sept. 1936	No. 458	£170	☐

Collectors are reminded that for issues from 1936 to date, prices in the unused column are for unmounted mint.

KING GEORGE VI

1936 (11 Dec.)–1952 (6 Feb.)

126 King George VI
and Queen Elizabeth

127

Coronation

1937 (13 May) *Wmk* **127**

461	**126**	1½d brown	30	30	☐	☐
		First Day Cover		35·00		☐

128

129

130

King George VI and National Emblems

1937–47 *Wmk* **127**

462	**128**	½d green	30	25	☐	☐
463		1d scarlet	30	25	☐	☐
464		1½d brown	30	25	☐	☐
465		2d orange	1·20	50	☐	☐
466		2½d blue	40	25	☐	☐
467		3d violet	5·00	1·00	☐	☐
468	**129**	4d green	60	75	☐	☐
469		5d brown	3·50	85	☐	☐
470		6d purple	1·50	60	☐	☐
471	**130**	7d green	5·00	60	☐	☐
472		8d red	7·50	80	☐	☐
473		9d deep green	6·50	80	☐	☐
474		10d blue	7·00	80	☐	☐
474a		11d plum	3·00	2·75	☐	☐
475		1s brown	9·00	75	☐	☐
	Set of 15	. . . .	45·00	10·00	☐	☐

First Day Covers

10 May 1937	Nos. 462/3, 466	45·00	☐
30 July 1937	No. 464	45·00	☐
31 Jan. 1938	Nos. 465, 467	95·00	☐
21 Nov. 1938	Nos. 468/9	60·00	☐
30 Jan. 1939	No. 470	55·00	☐
27 Feb. 1939	Nos. 471/2	80·00	☐
1 May 1939	Nos. 473/4, 475	£450	☐
29 Dec. 1947	No. 474a	50·00	☐

For later printings of the lower values in apparently lighter shades and different colours, see Nos. 485/90 and 503/8.

130a King George VI 131

132

132a

133

1939–48 *Wmk* **133** *Perf* 14

476	**130a**	2s 6d brown	. . . .	50·00	6·00	□	□
476*a*		2s 6d green	. . . .	11·00	1·50	□	□
477	**131**	5s red	. . . .	20·00	2·00	□	□
478	**132**	10s dark blue	. . . . . .	£225	20·00	□	□
478*a*		10s bright blue	. . . . .	35·00	5·00	□	□
478*b*	**132a**	£1 brown	. . . .	20·00	26·00	□	□
	Set of 6	. . . .		£300	55·00	□	□

First Day Covers

21 Aug. 1939	No. 477	. . . .	£750	□
4 Sept. 1939	No. 476	. . . .	£1500	□
30 Oct. 1939	No. 478	. . . .	£2750	□
9 Mar. 1942	No. 476*a*	. . . .	£1500	□
30 Nov. 1942	No. 478*a*	. . . .	£3250	□
1 Oct. 1948	No. 478*b*	. . . .	£275	□

134 Queen Victoria and King George VI

Centenary of First Adhesive Postage Stamps

1940 (6 MAY) *Wmk* **127** *Perf* $14\frac{1}{2} \times 14$

479	**134**	½d green	. . . .	30	75	□	□
480		1d red	. . . .	1·00	75	□	□
481		1½d brown	. . . .	50	1·50	□	□
482		2d orange	. . . .	1·00	75	□	□
483		2½d blue	. . . .	2·25	50	□	□
484		3d violet	. . . .	3·00	3·50	□	□
	Set of 6	. . . .	8·75	5·25	□	□
	First Day Cover	. . . .		55·00		□

Head as Nos. 462–7, but with lighter background

1941–42 *Wmk* **127**

485	**128**	½d pale green	. . . . . .	30	30	□	□
486		1d pale red	. . . .	30	30	□	□
487		1½d pale brown	. . . . . .	60	80	□	□
488		2d pale orange	. . . . .	50	50	□	□
489		2½d light blue	. . . .	30	30	□	□
490		3d pale violet	. . . . . .	2·50	1·00	□	□
	Set of 6	. . . .	3·50	2·75	□	□

First Day Covers

21 July 1941	No. 489	. . . .	45·00	□
11 Aug. 1941	No. 486	. . . .	22·00	□
1 Sept. 1941	No. 485	. . . .	22·00	□
6 Oct. 1941	No. 488	. . . .	60·00	□
3 Nov. 1941	No. 490	. . . .	£110	□
28 Sept. 1942	No. 487	. . . .	55·00	□

135 Symbols of Peace and Reconstruction

136 Symbols of Peace and Reconstruction

Victory

1946 (11 JUNE) *Wmk* **127**

491	**135**	2½d blue	. . . .	20	20	□	□
492	**136**	3d violet	. . . .	20	50	□	□
	First Day Cover	. . . .		65·00		□

137 King George VI and Queen Elizabeth

138 King George VI and Queen Elizabeth

Royal Silver Wedding

1948 (26 APR.) *Wmk* **127**

493	**137**	2½d blue	. . . .	35	20	□	□
494	**138**	£1 blue	. . . .	40·00	40·00	□	□
	First Day Cover	. . . .		£425		□

1948 (10 MAY)

Stamps of 1d and 2½d showing seaweed-gathering were on sale at eight Head Post Offices elsewhere in Great Britain, but were primarily for use in the Channel Islands and are listed there (see after Regional Issues).

139 Globe and Laurel Wreath

140 Speed

141 Olympic Symbol

142 Winged Victory

Olympic Games

1948 (29 JULY) *Wmk* **127**

495	**139**	2½d blue	35	10 □ □
496	**140**	3d violet	35	50 □ □
497	**141**	6d purple	1·25	40 □ □
498	**142**	1s brown	2·00	1·50 □ □
		Set of 4	3·50	2·00 □ □
		First Day Cover		45·00 □

143 Two Hemispheres

144 U.P.U. Monument, Berne

145 Goddess Concordia, Globe and Points of Compass

146 Posthorn and Globe

75th Anniversary of Universal Postal Union

1949 (10 OCT.) *Wmk* **127**

499	**143**	2½d blue	25	10 □ □
500	**144**	3d violet	25	50 □ □
501	**145**	6d purple	50	75 □ □
502	**146**	1s brown	1·00	1·25 □ □
		Set of 4	1·50	2·50 □ □
		First Day Cover		80·00 □

4d as No. 468 and others as Nos. 485/9, but colours changed

1950–51 *Wmk* **127**

503	**128**	½d pale orange	30	30 □ □
504		1d light blue	30	30 □ □
505		1½d pale green	65	60 □ □
506		2d pale brown	75	40 □ □
507		2½d pale red	60	40 □ □
508	**129**	4d light blue	2·00	1·75 □ □
		Set of 6	4·00	3·25 □ □

First Day Covers

2 Oct. 1950	No. 508	£120 □
3 May 1951	Nos. 503/7	55·00 □

147 HMS *Victory*

148 White Cliffs of Dover

149 St George and the Dragon

150 Royal Coat of Arms

1951 (3 MAY) *Wmk* **133** *Perf* 11 × 12

509	**147**	2s 6d green	2·00	1·00 □ □
510	**148**	5s red	40·00	1·00 □ □
511	**149**	10s blue	10·00	7·50 □ □
512	**150**	£1 brown	48·00	18·00 □ □
		Set of 4	95·00	25·00 □ □
		First Day Cover		£925 □

151 Commerce and Prosperity

152 Festival Symbol

Festival of Britain

1951 (3 MAY) *Wmk* **127**

513	**151**	2½d red	20	15 □ □
514	**152**	4d blue	30	35 □ □
		Set of 2	40	40 □ □
		First Day Cover		38·00 □

QUEEN ELIZABETH II
6 February, 1952

153 Tudor Crown

154

155

156

157

158

159

160

161

162

163

164

1952–54 *Wmk* **153**

515	**154**	½d orange		10	15 □ □
516		1d blue		20	20 □ □
517		1½d green		10	20 □ □
518		2d brown		20	20 □ □
519	**155**	2½d red		15	15 □ □
520		3d lilac		1·50	90 □ □
521	**156**	4d blue		3·25	1·25 □ □
		4½d *(See Nos.* 577, 594, 609 *and* 616*b)*			
522	**157**	5d brown		75	3·50 □ □
523		6d purple		4·00	1·00 □ □
524		7d green		9·50	5·50 □ □
525	**158**	8d magenta		75	85 □ □
526		9d bronze-green		23·00	4·75 □ □
527		10d blue		18·00	4·75 □ □
528		11d plum		35·00	15·00 □ □
529	**159**	1s bistre		80	50 □ □
530	**160**	1s 3d green		4·50	3·25 □ □
531	**159**	1s 6d indigo		14·00	3·75 □ □
	Set of 17			£100	40·00 □ □

First Day Covers

5 Dec. 1952	Nos. 517, 519		25·00 □
6 July 1953	Nos. 522, 525, 529		50·00 □
31 Aug. 1953	Nos. 515/16, 518		50·00 □
2 Nov. 1953	Nos. 521, 530/1		£170 □
18 Jan. 1954	Nos. 520, 523/4		£110 □
8 Feb. 1954	Nos. 526/8		£225 □

See also Nos. 540/56, 561/6, 570/94 and 599/618*a* and for stamps as Types **154/60** with face values in decimal currency see Nos. 2031/3, 2258/9, **MS**2326, **MS**2367 and 2378/9.

Coronation
1953 (3 JUNE) *Wmk* **153**

532	**161**	2½d red		20	25 □ □
533	**162**	4d blue		1·10	1·90 □ □
534	**163**	1s 3d green		5·00	3·00 □ □
535	**164**	1s 6d blue		10·00	4·75 □ □
	Set of 4			16·00	9·00 □ □
	First Day Cover			75·00	□

For £1 values as Type **163** see Nos. **MS**2147 and 2380.

165 St Edward's Crown

166 Carrickfergus Castle

167 Caernarvon Castle

168 Edinburgh Castle

169 Windsor Castle

1955 (1–23 SEPT.) *Wmk* **165** *Perf* 11 × 12

536	**166**	2s 6d brown		9·00	2·00 □ □
537	**167**	5s red		35·00	4·00 □ □

538	**168**	10s blue	85·00	14·00	□	□
539	**169**	£1 black	£130	35·00	□	□
		Set of 4	£225	50·00	□	□

First Day Cover (Nos. 538/9)
(1 Sept.) . . . . £800 □

First Day Cover (Nos. 536/7)
(23 Sept.) . . . . £600 □

See also Nos. 595a/8a and 759/62.

1955–58 *Wmk* **165**

540	**154**	½d orange	15	15	□	□
541		1d blue	30	15	□	□
542		1½d green	25	30	□	□
543		2d red-brown	25	35	□	□
543b		2d light red-brown . . .	20	20	□	□
544	**155**	2½d red	20	25	□	□
545		3d lilac	25	25	□	□
546	**156**	4d blue	1·25	25	□	□
547	**157**	5d brown	6·00	6·00	□	□
548		6d purple	4·50	1·25	□	□
549		7d green	50·00	10·00	□	□
550	**158**	8d magenta	7·00	1·25	□	□
551		9d bronze-green	20·00	2·75	□	□
552		10d blue	20·00	2·75	□	□
553		11d plum	50	1·10	□	□
554	**159**	1s bistre	22·00	65	□	□
555	**160**	1s 3d green	30·00	1·60	□	□
556	**159**	1s 6d indigo	23·00	1·60	□	□
		Set of 18	£160	27·00	□	□

170 Scout Badge and 'Rolling Hitch'

171 'Scouts coming to Britain'

172 Globe within a Compass

173

World Scout Jubilee Jamboree
1957 (1 Aug.) *Wmk* **165**

557	**170**	2½d red	50	50	□	□
558	**171**	4d blue	75	1·50	□	□
559	**172**	1s 3d green	4·50	4·50	□	□
		Set of 3	5·00	5·75	□	□
		First Day Cover		25·00		□

46th Inter Parliamentary Union Conference
1957 (12 Sept.) *Wmk* **165**

560	**173**	4d blue	1·00	1·00	□	□
		First Day Cover		£140		□

Graphite-lined and Phosphor Issues

These are used in connection with automatic sorting machinery, originally experimentally at Southampton but now also operating elsewhere. In such areas these stamps were the normal issue, but from mid 1967 *all* low-value stamps bear phosphor markings.

The graphite lines were printed in black on the back, beneath the gum; two lines per stamp except for the 2d *(see below)*.

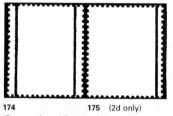

174   **175**   (2d only)
(Stamps viewed from back)

In November 1959, phosphor bands, printed on the front, replaced the graphite. They are wider than the graphite, not easy to see, but show as broad vertical bands at certain angles to the light.

Values representing the rate for printed papers (and second class mail from 1968) have one band and others have two, three or four bands according to size and format. From 1972 onwards some commemorative stamps were printed with 'all-over' phosphor.

In the small stamps the bands are on each side with the single band at left (except where otherwise stated). In the large-size commemorative stamps the single band may be at left, centre or right varying in different issues. The bands are vertical on both horizontal and vertical designs except where otherwise stated.

See also notes on page 37.

Graphite-lined issue

1957 (19 Nov.) *Two graphite lines on the back, except* 2d *value, which has one line. Wmk* **165**

561	**154**	½d orange	25	25	□	□
562		1d blue	40	40	□	□
563		1½d green	1·20	1·40	□	□
564		2d light red-brown . . .	1·60	2·25	□	□
565	**155**	2½d red	8·50	7·00	□	□
566		3d lilac	80	50	□	□
		Set of 6	12·00	10·50	□	□
		First Day Cover		85·00		□

See also Nos. 587/94.

176 Welsh Dragon

177 Flag and Games Emblem

178 Welsh Dragon

Sixth British Empire and Commonwealth Games, Cardiff
1958 (18 JULY) *Wmk* **165**

567	**176**	3d lilac	. . . .	20	20 ☐ ☐
568	**177**	6d mauve	. . . .	40	45 ☐ ☐
569	**178**	1s 3d green	. . . .	2·25	2·40 ☐ ☐
	Set of 3		. . . .	2·50	2·75 ☐ ☐
	First Day Cover	. . . .		75·00 ☐

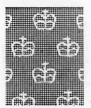

179 Multiple Crowns

WATERMARK. All the following issues to No. 755 are Watermark **179** (sideways on the vertical commemorative stamps) unless otherwise stated.

1958–65 *Wmk* **179**

570	**154**	½d orange	. . . .	10	10 ☐ ☐
571		1d blue	. . . .	10	10 ☐ ☐
572		1½d green	. . . .	10	15 ☐ ☐
573		2d light red-brown	. . .	10	10 ☐ ☐
574	**155**	2½d red	. . . .	10	20 ☐ ☐
575		3d lilac	. . . .	10	20 ☐ ☐
576a	**156**	4d blue	. . . .	15	15 ☐ ☐
577		4½d brown	. . . .	10	25 ☐ ☐
578	**157**	5d brown	. . . .	30	40 ☐ ☐
579		6d purple	. . . .	30	25 ☐ ☐
580		7d green	. . . .	50	45 ☐ ☐
581	**158**	8d magenta	. . . .	60	40 ☐ ☐
582		9d bronze-green	. . . . .	60	40 ☐ ☐
583		10d blue	. . . .	1·00	50 ☐ ☐
584	**159**	1s bistre	. . . .	45	30 ☐ ☐
585	**160**	1s 3d green	. . . .	45	30 ☐ ☐
586	**159**	1s 6d indigo	. . . .	4·00	40 ☐ ☐
	Set of 17		. . . .	8·00	4·25 ☐ ☐
	First Day Cover	(No. 577)			
	(9 Feb. 1959)	. . . .		£250 ☐

For full information on all future British issues, collectors should write to Royal Mail, Freepost EH3647, 21 South Gyle Crescent, Edinburgh EH12 9PE.

Graphite-lined issue
1958–59 *Two graphite lines on the back, except* 2d *value, which has one line. Wmk* **179**

587	**154**	½d orange	. . . .	3·25	4·00 ☐ ☐
588		1d blue	. . . .	1·50	1·50 ☐ ☐
589		1½d green	. . . .	60·00	48·00 ☐ ☐
590		2d light red-brown	. . .	9·00	3·50 ☐ ☐
591	**155**	2½d red	. . . .	10·00	10·00 ☐ ☐
592		3d lilac	. . . .	50	65 ☐ ☐
593	**156**	4d blue	. . . .	5·50	5·00 ☐ ☐
594		4½d brown	. . . .	6·50	5·00 ☐ ☐
	Set of 8		. . . .	85·00	70·00 ☐ ☐

The prices quoted for Nos. 587 and 589 are for examples with inverted watermark. Stamps with upright watermark are priced at: ½d £9 *mint*, £9 *used and* 1½d £90 *mint*, £80 *used*.

1959–63 *Wmk* **179** *Perf* 11 × 12

595a	**166**	2s 6d brown	. . . . . .	35	40 ☐ ☐
596a	**167**	5s red	. . . .	1·20	50 ☐ ☐
597a	**168**	10s blue	. . . .	4·50	4·50 ☐ ☐
598a	**169**	£1 black	. . . .	11·00	8·00 ☐ ☐
	Set of 4		. . . .	15·00	11·00 ☐ ☐

Phosphor-Graphite issue
1959 (18 Nov.) *Two phosphor bands on front and two graphite lines on back, except* 2d *value, which has one band on front and one line on back* (a) *Wmk* **165**

599	**154**	½d orange	. . . .	4·00	3·75 ☐ ☐
600		1d blue	. . . .	11·00	11·00 ☐ ☐
601		1½d green	. . . .	4·00	4·00 ☐ ☐

			(b) *Wmk* **179**			
605	**154**	2d light red-brown			
		(1 band)	. . . .	5·00	4·25 ☐ ☐
606	**155**	2½d red	. . . .	22·00	18·00 ☐ ☐
607		3d lilac	. . . .	10·00	8·00 ☐ ☐
608	**156**	4d blue	. . . .	20·00	16·00 ☐ ☐
609		4½d brown	. . . .	30·00	20·00 ☐ ☐
	Set of 8		. . . .	85·00	70·00 ☐ ☐

Phosphor issue
1960–67 *Two phosphor bands on front, except where otherwise stated. Wmk* **179**

610	**154**	½d orange	. . . .	10	15 ☐ ☐
611		1d blue	. . . .	10	10 ☐ ☐
612		1½d green	. . . .	15	15 ☐ ☐
613		2d light red-brown			
		(1 band)	. . . .	16·00	18·00 ☐ ☐
613a		2d light red-brown			
		(2 bands)	. . . .	10	15 ☐ ☐
614	**155**	2½d red (2 bands)	. . . .	20	30 ☐ ☐
614a		2½d red (1 band)	. . . .	60	75 ☐ ☐
615		3d lilac (2 bands)	. . . .	60	55 ☐ ☐
615c		3d lilac (1 side band)	. .	60	55 ☐ ☐
615e		3d lilac (1 centre band)		40	45 ☐ ☐
616a	**156**	4d blue	. . . .	25	25 ☐ ☐
616b		4½d brown	. . . .	25	30 ☐ ☐

616c	**157**	5d brown	. . . .	25		35	☐	☐
617		6d purple	. . . .	30		30	☐	☐
617a		7d green		55		50	☐	☐
617b	**158**	8d magenta	. . . . . .	40		45	☐	☐
617c		9d bronze-green	. . . .	60		55	☐	☐
617d		10d blue	. . . .	70		60	☐	☐
617e	**159**	1s bistre	. . . .	40		35	☐	☐
618	**160**	1s 3d green	. . . .	1·90		2·50	☐	☐
618a	**159**	1s 6d indigo	. . . . . .	2·00		2·00	☐	☐
		Set of 17 (one of each value)	. .	7·50		8·00	☐	☐

No. 615c exists with the phosphor band at the left or right of the stamp.

180   Postboy of 1660   **181**   Posthorn of 1660

Tercentenary of Establishment of 'General Letter Office'
1960 (7 July)

619	**180**	3d lilac	. . . .	50	50	☐	☐
620	**181**	1s 3d green	. . . .	3·75	4·25	☐	☐
		Set of 2	. . . .	3·75	4·25	☐	☐
		First Day Cover	. . . .		55·00		☐

182   Conference Emblem

First Anniversary of European Postal and Telecommunications Conference
1960 (19 Sept.)

621	**182**	6d green and purple	. .	1·50	50	☐	☐
622		1s 6d brown and blue	. . .	8·50	5·00	☐	☐
		Set of 2	. . . .	9·75	5·50	☐	☐
		First Day Cover	. . . .		55·00		☐

183   Thrift Plant   **184**   'Growth of Savings'

185   Thrift Plant

Centenary of Post Office Savings Bank
1961 (28 Aug.)

623A	**183**	2½d black and red	. . . .	25	25	☐	☐
624A	**184**	3d orange-brown and violet	. . . .	20	20	☐	☐
625A	**185**	1s 6d red and blue	. . . .	2·50	2·25	☐	☐
		Set of 3	. . . .	2·75	2·50	☐	☐
		First Day Cover	. . . .		65·00		☐

186   C.E.P.T. Emblem   **187**   Doves and Emblem

188   Doves and Emblem

European Postal and Telecommunications (C.E.P.T.) Conference, Torquay
1961 (18 Sept.)

626	**186**	2d orange, pink and brown	. . . .	15	10	☐	☐
627	**187**	4d buff, mauve and ultramarine	. . . . .	15	15	☐	☐
628	**188**	10d turquoise, green and blue	. . . .	15	50	☐	☐
		Set of 3	. . . .	40	60	☐	☐
		First Day Cover	. . . .		6·00		☐

189   Hammer Beam Roof, Westminster Hall   **190**   Palace of Westminster

Seventh Commonwealth Parliamentary Conference
1961 (25 SEPT.)

629	**189**	6d purple and gold ...	25	25 ☐ ☐
630	**190**	1s 3d green and blue ...	2·50	2·75 ☐ ☐
		Set of 2	2·75	3·00 ☐ ☐
		First Day Cover		30·00 ☐

191 'Units of Productivity'

192 'National Productivity'

193 'Unified Productivity'

National Productivity Year
1962 (14 Nov.) *Wmk* **179** (*inverted on* 2½d *and* 3d)

631	**191**	2½d green and red	20	20 ☐ ☐
		p. Phosphor	60	50 ☐ ☐
632	**192**	3d blue and violet	50	25 ☐ ☐
		p. Phosphor	1·50	80 ☐ ☐
633	**193**	1s 3d red, blue and green .	1·50	1·80 ☐ ☐
		p. Phosphor	35·00	22·00 ☐ ☐
		Set of 3 (*Ordinary*)	2·00	1·90 ☐ ☐
		Set of 3 (*Phosphor*)	30·00	22·00 ☐ ☐
		First Day Cover (*Ordinary*)		48·00 ☐
		First Day Cover (*Phosphor*) ...		£150 ☐

194 Campaign Emblem and Family

195 Children of Three Races

Freedom from Hunger
1963 (21 MAR.) *Wmk* **179** (*inverted*)

634	**194**	2½d crimson and pink ..	25	10 ☐ ☐
		p. Phosphor	3·00	1·25 ☐ ☐
635	**195**	1s 3d brown and yellow ..	1·90	1·90 ☐ ☐
		p. Phosphor	30·00	23·00 ☐ ☐
		Set of 2 (*Ordinary*)	2·00	2·00 ☐ ☐
		Set of 2 (*Phosphor*)	30·00	24·00 ☐ ☐
		First Day Cover (*Ordinary*)		32·00 ☐
		First Day Cover (*Phosphor*) ...		52·00 ☐

196 'Paris Conference'

Paris Postal Conference Centenary
1963 (7 MAY) *Wmk* **179** (*inverted*)

636	**196**	6d green and mauve ..	50	50 ☐ ☐
		p. Phosphor	6·00	7·00 ☐ ☐
		First Day Cover (*Ordinary*)		16·00 ☐
		First Day Cover (*Phosphor*) ...		37·00 ☐

197 Posy of Flowers

198 Woodland Life

National Nature Week
1963 (16 MAY)

637	**197**	3d multicoloured	15	15 ☐ ☐
		p. Phosphor	60	60 ☐ ☐
638	**198**	4½d multicoloured	35	35 ☐ ☐
		p. Phosphor	3·00	3·00 ☐ ☐
		Set of 2 (*Ordinary*)	50	50 ☐ ☐
		Set of 2 (*Phosphor*)	3·50	3·50 ☐ ☐
		First Day Cover (*Ordinary*)		22·00 ☐
		First Day Cover (*Phosphor*) ...		40·00 ☐

199 Rescue at Sea

200 19th-century Lifeboat

201 Lifeboatmen

Ninth International Lifeboat Conference, Edinburgh
1963 (31 MAY)

639	**199**	2½d blue, black and red .	25	25 ☐ ☐
		p. Phosphor	50	60 ☐ ☐
640	**200**	4d multicoloured	50	50 ☐ ☐
		p. Phosphor	50	60 ☐ ☐

641　**201**　1s 6d sepia, yellow and
blue . . . .　3·00　3·25 ☐ ☐
　　　　　p. Phosphor . . . .　48·00　28·00 ☐ ☐
Set of 3 (*Ordinary*) . . . .　3·25　3·50 ☐ ☐
Set of 3 (*Phosphor*) . . . .　48·00　28·00 ☐ ☐
First Day Cover (*Ordinary*) . . . .　35·00 ☐
First Day Cover (*Phosphor*) . . .　55·00 ☐

202　Red Cross　　**203**

204

Red Cross Centenary Congress
1963 (15 AUG.)
642　**202**　3d red and lilac . . . . .　25　25 ☐ ☐
　　　　　p. Phosphor . . . .　1·10　1·00 ☐ ☐
643　**203**　1s 3d red, blue and grey . .　3·00　3·00 ☐ ☐
　　　　　p. Phosphor . . . .　35·00　27·00 ☐ ☐
644　**204**　1s 6d red, blue and bistre . .　3·00　3·00 ☐ ☐
　　　　　p. Phosphor . . . .　35·00　27·00 ☐ ☐
Set of 3 (*Ordinary*) . . . .　5·00　5·75 ☐ ☐
Set of 3 (*Phosphor*) . . . .　65·00　55·00 ☐ ☐
First Day Cover (*Ordinary*) . . . .　40·00 ☐
First Day Cover (*Phosphor*) . . .　90·00 ☐

205　'Commonwealth Cable'

Opening of COMPAC (Trans-Pacific Telephone Cable)
1963 (3 DEC.)
645　**205**　1s 6d blue and black . . . .　2·75　2·50 ☐ ☐
　　　　　p. Phosphor . . . .　16·00　15·50 ☐ ☐
First Day Cover (*Ordinary*) . . . .　28·00 ☐
First Day Cover (*Phosphor*) . . .　40·00 ☐

206　Puck and Bottom　　**207**　Feste (*Twelfth Night*)
(*A Midsummer
Night's Dream*)

208　Balcony Scene　　**209**　'Eve of Agincourt'
(*Romeo and Juliet*)　　　(*Henry V*)

210　Hamlet contemplating
Yorick's skull (*Hamlet*)
and Queen Elizabeth II

Shakespeare Festival
1964 (23 APR.)　*Perf* 11 × 12 (2s 6d) *or* 15 × 14 (*others*)
646　**206**　3d bistre, black and
violet-blue . . . . . .　15　15 ☐ ☐
　　　　　p. Phosphor . . . .　25　30 ☐ ☐
647　**207**　6d multicoloured . . . .　30　30 ☐ ☐
　　　　　p. Phosphor . . . .　75　1·00 ☐ ☐
648　**208**　1s 3d multicoloured . . . .　75　1·00 ☐ ☐
　　　　　p. Phosphor . . . .　4·00　6·50 ☐ ☐
649　**209**　1s 6d multicoloured . . . .　1·00　85 ☐ ☐
　　　　　p. Phosphor . . . .　8·00　8·00 ☐ ☐
650　**210**　2s 6d deep slate-purple . . .　2·75　2·75 ☐ ☐
Set of 5 (*Ordinary*) . . . .　4·50　4·50 ☐ ☐
Set of 4 (*Phosphor*) . . . .　12·00　14·00 ☐ ☐
First Day Cover (*Ordinary*) . . . .　12·00 ☐
First Day Cover (*Phosphor*) . . .　17·00 ☐
Presentation Pack (*Ordinary*) . .　22·00　　☐

PRESENTATION PACKS were first introduced by the G.P.O. for the Shakespeare Festival issue. The packs include one set of stamps and details of the designs, the designer and the stamp printer. They were issued for almost all later definitive and special issues.

211　Flats near Richmond Park　**212**　Shipbuilding Yards, Belfast
('Urban Development')　　　　('Industrial Activity')

213　Beddgelert Forest Park,　**214**　Nuclear Reactor, Dounreay
Snowdonia ('Forestry')　　　　('Technological Development')

20th International Geographical Congress, London

1964 (1 JULY)

651	**211**	2½d multicoloured	10	10 □	□
		p. Phosphor	40	50 □	□
652	**212**	4d multicoloured	30	30 □	□
		p. Phosphor	1·25	1·25 □	□
653	**213**	8d multicoloured	75	85 □	□
		p. Phosphor	2·50	2·75 □	□
654	**214**	1s 6d multicoloured	3·50	3·50 □	□
		p. Phosphor	28·00	22·00 □	□
		Set of 4 (Ordinary)	4·50	4·50 □	□
		Set of 4 (Phosphor)	30·00	24·00 □	□
		First Day Cover (Ordinary)		22·00	□
		First Day Cover (Phosphor) . . .		40·00	□
		Presentation Pack (Ordinary) . .	£160		□

215 Spring Gentian

216 Dog Rose

217 Honeysuckle

218 Fringed Water Lily

Tenth International Botanical Congress, Edinburgh

1964 (5 AUG.)

655	**215**	3d violet, blue and green	25	25 □	□
		p. Phosphor	40	40 □	□
656	**216**	6d multicoloured	50	50 □	□
		p. Phosphor	2·50	2·75 □	□
657	**217**	9d multicoloured	1·75	2·25 □	□
		p. Phosphor	4·50	4·00 □	□
658	**218**	1s 3d multicoloured	2·50	2·50 □	□
		p. Phosphor	25·00	20·00 □	□
		Set of 4 (Ordinary)	4·50	4·50 □	□
		Set of 4 (Phosphor)	30·00	24·00 □	□
		First Day Cover (Ordinary)		24·00	□
		First Day Cover (Phosphor) . . .		40·00	□
		Presentation Pack (Ordinary) . .	£160		□

219 Forth Road Bridge

220 Forth Road and Railway Bridges

Opening of Forth Road Bridge

1964 (4 SEPT.)

659	**219**	3d black, blue and violet	10	10 □	□
		p. Phosphor	1·00	1·50 □	□
660	**220**	6d blackish lilac, blue and red	40	40 □	□
		p. Phosphor	4·50	4·75 □	□
		Set of 2 (Ordinary)	50	50 □	□
		Set of 2 (Phosphor)	5·00	5·75 □	□
		First Day Cover (Ordinary) . . .		7·00	□
		First Day Cover (Phosphor) . . .		18·00	□
		Presentation Pack (Ordinary) . .	£400		□

221 Sir Winston Churchill   **221a** Sir Winston Churchill

Churchill Commemoration

1965 (8 JULY)

661	**221**	4d black and drab	10	10 □	□
		p. Phosphor	25	25 □	□
662	**221a**	1s 3d black and grey	30	40 □	□
		p. Phosphor	2·50	3·00 □	□
		Set of 2 (Ordinary)	40	50 □	□
		Set of 2 (Phosphor)	2·75	3·25 □	□
		First Day Cover (Ordinary) . . .		7·00	□
		First Day Cover (Phosphor) . . .		9·00	□
		Presentation Pack (Ordinary) . .	70·00		□

**700th Anniversary of Parliament

222 Simon de Montfort's Seal

223 Parliament Buildings
(after engraving by Hollar, 1647)

700th Anniversary of Simon de Montfort's Parliament

1965 (19 JULY)

663	**222**	6d green	20	20 □	□
		p. Phosphor	60	1·00 □	□
664	**223**	2s 6d black, grey and drab	80	1·50 □	□
		Set of 2 (Ordinary)	1·00	1·25 □	□
		First Day Cover (Ordinary)		15·00	□
		First Day Cover (Phosphor) . . .		26·00	□
		Presentation Pack (Ordinary) . .	70·00		□

224 Bandsmen and Banner   225 Three Salvationists

Salvation Army Centenary
1965 (9 Aug.)

665	224	3d multicoloured	25	25 □	□
		p. Phosphor	25	40 □	□
666	225	1s 6d multicoloured	1·00	1·50 □	□
		p. Phosphor	2·50	2·75 □	□
		Set of 2 (Ordinary)	1·00	1·50 □	□
		Set of 2 (Phosphor)	2·50	3·00 □	□
		First Day Cover (Ordinary)		23·00	□
		First Day Cover (Phosphor) . . .		33·00	□

226 Lister's Carbolic Spray   227 Lister and Chemical Symbols

Centenary of Joseph Lister's Discovery of Antiseptic Surgery
1965 (1 Sept.)

667	226	4d indigo, chestnut and grey	25	15 □	□
		p. Phosphor	25	25 □	□
668	227	1s black, purple and blue	1·00	1·10 □	□
		p. Phosphor	2·00	2·50 □	□
		Set of 2 (Ordinary)	1·00	1·25 □	□
		Set of 2 (Phosphor)	2·25	2·50 □	□
		First Day Cover (Ordinary)		12·00	□
		First Day Cover (Phosphor) . . .		15·00	□

228 Trinidad Carnival Dancers   229 Canadian Folk Dancers

Commonwealth Arts Festival
1965 (1 Sept.)

669	228	6d black and orange . .	20	20 □	□
		p. Phosphor	30	30 □	□
670	229	1s 6d black and violet . . .	80	1·10 □	□
		p. Phosphor	2·50	3·50 □	□
		Set of 2 (Ordinary)	1·00	1·25 □	□
		Set of 2 (Phosphor)	2·75	3·50 □	□
		First Day Cover (Ordinary)		16·50	□
		First Day Cover (Phosphor) . . .		22·00	□

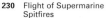

230 Flight of Supermarine Spitfires   231 Pilot in Hawker Hurricane Mk I

232 Wing-tips of Supermarine Spitfire and Messerschmitt Bf 109   233 Supermarine Spitfires attacking Heinkel HE 111H Bomber

234 Supermarine Spitfire attacking Junkers Ju 87B 'Stuka' Dive-bomber   235 Hawker Hurricanes Mk I over Wreck of Dornier Do-17Z Bomber

The above were issued together *se-tenant* in blocks of six (3 × 2) within the sheet.

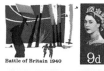

236 Anti-aircraft Artillery in Action   237 Air Battle over St Paul's Cathedral

25th Anniversary of Battle of Britain
1965 (13 Sept.)

671	230	4d olive and black	25	25 □	□
		a. Block of 6. Nos. 671/6	8·00	8·00 □	□
		p. Phosphor	50	50 □	□
		pa. Block of 6. Nos. 671p/6p	10·00	12·00 □	□
672	231	4d olive, blackish olive and black	25	25 □	□
		p. Phosphor	50	50 □	□
673	232	4d multicoloured	25	25 □	□
		p. Phosphor	50	50 □	□
674	233	4d olive and black	25	25 □	□
		p. Phosphor	50	50 □	□
675	234	4d olive and black	25	25 □	□
		p. Phosphor	50	50 □	□

676	235	4d multicoloured	25	25	□	□
		p. Phosphor	50	50	□	□
677	236	9d violet, orange and purple	1·75	1·75	□	□
		p. Phosphor	1·75	2·50	□	□
678	237	1s 3d multicoloured	1·75	1·75	□	□
		p. Phosphor	1·75	2·50	□	□
		Set of 8 (Ordinary)	8·50	8·50	□	□
		Set of 8 (Phosphor)	10·00	12·50	□	□
		First Day Cover (Ordinary)		25·00		□
		First Day Cover (Phosphor) ...		28·00		□
		Presentation Pack (Ordinary)	70·00		□	

238 Tower and Georgian Buildings   **239** Tower and Nash Terrace, Regent's Park

Opening of Post Office Tower
1965 (8 Oct.)

679	238	3d yellow, blue and green	10	15	□	□
		p. Phosphor	15	15	□	□
680	239	1s 3d green and blue ...	30	45	□	□
		p. Phosphor ...	30	50	□	□
		Set of 2 (Ordinary)	40	60	□	□
		Set of 2 (Phosphor)	45	65	□	□
		First Day Cover (Ordinary)		6·50		□
		First Day Cover (Phosphor)		7·00		□
		Presentation Pack (Ordinary) ..	6·50		□	
		Presentation Pack (Phosphor) ..	6·50		□	

240 U.N. Emblem   **241** I.C.Y. Emblem

20th Anniversary of UNO and International Co-operation Year
1965 (25 Oct.)

681	240	3d black, orange and blue	25	20	□	□
		p. Phosphor	25	30	□	□
682	241	1s 6d black, purple and blue	1·00	80	□	□
		p. Phosphor	2·75	3·00	□	□
		Set of 2 (Ordinary)	1·00	1·00	□	□
		Set of 2 (Phosphor)	2·50	3·25	□	□
		First Day Cover (Ordinary)		12·00		□
		First Day Cover (Phosphor) ...		14·00		□

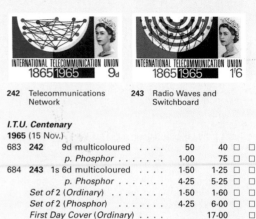

242 Telecommunications Network   **243** Radio Waves and Switchboard

I.T.U. Centenary
1965 (15 Nov.)

683	242	9d multicoloured	50	40	□	□
		p. Phosphor	1·00	75	□	□
684	243	1s 6d multicoloured	1·50	1·25	□	□
		p. Phosphor	4·25	5·25	□	□
		Set of 2 (Ordinary)	1·50	1·60	□	□
		Set of 2 (Phosphor)	4·25	6·00	□	□
		First Day Cover (Ordinary)		17·00		□
		First Day Cover (Phosphor) ...		20·00		□

244 Robert Burns (after Skirving chalk drawing)   **245** Robert Burns (after Nasmyth portrait)

Burns Commemoration
1966 (25 Jan.)

685	244	4d black, indigo and blue	15	15	□	□
		p. Phosphor	25	50	□	□
686	245	1s 3d black, blue and orange	40	70	□	□
		p. Phosphor	2·25	2·25	□	□
		Set of 2 (Ordinary)	55	85	□	□
		Set of 2 (Phosphor)	2·50	2·25	□	□
		First Day Cover (Ordinary)		4·00		□
		First Day Cover (Phosphor) ...		6·00		□
		Presentation Pack (Ordinary) ..	60·00		□	

246 Westminster Abbey   **247** Fan Vaulting, Henry VII Chapel

900th Anniversary of Westminster Abbey
1966 (28 Feb.) Perf 15 × 14 (3d) or 11 × 12 (2s 6d)

687	246	3d black, brown and blue	15	20	□	□
		p. Phosphor	20	25	□	□

688	**247**	2s 6d black	55	80	□	□
		Set of 2	70	1·00	□	□
		First Day Cover (Ordinary)		6·00		□
		First Day Cover (Phosphor) . . .		14·00		□
		Presentation Pack (Ordinary) . .	55·00			□

248 View near Hassocks, Sussex

249 Antrim, Northern Ireland

250 Harlech Castle, Wales

251 Cairngorm Mountains, Scotland

Landscapes
1966 (2 MAY)

689	**248**	4d black, yellow-green and blue	10	15	□	□
		p. Phosphor	10	15	□	□
690	**249**	6d black, green and blue	15	20	□	□
		p. Phosphor	15	20	□	□
691	**250**	1s 3d black, yellow and blue	25	35	□	□
		p. Phosphor	25	35	□	□
692	**251**	1s 6d black, orange and blue	40	35	□	□
		p. Phosphor	40	40	□	□
		Set of 4 (Ordinary)	80	95	□	□
		Set of 4 (Phosphor)	80	1·00	□	□
		First Day Cover (Ordinary)		7·00		□
		First Day Cover (Phosphor) . . .		8·50		□

252 Players with Ball

253 Goalmouth Mêlée   **254** Goalkeeper saving Goal

World Cup Football Championship
1966 (1 JUNE)

693	**252**	4d multicoloured	10	25	□	□
		p. Phosphor	10	25	□	□
694	**253**	6d multicoloured	15	25	□	□
		p. Phosphor	15	25	□	□
695	**254**	1s 3d multicoloured	50	1·00	□	□
		p. Phosphor	50	1·00	□	□
		Set of 3 (Ordinary)	70	1·00	□	□
		Set of 3 (Phosphor)	50	1·00	□	□
		First Day Cover (Ordinary)		20·00		□
		First Day Cover (Phosphor) . . .		22·00		□
		Presentation Pack (Ordinary) . .	15·00			□

255 Black-headed Gull   **256** Blue Tit

257 European Robin   **258** Blackbird

The above were issued *se-tenant* in blocks of four within the sheet.

British Birds
1966 (8 AUG.)

696	**255**	4d multicoloured	20	20	□	□
		a. Block of 4. *Nos.* 696/9	1·00	2·00	□	□
		p. Phosphor	20	20	□	□
		pa. Block of 4. *Nos.* 696p/9p	75	2·00	□	□
697	**256**	4d multicoloured	20	20	□	□
		p. Phosphor	20	20	□	□
698	**257**	4d multicoloured	20	20	□	□
		p. Phosphor	20	20	□	□
699	**258**	4d multicoloured	20	20	□	□
		p. Phosphor	20	20	□	□
		Set of 4 (Ordinary)	1·00	2·00	□	□
		Set of 4 (Phosphor)	75	2·00	□	□
		First Day Cover (Ordinary)		8·00		□
		First Day Cover (Phosphor) . . .		8·00		□
		Presentation Pack (Ordinary) . .	10·00			□

259 Cup Winners

England's World Cup Football Victory
1966 (18 Aug.)

700	**259**	4d multicoloured	. . . .	30	30 □	□
		First Day Cover	. . . .		13·00	□

260 Jodrell Bank Radio Telescope

261 British Motor-cars

262 SR N6 Hovercraft

263 Windscale Reactor

British Technology
1966 (19 Sept.)

701	**260**	4d black and lemon	. . .	15	10 □	□
		p. Phosphor		10	10 □	□
702	**261**	6d red, blue and orange		25	20 □	□
		p. Phosphor		15	25 □	□
703	**262**	1s 3d multicoloured	. . . .	50	40 □	□
		p. Phosphor		35	40 □	□
704	**263**	1s 6d multicoloured	. . . .	50	60 □	□
		p. Phosphor		50	60 □	□
		Set of 4 (Ordinary)		1·00	1·10 □	□
		Set of 4 (Phosphor)		1·00	1·10 □	□
		First Day Cover (Ordinary)			6·00	□
		First Day Cover (Phosphor) . . .			6·00	□
		Presentation Pack (Ordinary) . .		12·00		□

264　　　　**265**

266　　　　**267**

268　　　　**269**

The above show battle scenes, they were issued together *se-tenant* in horizontal strips of six within the sheet.

270 Norman Ship

271 Norman Horsemen attacking Harold's Troops

900th Anniversary of Battle of Hastings
1966 (14 Oct.) *Designs show scenes from Bayeux Tapestry*
Wmk **179** (*sideways on 1s 3d*)

705	**264**	4d multicoloured	. . . .	10	10 □	□
		a. Strip of 6. Nos. 705/10		1·90	2·25 □	□
		p. Phosphor		10	10 □	□
		pa. Strip of 6. Nos. 705p/10p		1·90	2·25 □	□
706	**265**	4d multicoloured	. . . .	10	10 □	□
		p. Phosphor		10	10 □	□
707	**266**	4d multicoloured	. . . .	10	10 □	□
		p. Phosphor		10	10 □	□
708	**267**	4d multicoloured	. . . .	10	10 □	□
		p. Phosphor		10	10 □	□
709	**268**	4d multicoloured	. . . .	10	10 □	□
		p. Phosphor		10	10 □	□
710	**269**	4d multicoloured	. . . .	10	10 □	□
		p. Phosphor		10	10 □	□

711	**270**	6d multicoloured	10	10 □ □
		p. Phosphor	10	10 □ □
712	**271**	1s 3d multicoloured	20	75 □ □
		p. Phosphor	20	75 □ □
		Set of 8 (Ordinary)	2·00	2·25 □ □
		Set of 8 (Phosphor)	2·00	2·25 □ □
		First Day Cover (Ordinary)		8·00 □
		First Day Cover (Phosphor) . . .		9·00 □
		Presentation Pack (Ordinary) . .	9·00	□

 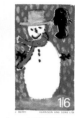

272 King of the Orient

273 Snowman

Christmas
1966 (1 Dec.) Wmk **179** (upright on 1s 6d)

713	**272**	3d multicoloured	10	25 □ □
		p. Phosphor	10	25 □ □
714	**273**	1s 6d multicoloured	30	50 □ □
		p. Phosphor	30	50 □ □
		Set of 2 (Ordinary)	40	40 □ □
		Set of 2 (Phosphor)	40	45 □ □
		First Day Cover (Ordinary)		2·50 □
		First Day Cover (Phosphor) . . .		2·00 □
		Presentation Pack (Ordinary) . .	12·00	□

274 Sea Freight

275 Air Freight

European Free Trade Association (EFTA)
1967 (20 Feb.)

715	**274**	9d multicoloured	25	20 □ □
		p. Phosphor	25	20 □ □
716	**275**	1s 6d multicoloured	50	45 □ □
		p. Phosphor	25	40 □ □
		Set of 2 (Ordinary)	50	65 □ □
		Set of 2 (Phosphor)	50	60 □ □
		First Day Cover (Ordinary)		3·00 □
		First Day Cover (Phosphor) . . .		3·00 □
		Presentation Pack (Ordinary) . .	3·50	□

276 Hawthorn and Bramble

277 Larger Bindweed and Viper's Bugloss

278 Ox-eye Daisy, Coltsfoot and Buttercup

279 Bluebell, Red Campion and Wood Anemone

The above sheet were issued together *se-tenant* in blocks of four within the sheet.

280 Dog Violet

281 Primroses

British Wild Flowers
1967 (24 Apr.)

717	**276**	4d multicoloured	20	20 □ □
		a. Block of 4. Nos. 717/20	80	2·25 □ □
		p. Phosphor	10	15 □ □
		pa Block of 4. Nos. 717p/ 20p	50	2·00 □ □
718	**277**	4d multicoloured	20	20 □ □
		p. Phosphor	10	15 □ □
719	**278**	4d multicoloured	20	20 □ □
		p. Phosphor	10	15 □ □
720	**279**	4d multicoloured	20	20 □ □
		p. Phosphor	10	15 □ □
721	**280**	9d multicoloured	20	25 □ □
		p. Phosphor	15	25 □ □
722	**281**	1s 9d multicoloured	25	35 □ □
		p. Phosphor	20	30 □ □
		Set of 6 (Ordinary)	1·00	2·25 □ □
		Set of 6 (Phosphor)	75	2·00 □ □
		First Day Cover (Ordinary)		5·00 □
		First Day Cover (Phosphor) . . .		5·00 □
		Presentation Pack (Ordinary) . .	5·25	□
		Presentation Pack (Phosphor) . .	5·25	□

282 (value at left)   **282a** (value at right)

I   II

Two *types* of the 2d.
 I. Value spaced away from left side of stamp.
 II. Value close to left side from new multi-positive. This results in the portrait appearing in the centre, thus conforming with the other values.

1967–69 *Two phosphor bands, except where otherwise stated. No wmk.*

723	**282**	½d orange-brown	10	20	☐	☐
724		1d olive (2 bands)	10	10	☐	☐
725		1d olive (1 centre band)	30	35	☐	☐
726		2d lake-brown (Type I) (2 bands)	10	15	☐	☐
727		2d lake-brown (Type II) (2 bands)	15	20	☐	☐
728		2d lake-brown (Type II) (1 centre band)	70	90	☐	☐
729		3d violet (1 centre band)	15	10	☐	☐
730		3d violet (2 bands) . . .	30	35	☐	☐
731		4d sepia (2 bands) . . .	10	10	☐	☐
732		4d olive-brown (1 centre band)	10	10	☐	☐
733		4d vermilion (1 centre band)	10	10	☐	☐
734		4d vermilion (1 side band)	1·50	1·90	☐	☐
735		5d blue	10	10	☐	☐
736		6d purple	20	25	☐	☐
737	**282a**	7d emerald	40	35	☐	☐
738		8d vermilion	20	45	☐	☐
739		8d turquoise-blue	50	60	☐	☐
740		9d green	40	25	☐	☐
741	**282**	10d drab	50	50	☐	☐
742		1s violet	45	25	☐	☐
743		1s 6d blue and deep blue .	50	50	☐	☐
		c. Phosphorised paper .	80	80	☐	☐
744		1s 9d orange and black . .	50	45	☐	☐
		Set of 16 (one of each value and colour)	4·00	4·00	☐	☐
		Presentation Pack (one of each value)	7·00		☐	
		Presentation Pack (German) . . .	£120		☐	

First Day Covers

5 June 1967	Nos. 731, 742, 744	. . . . .	3·00 ☐
8 Aug. 1967	Nos. 729, 740, 743	. . . . .	3·00 ☐
5 Feb. 1968	Nos. 723/4, 726, 736	. . . . .	3·00 ☐
1 July 1968	Nos. 735, 737/8, 741	. . . . .	3·00 ☐

No. 734 exists with phosphor band at the left or right.

283 'Master Lambton'   **284** 'Mares and Foals in a
      (Sir Thomas Lawrence)   Landscape' (George Stubbs)

285 'Children Coming Out
        of School' (L. S. Lowry)

British Paintings
1967 (10 July) *Two phosphor bands. No wmk*

748	**283**	4d multicoloured	10	10	☐	☐
749	**284**	9d multicoloured	15	15	☐	☐
750	**285**	1s 6d multicoloured	25	35	☐	☐
		Set of 3	30	50	☐	☐
		First Day Cover		3·00		☐
		Presentation Pack	5·50		☐	

286 *Gipsy Moth IV*

Sir Francis Chichester's World Voyage
1967 (24 July) *Three phosphor bands. No wmk*

751	**286**	1s 9d multicoloured . . .	20	20	☐	☐
		First Day Cover		1·25		

287 Radar Screen   **288** *Penicillium notatum*

289 Vickers VC-10 Jet Engines   **290** Television Equipment

British Discovery and Invention

1967 (19 SEPT.) *Two phosphor bands (except 4d. three bands).*
Wmk **179** (*sideways on 1s 9d*)

752	**287**	4d yellow, black and ver-				
		milion	10	10	□	□
753	**288**	1s multicoloured	10	20	□	□
754	**289**	1s 6d multicoloured	20	25	□	□
755	**290**	1s 9d multicoloured	20	30	□	□
		Set of 4	50	75	□	□
		First Day Cover		2·50		□
		Presentation Pack	4·00			□

NO WATERMARK. All the following issues are on un-watermarked paper unless otherwise stated.

291 'The Adoration of   **292** 'Madonna and
the Shepherds'   Child' (Murillo)
(School of Seville)

293 'The Adoration of the
Shepherds' (Louis Le Nain)

Christmas

1967 *Two phosphor bands (except 3d, one phosphor band)*

756	**291**	3d multicoloured				
		(27 Nov.)	10	15	□	□
757	**292**	4d multicoloured				
		(18 Oct.)	10	15	□	□

758	**293**	1s 6d multicoloured				
		(27 Nov.)	15	15	□	□
		Set of 3	30	30	□	□
		First Day Covers (2)		1·50		□

Gift Pack 1967

1967 (27 Nov.) *Comprises Nos.* 715p/22p *and* 748/58

GP758c	Gift Pack		3·00	□

1967–68 *No wmk. Perf* 11 × 12

759	**166**	2s 6d brown	30	45	□	□
760	**167**	5s red	70	75	□	□
761	**168**	10s blue	7·75	6·25	□	□
762	**169**	£1 black	7·50	6·00	□	□
		Set of 4	15·00	12·00	□	□

294 Tarr Steps, Exmoor   **295** Aberfeldy Bridge

296 Menai Bridge   **297** M4 Viaduct

British Bridges

1968 (29 APR.) *Two phosphor bands*

763	**294**	4d multicoloured	10	10	□	□
764	**295**	9d multicoloured	10	15	□	□
765	**296**	1s 6d multicoloured	15	25	□	□
766	**297**	1s 9d multicoloured	20	30	□	□
		Set of 4	50	70	□	□
		First Day Cover		1·50		□
		Presentation Pack	3·00			□

298 'TUC' and Trades Unionists   **299** Mrs Emmeline Pankhurst
(statue)

300 Sopwith Camel and English   **301** Captain Cook's *Endeavour*
Electric Lightning Fighters   and Signature

British Anniversaries. Events described on stamps
1968 (29 May) *Two phosphor bands*

767	**298**	4d multicoloured	10	10 □	□
768	**299**	9d violet, grey and			
		black	10	15 □	□
769	**300**	1s multicoloured	15	15 □	□
770	**301**	1s 9d ochre and brown . .	35	35 □	□
		Set of 4	50	50 □	□
		First Day Cover		4·00	□
		Presentation Pack	3·00		□

302 'Queen Elizabeth I' (Unknown Artist)

303 'Pinkie' (Lawrence)

304 'Ruins of St Mary Le Port' (Piper)

305 'The Hay Wain' (Constable)

British Paintings
1968 (12 Aug.) *Two phosphor bands*

771	**302**	4d multicoloured	10	10 □	□
772	**303**	1s multicoloured	10	20 □	□
773	**304**	1s 6d multicoloured	20	25 □	□
774	**305**	1s 9d multicoloured	25	40 □	□
		Set of 4	50	85 □	□
		First Day Cover		2·00	□
		Presentation Pack	3·50		□
		Presentation Pack (German) . . .	12·00		□

Gift Pack 1968
1968 (16 Sept.) *Comprises Nos. 763/74*

GP774c	*Gift Pack*	6·00		□
GP774d	*Gift Pack (German)*	35·00		□

Collectors Pack 1968
1968 (16 Sept.) *Comprises Nos. 752/8 and 763/74*

CP774e	*Collectors Pack*	7·00		□

306 Girl and Boy with Rocking Horse

307 Girl with Doll's House

308 Boy with Train Set

Christmas
1968 (25 Nov.) *Two phosphor bands (except 4d, one centre phosphor band)*

775	**306**	4d multicoloured	10	15 □	□
776	**307**	9d multicoloured	15	25 □	□
777	**308**	1s 6d multicoloured	15	50 □	□
		Set of 3	30	50 □	□
		First Day Cover		1·20	□
		Presentation Pack	5·00		□
		Presentation Pack (German) . . .	14·00		□

RMS Queen Elizabeth 2

309 Queen Elizabeth 2

310 Elizabethan Galleon

311 East Indiaman

312 Cutty Sark

SS Great Britain

313 *Great Britain*

RMS Mauretania

314 *Mauretania I*

The 9d and 1s values were arranged in horizontal strips of three and pairs respectively throughout the sheet.

British Ships

1969 (15 Jan.) *One horiz phosphor band (5d), two phosphor bands (9d) or two vert phosphor bands at right (1s)*

778	**309**	5d multicoloured	10	15	☐	☐
779	**310**	9d multicoloured	10	25	☐	☐
		a. Strip of 3. Nos. 779/81	1·25	1·50	☐	☐
780	**311**	9d multicoloured	10	25	☐	☐
781	**312**	9d multicoloured	10	25	☐	☐
782	**313**	1s multicoloured	40	35	☐	☐
		a. Pair. Nos. 782/3 . . .	1·25	1·50	☐	☐
783	**314**	1s multicoloured	40	35	☐	☐
		Set of 6	2·50	3·00	☐	☐
		First Day Cover		6·00		☐
		Presentation Pack	4·50		☐	
		Presentation Pack (German) . . .	40·00		☐	

315 Concorde in Flight

316 Plan and Elevation Views

317 Concorde's Nose and Tail

First Flight of Concorde

1969 (3 Mar.) *Two phosphor bands*

784	**315**	4d multicoloured	25	25	☐	☐
785	**316**	9d multicoloured	55	75	☐	☐

786	**317**	1s 6d deep blue, grey and light blue	75	1·00	☐	☐
		Set of 3	1·00	1·50	☐	☐
		First Day Cover		4·00		☐
		Presentation Pack	12·00		☐	
		Presentation Pack (German) . . .	40·00		☐	

318 (See also Type **357**)

1969 (5 Mar.) *P* 12

787	**318**	2s 6d brown	35	30	☐	☐
788		5s lake	1·75	60	☐	☐
789		10s ultramarine	6·00	7·00	☐	☐
790		£1 black	3·25	1·50	☐	☐
		Set of 4	10·00	8·50	☐	☐
		First Day Cover		9·50		☐
		Presentation Pack	16·00		☐	
		Presentation Pack (German) . . .	75·00		☐	

319 Page from the *Daily Mail,* and Vickers FB-27 Vimy Aircraft

320 Europa and C.E.P.T. Emblems

321 I.L.O. Emblem

322 Flags of N.A.T.O. Countries

323 Vickers FB-27 Vimy Aircraft and Globe showing Flight

Anniversaries. Events described on stamps

1969 (2 Apr.) *Two phosphor bands*

791	**319**	5d multicoloured	10	15	☐	☐
792	**320**	9d multicoloured	15	25	☐	☐

793	**321**	1s claret, red and blue .	15	25	☐	☐
794	**322**	1s 6d multicoloured	15	30	☐	☐
795	**323**	1s 9d olive, yellow and turquoise-green . . .	20	40	☐	☐
		Set of 5	50	1·00	☐	☐
		First Day Cover		3·00		☐
		Presentation Pack	3·50		☐	
		Presentation Pack (German) . . .	55·00		☐	

330 The King's Gate, Caernarvon Castle

331 The Eagle Tower, Caernarvon Castle

324 Durham Cathedral

325 York Minster

332 Queen Eleanor's Gate, Caernarvon Castle

333 Celtic Cross, Margam Abbey

The 5d values were printed *se-tenant* in strips of three throughout the sheet

326 St Giles' Cathedral, Edinburgh

327 Canterbury Cathedral

The above were issued together *se-tenant* in blocks of four within the sheet.

334 Prince Charles

Investiture of H.R.H. The Prince of Wales

1969 (1 JULY) *Two phosphor bands*

802	**330**	5d multicoloured	10	15	☐	☐
		a. Strip of 3. *Nos.* 802/4	50	1·00	☐	☐
803	**331**	5d multicoloured	10	15	☐	☐
804	**332**	5d multicoloured	10	15	☐	☐
805	**333**	9d multicoloured	15	30	☐	☐
806	**334**	1s black and gold	15	30	☐	☐
		Set of 5	50	1·00	☐	☐
		First Day Cover		1·50		☐
		Presentation Pack	2·50		☐	
		Presentation Pack (German) . . .	28·00		☐	

328 St Paul's Cathedral

329 Liverpool Metropolitan Cathedral

British Architecture (Cathedrals)

1969 (28 MAY) *Two phosphor bands*

796	**324**	5d multicoloured	10	10	☐	☐
		a. Block of 4. *Nos.* 796/9	1·10	1·30	☐	☐
797	**325**	5d multicoloured	10	10	☐	☐
798	**326**	5d multicoloured	10	10	☐	☐
799	**327**	5d multicoloured	10	10	☐	☐
800	**328**	9d multicoloured	25	30	☐	☐
801	**329**	1s 6d multicoloured	25	35	☐	☐
		Set of 6	1·10	1·30	☐	☐
		First Day Cover		3·00		☐
		Presentation Pack	3·25		☐	
		Presentation Pack (German) . . .	30·00		☐	

335 Mahatma Gandhi

Gandhi Centenary Year

1969 (13 Aug.) *Two phosphor bands*

807	**335**	1s 6d multicoloured	30	30	□ □
		First Day Cover		1·00	□

Collectors Pack 1969

1969 (15 Sept.) *Comprises Nos.* 775/86 *and* 791/807

CP807*b*	*Collectors Pack*	25·00	□

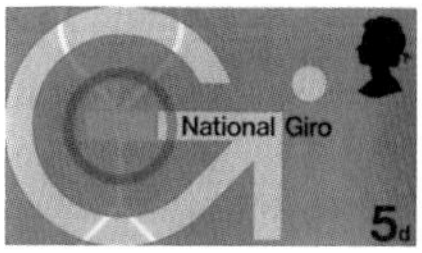

336 National Giro

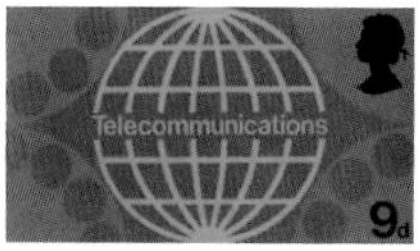

337 Telecommunications — International Subscriber Dialling

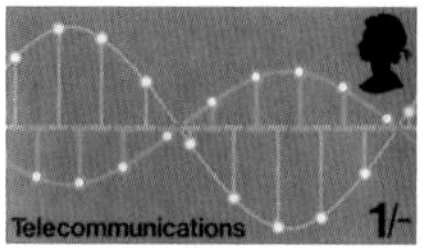

338 Telecommunications — Pulse Code Modulation

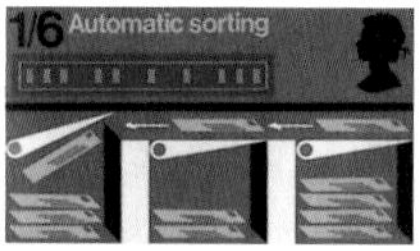

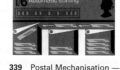

339 Postal Mechanisation — Automatic Sorting

British Post Office Technology

1969 (1 Oct.) *Two phosphor bands. Perf* $13\frac{1}{2} \times 14$

808	**336**	5d multicoloured	10	10	□ □
809	**337**	9d green, blue and black	15	20	□ □
810	**338**	1s green, lavender and black	15	20	□ □
811	**339**	1s 6d multicoloured	15	35	□ □
		Set of 4	50	75	□ □
		First Day Cover		1·50	□
		Presentation Pack	3·00		□

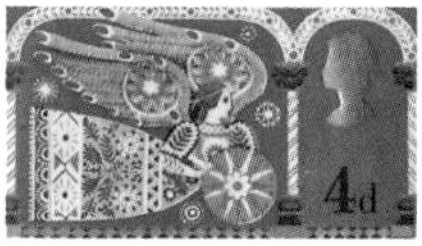

340 Herald Angel

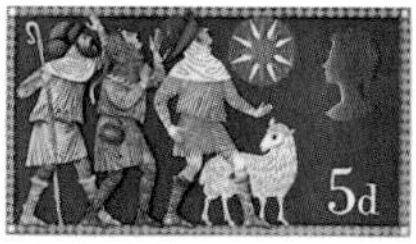

341 The Three Shepherds

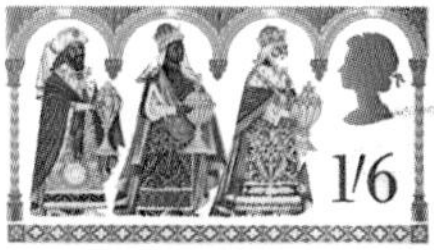

342 The Three Kings

Christmas

1969 (26 Nov.) *Two phosphor bands* (5*d*, 1*s* 6*d*) *or one centre band* (4*d*)

812	**340**	4d multicoloured	10	10	□ □
813	**341**	5d multicoloured	15	15	□ □
814	**342**	1s 6d multicoloured	20	20	□ □
		Set of 3	30	30	□ □
		First Day Cover		1·00	□
		Presentation Pack	3·00		□

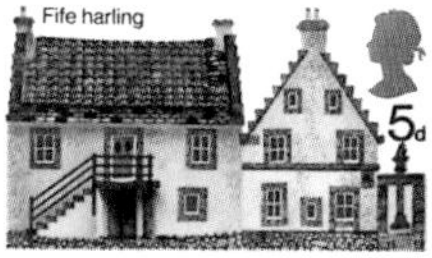

343 Fife Harling

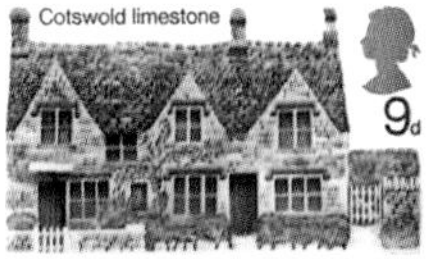

344 Cotswold Limestone

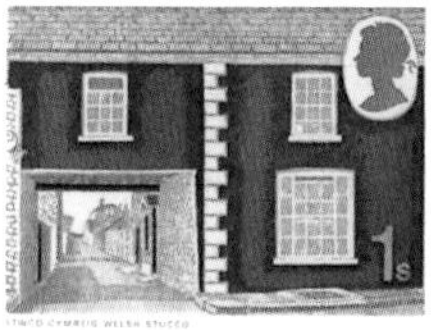

345 Welsh Stucco

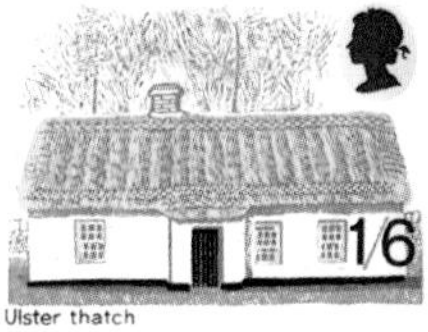

346 Ulster Thatch

British Rural Architecture

1970 (11 Feb.) *Two phosphor bands*

815	**343**	5d multicoloured	10	10	□ □
816	**344**	9d multicoloured	10	25	□ □
817	**345**	1s multicoloured	15	25	□ □
818	**346**	1s 6d multicoloured	20	40	□ □
		Set of 4	50	75	□ □
		First Day Cover		1·50	□
		Presentation Pack	4·00		□

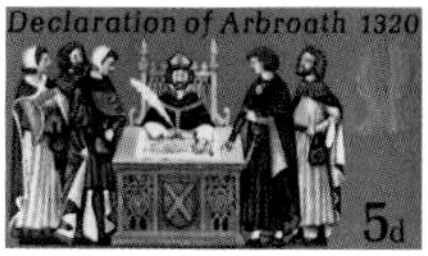

347 Signing the Declaration of Arbroath

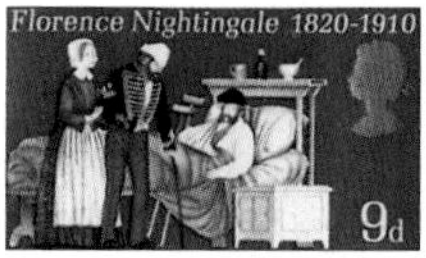

348 Florence Nightingale attending Patients

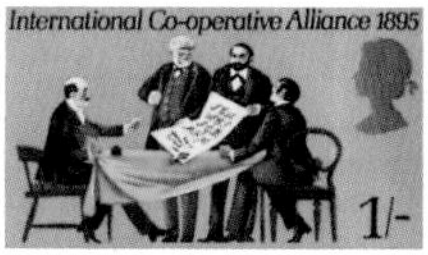

349 Signing of International Co-operative Alliance

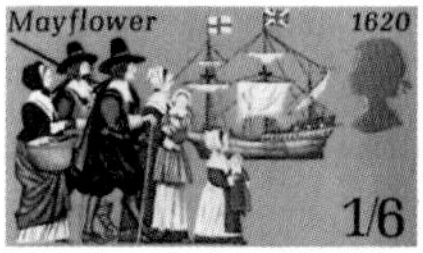

350 Pilgrims and *Mayflower*

351   Sir William Herschel, Francis Baily, Sir John Herschel and Telescope

Anniversaries. Events described on stamps

1970 (1 Apr.) *Two phosphor bands*

819	**347**	5d multicoloured	....	10	10	☐	☐
820	**348**	9d multicoloured	....	15	15	☐	☐
821	**349**	1s multicoloured	....	20	25	☐	☐
822	**350**	1s 6d multicoloured	....	20	30	☐	☐
823	**351**	1s 9d multicoloured	....	25	30	☐	☐
		Set of 5	....	75	1·00	☐	☐
		First Day Cover	....		2·00		☐
		Presentation Pack	....	3·00			☐

352   'Mr Pickwick and Sam' (*Pickwick Papers*)

353   'Mr and Mrs Micawber' (*David Copperfield*)

354   'David Copperfield and Betsy Trotwood' (*David Copperfield*)

355   'Oliver asking for more' (*Oliver Twist*)

356   'Grasmere' (from engraving by J. Farrington, R.A.)

The 5d values were issued together *se-tenant* in blocks of four within the sheet.

Literary Anniversaries. Events described on stamps

1970 (3 June) *Two phosphor bands*

824	**352**	5d multicoloured	....	10	25	☐	☐
		a. Block of 4. Nos. 824/7		75	1·50	☐	☐
825	**353**	5d multicoloured	....	10	25	☐	☐

826	**354**	5d multicoloured	....	10	25	☐	☐
827	**355**	5d multicoloured	....	10	25	☐	☐
828	**356**	1s 6d multicoloured	....	25	50	☐	☐
		Set of 5		1·00	1·50	☐	☐
		First Day Cover	....		2·00		☐
		Presentation Pack	....	3·00			☐

356a   357   (Value redrawn)

Decimal Currency

1970 (17 June)–**72** *10p and some printings of the 50p were issued on phosphor paper. Perf 12*

829	**356a**	10p cerise	....	50	75	☐	☐
830		20p olive-green	.....	60	25	☐	☐
831		50p ultramarine	.....	1·25	40	☐	☐
831*b*	**357**	£1 black (6 Dec. 1972)	.	3·50	80	☐	☐
		Set of 4	....	5·25	2·00	☐	☐
		First Day Cover (Nos. 829/31)	..		2·75		☐
		First Day Cover (No. 831*b*)	....		3·00		☐
		Presentation Pack (P.O. Pack No. 18)					
		(Nos. 829/31)	....	9·00			☐
		Presentation Pack (P.O. Pack No. 38)					
		(Nos. 830/1, 790 or 831b)	....	10·00			☐

358   Runners   359   Swimmers

360   Cyclists

Ninth British Commonwealth Games, Edinburgh

1970 (15 July) *Two phosphor bands. Perf 13½ × 14*

832	**358**	5d pink, emerald, greenish yellow and yellow-green	....	25	25	☐ ☐
833	**359**	1s 6d greenish blue, lilac, brown and Prussian blue	....	50	50	☐ ☐

834	360	1s 9d yellow-orange, lilac,					
		salmon and red-					
		brown	50	50	☐	☐	
		Set of 3	75	75	☐	☐	
		First Day Cover		1·20		☐	
		Presentation Pack	3·00			☐	

Collectors Pack 1970

1970 (14 Sept.) *Comprises Nos. 808/28 and 832/4*

CP834a	Collectors Pack	25·00		☐

361	1d Black	362	1s Green	363	4d Carmine
	(1840)		(1847)		(1855)

'Philympia 70' Stamp Exhibition

1970 (18 Sept.) *Two phosphor bands. Perf* 14 × 14½

835	361	5d multicoloured	25	10	☐	☐
836	362	9d multicoloured	25	30	☐	☐
837	363	1s 6d multicoloured	25	45	☐	☐
		Set of 3	50	75	☐	☐
		First Day Cover		1·50		☐
		Presentation Pack	3·00			☐

364	Shepherds and	365	Mary, Joseph and
	Apparition of the		Christ in the Manger
	Angel		

366	The Wise Men
	bearing Gifts

Christmas

1970 (25 Nov.) *Two phosphor bands* (5d, 1s 6d) *or one centre phosphor band* (4d)

838	364	4d multicoloured	15	10	☐	☐
839	365	5d multicoloured	15	15	☐	☐
840	366	1s 6d multicoloured	25	30	☐	☐
		Set of 3	50	50	☐	☐
		First Day Cover		1·50		☐
		Presentation Pack	2·75			☐

PRINTING PROCESSES

There is a basic distinction between stamps printed by photogravure and those printed by lithography. Sorting the two is not as difficult as it sounds and with a little experience it should become easy to tell which method of production was employed for a particular stamp.

The tiny dots of the printing screen give uneven edges to the values on photogravure stamps (right). *Litho values have clean, clear outlines* (left).

All you need is a reasonably good glass giving a magnification of ×4 or more (×10 is even better!).

The image on a photogravure stamp is created from a pattern or 'screen', of minute dots which are not evident when looking at the stamp without a glass but show up quite clearly under magnification, especially in the Queen's face and around the margin of the stamp design where it meets the white background of the paper. Now look at the value; here also, what looks to the naked eye like a straight line is in fact made up of rows of tiny little dots.

'Screens' of dots are also used in the production of litho printed stamps but they are only required where the printer is attempting to produce shades and tints as is necessary in the Queen's head portion of the stamp. Where solid colour is used, as in the background of the majority of values, there is no need to resort to a screen of dots and the background is printed as a solid mass of colour. If you look at the margins or the values of stamps produced in this way you will not see any evidence of dots—just a clear clean break between the inked portion of the stamp and the uninked white of the paper.

367    **367a**

Two types of the 3p., 10p. and 26p. (Nos. X930/c, X886/b and X971/b).

3p	3p	
I	II	
10p	10p	
I	II	
26p	26p	
I	II	

Decimal Currency

1971–96. *Type* **367**

(a) *Printed in photogravure by Harrison and Sons (except for some ptgs of Nos. X879 and X913 which were produced by Enschedé) with phosphor bands. Perf 15 × 14*

X841	½p	turquoise-blue (2 bands)	10	10	☐	☐
X842	½p	turquoise-blue (1 side band)	55·00	25·00	☐	☐
X843	½p	turquoise-blue (1 centre band)	40	25	☐	☐
X844	1p	crimson (2 bands)	10	15	☐	☐
X845	1p	crimson (1 centre band)	25	20	☐	☐
X846	1p	crimson ('all-over' phosphor)	15	25	☐	☐
X847	1p	crimson (1 side band)	1·00	1·25	☐	☐
X848	1½p	black (2 bands)	15	25	☐	☐
X849	2p	myrtle-green (face value as in T **367**) (2 bands)	15	20	☐	☐
X850	2p	myrtle-green (face value as in T **367**) ('all-over' phosphor)	25	30	☐	☐
X851	2½p	magenta (1 centre band)	20	15	☐	☐
X852	2½p	magenta (1 side band)	1·50	1·75	☐	☐
X853	2½p	magenta (2 bands)	25	50	☐	☐
X854	2½p	rose-red (2 bands)	40	60	☐	☐
X855	3p	ultramarine (2 bands)	20	25	☐	☐
X856	3p	ultramarine (1 centre band)	15	20	☐	☐
X857	3p	bright magenta (Type I) (2 bands)	35	35	☐	☐
X858	3½p	olive-grey (2 bands)	25	30	☐	☐
X859	3½p	olive-grey (1 centre band)	30	35	☐	☐
X860	3½p	purple-brown (1 centre band)	1·25	1·25	☐	☐
X861	4p	ochre-brown (2 bands)	20	25	☐	☐
X862	4p	greenish blue (2 bands)	1·75	2·00	☐	☐
X863	4p	greenish blue (1 centre band)	1·50	1·90	☐	☐
X864	4p	greenish blue (1 side band)	1·75	1·75	☐	☐
X865	4½p	grey-blue (2 bands)	25	30	☐	☐
X866	5p	pale violet (2 bands)	20	20	☐	☐
X867	5p	claret (1 centre band)	2·00	2·25	☐	☐
X868	5½p	violet (2 bands)	25	30	☐	☐
X869	5½p	violet (1 centre band)	25	30	☐	☐
X870	6p	light emerald (2 bands)	25	20	☐	☐
X871	6½p	greenish blue (2 bands)	30	35	☐	☐
X872	6½p	greenish blue (1 centre band)	25	20	☐	☐
X873Ea	6½p	greenish blue (1 side band)	55	55	☐	☐
X874	7p	purple-brown (2 bands)	30	35	☐	☐
X875	7p	purple-brown (1 centre band)	25	30	☐	☐
X876Ea	7p	purple-brown (1 side band)	45	50	☐	☐
X877	7½p	chestnut (2 bands)	25	35	☐	☐
X878	8p	rosine (2 bands)	25	30	☐	☐
X879	8p	rosine (1 centre band)	25	30	☐	☐
X880	8p	rosine (1 side band)	60	75	☐	☐
X881	8½p	yellowish green (2 bands)	30	25	☐	☐
X882	9p	yellow-orange and black (2 bands)	45	55	☐	☐
X883	9p	deep violet (2 bands)	35	25	☐	☐
X884	9½p	purple (2 bands)	35	45	☐	☐
X885	10p	orange-brown and chestnut (2 bands)	35	30	☐	☐
X886	10p	orange-brown (Type I) (2 bands)	35	25	☐	☐
		b. Type II	22·00	22·00	☐	☐
X887	10p	orange-brown (Type I) ('all-over' phosphor)	35	45	☐	☐
X888	10p	orange-brown (Type I) (1 centre band)	35	25	☐	☐
X889	10p	orange-brown (Type I) (1 side band)	70	80	☐	☐
X890	10½p	yellow (2 bands)	40	45	☐	☐
X891	10½p	blue (2 bands)	45	50	☐	☐
X892	11p	brown-red (2 bands)	40	30	☐	☐
X893	11½p	drab (1 centre band)	40	35	☐	☐
X894	11½p	drab (1 side band)	55	70	☐	☐
X895	12p	yellowish green (2 bands)	45	45	☐	☐
X896	12p	bright emerald (1 centre band)	45	45	☐	☐
X897	12p	bright emerald (1 side band)	80	85	☐	☐
X898	12½p	light emerald (1 centre band)	45	40	☐	☐
X899	12½p	light emerald (1 side band)	70	75	☐	☐
X900	13p	pale chestnut (1 centre band)	40	40	☐	☐
X901	13p	pale chestnut (1 side band)	50	60	☐	☐
X902	14p	grey-blue (2 bands)	75	80	☐	☐

No.	Description		
X903	14p deep blue (1 centre band)	40	50 □ □
X904	14p deep blue (1 side band)	4·00	4·00 □ □
X905	15p bright blue (1 centre band)	65	65 □ □
X906Ea	15p bright blue (1 side band)	3·00	3·00 □ □
X907	15½p pale violet (2 bands)	60	65 □ □
X908	16p olive-drab (2 bands)	1·25	1·40 □ □
X909	17p grey-blue (2 bands)	60	60 □ □
X910	17p deep blue (1 centre band)	80	85 □ □
X911Ea	17p deep blue (1 side band)	1·25	1·25 □ □
X912	18p deep olive-grey (2 bands)	70	80 □ □
X913	18p bright green (1 centre band)	60	50 □ □
X914	19p bright orange-red (2 bands)	1·50	1·50 □ □
X915	20p dull purple (2 bands)	1·20	90 □ □
X916	20p brownish black (2 bands)	1·50	1·60 □ □
X917	22p bright orange-red (2 bands)	1·50	1·25 □ □
X917a	25p rose-red (2 bands)	7·00	7·00 □ □
X918	26p rosine (Type I) (2 bands)	7·00	7·50 □ □
X919	31p purple (2 bands)	15·00	15·00 □ □
X920	34p ochre-brown (2 bands)	7·00	7·50 □ □
X921	50p ochre-brown (2 bands)	2·00	75 □ □
X922	50p ochre (2 bands)	4·50	4·50 □ □

(b) *Printed in photogravure by Harrison and Sons on phosphorised paper. Perf* 15 × 14

No.	Description		
X924	½p turquoise-blue	10	15 □ □
X925	1p crimson	10	15 □ □
X926	2p myrtle-green (face value as in T **367**)	15	20 □ □
X927	2p deep green (smaller value as in T **367a**)	15	20 □ □
X928	2p myrtle-green (smaller value as in T **367a**)	3·25	3·25 □ □
X929	2½p rose-red	15	20 □ □
X930	3p bright magenta (Type I)	20	25 □ □
	c. Type II	90	70 □ □
X931	3½p purple-brown	50	60 □ □
X932	4p greenish blue	25	40 □ □
X933	4p new blue	20	25 □ □
X934	5p pale violet	30	35 □ □
X935	5p dull red-brown	25	30 □ □
X936	6p yellow-olive	30	30 □ □
X937	7p brownish red	1·10	1·25 □ □
X938	8½p yellowish green	40	50 □ □
X939	10p orange-brown (Type I)	35	35 □ □
X940	10p dull orange (Type II)	40	35 □ □
X941	11p brown-red	70	80 □ □
X942	11½p ochre-brown	55	55 □ □
X943	12p yellowish green	45	45 □ □
X944	13p olive-grey	45	50 □ □
X945	13½p purple-brown	60	60 □ □
X946	14p grey-blue	50	50 □ □
X947	15p ultramarine	60	60 □ □
X948	15½p pale violet	60	50 □ □
X949	16p olive-drab	55	55 □ □
X950	16½p pale chestnut	80	75 □ □
X951	17p light emerald	60	60 □ □
X952	17p grey-blue	60	60 □ □
X953	17½p pale chestnut	70	75 □ □
X954	18p deep violet	70	70 □ □
X955	18p deep olive-grey	75	60 □ □
X956	19p bright orange-red	80	60 □ □
X957	19½p olive-grey	2·00	2·00 □ □
X958	20p dull purple	1·00	75 □ □
X959	20p turquoise-green	75	70 □ □
X960	20p brownish black	1·00	1·00 □ □
X961	20½p ultramarine	1·25	1·25 □ □
X962	22p blue	90	75 □ □
X963	22p yellow-green	90	80 □ □
X964	22p bright orange-red	90	80 □ □
X965	23p brown-red	1·25	1·00 □ □
X966	23p bright green	1·10	1·10 □ □
X967	24p violet	1·40	1·50 □ □
X968	24p Indian red	2·00	1·60 □ □
X969	24p chestnut	80	80 □ □
X970	25p purple	1·00	1·00 □ □
X971	26p rosine (Type I)	1·10	60 □ □
	b. Type II	3·50	4·00 □ □
X972	26p drab	1·50	1·25 □ □
X973	27p chestnut	1·25	1·25 □ □
X974	27p violet	1·50	1·25 □ □
X975	28p deep violet	1·25	1·25 □ □
X976	28p ochre	1·40	1·25 □ □
X977	28p deep bluish grey	1·40	1·25 □ □
X978	29p ochre-brown	1·75	1·75 □ □
X979	29p deep mauve	1·75	1·75 □ □
X980	30p deep olive-grey	1·25	1·25 □ □
X981	31p purple	1·25	1·25 □ □
X982	31p ultramarine	1·60	1·50 □ □
X983	32p greenish blue	1·90	1·75 □ □
X984	33p light emerald	1·75	1·60 □ □
X985	34p ochre-brown	1·75	1·75 □ □
X986	34p deep bluish grey	2·00	1·90 □ □
X987	34p deep mauve	1·75	1·75 □ □
X988	35p sepia	1·60	1·60 □ □
X989	35p yellow	1·75	1·60 □ □
X990	37p rosine	2·00	1·75 □ □
X991	39p bright mauve	1·75	1·75 □ □

(c) *Printed in photogravure by Harrison and Sons on ordinary paper. Perf* 15 × 14

No.	Description		
X992	50p ochre-brown	1·75	70 □ □
X993	75p grey-black (smaller values as T **367a**)	3·25	1·50 □ □

(d) *Printed in photogravure by Harrison and Sons on ordinary paper or phosphorised paper. Perf* 15 × 14

No.	Description		
X994	50p ochre	2·00	70 □ □

(e) *Printed in lithography by John Waddington. Perf* 14

No.	Description		
X996	4p greenish blue (2 bands)	25	35 □ □
X997	4p greenish blue (phosphorised paper)	45	40 □ □
X998	20p dull purple (2 bands)	1·25	1·20 □ □
X999	20p dull purple (phosphorised paper)	1·75	1·20 □ □

(f) *Printed in lithography by Questa. Perf* 14 (*Nos* X1000, X1003/4 *and* X1023) *or* 15 × 14 (*others*)

X1000	2p emerald-green (face value as in T **367**) (phosphorised paper)	20	25 □	□
	a. Perf 15 × 14	35	35 □	□
X1001	2p bright green and deep green (smaller value as in T **367a**) (phosphorised paper)	75	70 □	□
X1002	4p greenish blue (phosphorised paper)	70	75 □	□
X1003	5p light violet (phosphorised paper)	40	40 □	□
X1004	5p claret (phosphorised paper)	50	50 □	□
	a. Perf 15 × 14	65	60 □	□
X1005	13p pale chestnut (1 centre band)	70	75 □	□
X1006	13p pale chestnut (1 side band)	75	75 □	□
X1007	14p deep blue (1 centre band)	2·00	2·00 □	□
X1008	17p deep blue (1 centre band)	80	80 □	□
X1009	18p deep olive-grey (phosphorised paper)	90	95 □	□
X1010	18p deep olive-grey (2 bands)	7·50	7·50 □	□
X1011	18p bright green (1 centre band)	75	75 □	□
X1012	18p bright green (1 side band)	1·25	1·40 □	□
X1013	19p bright orange-red (phosphorised paper)	2·20	2·00 □	□
X1014	20p dull purple (phosphorised paper)	1·40	1·40 □	□
X1015	22p yellow-green (2 bands)	9·00	9·00 □	□
X1016	22p bright orange-red (phosphorised paper)	1·00	90 □	□
X1017	24p chestnut (phosphorised paper)	90	1·10 □	□
X1018	24p chestnut (2 bands)	1·40	1·40 □	□
X1019	33p light emerald (phosphorised paper)	2·50	2·50 □	□
X1020	33p light emerald (2 bands)	1·50	1·50 □	□
X1021	34p bistre-brown (2 bands)	7·50	7·50 □	□
X1022	39p bright mauve (2 bands)	1·50	1·60 □	□
X1023	75p black (face value as T **367**) (ordinary paper)	3·00	1·50 □	□
	a. Perf 15 × 14	3·50	2·25 □	□
X1024	75p brownish grey and black (smaller value as T **367a**) (ordinary paper)	9·00	8·50 □	□

(g) *Printed in lithography by Walsall. Perf* 14

X1050	2p deep green (phosphorised paper)	1·10	1·10 □	□
X1051	14p deep blue (1 side band)	4·50	4·50 □	□
X1052	19p bright orange-red (2 bands)	3·00	3·00 □	□
X1053	24p chestnut (phosphorised paper)	1·10	1·25 □	□
X1054	29p deep mauve (2 bands)	3·00	3·00 □	□
X1055	29p deep mauve (phosphorised paper)	4·50	4·50 □	□
X1056	31p ultramarine (phosphorised paper)	1·40	1·40 □	□
X1057	33p light emerald (phosphorised paper)	1·25	1·25 □	□
X1058	39p bright mauve (phosphorised paper)	1·60	1·60 □	□

Presentation Pack (*P.O. Pack No.* 26) (*contains* ½p (X841), 1p (X844), 1½p (X848), 2p (X849), 2½p (X851), 3p (X855), 3½p (X858), 4p (X861), 5p (X866), 6p (X870), 7½p (X877), 9p (X882)) .... 5·00 □

Presentation Pack (*'Scandinavia 71'*) (*contents as above*) .... 30·00 □

Presentation Pack (*P.O. Pack No.* 37) (*contains* ½p (X841), 1p (X844), 1½p (X848), 2p (X849), 2½p (X851), 3p (X855 *or* X856), 3½p (X858 *or* X859), 4p (X861), 4½p (X865), 5p (X866), 5½p (X868 *or* X869), 6p (X870), 7½p (X877), 8p (X878), 9p (X882), 10p (X885)) .. 8·00 □
Later issues of this pack included the 6½p (X871) or the 6½p (X872) and 7p (X874).

Presentation Pack (*P.O. Pack No.* 90) (*contains* ½p (X841), 1p (X844), 1½p (X848), 2p (X849), 2½p (X851), 3p (X856), 5p (X866), 6½p (X872), 7p (X874 *or* X875), 7½p (X877), 8p (X878), 8½p (X881), 9p (X883), 9½p (X884), 10p (X886), 10½p (X890), 11p (X892), 20p (X915), 50p (X921)) .... 5·00 □

Presentation Pack (*P.O. Pack No.* 129a) (*contains* 2½p (X929), 3p (X930), 4p (X996), 10½p (X891), 11½p (X893), 11½p (X942), 12p (X943), 13p (X944), 13½p (X945), 14p (X946), 15p (X947), 15½p (X948), 17p (X951), 17½p (X953), 18p (X954), 22p (X962), 25p (X970), 75p (X1023)) .... 20·00 □

Presentation Pack (*P.O. Pack No.* 1) (*contains* ½p (X924), 1p (X925), 2p (X1000), 3p (X930), 3½p (X931), 4p (X997), 5p (X1004), 10p (X888), 12½p (X898), 16p (X949), 16½p (X950), 17p (X952), 20p (X999), 20½p (X961), 23p (X965), 26p (X971), 28p (X975), 31p (X981), 50p (X992), 75p (X1023)) ... 40·00 □

Presentation Pack (*P.O. Pack No.* 5) (*contains* ½p (X924), 1p (X925), 2p (X1000a), 3p (X930), 4p (X997), 5p (X1004a), 10p (X939), 13p (X900), 16p

(X949), 17p (X952), 18p (X955), 20p
(X999), 22p (X963), 24p (X967), 26p
(X971), 28p (X975), 31p (X981), 34p
(X985), 50p (X992), 75p (X1023*a*)) . . . 34·00 □

Presentation Pack (P.O. Pack No. 9)
(*contains* 1p (X925), 2p (X1000*a*), 3p
(X930), 4p (X997), 5p (X1004*a*), 7p
(X937), 10p (X939), 12p (X896), 13p
(X900), 17p (X952), 18p (X955), 20p
(X999), 22p (X963), 24p (X967), 26p
(X971), 28p (X975), 31p (X981), 34p
(X985), 50p (X992), 75p (X1023*a*)) . 34·00 □

Presentation Pack (P.O. Pack No. 15)
(*contains* 14p (X903), 19p (X956), 20p
(X959), 23p (X966), 27p (X973), 28p
(X976), 32p (X983), 35p (X988)) . . . . 12·00 □

Presentation Pack (P.O. Pack No. 19)
(*contains* 15p (X905), 20p (X960), 24p
(X968), 29p (X979), 30p (X980), 34p
(X986), 37p (X990)) . . . . 10·00 □

Presentation Pack (P.O. Pack No. 22)
(*contains* 10p (X940), 17p (X910), 22p
(X964), 26p (X972), 27p (X974), 31p
(X982), 33p (X984)) . . . . 9·00 □

Presentation Pack (P.O. Pack No. 24)
(*contains* 1p (X925), 2p (X927), 3p
(X930), 4p (X933), 5p (X935), 10p
(X940), 17p (X910), 20p (X959), 22p
(X964), 26p (X972), 27p (X974), 30p
(X980), 31p (X982), 32p (X983), 33p
(X984), 37p (X990), 50p (X994), 75p
(X993)) . . . . 25·00 □

Presentation Pack (P.O. Pack No. 25)
(*contains* 6p (X936), 18p (X913), 24p
(X969), 28p (X977), 34p (X987), 35p
(X989), 39p (X991)) . . . . 9·00 □

First Day Covers

15 Feb. 1971	½p, 1p, 1½p, 2p, 2½p, 3p, 3½p, 4p, 5p, 6p, 7½p, 9p (*Nos.* X841, X844, X848/9, X851, X855, X858, X861, X866, X870, X877, X882) (*Covers carry* 'POSTING DELAYED BY THE POST OFFICE STRIKE 1971' *cachet*)	2·50	□
11 Aug. 1971	10p (*No.* X885)	1·50	□
24 Oct. 1973	4½p, 5½p, 8p (*Nos.* X865, X868, X878)	1·50	□
4 Sept. 1974	6½p (*No.* X871)	1·50	□
15 Jan. 1975	7p (*No.* X874)	1·00	□
24 Sept. 1975	8½p (*No.* X881)	1·50	□

25 Feb. 1976	9p, 9½p, 10p, 10½p, 11p, 20p (*Nos.* X883/4, X886, X890, X892, X915)	3·50	□
2 Feb. 1977	50p (*No.* X921)	1·75	□
26 April 1978	10½p (*No.* X891)	1·20	□
15 Aug. 1979	11½p, 13p, 15p (*Nos.* X942, X944, X947)	1·75	□
30 Jan. 1980	4p, 12p, 13½p, 17p, 17½p, 75p (*Nos.* X996, X943, X945, X951, X953, X1023)	3·25	□
22 Oct. 1980	3p, 22p (*Nos.* X930, X962) . . .	1·50	□
14 Jan. 1981	2½p, 11½p, 14p, 15½p, 18p, 25p (*Nos.* X929, X893, X946, X948, X954, X970)	2·00	□
27 Jan. 1982	5p, 12½p, 16½p, 19½p, 26p, 29p (*Nos.* X1004, X898, X950, X957, X971, X978)	3·50	□
30 Mar. 1983	3½p, 16p, 17p, 20½p, 23p, 28p, 31p (*Nos.* X931, X949, X952, X961, X965, X975, X981)	5·00	□
28 Aug. 1984	13p, 18p, 22p, 24p, 34p (*Nos.* X900, X955, X963, X967, X985)	3·00	□
29 Oct. 1985	7p, 12p (*Nos.* X937, X896) . . .	3·00	□
23 Aug. 1988	14p, 19p, 20p, 23p, 27p, 28p, 32p, 35p (*Nos.* X903, X956, X959, X966, X973, X976, X983, X988)	6·00	□
26 Sept. 1989	15p, 20p, 24p, 29p, 30p, 34p, 37p (*Nos.* X905, X960, X968, X979/80, X986, X990)	5·00	□
4 Sept. 1990	10p, 17p, 22p, 26p, 27p, 31p, 33p (*Nos.* X940, X910, X964, X972, X974, X982, X984)	5·50	□
10 Sept. 1991	6p, 18p, 24p, 28p, 34p, 35p, 39p (*Nos.* X936, X913, X969, X977, X987, X989, X991)	6·00	□

For similar stamps, but with elliptical perforations see Nos. Y1667/1803 in 1993.

PHOSPHOR BANDS. See notes on page 15.
Phosphor bands are applied to the stamps, after the design has been printed, by a separate cylinder. On issues with 'all-over' phosphor the 'band' covers the entire stamp. Parts of the stamp covered by phosphor bands, or the entire surface for 'all-over' phosphor versions, appear matt.

Nos. X847, X852, X864, X873, X876, X880, X889, X894, X897, X899, X901, X906, X911, X1006 and X1012 exist with the phosphor band at the left or right of the stamp.

PHOSPHORISED PAPER. First introduced as an experiment for a limited printing of the 1s 6d value (No. 743*c*) in 1969, this paper has the phosphor, to activate the automatic sorting machinery, added to the paper coating before the stamps were printed. Issues on this paper have a completely shiny surface. Although not adopted after this first trial further experiments on the 8½p in 1976 led to this paper being used for new printings of current values.

368 'A Mountain Road'
(T. P. Flanagan)

369 'Deer's Meadow'
(Tom Carr)

374 Servicemen and Nurse
of 1921

375 Roman Centurion

370 'Slieve na brock'
(Colin Middleton)

376 Rugby Football, 1871

'Ulster '71' Paintings

1971 (16 June) *Two phosphor bands*

881	368	3p multicoloured	. . . . .	25	25	□	□
882	369	7½p multicoloured	. . . . .	50	50	□	□
883	370	9p multicoloured	. . . . .	50	50	□	□
		Set of 3	. . . .	1·00	1·00	□	□
		First Day Cover			1·75		□
		Presentation Pack	. . . .	6·00			□

British Anniversaries. Events described on stamps

1971 (25 Aug.) *Two phosphor bands*

887	374	3p multicoloured	. . . . .	25	25	□	□
888	375	7½p multicoloured	. . . . .	50	50	□	□
889	376	9p multicoloured	. . . . .	50	50	□	□
		Set of 3	. . . .	1·00	1·00	□	□
		First Day Cover	. . . .		2·50		□
		Presentation Pack	. . . .	5·50			□

371 John Keats
(150th Death Anniv)

372 Thomas Gray
(Death Bicentenary)

377 Physical Sciences
Building, University
College of Wales,
Aberystwyth

378 Faraday Building,
Southampton
University

373 Sir Walter Scott (Birth
Bicentenary)

Literary Anniversaries. Events described above

1971 (28 July) *Two phosphor bands*

884	371	3p black, gold and blue	. .	25	10	□	□
885	372	5p black, gold and olive	.	45	50	□	□
886	373	7½p black, gold and brown		45	45	□	□
		Set of 3	. . . .	1·00	1·10	□	□
		First Day Cover	. . . .		2·00		□
		Presentation Pack	. . . .	5·50			□

379 Engineering Department,
Leicester University

380 Hexagon Restaurant,
Essex University

British Architecture (Modern University Buildings)

1971 (22 Sept.) *Two phosphor bands*

890	377	3p multicoloured	. . . . .	10	10	□	□
891	378	5p multicoloured	. . . . .	25	20	□	□

892	**379**	7½p ochre, black and				
		purple-brown	45	55	□	□
893	**380**	9p multicoloured	75	80	□	□
		Set of 4	1·25	1·50	□	□
		First Day Cover		2·00		□
		Presentation Pack	6·50			□

Collectors Pack 1971

1971 (29 SEPT.) *Comprises Nos. 835/40 and 881/93*

CP893*a*	Collectors Pack	50·00		□

381 Dream of the Wise Men

382 Adoration of the Magi

383 Ride of the Magi

Christmas

1971 (13 OCT.) *Two phosphor bands (3p, 7½p) or one centre phosphor band (2½p)*

894	**381**	2½p multicoloured	10	10	□	□
895	**382**	3p multicoloured	10	10	□	□
896	**383**	7½p multicoloured	55	75	□	□
		Set of 3	50	75	□	□
		First Day Cover		2·00		□
		Presentation Pack	4·50			□

384 Sir James Clark Ross

385 Sir Martin Frobisher

386 Henry Hudson

387 Capt. Robert F. Scott

British Polar Explorers

1972 (16 FEB.) *Two phosphor bands*

897	**384**	3p multicoloured	10	10	□	□
898	**385**	5p multicoloured	15	15	□	□
899	**386**	7½p multicoloured	45	50	□	□
900	**387**	9p multicoloured	70	85	□	□
		Set of 4	1·25	1·50	□	□
		First Day Cover		2·50		□
		Presentation Pack	5·25			□

388 Statuette of Tutankhamun

389 19th-century Coastguard

390 Ralph Vaughan Williams and Score

Anniversaries. Events described on stamps

1972 (26 APR.) *Two phosphor bands*

901	**388**	3p multicoloured	25	25	□	□
902	**389**	7½p multicoloured	50	50	□	□
903	**390**	9p multicoloured	50	50	□	□
		Set of 3	1·00	1·00	□	□
		First Day Cover		2·25		□
		Presentation Pack	4·25			□

For full information on all future British issues, collectors should write to Royal Mail, Freepost EH3647, 21 South Gyle Crescent, Edinburgh EH12 9PE.

391 St Andrew's, Greensted- juxta-Ongar, Essex

392 All Saints, Earls Barton, Northants

393 St Andrew's, Letheringsett, Norfolk

394 St Andrew's, Helpringham, Lincs

... St Mary the Virgin, Huish Episcopi, Somerset

395 St Mary the Virgin, Huish Episcopi, Somerset

British Architecture (Village Churches)

1972 (21 JUNE) *Two phosphor bands*

904	391	3p multicoloured	. . . . .	10	10	☐	☐
905	392	4p multicoloured	. . . . .	10	20	☐	☐
906	393	5p multicoloured	. . . . .	15	20	☐	☐
907	394	7½p multicoloured	. . . . .	50	75	☐	☐
908	395	9p multicoloured	. . . . .	50	80	☐	☐
		Set of 5	. . . .	1·25	1·90	☐	☐
		First Day Cover	. . . .		2·75	☐	
		Presentation Pack	. . . .	10·00		☐	

'Belgica '72' Souvenir Pack

1972 (24 JUNE) *Comprises Nos. 894/6 and 904/8*

CP908*b* Souvenir Pack . . . . 10·00   ☐

396 Microphones, 1924–69

397 Horn Loudspeaker

398 TV Camera, 1972

399 Oscillator and Spark Transmitter, 1897

Broadcasting Anniversaries. Events described on stamps

1972 (13 SEPT.) *Two phosphor bands*

909	396	3p multicoloured	. . . . .	10	10	☐	☐
910	397	5p multicoloured	. . . . .	10	20	☐	☐
911	398	7½p multicoloured	. . . . .	45	50	☐	☐
912	399	9p multicoloured	. . . . .	50	50	☐	☐
		Set of 4	. . . .	1·00	1·25	☐	☐
		First Day Cover	. . . .		2·75		☐
		Presentation Pack	. . . .	4·25		☐	

400 Angel holding Trumpet

401 Angel playing Lute

402 Angel playing Harp

Christmas

1972 (18 Oct.) *Two phosphor bands (3p, 7½p) or one centre phosphor band (2½p)*

913	**400**	2½p multicoloured	10	10 ☐ ☐
914	**401**	3p multicoloured	10	10 ☐ ☐
915	**402**	7½p multicoloured	50	45 ☐ ☐
		Set of 3	60	45 ☐ ☐
		First Day Cover		1·50 ☐
		Presentation Pack	4·00	☐

403 Queen Elizabeth II and Prince Philip

404 Europe

Royal Silver Wedding

1972 (20 Nov.) *3p 'all-over' phosphor, 20p without phosphor*

916	**403**	3p brownish black, deep blue and silver	25	25 ☐ ☐
917		20p brownish black, reddish purple and silver . . .	1·00	1·00 ☐ ☐
		Set of 2	1·00	1·00 ☐ ☐
		First Day Cover		1·50 ☐
		Presentation Pack	4·00	☐
		Presentation Pack (Japanese) . .	9·50	☐
		Souvenir Book	4·00	☐
		Gutter Pair (3p)	80	☐
		Traffic Light Gutter Pair (3p) . . .	20·00	☐

Collectors Pack 1972

1972 (20 Nov.) *Comprises Nos. 897/918*

CP918a   Collectors Pack . . . . 27·00   ☐

Nos. 920/1 were issued horizontally *se-tenant* throughout the sheet.

Britain's Entry into European Communities

1973 (3 Jan.) *Two phosphor bands*

919	**404**	3p multicoloured	25	25 ☐ ☐
920		5p multicoloured (blue jigsaw)	25	50 ☐ ☐
		a. Pair. Nos. 920/1	1·00	1·00 ☐ ☐
921		5p multicoloured (green jigsaw)	25	50 ☐ ☐
		Set of 3	1·00	1·00 ☐ ☐
		First Day Cover		2·00 ☐
		Presentation Pack	3·00	☐

405 Oak Tree

British Trees (1st Issue)

1973 (28 Feb.) *Two phosphor bands*

922	**405**	9p multicoloured	35	40 ☐ ☐
		First Day Cover		1·75 ☐
		Presentation Pack	2·75	☐

See also No. 949

406 David Livingstone

407 H. M. Stanley

The above were issued horizontally *se-tenant* throughout the sheet.

408 Sir Francis Drake

409 Sir Walter Raleigh

410 Charles Sturt

British Explorers

1973 (18 Apr.) *'All-over' phosphor*

923	**406**	3p multicoloured	40	25 ☐ ☐
		a. Pair. Nos. 923/4	80	1·00 ☐ ☐

924	**407**	3p multicoloured	. . . .	40	25 □ □
925	**408**	5p multicoloured	. . . .	40	50 □ □
926	**409**	7½p multicoloured	. . . .	40	50 □ □
927	**410**	9p multicoloured	. . . .	40	75 □ □
		Set of 5		1·50	2·50 □ □
		First Day Cover			2·50 □
		Presentation Pack		4·50	□

411　　　　　　　　　　**412**

413

County Cricket 1873–1973

1973 (16 MAY) *Designs show sketches of W. G. Grace by Harry Furniss. Queen's head in gold. 'All-over' phosphor*

928	**411**	3p black and brown	. . . .	25	25 □ □
929	**412**	7½p black and green	. . . .	75	75 □ □
930	**413**	9p black and blue	. . . .	1·25	1·00 □ □
		Set of 3		1·75	1·50 □ □
		First Day Cover			3·00 □
		Presentation Pack		4·50	□
		Souvenir Book		7·00	□
		PHQ Card (No. 928)		70·00	£275 □ □

The PHQ Card did not become available until mid-July. The used price quoted is for an example used in July or August 1973.

414 'Self-portrait' (Sir Joshua Reynolds)

415 'Self-portrait' (Sir Henry Raeburn)

416 'Nelly O'Brien' (Sir Joshua Reynolds)

417 'Rev R. Walker (The Skater)' (Sir Henry Raeburn)

Artistic Anniversaries. Events described on stamps

1973 (4 JULY) *'All-over' phosphor*

931	**414**	3p multicoloured	. . . .	10	10 □ □
932	**415**	5p multicoloured	. . . .	30	30 □ □
933	**416**	7½p multicoloured	. . . .	30	30 □ □
934	**417**	9p multicoloured	. . . .	60	60 □ □
		Set of 4		1·20	1·20 □ □
		First Day Cover			2·00 □
		Presentation Pack		3·25	□

418 Court Masque Costumes

419 St Paul's Church, Covent Garden

420 Prince's Lodging, Newmarket

421 Court Masque Stage Scene

The 3p and 5p values were printed horizontally *se-tenant* within the sheet.

400th Anniversary of the Birth of Inigo Jones (architect and designer)

1973 (15 AUG.) *'All-over' phosphor*

935	**418**	3p deep mauve, black and gold	. . . .	10	25 □ □
		a. Pair. Nos. 935/6		30	50 □ □
936	**419**	3p deep brown, black and gold	. . . .	10	25 □ □

937	**420**	5p blue, black and gold . .	35	50	☐	☐
		a. Pair. Nos. 937/8	1·00	1·00	☐	☐
938	**421**	5p grey-olive, black and gold	35	50	☐	☐
		Set of 4	1·25	1·25	☐	☐
		First Day Cover		2·00		☐
		Presentation Pack	3·50		☐	
		PHQ Card (No. 936)	£200	£200	☐	☐

422 Palace of Westminster seen from Whitehall

423 Palace of Westminster seen from Millbank

19th Commonwealth Parliamentary Conference

1973 (12 Sept.) *'All-over' phosphor*

939	**422**	8p black, grey and pale buff	45	50	☐	☐
940	**423**	10p gold and black	45	40	☐	☐
		Set of 2	75	75	☐	☐
		First Day Cover		1·50		☐
		Presentation Pack	3·00		☐	
		Souvenir Book	7·00		☐	
		PHQ Card (No. 939)	40·00	£150	☐	☐

14 November 1973   3½p

424 Princess Anne and Captain Mark Phillips

Royal Wedding

1973 (14 Nov.) *'All-over' phosphor*

941	**424**	3½p violet and silver	25	25	☐	☐
942		20p brown and silver . . .	1·00	75	☐	☐
		Set of 2	1·00	75	☐	☐
		First Day Cover		1·50		☐
		Presentation Pack	2·75		☐	
		PHQ Card (No. 941)	9·00	50·00	☐	☐
		Set of 2 Gutter Pairs	2·75		☐	
		Set of 2 Traffic Light Gutter Pairs	£110		☐	

425

426

427

428

429

430 'Good King Wenceslas, the Page and Peasant'

The 3p values depict the carol 'Good King Wenceslas' and were printed horizontally *se-tenant* within the sheet.

Christmas

1973 (28 Nov.) *One phosphor band (3p) or 'all-over' phosphor (3½p)*

943	**425**	3p multicoloured	20	25	☐	☐
		a. Strip of 5. Nos. 943/7 .	2·25	2·50	☐	☐
944	**426**	3p multicoloured	20	25	☐	☐
945	**427**	3p multicoloured	20	25	☐	☐
946	**428**	3p multicoloured	20	25	☐	☐
947	**429**	3p multicoloured	20	25	☐	☐
948	**430**	3½p multicoloured	20	25	☐	☐
		Set of 6	2·25	2·50	☐	☐
		First Day Cover		2·50		☐
		Presentation Pack	4·00		☐	

Collectors Pack 1973

1973 (28 Nov.) *Comprises Nos. 919/48*

CP948k	Collectors Pack	27·00		☐

10p

Horse Chestnut   Aesculus hippocastanum

431 Horse Chestnut

British Trees (2nd issue)

1974 (27 Feb.) *'All-over' phosphor*

949	**431**	10p multicoloured	40	35	☐	☐
		First Day Cover		1·25		☐
		Presentation Pack	2·50		☐	
		PHQ Card	£150	£150	☐	☐
		Gutter Pair	2·00		☐	
		Traffic Light Gutter Pair	65·00		☐	

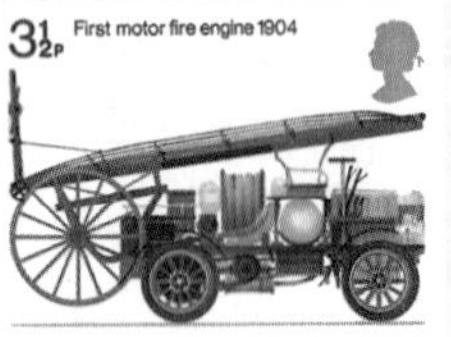

432 First Motor Fire-engine, 1904

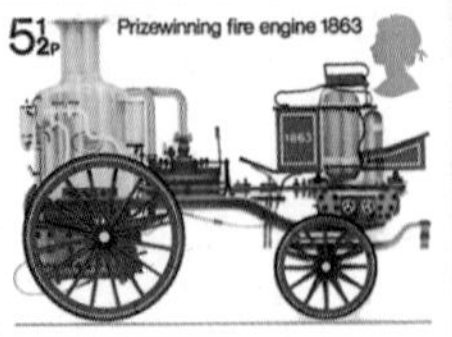

433 Prize-winning Fire-engine, 1863

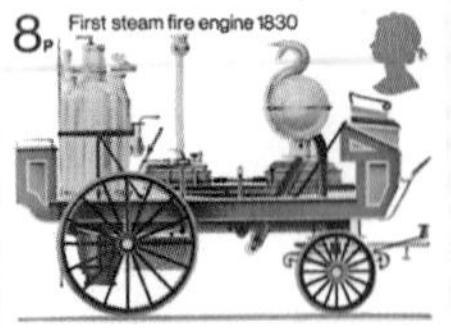

434 First Steam Fire-engine, 1830

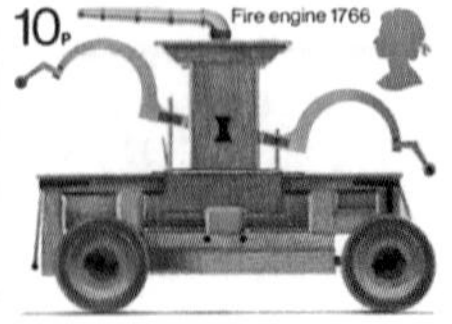

435 Fire-engine, 1766

Bicentenary of the Fire Prevention (Metropolis) Act

1974 (24 APR.) *'All-over' phosphor*

950	**432**	3½p multicoloured	25	10	□	□
951	**433**	5½p multicoloured	25	30	□	□
952	**434**	8p multicoloured	50	50	□	□
953	**435**	10p multicoloured	50	50	□	□
		Set of 4	1·25	1·25	□	□
		First Day Cover		3·00		□
		Presentation Pack	3·00		□	
		PHQ Card (*No.* 950)	£140	£150	□	□
		Set of 4 Gutter Pairs	4·00		□	
		Set of 4 Traffic Light Gutter Pairs	65·00		□	

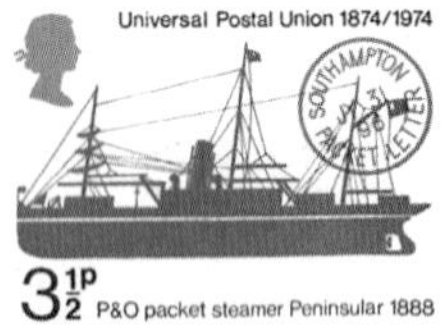

436 P & O Packet *Peninsular*, 1888

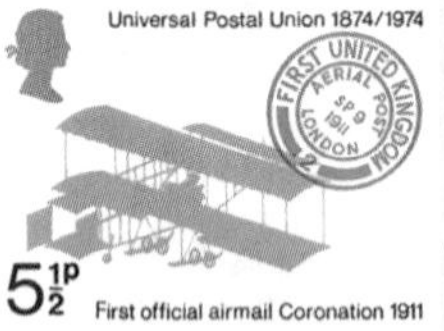

437 Farman H.F. III Biplane, 1911

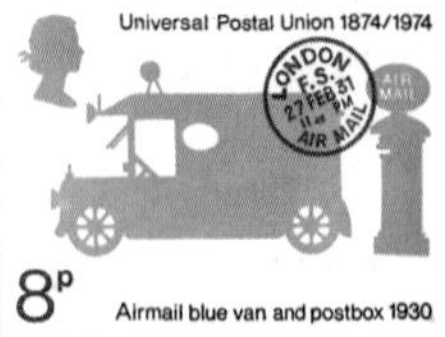

438 Airmail-blue Van and Postbox, 1930

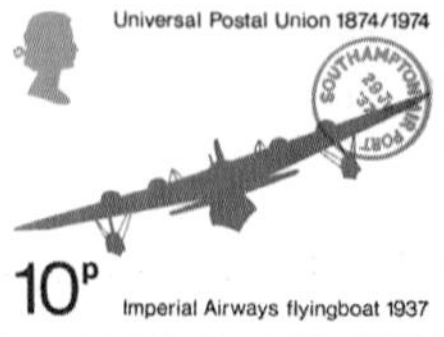

439 Imperial Airways Short S.21 Flying Boat *Maia*, 1937

Centenary of Universal Postal Union

1974 (12 JUNE) *'All-over' phosphor*

954	**436**	3½p multicoloured	25	10	□	□
955	**437**	5½p multicoloured	25	30	□	□
956	**438**	8p multicoloured	25	35	□	□
957	**439**	10p multicoloured	50	40	□	□
		Set of 4	1·00	1·00	□	□
		First Day Cover		2·00		□
		Presentation Pack	3·00		□	
		Set of 4 Gutter Pairs	3·00		□	
		Set of 4 Traffic Light Gutter Pairs	45·00		□	

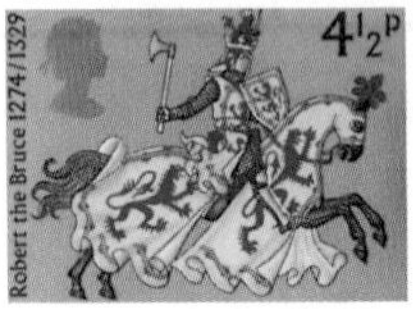

440 Robert the Bruce

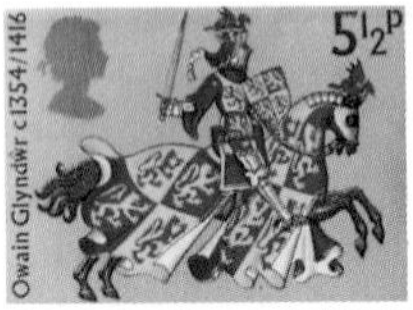

441 Owain Glyndŵr

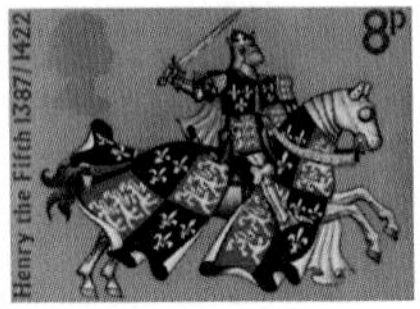

442 Henry V

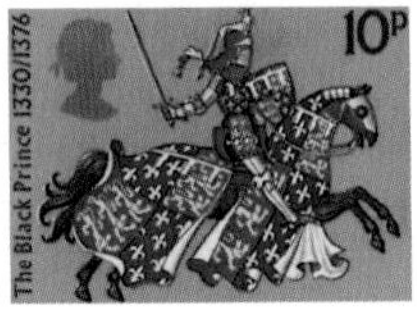

443 The Black Prince

Medieval Warriors

1974 (10 JULY) *'All-over' phosphor*

958	**440**	4½p multicoloured	25	10	□	□
959	**441**	5½p multicoloured	25	35	□	□
960	**442**	8p multicoloured	50	50	□	□
961	**443**	10p multicoloured	50	50	□	□
		Set of 4	1·25	1·25	□	□
		First Day Cover		3·00		□
		Presentation Pack	4·00		□	
		PHQ Cards (*set of* 4)	28·00	55·00	□	□
		Set of 4 Gutter Pairs	4·00		□	
		Set of 4 Traffic Light Gutter Pairs	70·00		□	

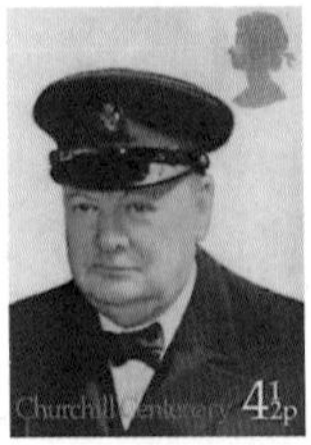

444 Churchill in Royal Yacht Squadron Uniform

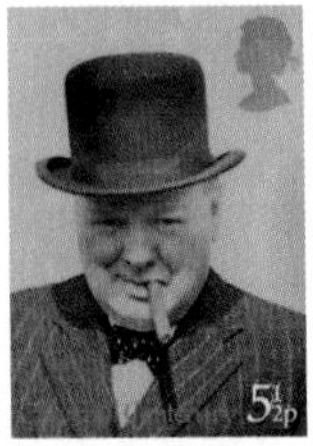

445 Prime Minister, 1940

446 Secretary for War
and Air, 1919

447 War Correspondent,
South Africa, 1899

Birth Centenary of Sir Winston Churchill
1974 (9 Oct.) *Queen's head and inscription in silver. 'All-over'
phosphor*

962	**444**	4½p green and blue	....	20	15 □	□
963	**445**	5½p grey and black	.....	35	35 □	□
964	**446**	8p rose and lake	....	60	50 □	□
965	**447**	10p stone and brown	...	60	50 □	□
	Set of 4	....		1·60	1·50 □	□
	First Day Cover	....			2·00	□
	Presentation Pack	....		3·00		□
	Souvenir Book	....		3·00		□
	PHQ Card (No. 963)	....		6·00	32·00 □	□
	Set of 4 Gutter Pairs	......		4·00		□
	Set of 4 Traffic Light Gutter Pairs			34·00		□

448 Adoration of the Magi
(York Minster, *c* 1355)

449 The Nativity (St Helen's
Church, Norwich, *c* 1480)

450 Virgin and Child (Ottery
St Mary Church, *c* 1350)

451 Virgin and Child (Worcester
Cathedral, *c* 1224)

Christmas
1974 (27 Nov.) *Designs show church roof bosses. One
phosphor band* (3½p) *or 'all-over' phosphor* (others)

966	**448**	3½p multicoloured	....	10	10 □	□
967	**449**	4½p multicoloured	....	10	10 □	□

968	**450**	8p multicoloured	....	25	50 □	□
969	**451**	10p multicoloured	.....	50	50 □	□
	Set of 4	.....		1·00	1·00 □	□
	First Day Cover	....			2·00	□
	Presentation Pack	....		2·75		□
	Set of 4 Gutter Pairs	....		3·50		□
	Set of 4 Traffic Light Gutter Pairs			36·00		□

Collectors Pack 1974
1974 (27 Nov.) *Comprises Nos. 949/69*

CP969a	*Collectors Pack*	....	13·00		□

452 Invalid in Wheelchair

Health and Handicap Funds
1975 (22 Jan.) *'All-over' phosphor*

970	**452**	4½p + 1½p azure and blue	..	25	25 □	□
	First Day Cover	....			1·00	□
	Gutter Pair	....		50		□
	Traffic Light Gutter Pair	.....		2·25		□

453 'Peace – Burial at Sea'

454 'Snowstorm – Steamer off
a Harbour's Mouth'

455 'The Arsenal, Venice'

456 'St Laurent'

Birth Bicentenary of J. M. W. Turner (painter)
1975 (19 Feb.) *'All-over' phosphor*

971	**453**	4½p multicoloured	.....	25	25 □	□
972	**454**	5½p multicoloured	.....	25	25 □	□

973	**455**	8p multicoloured	25	50	☐	☐
974	**456**	10p multicoloured	50	50	☐	☐
		Set of 4	1·00	1·00	☐	☐
		First Day Cover		1·50		☐
		Presentation Pack	2·75		☐	
		PHQ Card (No. 972)	42·00	34·00	☐	☐
		Set of 4 Gutter Pairs	2·25		☐	
		Set of 4 Traffic Light Gutter Pairs	11·50		☐	

457 Charlotte Square, Edinburgh

458 The Rows, Chester

The above were printed horizontally *se-tenant* throughout the sheet.

459 Royal Observatory, Greenwich

460 St George's Chapel, Windsor

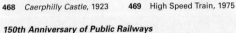

italic placeholder

461 National Theatre, London

European Architectural Heritage Year
1975 (23 Apr.) *'All-over' phosphor*

975	**457**	7p multicoloured	15	15	☐	☐
		a. Pair. Nos. 975/6	90	1·00	☐	☐
976	**458**	7p multicoloured	15	15	☐	☐
977	**459**	8p multicoloured	40	30	☐	☐
978	**460**	10p multicoloured	40	30	☐	☐
979	**461**	12p multicoloured	40	35	☐	☐
		Set of 5	1·50	1·40	☐	☐
		First Day Cover		2·50		☐
		Presentation Pack	3·00		☐	
		PHQ Cards (Nos. 975/7)	11·00	40·00	☐	☐
		Set of 5 Gutter Pairs	5·50		☐	
		Set of 5 Traffic Light Gutter Pairs	22·00		☐	

462 Sailing Dinghies

463 Racing Keel Boats

464 Cruising Yachts

465 Multihulls

Sailing
1975 (11 June) *'All-over' phosphor*

980	**462**	7p multicoloured	25	20	☐	☐
981	**463**	8p multicoloured	35	40	☐	☐
982	**464**	10p multicoloured	35	45	☐	☐
983	**465**	12p multicoloured	50	50	☐	☐
		Set of 4	1·25	1·25	☐	☐
		First Day Cover		2·00		☐
		Presentation Pack	2·50		☐	
		PHQ Card (No. 981)	5·75	30·00	☐	☐
		Set of 4 Gutter Pairs	2·50		☐	
		Set of 4 Traffic Light Gutter Pairs	25·00		☐	

466 Stephenson's *Locomotion*, 1825

467 *Abbotsford*, 1876

468 *Caerphilly Castle*, 1923

469 High Speed Train, 1975

150th Anniversary of Public Railways
1975 (13 Aug.) *'All-over' phosphor*

984	**466**	7p multicoloured	25	25	☐	☐
985	**467**	8p multicoloured	50	50	☐	☐

986	468	10p multicoloured	50	50 □ □
987	469	12p multicoloured	40	50 □ □
		Set of 4	1·50	1·50 □ □
		First Day Cover		2·50 □
		Presentation Pack	3·00	□
		Souvenir Book	4·00	□
		PHQ Cards (set of 4)	70·00	72·00 □ □
		Set of 4 Gutter Pairs	3·00	□
		Set of 4 Traffic Light Gutter Pairs	12·00	□

470 Palace of Westminster

62nd Inter-Parliamentary Union Conference

1975 (3 Sept.) *'All-over' phosphor*

988	470	12p multicoloured	50	40 □ □
		First Day Cover		80 □
		Presentation Pack	1·50	□
		Gutter Pair	1·00	□
		Traffic Light Gutter Pair	3·50	□

471 Emma and Mr
Woodhouse
(*Emma*)

472 Catherine Morland
(*Northanger Abbey*)

473 Mr Darcy
(*Pride and
Prejudice*)

474 Mary and Henry
Crawford (*Mansfield
Park*)

Birth Bicentenary of Jane Austen (novelist)

1975 (22 Oct.) *'All-over' phosphor*

989	471	8½p multicoloured	25	20 □ □
990	472	10p multicoloured	45	45 □ □

991	473	11p multicoloured	45	45 □ □
992	474	13p multicoloured	50	50 □ □
		Set of 4	1·50	1·25 □ □
		First Day Cover		2·50 □
		Presentation Pack	3·00	□
		PHQ Cards (set of 4)	24·00	42·00 □ □
		Set of 4 Gutter Pairs	2·50	□
		Set of 4 Traffic Light Gutter Pairs	9·00	□

475 Angels with
Harp and Lute

476 Angel with Mandolin

477 Angel with Horn

478 Angel with Trumpet

Christmas

1975 (26 Nov.) *One phosphor band (6½p). phosphor-inked (8½p)
(background) or 'all-over' phosphor (others)*

993	475	6½p multicoloured	25	25 □ □
994	476	8½p multicoloured	25	40 □ □
995	477	11p multicoloured	50	45 □ □
996	478	13p multicoloured	50	45 □ □
		Set of 4	1·25	1·25 □ □
		First Day Cover		1·50 □
		Presentation Pack	2·75	□
		Set of 4 Gutter Pairs	2·75	□
		Set of 4 Traffic Light Gutter Pairs	9·00	□

Collectors Pack 1975

1975 (26 Nov.) *Comprises Nos. 970/96*

CP996*a*	*Collectors Pack*	9·00	□

479 Housewife

480 Policeman

47

481 District Nurse **482** Industrialist

Telephone Centenary
1976 (10 MAR.) *'All-over' phosphor*

997	479	8½p multicoloured	25	20	☐	☐
998	480	10p multicoloured	40	40	☐	☐
999	481	11p multicoloured	50	50	☐	☐
1000	482	13p multicoloured	60	60	☐	☐
		Set of 4	1·50	1·50	☐	☐
		First Day Cover		1·50		☐
		Presentation Pack	2·50		☐	
		Set of 4 Gutter Pairs	2·75		☐	
		Set of 4 Traffic Light Gutter Pairs	9·00		☐	

483 Hewing Coal (Thomas Hepburn) **484** Machinery (Robert Owen)

485 Chimney Cleaning (Lord Shaftesbury) **486** Hands clutching Prison Bars (Elizabeth Fry)

Social Reformers
1976 (28 APR.) *'All-over' phosphor*

1001	483	8½p multicoloured	25	20	☐	☐
1002	484	10p multicoloured	40	40	☐	☐
1003	485	11p black, slate-grey and drab	50	50	☐	☐
1004	486	13p slate-grey, black and green	60	60	☐	☐
		Set of 4	1·50	1·50	☐	☐
		First Day Cover		1·50		☐
		Presentation Pack	2·50		☐	
		PHQ Card (No. 1001)	6·00	20·00	☐	☐
		Set of 4 Gutter Pairs	2·75		☐	
		Set of 4 Traffic Light Gutter Pairs	9·00		☐	

487 Benjamin Franklin (bust by Jean-Jacques Caffieri)

Bicentenary of American Revolution
1976 (2 JUNE) *'All-over' phosphor*

1005	487	11p multicoloured	50	50	☐	☐
		First Day Cover		1·50		☐
		Presentation Pack	1·25		☐	
		PHQ Card	4·25	20·00	☐	☐
		Gutter Pair	75		☐	
		Traffic Light Gutter Pair	3·00		☐	

488 'Elizabeth of Glamis' **489** 'Grandpa Dickson'

490 'Rosa Mundi' **491** 'Sweet Briar'

Centenary of Royal National Rose Society
1976 (30 JUNE) *'All-over' phosphor*

1006	488	8½p multicoloured	15	10	☐	☐
1007	489	10p multicoloured	40	40	☐	☐
1008	490	11p multicoloured	50	50	☐	☐
1009	491	13p multicoloured	65	65	☐	☐
		Set of 4	1·50	1·50	☐	☐
		First Day Cover		1·50		☐
		Presentation Pack	3·00		☐	
		PHQ Cards (set of 4)	28·00	35·00	☐	☐
		Set of 4 Gutter Pairs	3·00		☐	
		Set of 4 Traffic Light Gutter Pairs	12·00		☐	

492 Archdruid   **493** Morris Dancing

494 Scots Piper   **495** Welsh Harpist

British Cultural Traditions

1976 (4 Aug.) *'All-over' phosphor*

1010	**492**	8½p multicoloured	25	20	□	□
1011	**493**	10p multicoloured	40	40	□	□
1012	**494**	11p multicoloured	45	45	□	□
1013	**495**	13p multicoloured	60	60	□	□
		Set of 4	1·50	1·50	□	□
		First Day Cover		2·00		□
		Presentation Pack	2·50		□	
		PHQ Cards (set of 4)	18·00	28·00	□	□
		Set of 4 Gutter Pairs	3·00		□	
		Set of 4 Traffic Light Gutter Pairs	12·00		□	

496 The Canterbury   **497** The Tretyse of Love
Tales

For full information on all future British issues, collectors should write to Royal Mail, Freepost EH3647, 21 South Gyle Crescent, Edinburgh EH12 9PE.

498 *Game and Playe   **499** Early Printing Press
of Chesse*

500th Anniversary of British Printing

1976 (29 Sept.) *'All-over' phosphor*

1014	**496**	8½p black, blue and gold .	25	20	□	□
1015	**497**	10p black, olive-green and gold	40	40	□	□
1016	**498**	11p black, grey and gold .	45	45	□	□
1017	**499**	13p brown, ochre and gold	60	60	□	□
		Set of 4	1·50	1·50	□	□
		First Day Cover		1·75		□
		Presentation Pack	2·75		□	
		PHQ Cards (set of 4)	10·00	28·00	□	□
		Set of 4 Gutter Pairs	3·00		□	
		Set of 4 Traffic Light Gutter Pairs	8·00		□	

500 Virgin and Child   **501** Angel with Crown

502 Angel appearing to   **503** The Three Kings
Shepherds

Christmas

1976 (24 Nov.) *Designs show English medieval embroidery. One phosphor band (6½p) or 'all-over' phosphor (others)*

1018	**500**	6½p multicoloured	25	25	□	□
1019	**501**	8½p multicoloured	35	25	□	□
1020	**502**	11p multicoloured	40	45	□	□

1021	**503**	13p multicoloured	45	50 ☐ ☐
		Set of 4	1·25	1·25 ☐ ☐
		First Day Cover		1·50 ☐
		Presentation Pack	2·75	☐
		PHQ Cards (set of 4)	4·50	26·00 ☐ ☐
		Set of 4 Gutter Pairs	2·75	☐
		Set of 4 Traffic Light Gutter Pairs	8·00	☐

Collectors Pack 1976

1976 (24 Nov.) *Comprises Nos. 997/1021*

CP1021a	*Collectors Pack*	13·50	☐

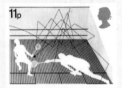

504 Lawn Tennis

505 Table Tennis

506 Squash

507 Badminton

Racket Sports

1977 (12 Jan.) *Phosphorised paper*

1022	**504**	8½p multicoloured	25	20 ☐ ☐
1023	**505**	10p multicoloured	40	40 ☐ ☐
1024	**506**	11p multicoloured	45	40 ☐ ☐
1025	**507**	13p multicoloured	45	50 ☐ ☐
		Set of 4	1·25	1·25 ☐ ☐
		First Day Cover		2·00 ☐
		Presentation Pack	2·50	☐
		PHQ Cards (set of 4)	8·00	24·00 ☐ ☐
		Set of 4 Gutter Pairs	3·00	☐
		Set of 4 Traffic Light Gutter Pairs	7·00	☐

508

1977 (2 Feb.)–87 *Type* **508** *Ordinary paper*

1026	£1 green and olive	3·00	25 ☐ ☐
1026b	£1·30 drab and deep greenish blue	5·50	6·00 ☐ ☐
1026c	£1·33 pale mauve and grey-black	7·50	7·00 ☐ ☐
1026d	£1·41 drab and deep greenish blue	8·50	8·50 ☐ ☐
1026e	£1·50 pale mauve and grey-black	6·00	5·00 ☐ ☐
1026f	£1·60 drab and deep greenish blue	6·50	7·00 ☐ ☐
1027	£2 green and brown	9·00	50 ☐ ☐
1028	£5 pink and blue	22·00	3·00 ☐ ☐
	Set of 8	60·00	32·00 ☐ ☐
	Presentation Pack (P.O. Pack No. 91 (small size)) (Nos. 1026, 1027/8)	48·00	☐
	Presentation Pack (P.O. Pack No.13 (large size)) (Nos. 1026, 1027/8)	£160	☐
	Presentation Pack (P.O. Pack No. 14) (No. 1026f)	12·00	☐
	Set of 8 Gutter Pairs	£150	☐
	Set of 8 Traffic Light Gutter Pairs	£180	☐

First Day Covers

2 Feb. 1977	Nos. 1026, 1027/8	14·00 ☐
3 Aug. 1983	No. 1026b	6·50 ☐
28 Aug. 1984	No. 1026c	8·00 ☐
17 Sept. 1985	No. 1026d	9·00 ☐
2 Sept. 1986	No. 1026e	6·50 ☐
15 Sept. 1987	No. 1026f	8·50 ☐

509 Steroids — Conformational Analysis

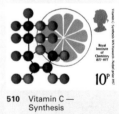

510 Vitamin C — Synthesis

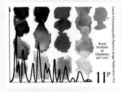

511 Starch — Chromatography

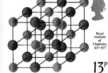

512 Salt — Crystallography

Centenary of Royal Institute of Chemistry

1977 (2 Mar.) *'All-over' phosphor*

1029	**509**	8½p multicoloured	25	20 ☐ ☐
1030	**510**	10p multicoloured	45	45 ☐ ☐
1031	**511**	11p multicoloured	45	45 ☐ ☐

1032	**512**	13p multicoloured	45	45 □ □
		Set of 4	1·25	1·25 □ □
		First Day Cover		1·50 □
		Presentation Pack	2·50	□
		PHQ Cards (set of 4)	8·00	18·00 □ □
		Set of 4 Gutter Pairs	3·00	□
		Set of 4 Traffic Light Gutter Pairs	8·00	□

513

518 Hedgehog   **519** Brown Hare

Silver Jubilee

1977 (11 MAY–15 JUNE) *'All-over' phosphor*

1033	**513**	8½p multicoloured	25	25 □ □
1034		9p multicoloured (15 June)	25	25 □ □
1035		10p multicoloured	25	25 □ □
1036		11p multicoloured	50	50 □ □
1037		13p multicoloured	50	50 □ □
		Set of 5	1·50	1·25 □ □
		First Day Covers (2)		2·00 □
		Presentation Pack (ex 9p)	2·00	□
		Souvenir Book (ex 9p)	3·00	□
		PHQ Cards (set of 5)	14·00	20·00 □ □
		Set of 5 Gutter Pairs	3·50	□
		Set of 5 Traffic Light Gutter Pairs	7·00	□

520 Red Squirrel   **521** Otter

522 Badger

T **518/22** were printed together, *se-tenant*, throughout the sheet.

British Wildlife

1977 (5 OCT.) *'All-over' phosphor*

1039	**518**	9p multicoloured	25	20 □ □
		a. Strip of 5. Nos.		
		1039/43	1·50	1·75 □ □
1040	**519**	9p multicoloured	25	20 □ □
1041	**520**	9p multicoloured	25	20 □ □
1042	**521**	9p multicoloured	25	20 □ □
1043	**522**	9p multicoloured	25	20 □ □
		Set of 5	1·50	1·75 □ □
		First Day Cover		3·00 □
		Presentation Pack	2·50	□
		PHQ Cards (set of 5)	3·00	7·00 □ □
		Gutter Strip of 10	3·00	□
		Traffic Light Gutter Strip of 10 .	5·00	□

517 'Gathering of Nations'

Commonwealth Heads of Government Meeting, London

1977 (8 JUNE) *'All-over' phosphor*

1038	**517**	13p black, deep green, rose		
		and silver	50	50 □ □
		First Day Cover		1·50 □
		Presentation Pack	1·50	□
		PHQ Card	3·00	6·00 □ □
		Gutter Pair	1·00	□
		Traffic Light Gutter Pair	2·00	□

523 'Three French Hens,
Two Turtle Doves and a
Partridge in a Pear Tree'

524 'Six Geese a laying,
Five Gold Rings,
Four Colly Birds'

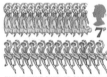

525 'Eight Maids a-milking,
Seven Swans a-
swimming'

526 'Ten Pipers piping,
Nine Drummers
drumming'

527 'Twelve Lords a-leaping,
Eleven Ladies dancing'

528 'A Partridge in a
Pear Tree'

T **523/8** depict the carol 'The Twelve Days of Christmas'.
T **523/7** were printed horizontally *se-tenant* throughout the sheet.

Christmas

1977 (23 Nov.) *One centre phosphor band* (7p) *or 'all-over'*
phosphor (9p)

1044	**523**	7p multicoloured	20	15	□	□
		a. Strip of 5. Nos. 1044/8	1·50	1·50	□	□
1045	**524**	7p multicoloured	20	15	□	□
1046	**525**	7p multicoloured	20	15	□	□
1047	**526**	7p multicoloured	20	15	□	□
1048	**527**	7p multicoloured	20	15	□	□
1049	**528**	9p multicoloured	35	30	□	□
		Set of 6	1·25	1·50	□	□
		First Day Cover		2·25	□	
		Presentation Pack	2·25		□	
		PHQ Cards (set of 6)	3·00	6·00	□	□
		Set of 6 Gutter Pairs	3·00		□	
		Set of 6 Traffic Light Gutter Pairs	5·00		□	

Collectors Pack 1977

1977 (23 Nov.) *Comprises Nos.* 1022/5, 1029/49
CP1049*b* Collectors Pack . . . . 9·00 □

529 Oil — North Sea
Production Platform

530 Coal — Modern
Pithead

531 Natural Gas —
Flame Rising
from Sea

532 Electricity — Nuclear
Power Station and
Uranium Atom

Energy Resources

1978 (25 Jan.) *'All-over' phosphor*

1050	**529**	9p multicoloured	25	25	□	□
1051	**530**	10½p multicoloured	25	25	□	□
1052	**531**	11p multicoloured	50	50	□	□
1053	**532**	13p multicoloured	50	50	□	□
		Set of 4	1·25	1·25	□	□
		First Day Cover		1·50		□
		Presentation Pack	2·00		□	
		PHQ Cards (set of 4)	3·00	6·00	□	□
		Set of 4 Gutter Pairs	2·75		□	
		Set of 4 Traffic Light Gutter Pairs	4·50		□	

533 Tower of London

534 Holyroodhouse

535 Caernarvon Castle

536 Hampton Court Palace

British Architecture (Historic Buildings)

1978 (1 Mar.) *'All-over' phosphor*

1054	**533**	9p multicoloured	25	20	□	□
1055	**534**	10½p multicoloured	25	40	□	□
1056	**535**	11p multicoloured	60	40	□	□
1057	**536**	13p multicoloured	60	40	□	□
		Set of 4	1·50	1·25	□	□
		First Day Cover		1·50		□
		Presentation Pack	2·00		□	
		PHQ Cards (set of 4)	3·00	6·00	□	□
		Set of 4 Gutter Pairs	3·00		□	
		Set of 4 Traffic Light Gutter Pairs	4·50		□	
MS1058	121 × 90 mm. Nos. 1054/7 . .		1·25	1·75	□	□
		First Day Cover		2·00		□

No. **MS**1058 was sold at 53½p, the premium being used for the London 1980 Stamp Exhibition.

537 State Coach

538 St Edward's Crown

539 The Sovereign's Orb

540 Imperial State Crown

25th Anniversary of Coronation

1978 (31 May) *'All-over' phosphor*

1059	**537**	9p gold and blue	35	25	□	□
1060	**538**	10½p gold and red	45	45	□	□
1061	**539**	11p gold and green	45	45	□	□
1062	**540**	13p gold and violet	50	50	□	□
		Set of 4	1·50	1·50	□	□
		First Day Cover		1·50		□
		Presentation Pack	2·00		□	
		Souvenir Book	3·00		□	
		PHQ Cards (set of 4)	3·00	6·00	□	□
		Set of 4 Gutter Pairs	3·00		□	
		Set of 4 Traffic Light Gutter Pairs	4·25		□	

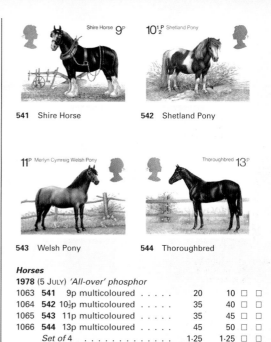

541 Shire Horse

542 Shetland Pony

543 Welsh Pony

544 Thoroughbred

Horses

1978 (5 July) *'All-over' phosphor*

1063	**541**	9p multicoloured	20	10	□	□
1064	**542**	10½p multicoloured	35	40	□	□
1065	**543**	11p multicoloured	35	45	□	□
1066	**544**	13p multicoloured	45	50	□	□
		Set of 4	1·25	1·25	□	□
		First Day Cover		1·50		□
		Presentation Pack	1·75		□	
		PHQ Cards (set of 4)	2·25	5·75	□	□
		Set of 4 Gutter Pairs	3·00		□	
		Set of 4 Traffic Light Gutter Pairs	4·50		□	

545 Penny-farthing and 1884 Safety Bicycle

546 1920 Touring Bicycles

547 Modern Small-wheel Bicycles

548 1978 Road-racers

Centenaries of Cyclists Touring Club and British Cycling Federation

1978 (2 Aug.) *'All-over' phosphor*

1067	545	9p multicoloured	25	20	□	□
1068	546	10½p multicoloured	35	40	□	□
1069	547	11p multicoloured	40	40	□	□
1070	548	13p multicoloured	50	50	□	□
		Set of 4	1·25	1·25	□	□
		First Day Cover		1·50		□
		Presentation Pack	1·75		□	
		PHQ Cards (set of 4)	2·25	5·00	□	□
		Set of 4 Gutter Pairs	2·75		□	
		Set of 4 Traffic Light Gutter Pairs	4·50		□	

549 Singing Carols round the Christmas Tree

550 The Waits

551 18th-Century Carol Singers

552 'The Boar's Head Carol'

Christmas

1978 (22 Nov.) *One centre phosphor band (7p) or 'all-over' phosphor (others)*

1071	549	7p multicoloured	25	25	□	□
1072	550	9p multicoloured	25	25	□	□
1073	551	11p multicoloured	50	50	□	□
1074	552	13p multicoloured	50	50	□	□
		Set of 4	1·25	1·25	□	□
		First Day Cover		1·50		□
		Presentation Pack	1·75		□	
		PHQ Cards (set of 4)	2·25	5·00	□	□
		Set of 4 Gutter Pairs	2·50		□	
		Set of 4 Traffic Light Gutter Pairs	4·25		□	

Collectors Pack 1978

1978 (22 Nov.) *Comprises Nos. 1050/7, 1059/74*

CP1074a	Collectors Pack	9·25		□

553 Old English Sheepdog

554 Welsh Springer Spaniel

555 West Highland Terrier

556 Irish Setter

Dogs

1979 (7 Feb.) *'All-over' phosphor*

1075	553	9p multicoloured	25	20	□	□
1076	554	10½p multicoloured	40	40	□	□
1077	555	11p multicoloured	40	40	□	□
1078	556	13p multicoloured	40	50	□	□
		Set of 4	1·25	1·25	□	□
		First Day Cover		1·50		□
		Presentation Pack	1·75		□	
		PHQ Cards (set of 4)	2·50	5·00	□	□
		Set of 4 Gutter Pairs	7·50		□	
		Set of 4 Traffic Light Gutter Pairs	4·25		□	

557 Primrose

558 Daffodil

559 Bluebell

560 Snowdrop

Spring Wild Flowers

1979 (21 Mar.) *'All-over' phosphor*

1079	**557**	9p multicoloured	25	20	☐	☐
1080	**558**	10½p multicoloured	25	45	☐	☐
1081	**559**	11p multicoloured	50	45	☐	☐
1082	**560**	13p multicoloured	50	40	☐	☐
		Set of 4	1·25	1·25	☐	☐
		First Day Cover		1·50		☐
		Presentation Pack	1·75		☐	
		PHQ Cards (set of 4)	2·50	4·50	☐	☐
		Set of 4 Gutter Pairs	2·50		☐	
		Set of 4 Traffic Light Gutter Pairs	4·25		☐	

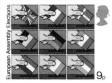

561

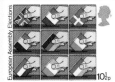

562

563

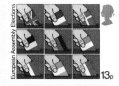

564

T **561/4** show hands placing the flags of the member nations into ballot boxes.

First Direct Elections to European Assembly

1979 (9 May) *Phosphorised paper*

1083	**561**	9p multicoloured	25	20	☐	☐
1084	**562**	10½p multicoloured	35	35	☐	☐
1085	**563**	11p multicoloured	40	40	☐	☐
1086	**564**	13p multicoloured	45	40	☐	☐
		Set of 4	1·25	1·25	☐	☐
		First Day Cover		1·50		☐
		Presentation Pack	1·75		☐	
		PHQ Cards (set of 4)	2·25	4·50	☐	☐
		Set of 4 Gutter Pairs	2·50		☐	
		Set of 4 Traffic Light Gutter Pairs	4·25		☐	

565 'Saddling "Mahmoud" for the Derby, 1936' (Sir Alfred Munnings)

566 'The Liverpool Great National Steeple Chase, 1839' (aquatint by F. C. Turner)

567 'The First Spring Meeting, Newmarket, 1793' (J. N. Sartorius)

568 'Racing at Dorsett Ferry, Windsor, 1684' (Francis Barlow)

Horseracing Paintings and Bicentenary of The Derby (9p)

1979 (6 June) *'All-over' phosphor*

1087	**565**	9p multicoloured	25	25	☐	☐
1088	**566**	10½p multicoloured	25	25	☐	☐
1089	**567**	11p multicoloured	50	50	☐	☐
1090	**568**	13p multicoloured	50	50	☐	☐
		Set of 4	1·25	1·25	☐	☐
		First Day Cover		1·50		☐
		Presentation Pack	1·75		☐	
		PHQ Cards (set of 4)	2·25	4·50	☐	☐
		Set of 4 Gutter Pairs	2·50		☐	
		Set of 4 Traffic Light Gutter Pairs	4·25		☐	

569 The Tale of Peter Rabbit (Beatrix Potter)

570 The Wind in the Willows (Kenneth Grahame)

571 Winnie-the-Pooh (A. A. Milne)

572 Alice's Adventures in in Wonderland (Lewis Carroll)

T **569/72** depict original illustrations from the four books.

International Year of the Child
1979 (11 July) *'All-over' phosphor*

1091	**569**	9p multicoloured	30	25	□	□
1092	**570**	10½p multicoloured	35	35	□	□
1093	**571**	11p multicoloured	40	40	□	□
1094	**572**	13p multicoloured	60	60	□	□
		Set of 4	1·50	1·50	□	□
		First Day Cover		1·50		□
		Presentation Pack	1·75		□	
		PHQ Cards (set of 4)	2·50	4·50	□	□
		Set of 4 Gutter Pairs	3·00		□	
		Set of 4 Traffic Light Gutter Pairs	4·25		□	

573 Sir Rowland Hill, 1795–1879

574 General Post, c 1839

575 London Post, c 1839

576 Uniform Postage, 1840

Death Centenary of Sir Rowland Hill (postal reformer)
1979 (22 Aug.–24 Oct.) *'All-over' phosphor*

1095	**573**	10p multicoloured	25	20	□	□
1096	**574**	11½p multicoloured	25	35	□	□
1097	**575**	13p multicoloured	50	45	□	□
1098	**576**	15p multicoloured	75	75	□	□
		Set of 4	1·50	1·50	□	□
		First Day Cover		1·50		□
		Presentation Pack	1·50		□	
		PHQ Cards (set of 4)	2·25	4·25	□	□
		Set of 4 Gutter Pairs	3·00		□	
		Set of 4 Traffic Light Gutter Pairs	4·25		□	
MS1099		89 × 121 mm. Nos. 1095/8 . .	1·25	1·50	□	□
		First Day Cover (24 Oct.)		1·50		□

No. **MS**1099 was sold at 59½p, the premium being used for the London 1980 Stamp Exhibition.

577 Policeman on the Beat

578 Policeman directing Traffic

579 Mounted Policewoman

580 River Patrol Boat

150th Anniversary of Metropolitan Police
1979 (26 Sept.) *Phosphorised paper*

1100	**577**	10p multicoloured	30	20	□	□
1101	**578**	11½p multicoloured	35	35	□	□
1102	**579**	13p multicoloured	40	55	□	□
1103	**580**	15p multicoloured	60	55	□	□
		Set of 4	1·50	1·50	□	□
		First Day Cover		1·50		□
		Presentation Pack	1·75		□	
		PHQ Cards (set of 4)	2·25	4·25	□	□
		Set of 4 Gutter Pairs	3·00		□	
		Set of 4 Traffic Light Gutter Pairs	4·25		□	

581 The Three Kings

582 Angel appearing to the Shepherds

583 The Nativity

584 Mary and Joseph travelling to Bethlehem

585 The Annunciation

Christmas

1979 (21 Nov.) *One centre phosphor band (8p) or phosphorised paper (others)*

1104	**581**	8p multicoloured	25	20	☐	☐
1105	**582**	10p multicoloured	25	25	☐	☐
1106	**583**	11½p multicoloured	25	35	☐	☐
1107	**584**	13p multicoloured	50	50	☐	☐
1108	**585**	15p multicoloured	50	50	☐	☐
		Set of 5	1·50	1·50	☐	☐
		First Day Cover		1·50		☐
		Presentation Pack	2·00		☐	
		PHQ Cards (set of 5)	2·50	4·25	☐	☐
		Set of 5 Gutter Pairs	3·50		☐	
		Set of 5 Traffic Light Gutter Pairs	4·50		☐	

Collectors Pack 1979

1979 (21 Nov.) *Comprises Nos. 1075/98, 1100/8*

CP1108*a*	*Collectors Pack*	12·00		☐

586 Common Kingfisher

587 Dipper

588 Moorhen

589 Yellow Wagtails

Centenary of Wild Bird Protection Act

1980 (16 Jan.) *Phosphorised paper*

1109	**586**	10p multicoloured	20	10	☐	☐
1110	**587**	11½p multicoloured	40	35	☐	☐

1111	**588**	13p multicoloured	50	55	☐	☐
1112	**589**	15p multicoloured	50	55	☐	☐
		Set of 4	1·50	1·50	☐	☐
		First Day Cover		1·50		☐
		Presentation Pack	1·50		☐	
		PHQ Cards (set of 4)	2·25	4·50	☐	☐
		Set of 4 Gutter Pairs	3·50		☐	

590 *Rocket* approaching Moorish Arch, Liverpool

591 First and Second Class Carriages passing through Olive Mount Cutting

592 Third Class Carriage and Sheep Truck crossing Chat Moss

593 Horsebox and Carriage Truck near Bridgewater Canal

594 Goods Truck and Mail-coach at Manchester

T **590/4** were printed together, *se-tenant*, in horizontal strips of 5 throughout the sheet.

150th Anniversary of Liverpool and Manchester Railway

1980 (12 Mar.) *Phosphorised paper*

1113	**590**	12p multicoloured	20	15	☐	☐
		a. Strip of 5. Nos. 1113/17	1·75	1·75	☐	☐
1114	**591**	12p multicoloured	20	15	☐	☐
1115	**592**	12p multicoloured	20	15	☐	☐
1116	**593**	12p multicoloured	20	15	☐	☐
1117	**594**	12p multicoloured	20	15	☐	☐
		Set of 5	1·75	1·75	☐	☐
		First Day Cover		1·75		☐
		Presentation Pack	2·00		☐	
		PHQ Cards (set of 5)	3·25	4·50	☐	☐
		Gutter block of 10	3·75		☐	

595 Montage of London Buildings

INTERNATIONAL STAMP EXHIBITION

'London 1980' International Stamp Exhibition

1980 (9 Apr.–7 May) *Phosphorised paper. Perf 14½ × 14*

1118	**595**	50p agate	. . . .	1·50	1·50	□	□
		First Day Cover	. . . .		1·50		□
		Presentation Pack	. . . .	1·75			□
		PHQ Card	. . . .	2·25	3·00	□	□
		Gutter Pair	. . . .	3·25			□
MS1119	90 × 123 mm. No. 1118	. . . .		1·50	1·75	□	□
		First Day Cover (7 May)			2·00		□

No. **MS**1119 was sold at 75p, the premium being used for the exhibition.

596 Buckingham Palace

597 The Albert Memorial

598 Royal Opera House

599 Hampton Court

600 Kensington Palace

London Landmarks

1980 (7 May) *Phosphorised paper*

1120	**596**	10½p multicoloured	. . . . .	25	10	□ □
1121	**597**	12p multicoloured	. . . . .	25	15	□ □
1122	**598**	13½p multicoloured	. . . . .	40	50	□ □
1123	**599**	15p multicoloured	. . . . .	50	75	□ □
1124	**600**	17½p multicoloured	. . . . .	75	75	□ □
		Set of 5	. . . .	2·00	2·00	□ □
		First Day Cover	. . . . .		2·00	□
		Presentation Pack	. . . . .	2·00		□
		PHQ Cards (set of 5)	. . . . .	2·25	3·00	□ □
		Set of 5 Gutter Pairs	. . . . .	4·25		□

601 Charlotte Brontë (*Jane Eyre*)

602 George Eliot (*The Mill on the Floss*)

603 Emily Brontë (*Wuthering Heights*)

604 Mrs Gaskell (*North and South*)

T **601/4** show authoresses and scenes from their novels. T **601/2** also include the 'Europa' C.E.P.T. emblem.

Famous Authoresses

1980 (9 July) *Phosphorised paper*

1125	**601**	12p multicoloured	. . . . .	35	20	□ □
1126	**602**	13½p multicoloured	. . . . .	40	45	□ □
1127	**603**	15p multicoloured	. . . . .	40	45	□ □
1128	**604**	17½p multicoloured	. . . . .	50	50	□ □
		Set of 4	. . . .	1·50	1·50	□ □
		First Day Cover	. . . . .		1·50	□
		Presentation Pack	. . . . .	1·75		□
		PHQ Cards (set of 4)	. . . . .	2·50	3·00	□ □
		Set of 4 Gutter Pairs	. . . . .	3·75		□

605 Queen Elizabeth the
Queen Mother

80th Birthday of Queen Elizabeth the Queen Mother
1980 (4 Aug.) *Phosphorised paper*

1129	**605**	12p multicoloured	75	75	□	□
		First Day Cover		1·50		□
		PHQ Card	2·25	1·75	□	□
		Gutter Pair	1·50		□	

606 Sir Henry Wood

607 Sir Thomas Beecham

608 Sir Malcolm Sargent

609 Sir John Barbirolli

British Conductors
1980 (10 Sept.) *Phosphorised paper*

1130	**606**	12p multicoloured	30	10	□	□
1131	**607**	13½p multicoloured	45	40	□	□
1132	**608**	15p multicoloured	50	55	□	□
1133	**609**	17½p multicoloured	50	55	□	□
		Set of 4	1·50	1·50	□	□
		First Day Cover		1·75		□
		Presentation Pack	1·75		□	
		PHQ Cards (set of 4)	2·25	3·75	□	□
		Set of 4 Gutter Pairs	3·75		□	

For full information on all future British issues, collectors should write to Royal Mail, Freepost EH3647, 21 South Gyle Crescent, Edinburgh EH12 9PE.

610 Running

611 Rugby

612 Boxing

613 Cricket

Sports Centenaries
1980 (10 Oct.) *Phosphorised paper. Perf* 14 × 14½

1134	**610**	12p multicoloured	25	20	□	□
1135	**611**	13½p multicoloured	50	50	□	□
1136	**612**	15p multicoloured	50	45	□	□
1137	**613**	17½p multicoloured	50	50	□	□
		Set of 4	1·50	1·50	□	□
		First Day Cover		1·75		□
		Presentation Pack	1·75		□	
		PHQ Cards (set of 4)	2·25	3·75	□	□
		Set of 4 Gutter Pairs	3·75		□	

Centenaries:—12p Amateur Athletics Association; 13½p Welsh Rugby Union; 15p Amateur Boxing Association; 17½p First England v Australia Test Match.

614 Christmas Tree

615 Candles

616 Apples and Mistletoe

617 Crown, Chains and Bell

618 Holly

Christmas

1980 (19 Nov.) *One centre phosphor band (10p) or phosphorised paper (others)*

1138	**614**	10p multicoloured	20	10	☐	☐
1139	**615**	12p multicoloured	20	20	☐	☐
1140	**616**	13½p multicoloured	40	40	☐	☐
1141	**617**	15p multicoloured	55	50	☐	☐
1142	**618**	17½p multicoloured	55	50	☐	☐
		Set of 5	1·75	1·50	☐	☐
		First Day Cover		1·75		☐
		Presentation Pack	2·00			☐
		PHQ Cards (set of 5)	2·25	4·00	☐	☐
		Set of 5 Gutter Pairs	4·50			☐

Collectors Pack 1980

1980 (19 Nov.) *Comprises Nos. 1109/18, 1120/42*

CP1142a	Collectors Pack	15·00	☐

619 St Valentine's Day

620 Morris Dancers

621 Lammastide

622 Medieval Mummers

T **619/20** also include the 'Europa' C.E.P.T. emblem.

Folklore

1981 (6 Feb.) *Phosphorised paper*

1143	**619**	14p multicoloured	25	25	☐	☐
1144	**620**	18p multicoloured	50	50	☐	☐
1145	**621**	22p multicoloured	75	80	☐	☐
1146	**622**	25p multicoloured	1·00	1·10	☐	☐
		Set of 4	2·25	2·50	☐	☐
		First Day Cover		2·00		☐
		Presentation Pack	2·25			☐
		PHQ Cards (set of 4)	2·25	3·25	☐	☐
		Set of 4 Gutter Pairs	5·25			☐

623 Blind Man with Guide Dog

624 Hands spelling 'Deaf' in Sign Language

625 Disabled Man in Wheelchair

626 Disabled Artist painting with Foot

International Year of the Disabled

1981 (25 Mar.) *Phosphorised paper*

1147	**623**	14p multicoloured	50	25	☐	☐
1148	**624**	18p multicoloured	50	50	☐	☐
1149	**625**	22p multicoloured	75	85	☐	☐
1150	**626**	25p multicoloured	1·00	1·00	☐	☐
		Set of 4	2·25	2·50	☐	☐
		First Day Cover		2·50		☐
		Presentation Pack	2·25			☐
		PHQ Cards (set of 4)	2·25	3·25	☐	☐
		Set of 4 Gutter Pairs	4·25			☐

Small Tortoiseshell

627 *Aglais urticae*

Large Blue

628 *Maculinea arion*

Peacock

629 *Inachis io*

Chequered Skipper

630 *Carterocephalus palaemon*

Butterflies

1981 (13 May) *Phosphorised paper*

1151	**627**	14p multicoloured	25	20	☐	☐
1152	**628**	18p multicoloured	75	70	☐	☐
1153	**629**	22p multicoloured	70	85	☐	☐
1154	**630**	25p multicoloured	75	85	☐	☐
		Set of 4	2·25	2·50	☐	☐
		First Day Cover		2·50		☐
		Presentation Pack	2·25		☐	
		PHQ Cards (set of 4)	2·25	6·00	☐	☐
		Set of 4 Gutter Pairs	4·75		☐	

631 Glenfinnan, Scotland

632 Derwentwater, England

633 Stackpole Head, Wales

634 Giant's Causeway, N. Ireland

635 St Kilda, Scotland

50th Anniversary of National Trust for Scotland (British landscapes)

1981 (24 June) *Phosphorised paper*

1155	**631**	14p multicoloured	15	25	☐	☐
1156	**632**	18p multicoloured	45	50	☐	☐
1157	**633**	20p multicoloured	70	75	☐	☐
1158	**634**	22p multicoloured	75	1·00	☐	☐
1159	**635**	25p multicoloured	90	1·00	☐	☐
		Set of 5	2·50	3·00	☐	☐
		First Day Cover		3·25		☐
		Presentation Pack	3·00		☐	
		PHQ Cards (set of 5)	2·50	5·00	☐	☐
		Set of 5 Gutter Pairs	6·00		☐	

636 Prince Charles and Lady Diana Spencer

Royal Wedding

1981 (22 July) *Phosphorised paper*

1160	**636**	14p multicoloured	75	25	☐	☐
1161		25p multicoloured	1·50	1·50	☐	☐
		Set of 2	2·25	1·50	☐	☐
		First Day Cover		2·75		☐
		Presentation Pack	3·00		☐	
		Souvenir Book	3·00		☐	
		PHQ Cards (set of 2)	2·50	5·00	☐	☐
		Set of 2 Gutter Pairs	4·00		☐	

637 'Expeditions'

638 'Skills'

639 'Service'

640 'Recreation'

25th Anniversary of Duke of Edinburgh's Award Scheme

1981 (12 Aug.) *Phosphorised paper. Perf 14*

1162	**637**	14p multicoloured	25	20	☐	☐
1163	**638**	18p multicoloured	45	50	☐	☐
1164	**639**	22p multicoloured	80	80	☐	☐
1165	**640**	25p multicoloured	90	1·00	☐	☐
		Set of 4	2·25	2·50	☐	☐
		First Day Cover		2·50		☐
		Presentation Pack	2·50		☐	
		PHQ Cards (set of 4)	2·50	4·50	☐	☐
		Set of 4 Gutter Pairs	5·00		☐	

641 Cockle-dredging from *Linsey II*

642 Hauling Trawl Net

643 Lobster Potting

644 Hoisting Seine Net

Fishing Industry

1981 (23 SEPT.) *Phosphorised paper*

1166	**641**	14p multicoloured	25	25	☐	☐
1167	**642**	18p multicoloured	50	50	☐	☐
1168	**643**	22p multicoloured	85	85	☐	☐
1169	**644**	25p multicoloured	85	85	☐	☐
		Set of 4	2·25	2·50	☐	☐
		First Day Cover		2·00		☐
		Presentation Pack	2·50		☐	
		PHQ Cards (set of 4)	2·25	4·50	☐	☐
		Set of 4 Gutter Pairs	5·00		☐	

Nos. 1166/9 were issued on the occasion of the centenary of Royal National Mission to Deep Sea Fishermen.

Samantha Brown, age 5

Tracy Jenkins, age 14

645 Father Christmas

646 Jesus Christ

Lucinda Blackmore, age 6

Stephen Moore, age 16

647 Flying Angel

648 Joseph and Mary arriving at Bethlehem

Sophie Sharp, age 8

649 Three Kings approaching Bethlehem

Christmas. Children's Pictures

1981 (18 NOV.) *One phosphor band* (11½p) *or phosphorised paper* (others)

1170	**645**	11½p multicoloured	25	20	☐	☐
1171	**646**	14p multicoloured	35	20	☐	☐
1172	**647**	18p multicoloured	50	60	☐	☐
1173	**648**	22p multicoloured	75	75	☐	☐
1174	**649**	25p multicoloured	85	85	☐	☐
		Set of 5	2·50	2·50	☐	☐
		First Day Cover		2·75		☐
		Presentation Pack	3·00		☐	
		PHQ Cards (set of 5)	2·25	5·50	☐	☐
		Set of 5 Gutter Pairs	5·50		☐	

Collectors Pack 1981

1981 (18 NOV.) *Comprises Nos. 1143/74*

CP1174a	*Collectors Pack*	17·50		☐

650 Charles Darwin and Giant Tortoises

651 Darwin and Marine Iguanas

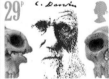

652 Darwin, Cactus Ground Finch and Large Ground Finch

653 Darwin and Prehistoric Skulls

Death Centenary of Charles Darwin

1982 (10 FEB.) *Phosphorised paper*

1175	**650**	15½p multicoloured	50	20	☐	☐
1176	**651**	19½p multicoloured	50	60	☐	☐
1177	**652**	26p multicoloured	75	85	☐	☐
1178	**653**	29p multicoloured	95	90	☐	☐
		Set of 4	2·50	2·50	☐	☐
		First Day Cover		2·75		☐
		Presentation Pack	3·00		☐	
		PHQ Cards (set of 4)	2·50	6·00	☐	☐
		Set of 4 Gutter Pairs	5·25		☐	

654 Boys' Brigade

655 Girls' Brigade

660 Hamlet

661 Opera Singer

Europa. British Theatre

1982 (28 Apr.) *Phosphorised paper*

1183	**658**	15½p multicoloured	25	15	☐	☐
1184	**659**	19½p multicoloured	50	50	☐	☐
1185	**660**	26p multicoloured	1·25	1·00	☐	☐
1186	**661**	29p multicoloured	1·50	1·00	☐	☐
		Set of 4	3·25	2·50	☐	☐
		First Day Cover		2·75		☐
		Presentation Pack	3·00		☐	
		PHQ Cards (set of 4)	2·50	6·00	☐	☐
		Set of 4 Gutter Pairs	8·00		☐	

656 Boy Scout Movement

657 Girl Guide Movement

Youth Organizations

1982 (24 Mar.) *Phosphorised paper*

1179	**654**	15½p multicoloured	25	15	☐	☐
1180	**655**	19½p multicoloured	50	50	☐	☐
1181	**656**	26p multicoloured	85	85	☐	☐
1182	**657**	29p multicoloured	1·00	1·10	☐	☐
		Set of 4	2·50	2·50	☐	☐
		First Day Cover		2·75		☐
		Presentation Pack	3·00		☐	
		PHQ Cards (set of 4)	2·50	6·00	☐	☐
		Set of 4 Gutter Pairs	5·50		☐	

Nos. 1179/82 were issued on the occasion of the 75th anniversary of the Boy Scout Movement, the 125th birth anniversary of Lord Baden-Powell and the centenary of the Boys' Brigade (1983).

662 Henry VIII and *Mary Rose*

663 Admiral Blake and *Triumph*

664 Lord Nelson and HMS *Victory*

665 Lord Fisher and HMS *Dreadnought*

658 Ballerina

659 Harlequin

666 Viscount Cunningham and HMS *Warspite*

Maritime Heritage

1982 (16 June) *Phosphorised paper*

1187	**662**	15½p multicoloured	35	25	☐	☐
1188	**663**	19½p multicoloured	50	50	☐	☐
1189	**664**	24p multicoloured	75	85	☐	☐
1190	**665**	26p multicoloured	75	85	☐	☐
1191	**666**	29p multicoloured	1·00	1·00	☐	☐
		Set of 5	3·00	3·50	☐	☐
		First Day Cover		3·75		☐
		Presentation Pack	3·50		☐	
		PHQ Cards (set of 5)	2·50	6·00	☐	☐
		Set of 5 Gutter Pairs	7·00		☐	

667 'Strawberry Thief'
(William Morris)

669 'Cherry Orchard'
(Paul Nash)

668 Untitled
(Steiner and Co)

670 'Chevron'
(Andrew Foster)

British Textiles

1982 (23 July) *Phosphorised paper*

1192	**667**	15½p multicoloured	25	25	☐	☐
1193	**668**	19½p multicoloured	75	75	☐	☐
1194	**669**	26p multicoloured	75	1·00	☐	☐
1195	**670**	29p multicoloured	1·00	1·25	☐	☐
		Set of 4	2·50	2·75	☐	☐
		First Day Cover		3·00		☐
		Presentation Pack	2·75		☐	
		PHQ Cards (set of 4)	2·50	6·00	☐	☐
		Set of 4 Gutter Pairs	5·50		☐	

Nos 1192/5 were issued on the occasion of the 250th birth anniversary of Sir Richard Arkwright (inventor of spinning machine).

For full information on all future British issues, collectors should write to Royal Mail, Freepost EH3647, 21 South Gyle Crescent, Edinburgh EH12 9PE.

671 Development of Communications

672 Modern Technological Aids

Information Technology

1982 (8 Sept.) *Phosphorised paper. Perf* 14 × 15

1196	**671**	15½p multicoloured	75	25	☐	☐
1197	**672**	26p multicoloured	50	1·00	☐	☐
		Set of 2	1·25	1·25	☐	☐
		First Day Cover		1·75		☐
		Presentation Pack	1·50		☐	
		PHQ Cards (set of 2)	2·00	5·25	☐	☐
		Set of 2 Gutter Pairs	2·75		☐	

673 Austin 'Seven' and 'Metro'

674 Ford 'Model T' and 'Escort'

675 Jaguar 'SS1' and 'XJ6'

676 Rolls-Royce 'Silver Ghost' and 'Silver Spirit'

British Motor Industry

1982 (13 Oct.) *Phosphorised paper. Perf* 14½ × 14

1198	**673**	15½p multicoloured	50	25	☐	☐
1199	**674**	19½p multicoloured	75	75	☐	☐
1200	**675**	26p multicoloured	75	75	☐	☐
1201	**676**	29p multicoloured	1·00	1·00	☐	☐
		Set of 4	2·50	2·50	☐	☐
		First Day Cover		2·50		☐
		Presentation Pack	3·00		☐	
		PHQ Cards (set of 4)	2·50	6·00	☐	☐
		Set of 4 Gutter Pairs	6·25		☐	

677 'While Shepherds Watched'

684 Brown Trout

685 Eurasian Perch

678 'The Holly and the Ivy'

British River Fishes

1983 (26 Jan.) *Phosphorised paper*

1207	**682**	15½p multicoloured	30	10	☐	☐
1208	**683**	19½p multicoloured	60	60	☐	☐
1209	**684**	26p multicoloured	75	85	☐	☐
1210	**685**	29p multicoloured	1·00	1·10	☐	☐
		Set of 4	2·50	2·50	☐	☐
		First Day Cover		2·50		☐
		Presentation Pack	2·75		☐	
		PHQ Cards (set of 4)	3·00	7·00	☐	☐
		Set of 4 Gutter Pairs	5·00		☐	

679 'I Saw Three Ships'

680 'We Three Kings'

681 'Good King Wenceslas'

Christmas. Carols

1982 (17 Nov.) *One phosphor band (12½p) or phosphorised paper (others).*

1202	**677**	12½p multicoloured	25	20	☐	☐
1203	**678**	15½p multicoloured	50	20	☐	☐
1204	**679**	19½p multicoloured	65	75	☐	☐
1205	**680**	26p multicoloured	75	80	☐	☐
1206	**681**	29p multicoloured	1·00	90	☐	☐
		Set of 5	3·00	2·50	☐	☐
		First Day Cover		2·50		☐
		Presentation Pack	3·25		☐	
		PHQ Cards (set of 5)	2·50	6·00	☐	☐
		Set of 5 Gutter Pairs	5·25		☐	

Collectors Pack 1982

1982 (17 Nov.) *Comprises Nos. 1175/1206*

CP1206a	*Collectors Pack*	26·00		☐

686 Tropical Island

687 Desert

688 Temperate Farmland

689 Mountain Range

Commonwealth Day. Geographical Regions

1983 (9 Mar.) *Phosphorised paper*

1211	**686**	15½p multicoloured	40	25	☐	☐
1212	**687**	19½p multicoloured	75	75	☐	☐
1213	**688**	26p multicoloured	75	75	☐	☐
1214	**689**	29p multicoloured	1·00	1·00	☐	☐
		Set of 4	2·50	2·50	☐	☐
		First Day Cover		2·50		☐
		Presentation Pack	3·00		☐	
		PHQ Cards (set of 4)	2·50	6·50	☐	☐
		Set of 4 Gutter Pairs	6·00		☐	

682 Atlantic Salmon

683 Northern Pike

690 Humber Bridge

691 Thames Flood Barrier

697 Paratroopers, The Parachute Regiment (1983)

692 *Iolair* (oilfield emergency support vessel)

Europa. Engineering Achievements

1983 (25 MAY) *Phosphorised paper*

1215	**690**	16p multicoloured	. . . . .	50	25	☐	☐
1216	**691**	20½p multicoloured	. . . . .	1·00	1·00	☐	☐
1217	**692**	28p multicoloured	. . . . .	1·00	1·00	☐	☐
		Set of 3	. . . .	2·25	2·00	☐	☐
		First Day Cover	. . . .		2·25		☐
		Presentation Pack	. . . .	2·50		☐	
		PHQ Cards (set of 3)	. . . . .	2·50	5·75	☐	☐
		Set of 3 Gutter Pairs	. . . . . .	7·00		☐	

British Army Uniforms

1983 (6 JULY) *Phosphorised paper*

1218	**693**	16p multicoloured	. . . . .	50	10	☐	☐
1219	**694**	20½p multicoloured	. . . . .	50	60	☐	☐
1220	**695**	26p multicoloured	. . . . .	75	90	☐	☐
1221	**696**	28p multicoloured	. . . . .	75	90	☐	☐
1222	**697**	31p multicoloured	. . . . .	75	85	☐	☐
		Set of 5	. . . .	3·00	3·25	☐	☐
		First Day Cover	. . . .		3·25		☐
		Presentation Pack	. . . .	3·50		☐	
		PHQ Cards (set of 5)	. . . . .	3·50	6·50	☐	☐
		Set of 5 Gutter Pairs	. . . . . .	7·50		☐	

Nos. 1218/22 were issued on the occasion of the 350th anniversary of The Royal Scots, the senior line regiment of the British Army.

693 Musketeer and Pikeman, The Royal Scots (1633)

694 Fusilier and Ensign, The Royal Welch Fusiliers (mid-18th century)

698 20th-Century Garden, Sissinghurst

699 19th-Century Garden, Biddulph Grange

695 Riflemen, 95th Rifles (The Royal Green Jackets) (1805)

696 Sergeant (khaki service uniform) and Guardsman full dress), The Irish Guards (1900).

700 18th-Century Garden, Blenheim

701 17th-Century Garden, Pitmedden

British Gardens

1983 (24 Aug.) *Phosphorised paper. Perf* 14

1223	698	16p multicoloured	50	10	☐	☐
1224	699	20½p multicoloured	50	55	☐	☐
1225	700	28p multicoloured	75	90	☐	☐
1226	701	31p multicoloured	1·00	90	☐	☐
		Set of 4	2·50	2·25	☐	☐
		First Day Cover		2·25	☐	
		Presentation Pack	3·00		☐	
		PHQ Cards (set of 4)	3·00	6·25	☐	☐
		Set of 4 Gutter Pairs	6·00		☐	

702 Merry-go-round

703 Big Wheel, Helter-skelter and Performing Animals

704 Side-shows

705 Early Produce Fair

British Fairs

1983 (5 Oct.) *Phosphorised paper*

1227	702	16p multicoloured	35	25	☐	☐
1228	703	20½p multicoloured	75	75	☐	☐
1229	704	28p multicoloured	75	1·00	☐	☐
1230	705	31p multicoloured	1·00	1·00	☐	☐
		Set of 4	2·50	2·75	☐	☐
		First Day Cover		3·00	☐	
		Presentation Pack	3·00		☐	
		PHQ Cards (set of 4)	3·00	6·25	☐	☐
		Set of 4 Gutter Pairs	6·00		☐	

Nos. 1227/30 were issued to mark the 850th anniversary of St Bartholomew's Fair, Smithfield, London.

706 'Christmas Post' (pillar-box)

707 'The Three Kings' (chimney-pots)

708 'World at Peace' (Dove and Blackbird)

709 'Light of Christmas' (street lamp)

710 'Christmas Dove' (hedge sculpture)

Christmas

1983 (16 Nov.) *One phosphor band (12½p) or phosphorised paper (others)*

1231	706	12½p multicoloured	25	25	☐	☐
1232	707	16p multicoloured	50	25	☐	☐
1233	708	20½p multicoloured	75	1·00	☐	☐
1234	709	28p multicoloured	75	1·00	☐	☐
1235	710	31p multicoloured	1·25	1·25	☐	☐
		Set of 5	3·25	3·25	☐	☐
		First Day Cover		3·50	☐	
		Presentation Pack	3·50		☐	
		PHQ Cards (set of 5)	3·00	6·25	☐	☐
		Set of 5 Gutter Pairs	6·50		☐	

Collectors Pack 1983

1983 (16 Nov.) *Comprises Nos.* 1207/35

CP1235*a*	*Collectors Pack*	32·00		☐

711 Arms of the College of Arms

712 Arms of King Richard III (founder)

713 Arms of the Earl Marshal of England

714 Arms of the City of London

500th Anniversary of College of Arms

1984 (17 Jan.) *Phosphorised paper. Perf 14½*

1236	**711**	16p multicoloured	50	15	□	□
1237	**712**	20½p multicoloured	50	65	□	□
1238	**713**	28p multicoloured	1·00	1·10	□	□
1239	**714**	31p multicoloured	1·25	1·25	□	□
		Set of 4	3·00	3·00	□	□
		First Day Cover		3·00		□
		Presentation Pack	3·25			□
		PHQ Cards (set of 4)	3·00	6·50	□	□
		Set of 4 Gutter Pairs	6·25			□

16ᵖ   Highland Cow

715 Highland Cow

20½ᵖ   Chillingham Wild Bull

716 Chillingham Wild Bull

26ᵖ   Hereford Bull

717 Hereford Bull

28ᵖ   Welsh Black Bull

718 Welsh Black Bull

31ᵖ   Irish Moiled Cow

719 Irish Moiled Cow

British Cattle

1984 (6 Mar.) *Phosphorised paper*

1240	**715**	16p multicoloured	35	15	□	□
1241	**716**	20½p multicoloured	60	60	□	□
1242	**717**	26p multicoloured	80	80	□	□
1243	**718**	28p multicoloured	90	90	□	□
1244	**719**	31p multicoloured	1·00	1·20	□	□
		Set of 5	3·50	3·50	□	□
		First Day Cover		3·50		□
		Presentation Pack	4·00			□
		PHQ Cards (set of 5)	3·00	6·50	□	□
		Set of 5 Gutter Pairs	7·25			□

Nos. 1240/4 marked the centenary of the Highland Cattle Society and the bicentenary of the Royal Highland and Agricultural Society of Scotland.

720 Festival Hall, Liverpool

721 Milburngate Shopping Centre, Durham

722 Bush House, Bristol

723 Commercial Street Housing Scheme, Perth

Urban Renewal

1984 (10 Apr.) *Phosphorised paper*

1245	**720**	16p multicoloured	30	10	□	□
1246	**721**	20½p multicoloured	50	60	□	□
1247	**722**	28p multicoloured	1·00	1·00	□	□
1248	**723**	31p multicoloured	1·00	1·00	□	□
		Set of 4	2·50	2·50	□	□
		First Day Cover		2·50		□
		Presentation Pack	3·00			□
		PHQ Cards (set of 4)	3·00	6·25	□	□
		Set of 4 Gutter Pairs	6·50			□

Nos. 1245/8 marked the opening of the International Gardens Festival, Liverpool, and the 150th anniversaries of the Royal Institute of British Architects and the Chartered Institute of Building.

724 C.E.P.T. 25th Anniversary Logo

725 Abduction of Europa

Nos. 1249/50 and 1251/2 were each printed together, *se-tenant*, in horizontal pairs throughout the sheets.

For full information on all future British issues, collectors should write to Royal Mail, Freepost EH3647, 21 South Gyle Crescent, Edinburgh EH12 9PE.

Europa. 25th Anniversary of C.E.P.T. and 2nd European Parliamentary Elections

1984 (15 May) *Phosphorised paper*

1249	724	16p greenish slate, deep blue and gold	50	25	□	□
		a. Horiz pair. Nos. 1249/50	1·50	1·50	□	□
1250	725	16p greenish slate, deep blue, black and gold .	50	25	□	□
1251	724	20½p Venetian red, deep magenta and gold . .	70	40	□	□
		a. Horiz pair. Nos. 1251/2	2·50	2·50	□	□
1252	725	20½p Venetian red, deep magenta, black and gold	70	40	□	□
		Set of 4	3·00	3·00	□	□
		First Day Cover		3·50		□
		Presentation Pack	4·00		□	
		PHQ Cards (set of 4)	3·00	6·25	□	□
		Set of 2 Gutter Blocks of 4 . . .	8·00		□	

726 Lancaster House

London Economic Summit Conference

1984 (5 June) *Phosphorised paper*

1253	726	31p multicoloured	1·25	1·25	□	□
		First Day Cover		2·25		□
		PHQ Card	1·00	3·50	□	□
		Gutter Pair	2·50		□	

727   View of Earth from 'Apollo 11'

728   Navigational Chart of English Channel

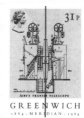

729   Greenwich Observatory

730   Sir George Airey's Transit Telescope

Centenary of Greenwich Meridian

1984 (26 June) *Phosphorised paper. Perf 14 × 14½*

1254	727	16p multicoloured	50	25	□	□
1255	728	20½p multicoloured	75	80	□	□
1256	729	28p multicoloured	1·00	1·00	□	□
1257	730	31p multicoloured	1·00	1·10	□	□
		Set of 4	3·00	3·00	□	□
		First Day Cover		3·00		□
		Presentation Pack	3·50		□	
		PHQ Cards (set of 4)	3·00	6·25	□	□
		Set of 4 Gutter Pairs	6·50		□	

731   Bath Mail Coach, 1784

732   Attack on Exeter Mail, 1816

733   Norwich Mail in Thunderstorm, 1827

734   Holyhead and Liverpool Mails leaving London, 1828

735   Edinburgh Mail Snowbound, 1831

T **731/5** were printed together, *se-tenant,* in horizontal strips of 5 throughout the sheet.

Bicentenary of First Mail Coach Run, Bath and Bristol to London

1984 (31 JULY) *Phosphorised paper*

1258	**731**	16p multicoloured	40	35	☐	☐
		a. *Horiz strip of 5. Nos.*				
		1258/62	2·50	2·75	☐	☐
1259	**732**	16p multicoloured	40	35	☐	☐
1260	**733**	16p multicoloured	40	35	☐	☐
1261	**734**	16p multicoloured	40	35	☐	☐
1262	**735**	16p multicoloured	40	35	☐	☐
		Set of 5	2·50	2·75	☐	☐
		First Day Cover		3·00		☐
		Presentation Pack	3·00		☐	
		Souvenir Book	7·50		☐	
		PHQ Cards (set of 5)	3·00	6·50	☐	☐
		Gutter Block of 10	6·50		☐	

736 Nigerian Clinic

737 Violinist and Acropolis, Athens

738 Building Project, Sri Lanka

739 British Council Library

50th Anniversary of The British Council

1984 (25 SEPT.) *Phosphorised paper*

1263	**736**	17p multicoloured	50	25	☐	☐
1264	**737**	22p multicoloured	85	1·00	☐	☐
1265	**738**	31p multicoloured	85	1·00	☐	☐
1266	**739**	34p multicoloured	1·00	1·00	☐	☐
		Set of 4	3·00	3·00	☐	☐
		First Day Cover		3·00		☐
		Presentation Pack	3·25		☐	
		PHQ Cards (set of 4)	3·00	6·25	☐	☐
		Set of 4 Gutter Pairs	6·50		☐	

For full information on all future British issues, collectors should write to Royal Mail, Freepost EH3647, 21 South Gyle Crescent, Edinburgh EH12 9PE.

740 The Holy Family   **741** Arrival in Bethlehem

742 Shepherd and Lamb   **743** Virgin and Child

744 Offering of Frankincense

Christmas

1984 (20 NOV.) *One phosphor band* (13p) *or phosphorised paper* (others)

1267	**740**	13p multicoloured	25	25	☐	☐
1268	**741**	17p multicoloured	50	50	☐	☐
1269	**742**	22p multicoloured	75	75	☐	☐
1270	**743**	31p multicoloured	1·00	1·00	☐	☐
1271	**744**	34p multicoloured	1·00	1·00	☐	☐
		Set of 5		3·25	3·25	☐	☐
		First Day Cover		3·25		☐
		Presentation Pack	3·75		☐	
		PHQ Cards (set of 5)	3·00	6·25	☐	☐
		Set of 5 Gutter Pairs	7·00		☐	

Collectors Pack 1984

1984 (20 NOV.) *Comprises Nos.* 1236/71

CP1271a	*Collectors Pack*	37·00		☐

Post Office Yearbook

1984 *Comprises Nos. 1236/71 in hardbound book with slip case*

YB1271a	*Yearbook*	90·00		☐

17P

FLYING SCOTSMAN

745 'Flying Scotsman'

22P

GOLDEN ARROW

746 'Golden Arrow'

29p

Wart-Biter Bush-Cricket

752 *Decticus verrucivorus*
(bush-cricket)

31P

Stag Beetle

753 *Lucanus cervus*
(stag beetle)

29P

CHELTENHAM FLYER

747 'Cheltenham Flyer'

31P

ROYAL SCOT

748 'Royal Scot'

34P

Emperor Dragonfly

754 *Anax imperator* (dragonfly)

34P

CORNISH RIVIERA

749 'Cornish Riviera'

Famous Trains
1985 (22 JAN.) *Phosphorised paper*

1272	**745**	17p multicoloured	. . . . .	75	25	☐	☐
1273	**746**	22p multicoloured	. . . . .	75	1·00	☐	☐
1274	**747**	29p multicoloured	. . . . .	1·00	1·25	☐	☐
1275	**748**	31p multicoloured	. . . . .	1·25	1·50	☐	☐
1276	**749**	34p multicoloured	. . . . .	2·50	2·50	☐	☐
		Set of 5	. . . .	6·00	6·00	☐	☐
		First Day Cover	. . . .		6·00		☐
		Presentation Pack	. . . .	6·00		☐	
		PHQ Cards (set of 5)	. . . . . .	6·00	15·00	☐	☐
		Set of 5 Gutter Pairs	. . . . . .	12·00		☐	

Nos. 1272/6 were issued on the occasion of the 150th anniversary of the Great Western Railway Company.

Insects
1985 (12 MAR.) *Phosphorised paper*

1277	**750**	17p multicoloured	. . . . .	40	10	☐	☐
1278	**751**	22p multicoloured	. . . . .	60	55	☐	☐
1279	**752**	29p multicoloured	. . . . .	85	90	☐	☐
1280	**753**	31p multicoloured	. . . . .	1·00	1·00	☐	☐
1281	**754**	34p multicoloured	. . . . .	1·00	90	☐	☐
		Set of 5	. . . .	3·25	3·25	☐	☐
		First Day Cover	. . . .		3·50		☐
		Presentation Pack	. . . .	4·50		☐	
		PHQ Cards (set of 5)	. . . . . .	3·00	7·50	☐	☐
		Set of 5 Gutter Pairs	. . . . . .	8·75		☐	

Nos. 1277/81 were issued on the occasion of the centenaries of the Royal Entomological Society of London's Royal Charter and of the Selborne Society.

17P

Buff Tailed Bumble Bee

750 *Bombus terrestris*
(bee)

22P

Seven Spotted Ladybird

751 *Coccinella septempunctata*
(ladybird)

SEVENTEEN·PENCE

WATER·MUSIC
George Frideric Handel

755 'Water Music',
by Handel

TWENTY·TWO·PENCE

THE·PLANETS·SUITE
Gustav Holst

756 'The Planets',
by Holst

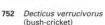

THE·FIRST·CUCKOO
Frederick Delius

SEA·PICTURES
Edward Elgar

757 'The First Cuckoo',   **758** 'Sea Pictures',
by Delius   by Elgar

Europa. European Music Year
1985 (14 MAY) *Phosphorised paper. Perf* 14½

1282	755	17p multicoloured	55	10	□	□
1283	756	22p multicoloured	75	90	□	□
1284	757	31p multicoloured	1·50	1·25	□	□
1285	758	34p multicoloured	1·50	1·25	□	□
		Set of 4	4·00	3·25	□	□
		First Day Cover		4·00		□
		Presentation Pack	4·75		□	
		PHQ Cards (set of 4)	3·00	6·50	□	□
		Set of 4 Gutter Pairs	10·00		□	

Nos. 1282/5 were issued on the occasion of the 300th birth anniversary of Handel.

759 R.N.L.I. Lifeboat and   **760** Beachy Head Lighthouse
Signal Flags   and Chart

761 'Marecs A'   **762** Buoys
Communications Satelite
and Dish Aerials

Safety at Sea
1985 (18 JUNE) *Phosphorised paper. Perf* 14

1286	759	17p multicoloured	40	25	□	□
1287	760	22p multicoloured	60	75	□	□

1288	761	31p multicoloured	1·00	1·00	□	□
1289	762	34p multicoloured	1·50	1·25	□	□
		Set of 4	3·00	3·00	□	□
		First Day Cover		3·00		□
		Presentation Pack	3·75		□	
		PHQ Cards (set of 4)	3·00	6·50	□	□
		Set of 4 Gutter Pairs	7·00		□	

Nos. 1286/9 were issued to mark the bicentenary of the unimmersible lifeboat and the 50th anniversary of Radar.

763 Datapost Motorcyclist,   **764** Rural Postbus
City of London

765 Parcel Delivery   **766** Town Letter Delivery
in Winter

350 Years of Royal Mail Public Postal Service
1985 (30 JULY) *Phosphorised paper*

1290	763	17p multicoloured	50	10	□	□
1291	764	22p multicoloured	75	70	□	□
1292	765	31p multicoloured	1·00	1·00	□	□
1293	766	34p multicoloured	1·00	1·00	□	□
		Set of 4	2·75	2·50	□	□
		First Day Cover		3·25		□
		Presentation Pack	3·75		□	
		PHQ Cards (set of 4)	3·00	6·50	□	□
		Set of 4 Gutter Pairs	7·00		□	

767 King Arthur and Merlin   **768** The Lady of the Lake

769 Queen Guinevere and Sir Lancelot   **770** Sir Galahad

Arthurian Legends

1985 (3 SEPT.) *Phosphorised paper*

1294	**767**	17p multicoloured	. . . . .	50	25	□	□
1295	**768**	22p multicoloured	. . . . .	75	75	□	□
1296	**769**	31p multicoloured	. . . . .	1·25	1·25	□	□
1297	**770**	34p multicoloured	. . . . .	1·25	1·25	□	□
		Set of 4	. . . .	3·50	3·00	□	□
		First Day Cover	. . . .		3·50		□
		Presentation Pack	. . . .	4·00		□	
		PHQ Cards (set of 4)	. . . . . .	3·00	6·50	□	□
		Set of 4 Gutter Pairs	. . . . . .	7·00		□	

Nos. 1294/7 were issued to mark the 500th anniversary of the printing of Sir Thomas Malory's *Morte d'Arthur*.

771 Peter Sellers (from photo by Bill Brandt)   **772** David Niven (from photo by Cornell Lucas)

773 Charlie Chaplin (from photo by Lord Snowdon)   **774** Vivien Leigh (from photo by Angus McBean)

775 Alfred Hitchcock (from photo by Howard Coster)

British Film Year

1985 (8 OCT.) *Phosphorised paper. Perf 14½*

1298	**771**	17p multicoloured	. . . . .	45	25	□	□
1299	**772**	22p multicoloured	. . . . .	60	75	□	□
1300	**773**	29p multicoloured	. . . . .	1·00	1·25	□	□
1301	**774**	31p multicoloured	. . . . .	1·10	1·50	□	□
1302	**775**	34p multicoloured	. . . . .	1·40	1·50	□	□
		Set of 5	. . . .	4·00	4·50	□	□
		First Day Cover	. . . .		5·00		□
		Presentation Pack	. . . .	5·50		□	
		Souvenir Book	. . . .	11·50		□	
		PHQ Cards (set of 5)	. . . . . .	3·00	8·50	□	□
		Set of 5 Gutter Pairs	. . . . . .	10·50		□	

776 Principal Boy   **777** Genie

778 Dame   **779** Good Fairy

780 Pantomime Cat

Christmas. Pantomime Characters

1985 (19 NOV.) *One phosphor band* (12p) *or phosphorised paper* (*others*)

1303	**776**	12p multicoloured	. . . . .	50	15	□	□
1304	**777**	17p multicoloured	. . . . .	50	25	□	□
1305	**778**	22p multicoloured	. . . . .	75	1·10	□	□
1306	**779**	31p multicoloured	. . . . .	1·25	1·40	□	□
1307	**780**	34p multicoloured	. . . . .	1·25	1·40	□	□
		Set of 5	. . . .	4·00	4·00	□	□
		First Day Cover	. . . .		4·50		□
		Presentation Pack	. . . .	4·25		□	
		PHQ Cards (Set of 5)	. . . . . .	3·00	6·50	□	□
		Set of 5 Gutter Pairs	. . . . . .	8·00		□	

Collectors Pack 1985

1985 (19 Nov.) *Comprises Nos. 1272/1307*

CP1307*a* Collectors Pack . . . . 35·00 ☐

Post Office Yearbook

1985 *Comprises Nos. 1272/1307 in hardbound book with slip case*

YB1307*a* Yearbook . . . . 80·00 ☐

17 PENCE · INDUSTRY YEAR 1986

22 PENCE · INDUSTRY YEAR 1986

781 Light Bulb and North Sea Oil Drilling Rig (Energy)

782 Thermometer and Pharmaceutical Laboratory (Health)

31 PENCE · INDUSTRY YEAR 1986

34 PENCE · INDUSTRY YEAR 1986

783 Garden Hoe and Steel Works (Steel)

784 Loaf of Bread and and Cornfield (Agriculture)

Industry Year

1986 (14 Jan.) *Phosphorised paper. Perf* $14\frac{1}{2} \times 14$

1308	**781**	17p multicoloured	75	25 ☐ ☐
1309	**782**	22p multicoloured	50	75 ☐ ☐
1310	**783**	31p multicoloured	1·25	1·40 ☐ ☐
1311	**784**	34p multicoloured	1·25	1·40 ☐ ☐
		Set of 4	3·50	3·50 ☐ ☐
		First Day Cover		3·50 ☐
		Presentation Pack	3·75	☐
		PHQ Cards (set of 4)	3·50	6·50 ☐ ☐
		Set of 4 Gutter Pairs	7·00	☐

785 Dr Edmond Halley as Comet

786 *Giotto* Spacecraft approaching Comet

787 'Twice in a Lifetime'

788 Comet orbiting Sun and Planets

Appearance of Halley's Comet

1986 (18 Feb.) *Phosphorised paper*

1312	**785**	17p multicoloured	50	25 ☐ ☐
1313	**786**	22p multicoloured	75	75 ☐ ☐
1314	**787**	31p multicoloured	1·25	1·25 ☐ ☐
1315	**788**	34p multicoloured	1·25	1·40 ☐ ☐
		Set of 4	3·50	3·50 ☐ ☐
		First Day Cover		3·50 ☐
		Presentation Pack	3·75	☐
		PHQ Cards (set of 4)	3·50	6·50 ☐ ☐
		Set of 4 Gutter Pairs	7·00	☐

HER MAJESTY THE QUEEN
Sixtieth Birthday 17p

HER MAJESTY THE QUEEN
Sixtieth Birthday 17p

789 Queen Elizabeth II in 1928, 1942 and 1952

790 Queen Elizabeth II in 1958, 1973 and 1982

Nos. 1316/17 and 1318/19 were each printed together, *se-tenant*, in horizontal pairs throughout the sheets.

60th Birthday of Queen Elizabeth II

1986 (21 Apr.) *Phosphorised paper*

1316	**789**	17p multicoloured	60	25 ☐ ☐
		a. Horiz pair. Nos. 1316/17	1·50	1·50 ☐ ☐
1317	**790**	17p multicoloured	60	25 ☐ ☐
1318	**789**	34p multicoloured	70	50 ☐ ☐
		a. Horiz pair. Nos. 1318/19	3·00	4·00 ☐ ☐
1319	**790**	34p multicoloured	70	50 ☐ ☐
		Set of 4	4·50	5·00 ☐ ☐
		First Day Cover		5·00 ☐
		Presentation Pack	5·50	☐
		Souvenir Book	8·50	☐
		PHQ Cards (set of 4)	5·00	6·50 ☐ ☐
		Set of 2 Gutter Blocks of 4 . . .	11·00	☐

For full information on all future British issues, collectors should write to Royal Mail, Freepost EH3647, 21 South Gyle Crescent, Edinburgh EH12 9PE.

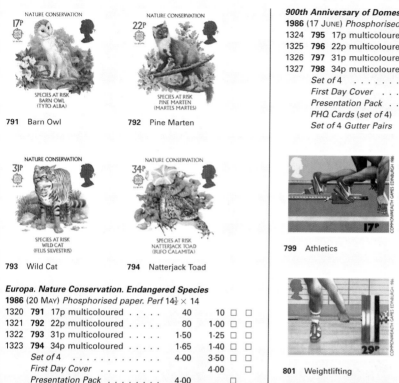

NATURE CONSERVATION
17p

SPECIES AT RISK
BARN OWL
(TYTO ALBA)

791 Barn Owl

NATURE CONSERVATION
22p

SPECIES AT RISK
PINE MARTEN
(MARTES MARTES)

792 Pine Marten

NATURE CONSERVATION
31p

SPECIES AT RISK
WILD CAT
(FELIS SILVESTRIS)

793 Wild Cat

NATURE CONSERVATION
34p

SPECIES AT RISK
NATTERJACK TOAD
(BUFO CALAMITA)

794 Natterjack Toad

Europa. Nature Conservation. Endangered Species

1986 (20 May) *Phosphorised paper. Perf 14½ × 14*

1320	**791**	17p multicoloured	40	10	☐	☐
1321	**792**	22p multicoloured	80	1·00	☐	☐
1322	**793**	31p multicoloured	1·50	1·25	☐	☐
1323	**794**	34p multicoloured	1·65	1·40	☐	☐
		Set of 4	4·00	3·50	☐	☐
		First Day Cover		4·00		☐
		Presentation Pack	4·00		☐	
		PHQ Cards (set of 4)	3·50	6·50	☐	☐
		Set of 4 Gutter Pairs	10·00		☐	

795 Peasants Working in Fields

796 Freemen working at Town Trades

797 Knight and Retainers

798 Lord at Banquet

900th Anniversary of Domesday Book

1986 (17 June) *Phosphorised paper*

1324	**795**	17p multicoloured	40	10	☐	☐
1325	**796**	22p multicoloured	85	85	☐	☐
1326	**797**	31p multicoloured	1·25	1·40	☐	☐
1327	**798**	34p multicoloured	1·25	1·40	☐	☐
		Set of 4	3·50	3·50	☐	☐
		First Day Cover		4·00		☐
		Presentation Pack	4·00		☐	
		PHQ Cards (set of 4)	3·50	6·50	☐	☐
		Set of 4 Gutter Pairs	7·00		☐	

799 Athletics

800 Rowing

801 Weightlifting

802 Rifle-shooting

803 Hockey

Thirteenth Commonwealth Games, Edinburgh (Nos. 1328/31) and World Men's Hockey Cup, London (No. 1332)

1986 (15 July) *Phosphorised paper*

1328	**799**	17p multicoloured	40	25	☐	☐
1329	**800**	22p multicoloured	55	75	☐	☐
1330	**801**	29p multicoloured	75	1·00	☐	☐
1331	**802**	31p multicoloured	1·00	1·25	☐	☐
1332	**803**	34p multicoloured	1·25	1·25	☐	☐
		Set of 5	3·50	3·50	☐	☐
		First Day Cover		3·50		☐
		Presentation Pack	3·50		☐	
		PHQ Cards (set of 5)	3·50	7·50	☐	☐
		Set of 5 Gutter Pairs	8·75		☐	

No. 1332 also marked the centenary of the Hockey Association.

804 Prince Andrew and Miss Sarah Ferguson 805

Royal Wedding

1986 (22 July) *One side band* (12p) *or phosphorised paper* (17p)

1333	**804**	12p multicoloured	50	30	□	□
1334	**805**	17p multicoloured	1·00	1·25	□	□
		Set of 2	1·50	1·50	□	□
		First Day Cover		2·00		□
		Presentation Pack	1·75		□	
		PHQ Cards (set of 2)	2·25	5·00	□	□
		Set of 2 Gutter Pairs	3·00		□	

806 Stylised Cross on Ballot Paper

32nd Commonwealth Parliamentary Conference, London

1986 (19 Aug.) *Phosphorised paper. Perf* 14 × 14½

1335	**806**	34p multicoloured	1·25	1·25	□	□
		First Day Cover		1·75		□
		PHQ Card	1·00	3·00	□	□
		Gutter Pair	2·75		□	

807 Lord Dowding and Hawker Hurricane Mk. I

808 Lord Tedder and Hawker Typhoon 1B

809 Lord Trenchard and De Havilland D.H.9A

810 Sir Arthur Harris and Avro Type 683 Lancaster

811 Lord Portal and De Havilland D.H.98 Mosquito

History of the Royal Air Force

1986 (16th Sept.) *Phosphorised paper. Perf* 14½ × 14

1336	**807**	17p multicoloured	50	10	□	□
1337	**808**	22p multicoloured	75	95	□	□
1338	**809**	29p multicoloured	1·25	1·25	□	□
1339	**810**	31p multicoloured	1·75	1·60	□	□
1340	**811**	34p multicoloured	1·75	1·90	□	□
		Set of 5	5·00	5·50	□	□
		First Day Cover		5·50		□
		Presentation Pack	5·50		□	
		PHQ Cards (set of 5)	4·50	10·00	□	□
		Set of 5 Gutter Pairs	12·00		□	

Nos. 1336/40 were issued to celebrate the 50th anniversary of the first R.A.F. Commands.

812 The Glastonbury Thorn

813 The Tanad Valley Plygain

814 The Hebrides Tribute

815 The Dewsbury Church Knell

816 The Hereford Boy Bishop

Christmas. Folk Customs

1986 (18 Nov.–2 Dec.) One phosphor band (12p, 13p) or phosphorised paper (others)

1341	**812**	12p multicoloured (2 Dec.)	50	50 □ □
1342		13p multicoloured	25	15 □ □
1343	**813**	18p multicoloured	50	15 □ □
1344	**814**	22p multicoloured	1·00	1·00 □ □
1345	**815**	31p multicoloured	1·25	1·00 □ □
1346	**816**	34p multicoloured	1·25	1·10 □ □
		Set of 6	3·50	3·50 □ □
		First Day Covers (2)		3·75 □
		Presentation Pack (Nos. 1342/6)	3·75	□
		PHQ Cards (set of 5) (Nos. 1342/6)	3·50	6·50 □ □
		Set of 6 Gutter Pairs	9·00	□

Collectors Pack 1986

1986 (18 Nov.) Comprises Nos. 1308/40, 1342/6
CP1346a   Collectors Pack . . . . 37·00   □

Post Office Yearbook

1986 Comprises Nos. 1308/40, 1342/6 in hardbound book with slip case
YB1346a   Yearbook . . . . 70·00   □

817 North American Blanket Flower

819 Echeveria

Flower Photographs by Alfred Lammer

1987 (20 Jan.) Phosphorised paper. Perf $14\frac{1}{2} \times 14$

1347	**817**	18p multicoloured	40	10 □ □
1348	**818**	22p multicoloured	70	85 □ □
1349	**819**	31p multicoloured	1·10	1·25 □ □
1350	**820**	34p multicoloured	1·10	1·25 □ □
		Set of 4	3·25	3·25 □ □
		First Day Cover		3·50 □
		Presentation Pack	4·00	□
		PHQ Cards (set of 4)	3·00	7·00 □ □
		Set of 4 Gutter Pairs	7·50	□

821   The Principia Mathematica

822   Motion of Bodies in Ellipses

823   Optick Treatise

824   The System of the World

300th Anniversary of The Principia Mathematica by Sir Isaac Newton

1987 (24 Mar.) Phosphorised paper

1351	**821**	18p multicoloured	50	15 □ □
1352	**822**	22p multicoloured	75	75 □ □
1353	**823**	31p multicoloured	1·25	1·50 □ □
1354	**824**	34p multicoloured	1·25	1·25 □ □
		Set of 4	3·50	3·25 □ □
		First Day Cover		3·75 □
		Presentation Pack	4·00	□
		PHQ Cards (set of 4)	3·00	6·50 □ □
		Set of 4 Gutter Pairs	8·00	□

818   Globe Thistle

820   Autumn Crocus

For full information on all future British issues, collectors should write to Royal Mail, Freepost EH3647, 21 South Gyle Crescent, Edinburgh EH12 9PE.

825 Willis Faber and Dumas Building, Ipswich

826 Pompidou Centre, Paris

827 Staatsgalerie, Stuttgart

828 European Investment Bank, Luxembourg

Europa. British Architects in Europe
1987 (12 MAY) *Phosphorised paper*

1355	825	18p multicoloured	50		15	☐	☐
1356	826	22p multicoloured	75		75	☐	☐
1357	827	31p multicoloured	1·25		1·25	☐	☐
1358	828	34p multicoloured	1·75		1·25	☐	☐
		Set of 4	4·00		3·25	☐	☐
		First Day Cover			3·75		☐
		Presentation Pack	4·00			☐	
		PHQ Cards (set of 4)	3·00		6·50	☐	☐
		Set of 4 Gutter Pairs	9·50			☐	

829 Brigade Members with Ashford Litter, 1887

830 Bandaging Blitz Victim, 1940

831 Volunteer with fainting Girl, 1965

832 Transport of Transplant Organ by Air Wing, 1987

Centenary of St John Ambulance Brigade
1987 (16 JUNE) *Phosphorised paper. Perf 14 × 14½*

1359	829	18p multicoloured	40		25	☐	☐
1360	830	22p multicoloured	60		75	☐	☐
1361	831	31p multicoloured	1·25		1·25	☐	☐
1362	832	34p multicoloured	1·25		1·25	☐	☐
		Set of 4	3·25		3·25	☐	☐
		First Day Cover			3·75		☐
		Presentation Pack	4·00			☐	
		PHQ Cards (set of 4)	3·00		6·50	☐	☐
		Set of 4 Gutter Pairs	7·50			☐	

833 Arms of the Lord Lyon King of Arms

834 Scottish Heraldic Banner of Prince Charles

835 Arms of Royal Scottish Academy of Painting, Sculpture and Architecture

836 Arms of Royal Society of Edinburgh

300th Anniversary of Revival of Order of the Thistle
1987 (21 JULY) *Phosphorised paper. Perf 14½*

1363	833	18p multicoloured	50		10	☐	☐
1364	834	22p multicoloured	75		90	☐	☐
1365	835	31p multicoloured	1·40		1·40	☐	☐
1366	836	34p multicoloured	1·50		1·40	☐	☐
		Set of 4	3·75		3·50	☐	☐
		First Day Cover			3·75		☐
		Presentation Pack	4·00			☐	
		PHQ Cards (set of 4)	3·00		6·50	☐	☐
		Set of 4 Gutter Pairs	8·00			☐	

For full information on all future British issues, collectors should write to Royal Mail, Freepost EH3647, 21 South Gyle Crescent, Edinburgh EH12 9PE.

837 Crystal Palace, 'Monarch of the Glen' (Landseer) and Grace Darling

838 Great Eastern, Beeton's Book of Household Management and Prince Albert

839 Albert Memorial, Ballot Box and Disraeli

840 Diamond Jubilee Emblem, Morse Key and Newspaper Placard for Relief of Mafeking

150th Anniversary of Queen Victoria's Accession

1987 (8 SEPT.) *Phosphorised paper*

1367	**837**	18p multicoloured	50	10	☐	☐
1368	**838**	22p multicoloured	80	75	☐	☐
1369	**839**	31p multicoloured	1·25	1·50	☐	☐
1370	**840**	34p multicoloured	1·35	1·60	☐	☐
		Set of 4	3·50	3·50	☐	☐
		First Day Cover		3·75		☐
		Presentation Pack	4·25		☐	
		PHQ Cards (set of 4)	3·00	6·50	☐	☐
		Set of 4 Gutter Pairs	9·00		☐	

841 Pot by Bernard Leach

842 Pot by Elizabeth Fritsch

843 Pot by Lucie Rie

844 Pot by Hans Coper

Studio Pottery

1987 (13 OCT.) *Phosphorised paper. Perf* 14½ × 14

1371	**841**	18p multicoloured	50	25	☐	☐
1372	**842**	26p multicoloured	70	75	☐	☐
1373	**843**	31p multicoloured	1·25	1·25	☐	☐
1374	**844**	34p multicoloured	1·40	1·50	☐	☐
		Set of 4	3·50	3·50	☐	☐
		First Day Cover		3·75		☐
		Presentation Pack	3·50		☐	
		PHQ Cards (set of 4)	3·00	6·50	☐	☐
		Set of 4 Gutter Pairs	8·50		☐	

Nos. 1371/4 also mark the birth centenary of Bernard Leach, the potter.

845 Decorating the Christmas Tree

846 Waiting for Father Christmas

847 Sleeping Child and Father Christmas in Sleigh

848 Child reading

849 Child playing Flute and Snowman

Christmas

1987 (17 NOV.) *One phosphor band* (13p) *or phosphorised paper*

1375	**845**	13p multicoloured	30	10	☐	☐
1376	**846**	18p multicoloured	40	20	☐	☐
1377	**847**	26p multicoloured	80	1·00	☐	☐
1378	**848**	31p multicoloured	1·10	1·25	☐	☐
1379	**849**	34p multicoloured	1·25	1·50	☐	☐
		Set of 5	3·50	3·75	☐	☐
		First Day Cover		3·75		☐
		Presentation Pack	3·50		☐	
		PHQ Cards (set of 5)	3·00	6·50	☐	☐
		Set of 5 Gutter Pairs	8·50		☐	

Collectors Pack 1987

1987 (17 Nov.) Comprises Nos. 1347/79

CP1379a   Collectors Pack . . . .   37·00   □

Post Office Yearbook

1987 Comprises Nos. 1347/79 in hardbound book with slip case

YB1379a   Yearbook . . . .   35·00   □

850 Short-spined
Seascorpion ('Bull-rout')
(Jonathan Couch)

851 Yellow Waterlily
(Major Joshua Swatkin)

852 Whistling ('Bewick's')
Swan (Edward Lear)

853 Morchella esculenta
(James Sowerby)

Bicentenary of Linnean Society. Archive Illustrations

1988 (19 Jan.) Phosphorised paper

1380	**850**	18p multicoloured	55	10	□	□
1381	**851**	26p multicoloured	85	1·00	□	□
1382	**852**	31p multicoloured	1·10	1·25	□	□
1383	**853**	34p multicoloured	1·25	1·40	□	□
		Set of 4	3·25	3·25	□	□
		First Day Cover		3·75	□	
		Presentation Pack	4·00		□	
		PHQ Cards (set of 4)	3·00	6·50	□	□
		Set of 4 Gutter Pairs	8·00		□	

854 Revd William
Morgan (Bible
translator, 1588)

855 William Salesbury
(New Testament
translator, 1567)

856 Bishop Richard
Davies (New
Testament translator,
1567)

857 Bishop Richard Parry
(editor of Revised
Welsh Bible, 1620)

400th Anniversary of Welsh Bible

1988 (1 Mar.) Phosphorised paper. Perf 14½ × 14

1384	**854**	18p multicoloured	40	10	□	□
1385	**855**	26p multicoloured	70	95	□	□
1386	**856**	31p multicoloured	1·25	1·25	□	□
1387	**857**	34p multicoloured	1·40	1·25	□	□
		Set of 4	3·25	3·25	□	□
		First Day Cover		3·75		□
		Presentation Pack	4·00		□	
		PHQ Cards (set of 4)	3·00	6·50	□	□
		Set of 4 Gutter Pairs	8·00		□	

858 Gymnastics
(Centenary of British
Amateur Gymnastics
Association)

859 Downhill Skiing
(Ski Club of
Great Britain)

860 Tennis (Centenary
of Lawn Tennis
Association)

861 Football (Centenary
of Football League)

Sports Organizations

1988 (22 MAR.) *Phosphorised paper. Perf 14½*

1388	858	18p multicoloured	40	15	□	□
1389	859	26p multicoloured	70	80	□	□
1390	860	31p multicoloured	1·10	1·25	□	□
1391	861	34p multicoloured	1·25	1·25	□	□
		Set of 4	3·25	3·25	□	□
		First Day Cover		3·50		□
		Presentation Pack	4·00		□	
		PHQ Cards (set of 4)	2·50	6·00	□	□
		Set of 4 Gutter Pairs	8·00		□	

862 *Mallard* and Mailbags on Pick-up Arms

863 Loading Transatlantic Mail on Liner *Queen Elizabeth*

864 Glasgow Tram No. 1173 and Pillar Box

865 Imperial Airways Handley Page H.P.45 *Horatius* and Airmail Van

Europa. Transport and Mail Services in 1930's

1988 (10 MAY) *Phosphorised paper*

1392	862	18p multicoloured	50	15	□	□
1393	863	26p multicoloured	1·00	1·00	□	□
1394	864	31p multicoloured	1·25	1·25	□	□
1395	865	34p multicoloured	1·60	1·50	□	□
		Set of 4	4·00	3·50	□	□
		First Day Cover		3·75		□
		Presentation Pack	4·25		□	
		PHQ Cards (set of 4)	2·25	6·00	□	□
		Set of 4 Gutter Pairs	11·00		□	

866 Early Settler and Sailing Clipper

867 Queen Elizabeth II with British and Australian Parliament Buildings

868 W. G. Grace (cricketer) and Tennis Racquet

869 Shakespeare, John Lennon (entertainer) and Sydney Landmarks

Nos. 1396/7 and 1398/9 were each printed together, *se-tenant,* in horizontal pairs throughout the sheets, each pair showing a background design of the Australian flag.

Bicentenary of Australian Settlement

1988 (21 JUNE) *Phosphorised paper. Perf 14½*

1396	866	18p multicoloured	30	25	□	□
		a. Horiz pair. Nos. 1396/7	1·25	1·50	□	□
1397	867	18p multicoloured	30	25	□	□
1398	868	34p multicoloured	60	50	□	□
		a. Horiz pair. Nos. 1398/9	2·50	2·50	□	□
1399	869	34p multicoloured	60	50	□	□
		Set of 4	3·50	3·50	□	□
		First Day Cover		3·75		□
		Presentation Pack	4·00		□	
		Souvenir Book	15·00		□	
		PHQ Cards (set of 4)	2·25	6·00	□	□
		Set of 2 Gutter Blocks of 4 . . .	8·25		□	

Stamps in similar designs were also issued by Australia. These are included in the Souvenir Book.

870 Spanish Galeasse off The Lizard

871 English Fleet leaving Plymouth

872 Engagement off Isle of Wight

873 Attack of English Fire-ships, Calais

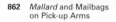

ARMADA · NORTH SEA · 30 JULY–2 AUG 1588

874   Armada in Storm, North Sea

Nos. 1400/4 were printed together, *se-tenant*, in horizontal strips of 5 throughout the sheet, forming a composite design.

400th Anniversary of Spanish Armada

1988 (19 JULY) *Phosphorised paper*

1400	870	18p multicoloured	30	25	□	□
		a. Horiz strip of 5. Nos. .				
		1400/4	3·00	3·00	□	□
1401	871	18p multicoloured	30	25	□	□
1402	872	18p multicoloured	30	25	□	□
1403	873	18p multicoloured	30	25	□	□
1404	874	18p multicoloured	30	25	□	□
		Set of 5	3·00	3·00	□	□
		First Day Cover		3·75	□	
		Presentation Pack	3·75		□	
		PHQ Cards (set of 5)	2·75	7·00	□	□
		Gutter Block of 10	8·00		□	

The Owl and the Pussy-cat went to sea
In a beautiful pea-green boat,
EDWARD LEAR • 1812–1888

C c
'It was a lovely Pussy-Cat . . .'
EDWARD LEAR • 1812–1888

875   'The Owl and the Pussy-cat'

876   'Edward Lear as a Bird' (self-portrait)

877   'Cat' (from alphabet book)

878   'There was a Young Lady whose Bonnet . . .' (limerick)

Death Centenary of Edward Lear (artist and author)

1988 (6–27 SEPT.) *Phosphorised paper*

1405	875	19p black, pale cream and carmine	65	20	□	□
1406	876	27p black, pale cream and yellow	1·00	1·00	□	□
1407	877	32p black, pale cream and emerald	1·25	1·40	□	□
1408	878	35p black, pale cream and blue	1·40	1·40	□	□
		Set of 4	4·00	3·50	□	□
		First Day Cover		3·75	□	
		Presentation Pack	4·25		□	
		PHQ Cards (set of 4)	2·25	6·00	□	□
		Set of 4 Gutter Pairs	9·00		□	
MS1409		122 × 90 mm. Nos. 1405/8 . .	7·00	8·50	□	□
		First Day Cover (27 Sept.) . . .		8·50	□	

No. **MS**1409 was sold at £1·35, the premium being used for the 'Stamp World London 90' International Stamp Exhibition.

CARRICKFERGUS CASTLE

879   Carrickfergus Castle

CAERNARFON CASTLE

880   Caernarvon Castle

EDINBURGH CASTLE

881   Edinburgh Castle

WINDSOR CASTLE

882   Windsor Castle

1988 (18 OCT.) *Ordinary paper*

1410	879	£1 deep green	4·25	60	□	□
1411	880	£1·50 maroon	4·50	1·25	□	□
1412	881	£2 indigo	8·00	1·50	□	□
1413	882	£5 deep brown	21·00	5·50	□	□
		Set of 4	35·00	8·00	□	□
		First Day Cover		35·00	□	
		Presentation Pack	35·00		□	
		Set of 4 Gutter pairs	70·00		□	

For similar designs, but with silhouette of Queen's head see Nos. 1611/14 and 1993/6.

> **Minimum Price.** The minimum price quoted is 10p. This represents a handling charge rather than a basis for valuing common stamps. Where the actual value of a stamp is less than 10p this may be apparent when set prices are shown, particularly for sets including a number of 10p stamps. It therefore follows that in valuing common stamps the 10p catalogue price should not be reckoned automatically since it covers a variation in real scarcity.

883   Journey to Bethlehem

884   Shepherds and Star

885   Three Wise Men

886   Nativity

887   The Annunciation

Christmas

1988 (15 Nov.) *One phosphor band (14p) or phosphorised paper (others)*

1414	**883**	14p multicoloured	. . . .	45	25	□ □
1415	**884**	19p multicoloured	. . . .	50	25	□ □
1416	**885**	27p multicoloured	. . . .	90	1·00	□ □
1417	**886**	32p multicoloured	. . . .	1·10	1·25	□ □
1418	**887**	35p multicoloured	. . . .	1·40	1·25	□ □
		Set of 5	. . . .	4·00	3·75	□ □
		First Day Cover	. . . .		3·75	□
		Presentation Pack	. . . .	4·00		□
		PHQ Cards (set of 5)	. . . . . .	3·00	6·00	□ □
		Set of 5 Gutter Pairs	. . . . . .	9·50		□

Collectors Pack 1988

1988 (15 Nov.) *Comprises Nos.* 1380/1408, 1414/18
CP1418*a*   *Collectors Pack* . . . .   35·00   □

Post Office Yearbook

1988 *Comprises Nos.* 1380/1404, **MS**1409, 1414/18 *in hardbound book with slip case*
YB1418*a*   *Yearbook* . . . .   37·00   □

888   Atlantic Puffin

889   Avocet

890   Oystercatcher

891   Northern Gannet

Centenary of Royal Society for the Protection of Birds

1989 (17 Jan.) *Phosphorised paper*

1419	**888**	19p multicoloured	. . . .	25	20	□ □
1420	**889**	27p multicoloured	. . . .	1·25	1·25	□ □
1421	**890**	32p multicoloured	. . . .	1·25	1·25	□ □
1422	**891**	35p multicoloured	. . . .	1·25	1·25	□ □
		Set of 4	. . . .	3·50	3·50	□ □
		First Day Cover	. . . .		4·00	□
		Presentation Pack	. . . .	4·00		□
		PHQ Cards (set of 4)	. . . . . .	3·00	7·00	□ □
		Set of 4 Gutter Pairs	. . . . . .	9·50		□

892   Rose

893   Cupid

894   Yachts

895   Fruit

896 Teddy Bear

Nos. 1423/7 were printed together, *se-tenant*, in horizontal strips of five, two such strips forming the booklet pane with twelve half stamp-size labels.

Greetings Booklet Stamps

1989 (31 Jan.) *Phosphorised paper*

1423	892	19p multicoloured	50	30 □	□	
		a. Booklet pane. Nos.				
		1423/7 × 2	50·00	□		
		b. Horiz strip of 5. Nos.				
		1423/7	25·00	25·00 □		
1424	893	19p multicoloured	50	30 □	□	
1425	894	19p multicoloured	50	30 □	□	
1426	895	19p multicoloured	50	30 □	□	
1427	896	19p multicoloured	50	30 □	□	
		Set of 5	25·00	25·00 □		
		First Day Cover		25·00	□	

897 Fruit and Vegetables   898 Meat Products

899 Dairy Produce   900 Cereal Products

Food and Farming Year

1989 (7 Mar.) *Phosphorised paper. Perf* 14 × 14½

1428	897	19p multicoloured	45	15 □	□	
1429	898	27p multicoloured	90	85 □	□	
1430	899	32p multicoloured	1·25	1·40 □	□	
1431	900	35p multicoloured	1·40	1·50 □	□	
		Set of 4	3·50	3·50 □	□	
		First Day Cover		3·75	□	
		Presentation Pack	4·00		□	
		PHQ Cards (set of 4)	2·25	6·50 □	□	
		Set of 4 Gutter Pairs	8·50		□	

901 Mortar Board (150th Anniv of Public Education in England)	902 Cross on Ballot Paper (3rd Direct Elections to European Parliament)

903 Posthorn (26th Postal, Telegraph and Telephone International Congress, Brighton)	904 Globe (Inter-Parliamentary Union Centenary Conference, London)

Nos. 1432/3 and 1434/5 were each printed together, *se-tenant*, in horizontal pairs throughout the sheets.

Anniversaries

1989 (11 Apr.) *Phosphorised paper. Perf* 14 × 14½

1432	901	19p multicoloured	50	25 □	□	
		a. Horiz pair. Nos. 1432/3	1·50	1·50 □	□	
1433	902	19p multicoloured	50	25 □	□	
1434	903	35p multicoloured	75	50 □	□	
		a. Horiz pair. Nos. 1434/5	2·50	2·50 □	□	
1435	904	35p multicoloured	75	50 □	□	
		Set of 4	3·50	3·50 □	□	
		First Day Cover		4·50	□	
		Presentation Pack	4·00		□	
		PHQ Cards (set of 4)	2·25	6·50 □	□	
		Set of 2 Gutter Strips of 4 . . .	9·00		□	

905 Toy Train and Airplane Airplane	906 Building Bricks

907   Dice and Board   908   Toy Robot, Boat
      Games   and Doll's House

Europa. Games and Toys

1989 (16 May) *Phosphorised paper*

1436	**905**	19p multicoloured	65	25	☐	☐
1437	**906**	27p multicoloured	95	1·00	☐	☐
1438	**907**	32p multicoloured	1·40	1·25	☐	☐
1439	**908**	35p multicoloured	1·50	1·25	☐	☐
		Set of 4	4·00	3·50	☐	☐
		First Day Cover		3·75		☐
		Presentation Pack	4·25		☐	
		PHQ Cards (*set of* 4)	2·25	6·50	☐	☐
		Set of 4 *Gutter Pairs*	10·50		☐	

909   Ironbridge, Shropshire   910   Tin Mine. St Agnes
                                  Head, Cornwall

911   Cotton Mills,   912   Pontcysylite Aqueduct,
      New Lanark,   Clwyd
      Strathclyde

912a

Industrial Archaeology

1989 (4–25 July) *Phosphorised paper*

1440	**909**	19p multicoloured	60	15	☐	☐
1441	**910**	27p multicoloured	1·00	1·10	☐	☐
1442	**911**	32p multicoloured	1·10	1·25	☐	☐
1443	**912**	35p multicoloured	1·25	1·50	☐	☐
		Set of 4	3·50	3·50	☐	☐
		First Day Cover		3·75		☐
		Presentation Pack	4·00		☐	
		PHQ Cards (*set of* 4)	2·25	6·50	☐	☐
		Set of 4 *Gutter Pairs*	8·50		☐	
MS1444		122 × 90 mm. **912a** As Nos.				
		1440/3 but designs horizontal .	6·00	6·50	☐	☐
		First Day Cover (25 July) . . .		6·50		☐

No. **MS**1444 was sold at £1·40, the premium being used for the 'Stamp World London 90' International Stamp Exhibition.

913   914

Booklet Stamps

1989 (22 Aug.)–**92** (*a*) *Printed in photogravure by Harrison and Sons. Perf* 15 × 14

1445	**913**	(2nd) bright blue (1 centre band)	1·00	1·00	☐	☐
1446		(2nd) bright blue (1 side band) (20.3.90)	3·00	3·25	☐	☐
1447	**914**	(1st) black (phosphorised paper)	1·75	1·00	☐	☐
1448		(1st) brownish black (2 bands) (20.3.90)	3·25	3·00	☐	☐

(*b*) *Printed in lithography by Walsall. Perf* 14

1449	**913**	(2nd) bright blue (1 centre band)	1·00	90	☐	☐
1450	**914**	(1st) black (2 bands)	2·50	2·40	☐	☐

(c) Printed in lithography by Questa. Perf 15 × 14

1451	913	(2nd) bright blue (1 centre band) (19.9.89)	1·00	1·00 □ □
1451a		(2nd) bright blue (1 side band) (25.2.92)	3·00	3·00 □ □
1452	914	(1st) black (phosphorised paper) (19.9.89)	2·50	2·50 □ □
		First Day Cover (Nos. 1445, 1447)		5·00 □

For similar stamps showing changed colours see Nos. 1511/16, for those with elliptical perforations Nos. 1664/71 and for self-adhesive versions Nos. 2039/40.

No. 1451a exists with the phosphor band at the left or right of the stamp.

919 Royal Mail Coach

920 Escort of Blues and Royals

921 Lord Mayor's Coach

922 Coach Team passing St Paul's

915 Snowflake (×10)

916 *Calliphora erythrocephala (fly)* (×5)

923 Blues and Royals Drum Horse

Nos. 1457/61 were printed together, *se-tenant,* in horizontal strips of 5 throughout the sheet, forming a composite design.

Lord Mayor's Show, London

1989 (17 OCT.) *Phosphorised paper*

1457	919	20p multicoloured	40	30 □ □
		a. Horiz strip of 5. Nos. 1457/61	3·00	3·00 □ □
1458	920	20p multicoloured	40	30 □ □
1459	921	20p multicoloured	40	30 □ □
1460	922	20p multicoloured	40	30 □ □
1461	923	20p multicoloured	40	30 □ □
		Set of 5	3·00	3·00 □ □
		First Day Cover		3·50 □
		Presentation Pack	3·00	□
		PHQ Cards (set of 5)	3·00	6·50 □ □
		Gutter Strip of 10	8·00	□

Nos. 1457/61 commemorate the 800th anniversary of the installation of the first Lord Mayor of London.

915 Snowflake (×10)

916 *Calliphora erythrocephala (fly)* (×5)

917 Blood Cells (×500)

918 Microchip (×600)

150th Anniversary of Royal Microscopical Society

1989 (5 SEPT.) *Phosphorised paper. Perf* 14½ × 14

1453	915	19p multicoloured	45	25 □ □
1454	916	27p multicoloured	95	1·00 □ □
1455	917	32p multicoloured	1·10	1·25 □ □
1456	918	35p multicoloured	1·25	1·25 □ □
		Set of 4	3·50	3·50 □ □
		First Day Cover		3·50 □
		Presentation Pack	4·00	□
		PHQ Cards (set of 4)	2·25	6·50 □ □
		Set of 4 Gutter Pairs	8·50	□

924 14th-century Peasants from Stained-glass Window

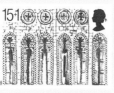

925 Arches and Roundels, West Front

926 Octagon Tower

927 Arcade from West Transept

928 Triple Arch from West Front

Christmas. 800th Anniversary of Ely Cathedral

1989 (14 Nov.) One phosphor band (Nos. 1462/3) or phosphorised paper (others)

1462	**924**	15p gold, silver and blue .	40	15 ☐ ☐
1463	**925**	15p + 1p gold, silver and blue	50	40 ☐ ☐
1464	**926**	20p + 1p gold, silver and rosine	65	80 ☐ ☐
1465	**927**	34p + 1p gold, silver and emerald	1·25	1·75 ☐ ☐
1466	**928**	37p + 1p gold, silver and yellow-olive	1·40	1·90 ☐ ☐
		Set of 5	3·75	4·50 ☐ ☐
		First Day Cover		4·50 ☐
		Presentation Pack	4·50	☐
		PHQ Cards (set of 5)	3·00	6·00 ☐ ☐
		Set of 5 Gutter Pairs	9·00	☐

Collectors Pack 1989

1989 (14 Nov.) Comprises Nos. 1419/22, 1428/43 and 1453/66

CP1466a Collectors Pack . . . . 38·00 ☐

Post Office Yearbook

1989 (14 Nov.) Comprises Nos. 1419/22, 1428/44 and 1453/66 in hardback book with slip case

YB1466a Yearbook . . . . 42·00 ☐

929 Queen Victoria and Queen Elizabeth II

150th Anniversary of the Penny Black

1990 (10 Jan.–17 Apr.) (a) Printed in photogravure by Harrison and Sons (Nos. 1468, 1470, 1472 from booklets only). Perf 15 × 14

1467	**929**	15p bright blue (1 centre band)	80	80 ☐ ☐
1468		15p bright blue (1 side band) (30 Jan.)	3·75	3·75 ☐ ☐
1469		20p brownish black and cream (phosphorised paper)	1·00	1·00 ☐ ☐
1470		20p brownish black and cream (2 bands) (30 Jan.)	2·75	2·75 ☐ ☐
1471		29p deep mauve (phosphorised paper)	1·75	1·75 ☐ ☐
1472		29p deep mauve (2 bands) (20 Mar.)	9·00	9·00 ☐ ☐
1473		34p deep bluish grey (phosphorised paper)	2·00	2·00 ☐ ☐
1474		37p rosine (phosphorised paper)	2·25	2·25 ☐ ☐
		Set of 5 (Nos. 1467, 1469, 1471, 1473/4)	7·00	7·00 ☐ ☐
		First Day Cover (Nos. 1467, 1469, 1471, 1473/4)		7·00 ☐
		Presentation Pack (Nos. 1467, 1469, 1471, 1473/4)	9·00	☐

(b) Litho Walsall (booklets). Perf 14 (30 Jan.)

1475	**929**	15p bright blue (1 centre band)	1·50	1·75 ☐ ☐
1476		20p brownish black and cream (phosphorised paper)	1·60	1·75 ☐ ☐

(c) Litho Questa (booklets). Perf 15 × 14 (17 Apr.)

1477	**929**	15p bright blue (1 centre band)	2·25	2·25 ☐ ☐
1478		20p brownish black (phosphorised paper)	2·00	2·25 ☐ ☐

No. 1468 exists with the phosphor band at the left or right of the stamp.

For Type **929** redrawn with "1st" face value see No. 2133.

930 Kitten

931 Rabbit

932 Duckling

933 Puppy

150th Anniversary of Royal Society for Prevention of Cruelty to Animals

1990 (23 JAN.) *Phosphorised paper. Perf 14 × 14½*

1479	930	20p multicoloured	75	50	☐ ☐
1480	931	29p multicoloured	1·25	1·25	☐ ☐
1481	932	34p multicoloured	1·25	1·50	☐ ☐
1482	933	37p multicoloured	1·50	1·50	☐ ☐
		Set of 4	4·50	4·25	☐ ☐
		First Day Cover		4·25	☐
		Presentation Pack	4·50		☐
		PHQ Cards (set of 4)	3·00	7·50	☐ ☐
		Set of 4 Gutter Pairs	9·50		☐

934 Teddy Bear

935 Dennis the Menace

936 Punch

937 Cheshire Cat

938 The Man in the Moon

939 The Laughing Policeman

940 Clown

941 Mona Lisa

942 Queen of Hearts

943 Stan Laurel (comedian)

T **934**/43 were printed together, *se-tenant*, in booklet panes of 10.

Greetings Booklet Stamps. 'Smiles'

1990 (6 FEB.) *Two phosphor bands*

1483	934	20p multicoloured	60	50	☐ ☐
		a. Booklet pane. Nos. 1483/92	30·00		☐
1484	935	20p multicoloured	60	50	☐ ☐
1485	936	20p multicoloured	60	50	☐ ☐
1486	937	20p multicoloured	60	50	☐ ☐
1487	938	20p multicoloured	60	50	☐ ☐
1488	939	20p multicoloured	60	50	☐ ☐
1489	940	20p multicoloured	60	50	☐ ☐
1490	941	20p multicoloured	60	50	☐ ☐
1491	942	20p multicoloured	60	50	☐ ☐
1492	943	20p gold and grey-black .	60	50	☐ ☐
		Set of 10	30·00	26·00	☐ ☐
		First Day Cover		28·00	☐

For these designs with the face value expressed as '1st' see Nos. 1550/9.

For an explanation of the pricing of *se-tenant* combinations, please see the introduction to this catalogue.

944 Alexandra Palace
('Stamp World London
90' Exhibition)

945 Glasgow School
of Art

946 British Philatelic
Bureau, Edinburgh

947 Templeton Carpet
Factory, Glasgow

**Europa (Nos. 1493 and 1495) and 'Glasgow 1990 European City
of Culture' (Nos. 1494 and 1496)**

1990 (6 MAR.) *Phosphorised paper*

1493	**944**	20p multicoloured	50	25	□	□
1494	**945**	20p multicoloured	50	25	□	□
1495	**946**	29p multicoloured	1·25	1·75	□	□
1496	**947**	37p multicoloured	1·50	1·75	□	□
		Set of 4	3·50	3·50	□	□
		First Day Cover		3·50	□	
		Presentation Pack	4·25		□	
		PHQ Cards (set of 4)	3·00	6·00	□	□
		Set of 4 Gutter Pairs	10·00		□	

948 Export Achievement
Award

949 Technological
Achievement Award

Nos. 1497/8 and 1499/500 were each printed together,
se-tenant, in horizontal pairs throughout the sheets.

**25th Anniversary of Queen's Awards for Export and
Technology**

1990 (10 APR.) *Phosphorised paper. Perf* 14 × 14½

1497	**948**	20p multicoloured	40	30	□	□
		a. Horiz pair. Nos. 1497/8	1·40	1·60	□	□
1498	**949**	20p multicoloured	40	30	□	□
1499	**948**	37p multicoloured	50	50	□	□
		a. Horiz pair. Nos.				
		1499/1500	3·00	3·00	□	□
1500	**949**	37p multicoloured	50	50	□	□
		Set of 4	4·00	4·25	□	□
		First Day Cover		4·50		□
		Presentation Pack	4·50		□	
		PHQ Cards (set of 4)	3·00	6·00	□	□
		Set of 2 Gutter Strips of 4 . . .	8·50		□	

949a

**'Stamp World London 90' International Stamp Exhibition,
London**

1990 (3 MAY) *Sheet* 122 × 90 *mm. Phosphorised paper*

MS1501	**949a**	20p brownish black and				
		cream	5·50	5·50	□	□
		First Day Cover		5·75		□
		Souvenir Book (Nos. 1467, 1469,				
		1471, 1473/4 and **MS**1501 . .	20·00		□	

No. **MS**1501 was sold at £1, the premium being used for the
exhibition.

950 Cycad and Sir Joseph
Banks Building

951 Stone Pine and Princess
of Wales Conservatory

952 Willow Tree and Palm House

953 Cedar Tree and Pagoda

957 Elizabeth, Duchess of York

958 Lady Elizabeth Bowes-Lyon

150th Anniversary of Kew Gardens

1990 (5 JUNE) *Phosphorised paper*

1502	**950**	20p multicoloured	55	15	□	□
1503	**951**	29p multicoloured	75	1·00	□	□
1504	**952**	34p multicoloured	1·25	1·60	□	□
1505	**953**	37p multicoloured	1·50	1·50	□	□
		Set of 4	3·50	3·75	□	□
		First Day Cover		3·75		□
		Presentation Pack	4·00		□	
		PHQ Cards (set of 4)	3·00	6·00	□	□
		Set of 4 Gutter Pairs	9·00		□	

90th Birthday of Queen Elizabeth the Queen Mother

1990 (2 AUG.) *Phosphorised paper*

1507	**955**	20p multicoloured	95	25	□	□
1508	**956**	29p silver, indigo and grey-blue	1·40	1·50	□	□
1509	**957**	34p multicoloured	2·00	2·50	□	□
1510	**958**	37p silver, sepia and stone	2·25	2·50	□	□
		Set of 4	6·00	6·25	□	□
		First Day Cover		6·25		□
		Presentation Pack	7·00		□	
		PHQ Cards (set of 4)	5·50	8·00	□	□
		Set of 4 Gutter Pairs	15·00		□	

For these designs with Queen's head and frame in black see Nos. 2280/3.

954 Thomas Hardy and Clyffe Clump, Dorset

150th Birth Anniversary of Thomas Hardy (author)

1990 (10 JULY) *Phosphorised paper*

1506	**954**	20p multicoloured	80	75	□	□
		First Day Cover		1·50		□
		Presentation Pack	1·50		□	
		PHQ Card	1·00	2·25	□	□
		Gutter Pair	1·75		□	

Booklet Stamps

1990 (7 AUG.)–**92** *As Types* **913/14**, *but colours changed*

(a) Photo Harrison. Perf 15 × 14

1511	**913**	(2nd) deep blue (1 centre band)	1·50	1·50	□	□
1512	**914**	(1st) bright orange-red (phosphorised paper)	1·50	1·50	□	□

(b) Litho Questa. Perf 15 × 14

1513	**913**	(2nd) deep blue (1 centre band)	2·50	2·50	□	□
1514	**914**	(1st) bright orange-red (phosphorised paper)	˙1·00	1·00	□	□
1514a		(1st) bright orange-red (2 bands) (25.2.92) . . .	2·25	2·25	□	□

(c) Litho Walsall. Perf 14

1515	**913**	(2nd) deep blue (1 centre band)	1·00	1·00	□	□
1516	**914**	(1st) bright orange-red (phosphorised paper)	1·25	1·25	□	□
		c. Perf 13	2·75	3·00	□	□
		First Day Cover (Nos. 1515/16) .		5·00		□

For similar stamps with elliptical perforations see Nos. 1664/71.

955 Queen Elizabeth the Queen Mother

956 Queen Elizabeth

For full information on all future British issues, collectors should write to Royal Mail, Freepost EH3647, 21 South Syle Crescent, Edinburgh EH12 9PE.

959 Victoria Cross

960 George Cross

961 Distinguished Service Cross and Distinguished Service Medal

962 Military Cross and Military Medal

963 Distinguished Flying Cross and Distinguished Flying Medal

Gallantry Awards

1990 (11 Sept.) *Phosphorised paper*

1517	959	20p multicoloured	80	75	☐	☐
1518	960	20p multicoloured	80	75	☐	☐
1519	961	20p multicoloured	80	75	☐	☐
1520	962	20p multicoloured	80	75	☐	☐
1521	963	20p multicoloured	80	75	☐	☐
		Set of 5	3·75	3·50	☐	☐
		First Day Cover		3·75		☐
		Presentation Pack	4·00			☐
		PHQ Cards (set of 5)	3·00	8·00	☐	☐
		Set of 5 Gutter Pairs	9·25			☐

For Type **959** with "all-over" phosphor and perf 14 × 14½ see No. 2666.

964 Armagh Observatory, Jodrell Bank Radio Telescope and La Palma Telescope

965 Newton's Moon and Tides Diagram with Early Telescopes

966 Greenwich Old Observatory and Early Astronomical Equipment

967 Stonehenge, Gyroscope and Navigating by Stars

Astronomy

1990 (16 Oct.) *Phosphorised paper. Perf* 14 × 14½

1522	964	22p multicoloured	65	15	☐	☐
1523	965	26p multicoloured	1·00	1·10	☐	☐
1524	966	31p multicoloured	1·25	1·40	☐	☐
1525	967	37p multicoloured	1·50	1·40	☐	☐
		Set of 4	3·75	3·75	☐	☐
		First Day Cover		4·00		☐
		Presentation Pack	4·50			☐
		PHQ Cards (set of 4)	3·00	7·00	☐	☐
		Set of 4 Gutter Pairs	9·25			☐

Nos. 1522/5 commemorate the centenary of the British Astronomical Association and the bicentenary of the Armagh Observatory.

968 Building a Snowman

969 Fetching the Christmas Tree

970 Carol Singing

971 Tobogganing

972 Ice-skating

Christmas

1990 (13 Nov.) *One phosphor band (17p) or phosphorised paper (others)*

1526	**968**	17p multicoloured	50	15	☐	☐
1527	**969**	22p multicoloured	70	20	☐	☐
1528	**970**	26p multicoloured	70	1·10	☐	☐
1529	**971**	31p multicoloured	1·25	1·50	☐	☐
1530	**972**	37p multicoloured	1·25	1·50	☐	☐
		Set of 5	4·00	4·00	☐	☐
		First Day Cover		4·00		☐
		Presentation Pack	4·50		☐	
		PHQ Cards (*set of* 5)	3·00	7·00	☐	☐
		Set of 5 Gutter Pairs	10·00		☐	

Collectors Pack 1990

1990 (13 Nov.) *Comprises Nos. 1479/82, 1493/1510 and 1517/30*
CP1530*a* Collectors Pack . . . . 40·00   ☐

Post Office Yearbook

1990 *Comprises Nos. 1479/82, 1493/1500, 1502/10 and 1517/30 in hardback book with slip case*
YB1530*a* Yearbook . . . . 45·00   ☐

'King Charles Spaniel'

973 'King Charles Spaniel'

974 'A Pointer'

975 'Two Hounds in a Landscape'

976 'A Rough Dog'

977 'Fino and Tiny'

Dogs. Paintings by George Stubbs

1991 (8 JAN.) *Phosphorised paper. Perf* $14 \times 14\frac{1}{2}$

1531	**973**	22p multicoloured	50	15	☐	☐
1532	**974**	26p multicoloured	75	1·25	☐	☐

1533	**975**	31p multicoloured	1·00	1·25	☐	☐
1534	**976**	33p multicoloured	1·25	1·25	☐	☐
1535	**977**	37p multicoloured	1·25	1·25	☐	☐
		Set of 5	4·50	4·50	☐	☐
		First Day Cover		5·00		☐
		Presentation Pack	5·00		☐	
		PHQ Cards (*set of* 5)	3·50	7·00	☐	☐
		Set of 5 Gutter Pairs	11·00		☐	

978 Thrush's Nest

979 Shooting Star and Rainbow

980 Magpies and Charm Bracelet

981 Black Cat

982 Common Kingfisher with Key

983 Mallard and Frog

984 Four-leaf Clover in Boot and Match Box

985 Pot of Gold at End of Rainbow

986 Heart-shaped Butterflies

987 Wishing Well and Sixpence

T **978/87** were printed together, *se-tenant,* in booklet panes of 10 stamps and 12 half stamp-size labels, the backgrounds of the stamps forming a composite design.

Greetings Booklet Stamps. 'Good Luck'

1991 (5 Feb.) *Two phosphor bands*

1536	**978**	(1st) multicoloured	50	50	□	□
		a. Booklet pane. Nos.				
		1536/45	15·00	17·00	□	□
1537	**979**	(1st) multicoloured	50	50	□	□
1538	**980**	(1st) multicoloured	50	50	□	□
1539	**981**	(1st) multicoloured	50	50	□	□
1540	**982**	(1st) multicoloured	50	50	□	□
1541	**983**	(1st) multicoloured	50	50	□	□
1542	**984**	(1st) multicoloured	50	50	□	□
1543	**985**	(1st) multicoloured	50	50	□	□
1544	**986**	(1st) multicoloured	50	50	□	□
1545	**987**	(1st) multicoloured	50	50	□	□
		Set of 10	15·00	17·00	□	□
		First Day Cover		19·00		□

988   Michael Faraday (inventor of electric motor) (Birth Bicentenary)

989   Charles Babbage (computer science pioneer) (Birth Bicentenary)

990   Radar Sweep of East Anglia (50th Anniv of Discovery by Sir Robert Watson-Watt)

991   Gloster Whittle E28/39 Aircraft over East Anglia (50th Anniv of First Flight of Sir Frank Whittle's Jet Engine)

Scientific Achievements

1991 (5 Mar.) *Phosphorised paper*

1546	**988**	22p multicoloured	60	50	□	□
1547	**989**	22p multicoloured	60	50	□	□
1548	**990**	31p multicoloured	1·20	1·50	□	□
1549	**991**	37p multicoloured	1·35	1·75	□	□
		Set of 4	3·50	4·00	□	□
		First Day Cover		4·00		□
		Presentation Pack	4·25		□	
		PHQ Cards (*set of 4*)	3·50	7·00	□	□
		Set of 4 Gutter Pairs	8·50		□	

992   Teddy Bear

Nos. 1550/9 were originally printed together, *se-tenant,* in booklet panes of 10 stamps and 12 half stamp-size labels.

Greetings Booklet Stamps. 'Smiles'

1991 (26 Mar.) *As Nos. 1483/92, but inscribed '1st' as T* **992**. *Two phosphor bands. Perf 15 × 14*

1550	**992**	(1st) multicoloured	40	40	□	□
		a. Booklet pane. Nos.				
		1550/9	12·00	13·00	□	□
1551	**935**	(1st) multicoloured	40	40	□	□
1552	**936**	(1st) multicoloured	40	40	□	□
1553	**937**	(1st) multicoloured	40	40	□	□
1554	**938**	(1st) multicoloured	40	40	□	□
1555	**939**	(1st) multicoloured	40	40	□	□
1556	**940**	(1st) multicoloured	40	40	□	□
1557	**941**	(1st) multicoloured	40	40	□	□
1558	**942**	(1st) multicoloured	40	40	□	□
1559	**943**	(1st) multicoloured	40	40	□	□
		Set of 10	12·00	13·00	□	□
		First Day Cover		13·00		□

The stamps were re-issued in sheets of 10 each with *se-tenant* label on 22 May 2000 in connection with 'customised' stamps available at 'Stamp Show 2000'. The labels show either a pattern of ribbons or a personal photograph.

A similar sheet, but in lithography instead of photogravure, and perforated $14\frac{1}{2} \times 14$, appeared on 3 July 2001 with the labels showing either greetings or a personal photograph.

Three further sheets, also in lithography, appeared on 1 October 2002. One contained Nos. 1550/1 each ×10 with greetings labels. Both designs were also available in sheets of 20 with personal photographs.

993   Man looking at Space   **994**

995 Space looking at Man **996**

Nos. 1560/1 and 1562/3 were each printed together, *se-tenant,* in horizontal pairs throughout the sheets, each pair forming a composite design.

Europa. Europe in Space

1991 (23 APR.) *Phosphorised paper*

1560	**993**	22p multicoloured	40	30	□	□
		a. Horiz pair. Nos. 1560/1	1·50	1·50	□	□
1561	**994**	22p multicoloured	40	30	□	□
1562	**995**	37p multicoloured	50	40	□	□
		a. Horiz pair. Nos. 1562/3	3·50	3·00	□	□
1563	**996**	37p multicoloured	50	40	□	□
		Set of 4	4·00	3·50	□	□
		First Day Cover		4·50		□
		Presentation Pack	5·00		□	
		PHQ Cards (set of 4)	3·00	7·00	□	□
		Set of 2 Gutter Strips of 4 . . .	12·00		□	

997 Fencing

998 Hurdling

999 Diving

1000 Rugby

World Student Games, Sheffield (Nos. 1564/6) and World Cup Rugby Championship, London (No. 1567)

1991 (11 JUNE) *Phosphorised paper. Perf 14½ × 14*

1564	**997**	22p multicoloured	60	20	□	□
1565	**998**	26p multicoloured	1·00	1·00	□	□

1566	**999**	31p multicoloured	1·25	1·25	□	□
1567	**1000**	37p multicoloured	1·50	1·50	□	□
		Set of 4	3·50	3·50	□	□
		First Day Cover		4·00		□
		Presentation Pack	4·50		□	
		PHQ Cards (set of 4)	3·00	7·00	□	□
		Set of 4 Gutter Pairs	9·00		□	

1001 'Silver Jubilee'   **1002** 'Mme Alfred Carrière'

1003 *Rosa moyesii*   **1004** 'Harvest Fayre'

1005 'Mutabilis'

9th World Congress of Roses, Belfast

1991 (16 JULY) *Phosphorised paper. Perf 14½ × 14*

1568	**1001**	22p multicoloured	50	20	□	□
1569	**1002**	26p multicoloured	75	1·25	□	□
1570	**1003**	31p multicoloured	1·00	1·25	□	□
1571	**1004**	33p multicoloured	1·25	1·50	□	□
1572	**1005**	37p multicoloured	1·50	1·50	□	□
		Set of 5	4·50	5·00	□	□
		First Day Cover		5·00		□
		Presentation Pack	5·00		□	
		PHQ Cards (set of 5)	3·00	9·00	□	□
		Set of 5 Gutter Pairs	11·00		□	

1006 Iguanodon

1007 Stegosaurus

1008 Tyrannosaurus

1009 Protoceratops

1010 Triceratops

150th Anniversary of Dinosaurs' Identification by Owen

1991 (20 Aug.) *Phosphorised paper. Perf* 14½ × 14

1573	**1006**	22p multicoloured	. . . .	60	20	☐	☐
1574	**1007**	26p multicoloured	. . . .	1·10	1·25	☐	☐
1575	**1008**	31p multicoloured	. . . .	1·25	1·25	☐	☐
1576	**1009**	33p multicoloured	. . . .	1·50	1·50	☐	☐
1577	**1010**	37p multicoloured	. . . .	1·60	1·50	☐	☐
		Set of 5	. . . .	5·75	5·00	☐	☐
		First Day Cover	. . . .		5·50		☐
		Presentation Pack	. . . .	6·00		☐	
		PHQ Cards (set of 5)	. . . . . .	3·00	9·00	☐	☐
		Set of 5 Gutter Pairs	. . . . . .	12·00		☐	

1011 Map of 1816

1012 Map of 1906

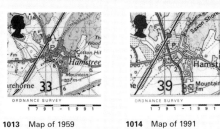

1013 Map of 1959 **1014** Map of 1991

Bicentenary of Ordnance Survey. Maps of Hamstreet, Kent

1991 (17 Sept.) *Phosphorised paper. Perf* 14½ × 14

1578	**1011**	24p multicoloured	. . . .	60	20	☐	☐
1579	**1012**	28p multicoloured	. . . .	1·00	95	☐	☐
1580	**1013**	33p multicoloured	. . . .	1·25	1·40	☐	☐
1581	**1014**	39p multicoloured	. . . .	1·50	1·40	☐	☐
		Set of 4	. . . .	3·50	3·50	☐	☐
		First Day Cover	. . . .		4·25		☐
		Presentation Pack	. . . .	4·50		☐	
		PHQ Cards (set of 4)	. . . . . .	3·00	7·00	☐	☐
		Set of 4 Gutter Pairs	. . . . . .	10·00		☐	

1015 Adoration of the Magi

1016 Mary and Baby Jesus in Stable

1017 Holy Family and Angel

1018 The Annunciation

1019 The Flight into Egypt

Christmas. Illuminated Manuscripts from the Bodleian Library, Oxford

1991 (12 Nov.) *One phosphor band* (18p) *or phosphorised paper* (*others*)

1582	**1015**	18p multicoloured	. . . .	75	10 ☐ ☐
1583	**1016**	24p multicoloured	. . . .	90	10 ☐ ☐
1584	**1017**	28p multicoloured	. . . .	95	1·25 ☐ ☐
1585	**1018**	33p multicoloured	. . . .	1·10	1·50 ☐ ☐
1586	**1019**	39p multicoloured	. . . .	1·25	1·75 ☐ ☐
		Set of 5		4·50	4·50 ☐ ☐
		First Day Cover			4·50 ☐
		Presentation Pack		4·50	☐
		PHQ Cards (set of 5)		3·00	7·50 ☐ ☐
		Set of 5 Gutter Pairs		11·00	☐

Collectors Pack 1991

1991 (12 Nov.) *Comprises Nos. 1531/5, 1546/9 and 1560/86*

CP1586*a*   Collectors Pack . . . .   40·00   ☐

Post Office Yearbook

1991 *Comprises Nos. 1531/5, 1546/9 and 1560/86 in hardback book with slip case*

YB1586*a*   Yearbook . . . .   45·00   ☐

1020   Fallow Deer in Scottish Forest

1021   Hare on North Yorkshire Moors

1022   Fox in the Fens

1023   Redwing and Home Counties Village

1024   Welsh Mountain Sheep in Snowdonia

The Four Seasons. Wintertime

1992 (14 Jan.) *One phosphor band* (18p) *or phosphorised paper* (*others*)

1587	**1020**	18p multicoloured	. . . .	55	25 ☐ ☐
1588	**1021**	24p multicoloured	. . . .	75	25 ☐ ☐
1589	**1022**	28p multicoloured	. . . .	1·00	1·25 ☐ ☐
1590	**1023**	33p multicoloured	. . . .	1·25	1·50 ☐ ☐
1591	**1024**	39p multicoloured	. . . .	1·40	1·75 ☐ ☐
		Set of 5		4·50	4·50 ☐ ☐
		First Day Cover			4·50 ☐
		Presentation Pack		4·50	☐
		PHQ Cards (set of 5)		3·00	8·00 ☐ ☐
		Set of 5 Gutter Pairs		11·00	☐

1025   Flower Spray

1026   Double Locket

1027   Key

1028   Model Car and Cigarette Cards

1029   Compass and Map

1030   Pocket Watch

1031   1854 1d. Red Stamp and Pen

1032   Pearl Necklace

1033 Marbles

1034 Bucket, Spade and Starfish

T **1025/34** were printed together, *se-tenant*, in booklet panes of 10 stamps and 12 half stamp-size labels, the backgrounds of the stamps forming a composite design.

Greetings Stamps. 'Memories'

1992 (28 JAN.) *Two phosphor bands*

1592	**1025**	(1st) multicoloured	50	50	□	□
		a. Booklet pane. Nos.				
		1592/1601	13·00	13·00	□	□
1593	**1026**	(1st) multicoloured	50	50	□	□
1594	**1027**	(1st) multicoloured	50	50	□	□
1595	**1028**	(1st) multicoloured	50	50	□	□
1596	**1029**	(1st) multicoloured	50	50	□	□
1597	**1030**	(1st) multicoloured	50	50	□	□
1598	**1031**	(1st) multicoloured	50	50	□	□
1599	**1032**	(1st) multicoloured	50	50	□	□
1600	**1033**	(1st) multicoloured	50	50	□	□
1601	**1034**	(1st) multicoloured	50	50	□	□
		Set of 10	13·00	13·00	□	□
		First Day Cover		13·00		□
		Presentation Pack	17·00		□	

1035 Queen Elizabeth in Coronation Robes and Parliamentary Emblem

1036 Queen Elizabeth in Garter Robes and Archiepiscopal Arms

1037 Queen Elizabeth with Baby Prince Andrew and Royal Arms

1038 Queen Elizabeth at Trooping the Colour and Service Emblems

1039 Queen Elizabeth and Commonwealth Emblem

Nos. 1602/6 were printed together, *se-tenant*, in horizontal strips of 5 throughout the sheet.

40th Anniversary of Accession

1992 (6 FEB.) *Two phosphor bands. Perf* $14\frac{1}{2} \times 14$

1602	**1035**	24p multicoloured	50	50	□	□
		a. Horiz strip of 5. Nos.				
		1602/6	6·00	6·00	□	□
1603	**1036**	24p multicoloured	50	50	□	□
1604	**1037**	24p multicoloured	50	50	□	□
1605	**1038**	24p multicoloured	50	50	□	□
1606	**1039**	24p multicoloured	50	50	□	□
		Set of 5	6·00	6·00	□	□
		First Day Cover		6·00		□
		Presentation Pack	7·00		□	
		PHQ Cards (set of 5)	3·00	7·50	□	□
		Gutter Block of 10	15·00		□	

1040 Tennyson in 1888 and 'The Beguiling of Merlin' (Sir Edward Burne-Jones)

1041 Tennyson in 1856 and 'April Love' (Arthur Hughes)

1042 Tennyson in 1864 and 'I am Sick of the Shadows' (John Waterhouse)

1043 Tennyson as a Young Man and 'Mariana' (Dante Gabriel Rossetti)

Death Centenary of Alfred, Lord Tennyson (poet)

1992 (10 MAR.) *Phosphorised paper. Perf 14½ × 14*

1607	**1040**	24p multicoloured	60	20	□	□
1608	**1041**	28p multicoloured	85	85	□	□
1609	**1042**	33p multicoloured	1·40	1·60	□	□
1610	**1043**	39p multicoloured	1·50	1·60	□	□
		Set of 4	4·00	3·75	□	□
		First Day Cover		4·25		□
		Presentation Pack	4·50		□	
		PHQ Cards (set of 4)	3·00	7·00	□	□
		Set of 4 Gutter Pairs	10·00		□	

CARRICKFERGUS CASTLE

1044 Carrickfergus Castle

1992 (24 MAR.)–**95**. *Designs as Nos. 1410/13, but showing Queen's head in silhouette as T **1044**. Perf 15 × 14 (with one elliptical hole on each vertical side)*

1611	**1044**	£1 bottle green and gold†	5·50	1·00	□	□
1612	**880**	£1·50 maroon and gold†	5·50	1·00	□	□
1613	**881**	£2 indigo and gold† . . .	7·50	1·00	□	□
1613*a*	**1044**	£3 reddish violet and gold†	18·50	3·00	□	□
1614	**882**	£5 deep brown and gold†	17·00	3·00	□	□
		Set of 5	48·00	8·00	□	□
		First Day Cover (*Nos. 1611/13, 1614*)		35·00		□
		First Day Cover (22 Aug. 1995) (*No. 1613a*)		10·00		□
		Presentation Pack (*P.O. Pack No. 27*) (*Nos. 1611/13, 1614*) . . .	38·00		□	
		Presentation Pack (*P.O. Pack No. 33*) (*No. 1613a*)	30·00		□	
		PHQ Cards (*Nos. 1611/14*) . . .	12·00		□	
		PHQ Card (*No. 1613a*)	6·00	22·00	□	□
		Set of 5 Gutter Pairs	98·00		□	

†The Queen's head on these stamps is printed in optically variable ink which changes colour from gold to green when viewed from different angles.

PHQ cards for Nos. 1611/13 and 1614 were not issued until 16 February 1993.

Nos. 1611/14 were printed by Harrison. For stamps with different lettering by Enschedé see Nos. 1993/6.

For full information on all future British issues, collectors should write to Royal Mail, Freepost EH3647, 21 South Gyle Crescent, Edinburgh EH12 9PE.

1045 British Olympic Association Logo (Olympic Games, Barcelona)

1046 British Paralympic Association Symbol (Paralympics '92, Barcelona)

1047 *Santa Maria* (500th Anniv of Discovery of America by Columbus)

1048 *Kaisei* (Japanese cadet brigantine) (Grand Regatta Columbus, 1992)

1049 British Pavilion, 'EXPO 92', Seville

Nos. 1615/16 were printed together, *se-tenant*, in horizontal pairs throughout the sheet.

Europa. International Events

1992 (7 APR.) *Phosphorised paper. Perf 14 × 14½*

1615	**1045**	24p multicoloured	50	40	□	□
		a. *Horiz pair. Nos.* 1615/16	2·25	1·75	□	□
1616	**1046**	24p multicoloured	50	40	□	□
1617	**1047**	24p multicoloured	1·00	75	□	□
1618	**1048**	39p multicoloured	1·40	1·50	□	□
1619	**1049**	39p multicoloured	1·40	1·50	□	□
		Set of 5	4·50	4·50	□	□
		First Day Cover		5·00		□
		Presentation Pack	5·25		□	
		PHQ Cards (set of 5)	3·00	7·00	□	□
		Set of 3 Gutter Pairs and a Gutter Strip of 4	13·00		□	

1050 Pikeman

1051 Drummer

1052 Musketeer

1053 Standard Bearer

1058 Iolanthe

350th Anniversary of the Civil War

1992 (16 JUNE) *Phosphorised paper. Perf* $14\frac{1}{2} \times 14$

1620	**1050**	24p multicoloured	. . . .	60	20	☐	☐
1621	**1051**	28p multicoloured	. . . .	85	85	☐	☐
1622	**1052**	33p multicoloured	. . . .	1·40	1·50	☐	☐
1623	**1053**	39p multicoloured	. . . .	1·50	1·75	☐	☐
		Set of 4	. . . .	4·00	4·00	☐	☐
		First Day Cover	. . . .		4·00		☐
		Presentation Pack	. . . .	4·50		☐	
		PHQ Cards (set of 4)	. . . . . .	3·00	7·00	☐	☐
		Set of 4 Gutter Pairs	. . . . . .	10·50		☐	

150th Birth Anniversary of Sir Arthur Sullivan (composer). Gilbert and Sullivan Operas

1992 (21 JULY) *One phosphor band* (18p) *or phosphorised paper* (*others*). *Perf* $14\frac{1}{2} \times 14$

1624	**1054**	18p multicoloured	. . . .	50	20	☐	☐
1625	**1055**	24p multicoloured	. . . .	80	20	☐	☐
1626	**1056**	28p multicoloured	. . . .	95	1·00	☐	☐
1627	**1057**	33p multicoloured	. . . .	1·50	1·60	☐	☐
1628	**1058**	39p multicoloured	. . . .	1·60	1·60	☐	☐
		Set of 5	. . . .	4·50	4·25	☐	☐
		First Day Cover	. . . .		4·50		☐
		Presentation Pack	. . . .	4·50			☐
		PHQ Cards (set of 5)	. . . . . .	3·00	6·25		☐
		Set of 5 Gutter Pairs	. . . . . .	10·50			☐

1054 The Yeomen of the Guard

1055 The Gondoliers

1056 The Mikado

1057 The Pirates of Penzance

1059 'Acid Rain Kills'

1060 'Ozone Layer'

1061 'Greenhouse Effect'

1062 'Bird of Hope'

Protection of the Environment. Children's Paintings

1992 (15 SEPT.) *Phosphorised paper. Perf* $14 \times 14\frac{1}{2}$

1629	**1059**	24p multicoloured	. . . .	70	25	☐	☐
1630	**1060**	28p multicoloured	. . . .	1·10	1·25	☐	☐
1631	**1061**	33p multicoloured	. . . .	1·25	1·50	☐	☐
1632	**1062**	39p multicoloured	. . . .	1·40	1·50	☐	☐
		Set of 4	. . . .	4·00	4·00	☐	☐
		First Day Cover	. . . .		4·00		☐
		Presentation Pack	. . . .	4·50		☐	
		PHQ Cards (set of 4)	. . . . . .	3·00	6·25	☐	☐
		Set of 4 Gutter Pairs	. . . . . .	10·00		☐	

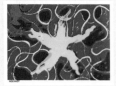

1063 European Star

Single European Market

1992 (13 Oct.) *Phosphorised paper*

1633	**1063**	24p multicoloured	1·00	1·00 □	□
		First Day Cover		1·50	□
		Presentation Pack	1·50		□
		PHQ Card	1·50	4·00 □	□
		Gutter Pair	2·25		□

1064 'Angel Gabriel', St James's, Pangbourne

1065 'Madonna and Child', St. Mary's, Bibury

1066 'King with Gold', Our Lady and St Peter, Leatherhead

1067 'Shepherds', All Saints, Porthcawl

1068 'Kings with Frankincense and Myrrh', Our Lady and St Peter, Leatherhead

Christmas. Stained Glass Windows

1992 (10 Nov.) *One phosphor band* (18p) *or phosphorised paper* (*others*)

1634	**1064**	18p multicoloured	50	15 □	□
1635	**1065**	24p multicoloured	75	15 □	□
1636	**1066**	28p multicoloured	1·00	1·10 □	□
1637	**1067**	33p multicoloured	1·25	1·50 □	□
1638	**1068**	39p multicoloured	1·25	1·50 □	□
		Set of 5	4·25	4·25 □	□
		First Day Cover		4·50	□
		Presentation Pack	4·50		□
		PHQ Cards (set of 5)	3·00	7·50 □	□
		Set of 5 Gutter Pairs	10·00		□

Collectors Pack 1992

1992 (10 Nov.) *Comprises Nos. 1587/91, 1602/10 and 1615/38*
CP1638a   Collectors Pack . . . .   45·00   □

Post Office Yearbook

1992 (11 Nov.) *Comprises Nos. 1587/91, 1602/10 and 1615/38 in hardback book with slip case*
YB1638a   Yearbook . . . .   55·00   □

1069 Mute Swan Cob and St Catherine's, Abbotsbury

1070 Cygnet and Decoy

1071 Swans and Cygnet

1072 Eggs in Nest and Tithe Barn, Abbotsbury

1073 Young Swan and the Fleet

600th Anniversary of Abbotsbury Swannery

1993 (19 Jan.) *One phosphor band* (18p) *or phosphorised paper* (*others*)

1639	**1069**	18p multicoloured	1·25	25 □	□
1640	**1070**	24p multicoloured	1·10	25 □	□
1641	**1071**	28p multicoloured	1·40	2·25 □	□
1642	**1072**	33p multicoloured	1·75	2·50 □	□
1643	**1073**	39p multicoloured	1·90	2·50 □	□
		Set of 5	6·50	7·50 □	□
		First Day Cover		7·50	□
		Presentation Pack	7·00		□
		PHQ Cards (set of 5)	4·25	8·50 □	□
		Set of 5 Gutter Pairs	15·00		□

1074 Long John Silver and Parrot (*Treasure Island*)

1075 Tweedledum and Tweedledee (*Alice Through the Looking-Glass*)

1076 William (*William* books)

1077 Mole and Toad (*The Wind in the Willows*)

1078 Teacher and Wilfrid ('The Bash Street Kids')

1079 Peter Rabbit and Mrs Rabbit (*The Tale of Peter Rabbit*)

1080 Snowman (*The Snowman*) and Father Christmas (*Father Christmas*)

1081 The Big Friendly Giant and Sophie (*The BFG*)

1082 Bill Badger and Rupert Bear

1083 Aladdin and the Genie

T **1074/83** were printed together, *se-tenant*, in booklet panes of 10 stamps and 20 half stamp-size labels.

Greetings Stamps. 'Gift Giving'

1993 (2 Feb.) *Two phosphor bands. Perf* 15 × 14 (*with one elliptical hole on each vertical side*)

1644	**1074**	(1st) multicoloured	50	40	□	□
		a. Booklet pane. Nos.				
		1644/53	11·00	12·00	□	□
1645	**1075**	(1st) gold, cream and				
		black	50	40	□	□
1646	**1076**	(1st) multicoloured	50	40	□	□
1647	**1077**	(1st) multicoloured	50	40	□	□
1648	**1078**	(1st) multicoloured	50	40	□	□
1649	**1079**	(1st) multicoloured	50	40	□	□
1650	**1080**	(1st) multicoloured	50	40	□	□
1651	**1081**	(1st) multicoloured	50	40	□	□
1652	**1082**	(1st) multicoloured	50	40	□	□
1653	**1083**	(1st) multicoloured	50	40	□	□
		Set of 10	11·00	12·00	□	□
		First Day Cover		12·00		□
		Presentation Pack	16·00		□	
		PHQ Cards (*set of* 10)	13·50	28·00	□	□

1084 Decorated Enamel Dial

1085 Escapement, Remontoire and Fusee

1086 Balance, Spring and Temperature Compensator

1087 Back of Movement

300th Birth Anniversary of John Harrison (inventor of the marine chronometer). Details of 'H4' Clock

1993 (16 Feb.) *Phosphorised paper. Perf* 14½ × 14

1654	**1084**	24p multicoloured	60	25	□	□
1655	**1085**	28p multicoloured	1·00	1·25	□	□
1656	**1086**	33p multicoloured	1·40	1·25	□	□
1657	**1087**	39p multicoloured	1·50	1·50	□	□
		Set of 4	4·00	4·00	□	□
		First Day Cover		4·00		□
		Presentation Pack	4·25		□	
		PHQ Cards (*set of 4*)	4·25	7·00	□	□
		Set of 4 Gutter Pairs	10·00		□	

1088 Britannia

1993 (2 MAR.) *Granite paper. Perf* 14 × 14½ (*with two elliptical holes on each horizontal side*)

1658	**1088**	£10 multicoloured	40·00	12·00	□	□
		First Day Cover		25·00		□
		Presentation Pack	36·00		□	
		PHQ Card	5·00	35·00	□	□

1089 *Dendrobium hellwigianum*

1090 *Paphiopedilum Maudiae 'Magnifcum'*

1091 *Cymbidium lowianum*

1092 *Vanda* Rothschildiana

1093 *Dendrobium vexillarius var albiviride*

1093a

14th World Orchid Conference, Glasgow

1993 (16 MAR.) *One phosphor band* (18p) *or phosphorised paper* (*others*)

1659	**1089**	18p multicoloured	45	25	□	□
1660	**1090**	24p multicoloured	75	25	□	□
1661	**1091**	28p multicoloured	1·00	1·25	□	□
1662	**1092**	33p multicoloured	1·25	1·50	□	□
1663	**1093**	39p multicoloured	1·60	1·50	□	□
		Set of 5	4·50	4·50	□	□
		First Day Cover		4·50		□
		Presentation Pack	5·00		□	
		PHQ Cards (set of 5)	4·50	7·00	□	□
		Set of 5 Gutter Pairs	10·00		□	

Booklet Stamps

1993 (6 APR.)–**2005** *As T* 913/14 *and* 1093a, *but Perf* 14 (*No.* 1665) *or* 15 × 14 (*others*) (*both with one elliptical hole on each vertical side*)

(a) *Photo*
 Harrison (*No.* 1666)
 Questa (*Nos.* 1664ab, 1667ab)
 Walsall (*No.* 1665)
 Harrison (later *De La Rue*), Questa or Walsall (*No.* 1667)
 Harrison (later *De La Rue*), Enschedé, Questa or Walsall (*Nos.* 1664, 1668, 1669)

1664	**913**	(2nd) bright blue (1 centre band)	1·00	1·00	□	□
		a. Perf 14	1·10	1·10	□	□
1665		(2nd) bright blue (1 side band)	1·10	1·10	□	□
1666	**914**	(1st) bright orange-red (phosphorised paper)	1·50	1·25	□	□
1667		(1st) bright orange-red (2 phosphor bands) . .	1·10	1·10	□	□
		a. Perf 14	1·50	1·50	□	□
1668		(1st) gold (2 phosphor bands)	1·00	1·00	□	□
1669	**1093a**	(E) deep blue (2 phosphor bands) . .	1·25	1·25	□	□

(b) *Litho Questa or Walsall* (*No.* 1671 *also Enschedé*)

1670	**913**	(2nd) bright blue (1 centre band)	90	90	□	□
1671	**914**	(1st) bright orange-red (2 phosphor bands) . .	1·00	1·00	□	□

First Day Covers

21 Apr. 1997	(1st), 26p (Nos 1668, Y1686) . .	£3·50	□
19 Jan. 1999	(E) (No 1669)	£3·50	□

Nos. 1664, 1667, 1669 and 1670/1 also come from sheets.

No. 1665 exists with the phosphor band at the left or right of the stamp and was only issued in booklets.

No. 1668 was issued by Harrison in booklets and Walsall in sheets and booklets for the Queen's Golden Wedding on 21 April 1997. The gold colour was later adopted for the (1st) class rate, replacing bright orange-red.

For No. 1668 in presentation pack see Pack No. 38 listed below, No. Y1667 etc.

No. 1669 was valid for the basic European airmail rate, initially 30p.

For self-adhesive versions in these colours see Nos. 2039/40 and 2295/8.

1993–2006 *As Nos.* X841 *etc, but perf* 14 (*No.* Y1678) *or* 15 × 14 (*others*) (*both with one elliptical hole on each vertical side*)

(a) *Photo*
Enschedé:— 20p (Y1679), 29p, 35p (Y1692), 36p, 38p (Y1700), 41p (Y1706), 43p (Y1710)
Harrison:— 20p (Y1681), 25p (Y1683), 26p (Y1686), 35p (Y1693), 41p (Y1707), 43p (Y1711)
Walsall:— 10p (Y1676), 19p (Y1678), 38p (Y1701a), 43p (Y1711a)
Enschedé or Harrison (later *De La Rue*):— 4p, 5p, 6p, 10p (Y1676), 25p (Y1684), 31p, 39p (Y1702), £1

Enschedé, Harrison (later De La Rue) or Questa:— 1p, 2p
Enschedé, Harrison (later De La Rue) or Walsall:— 30p, 37p (Y1697), 42p, 50p, 63p
Harrison (later De La Rue) or Questa:— 19p (Y1677), 20p (Y1680), 26p (Y1685)
De La Rue or Walsall:— 38p (Y1701), 39p (Y1703), 40p (Y1704), 64p, 65p, 68p
De La Rue:— 7p, 8p, 9p, 12p, 14p, 20p (Y1682), 33p, 34p, 35p (Y1694), 37p (Y1698/9), 40p (Y1708), 41p (Y1708), 43p (Y1712), 44p, 45p, 46p, 49p, 72p, £1·50, £2, £3, £5
Enschedé or De La Rue:— 35p (Y1695), 47p

Y1667	**367**	1p crimson (2 bands) .	25	25	☐	☐
Y1668		2p deep green (2 bands)	25	25	☐	☐
Y1669		4p new blue (2 bands) .	25	25	☐	☐
Y1670		5p dull red-brown (2 bands)	25	25	☐	☐
Y1671		6p yellow-olive (2 bands)	25	30	☐	☐
Y1672		7p grey (2 bands)	35	35	☐	☐
Y1673		7p bright magenta (2 bands)	25	25	☐	☐
Y1674		8p yellow (2 bands) . .	35	35	☐	☐
Y1675		9p yellow-orange (2 bands)	15	20	☐	☐
Y1676		10p dull orange (2 bands)	35	35	☐	☐
		a. Perf 14	2·00	2·00	☐	☐
Y1676b		12p greenish blue (2 bands)	20	25	☐	☐
Y1676c		14p rose-red (2 bands) .	20	25	☐	☐
Y1677		19p bistre (1 centre band)	75	75	☐	☐
Y1678 *a*		19p bistre (1 side band) .	2·00	2·00	☐	☐
Y1679		20p turquoise-green (2 bands)	90	90	☐	☐
Y1680		20p bright green (1 centre band)	70	70	☐	☐
Y1681		20p bright green (1 side band)	1·50	1·50	☐	☐
Y1682		20p bright green (2 bands)	75	75	☐	☐
Y1683		25p rose-red (phosphorised paper)	1·10	1·10	☐	☐
Y1684		25p rose-red (2 bands) .	1·10	1·10	☐	☐
Y1685		26p red-brown (2 bands)	1·10	1·10	☐	☐
Y1686		26p gold (2 bands)	1·10	1·10	☐	☐
Y1687		29p grey (2 bands)	1·25	1·25	☐	☐
Y1688		30p deep olive-grey (2 bands)	1·10	1·10	☐	☐
Y1689		31p deep mauve (2 bands)	1·20	1·20	☐	☐
Y1690		33p grey-green (2 bands)	1·50	1·50	☐	☐
Y1691		34p yellow-olive (2 bands)	1·25	1·00	☐	☐
Y1692		35p yellow (2 bands) . .	1·50	1·50	☐	☐
Y1693		35p yellow (phosphorised paper)	7·50	7·50	☐	☐
Y1694		35p sepia (2 bands) . . .	1·10	1·10	☐	☐
Y1695		35p yellow-olive (1 centre band)	50	55	☐	☐
Y1696		36p bright ultramarine (2 bands)	1·50	1·50	☐	☐
Y1697		37p bright mauve (2 bands)	1·40	1·40	☐	☐
Y1698		37p grey-black (2 bands)	1·40	1·40	☐	☐
Y1699		37p brown-olive (1 centre band)	60	65	☐	☐
Y1700		38p rosine (2 bands) . .	1·50	1·50	☐	☐
Y1701		38p ultramarine (2 bands)	2·00	2·00	☐	☐
		a. Perf 14	7·50	7·50	☐	☐
Y1702		39p bright magenta (2 bands)	1·50	1·50	☐	☐
Y1703		39p grey (2 bands)	1·20	1·20	☐	☐
Y1704		40p deep azure (2 bands)	1·40	1·40	☐	☐
Y1705		40p turquoise-blue (2 bands)	1·30	1·30	☐	☐
Y1706		41p grey-brown (2 bands)	1·75	1·75	☐	☐
Y1707		41p drab (phosphorised paper)	7·50	7·50	☐	☐
Y1708		41p rosine (2 bands) . . .	1·40	1·40	☐	☐
Y1709		42p deep olive-grey (2 bands)	1·40	1·40	☐	☐
Y1710		43p deep olive-brown (2 bands)	1·75	1·75	☐	☐
Y1711		43p sepia (2 bands) . . .	2·50	2·50	☐	☐
		a. Perf 14	2·50	2·50	☐	☐
Y1712		43p emerald (2 bands) .	1·40	1·40	☐	☐
Y1713		44p grey-brown (2 bands)	4·25	4·25	☐	☐
Y1714		44p deep bright blue (2 bands)	70	75	☐	☐
Y1715		45p bright mauve (2 bands)	1·50	1·50	☐	☐
Y1716		46p yellow (2 bands) . .	70	75	☐	☐
Y1717		47p turquoise-green (2 bands)	1·75	1·75	☐	☐
Y1718		49p red-brown (2 bands)	75	80	☐	☐
Y1719		50p ochre (2 bands) . . .	1·75	1·20	☐	☐
Y1720		63p light emerald (2 bands)	2·00	2·00	☐	☐
Y1721		64p turquoise-green (2 bands)	2·25	2·25	☐	☐
Y1722		65p greenish blue (2 bands)	2·10	2·10	☐	☐
Y1723		68p grey-brown (2 bands)	2·10	2·10	☐	☐
Y1724		72p rosine (2 bands) . .	1·10	1·20	☐	☐
Y1725		£1 bluish violet (2 bands)	3·25	3·00	☐	☐
Y1726		£1·50 brown-red (2 bands)	3·50	3·50	☐	☐
Y1727		£2 deep blue-green (2 bands)	5·00	5·00	☐	☐
Y1728		£3 deep mauve (2 bands)	7·50	5·00	☐	☐
Y1729		£5 azure (2 bands) . . .	12·00	6·00	☐	☐

(b) *Litho Walsall* (37p, 60p, 63p), *Questa or Walsall* (25p, 35p, 41p), *Questa* (others)

Y1743	**367**	1p lake (2 bands)	40	40	☐	☐
Y1748		6p yellow-olive (2 bands)	12·00	13·00	☐	☐
Y1749		10p dull orange (2 bands)	5·00	5·00	☐	☐
Y1750		19p bistre (1 side band) .	1·90	1·75	☐	☐
Y1751		20p bright yellow-green (1 centre band) . . .	2·25	2·25	☐	☐

Y1752	25p red (2 bands)	1·10	1·10 ☐ ☐
Y1753	26p chestnut (2 bands)	1·00	1·00 ☐ ☐
Y1754	30p olive-grey (2 bands)	4·25	4·25 ☐ ☐
Y1755	35p yellow (2 bands)	1·60	1·60 ☐ ☐
Y1756	37p bright mauve (2 bands)	2·40	2·40 ☐ ☐
Y1757	41p drab (2 bands) . . .	1·75	1·75 ☐ ☐
Y1758	60p dull blue-grey (2 bands)	2·50	2·50 ☐ ☐
Y1759	63p light emerald (2 bands)	3·00	3·00 ☐ ☐

(c) Recess Enschedé or De La Rue

Y1800	**367**	£1·50 red	4·25	2·00 ☐ ☐
Y1801		£2 dull blue	6·00	2·25 ☐ ☐
Y1802		£3 dull violet	9·00	3·00 ☐ ☐
Y1803		£5 brown	15·00	5·00 ☐ ☐

PHQ Card (No. Y1725) . . . . . 40 3·00 ☐ ☐

Presentation Pack (P.O. Pack No. 30) (contains 19p (Y1677), 25p (Y1683), 29p (Y1687), 36p (Y1696), 38p (Y1700), 41p (Y1706)) . . 7·00 ☐

Presentation Pack (P.O. Pack No. 34) (contains 1p (Y1667), 2p (Y1668), 4p (Y1669), 5p (Y1670), 6p (Y1671), 10p (Y1676), 19p (Y1677), 20p (Y1679), 25p (Y1684), 29p (Y1687), 30p (Y1688), 35p (Y1692), 36p (Y1696), 38p (Y1700), 41p (Y1706), 50p (Y1719), 60p (Y1758), £1 (Y1725)) . . . . . 30·00 ☐

Presentation Pack (P.O. Pack No. 35) (contains 20p (Y1680), 26p (Y1685), 31p (Y1689), 37p (Y1697), 39p (Y1702), 43p (Y1710), 63p (Y1720)) . . . . 9·50 ☐

Presentation Pack (P.O. Pack No. 38) (contains 1st (1668), 26p (Y1686)) 7·50 . . . .☐

Presentation Pack (P.O. Pack No. 41) (contains 2nd (1664), 1st (1667), 1p (Y1667), 2p (Y1668), 4p (Y1669), 5p (Y1670), 6p (Y1671), 10p (Y1676), 20p (Y1680), 26p (Y1685), 30p (Y1688), 31p (Y1689), 37p (Y1697), 39p (Y1702), 43p (Y1711), 50p (Y1719), 63p (Y1720), £1 (Y1725)) . . . . 16·00 ☐

Presentation Pack (P.O. Pack No. 43 or 43A) (contains £1·50 (Y1800), £2 (Y1801), £3 (Y1802), £5 (Y1803)) . . . . 55·00 ☐

Presentation Pack (P.O. Pack No. 44) contains 7p (Y1672), 19p (Y1677), 38p (Y1701), 44p (Y1713), 64p (Y1721)) . . . . 11·00 ☐

Presentation Pack (P.O. Pack No. 49) (contains 8p (Y1674), 33p (Y1690), 40p (Y1704), 41p (Y1708), 45p (Y1715), 65p (Y1722)) . . . . 10·00 ☐

Presentation Pack (P.O. Pack No. 57) (contains 2nd (1664), 1st (1667), E (1669), 1p (Y1667), 2p (Y1668), 4p (Y1669), 5p (Y1670), 8p (Y1674), 10p (Y1676), 20p (Y1682), 33p (Y1690), 40p (Y1704), 41p (Y1708), 45p (Y1715), 50p (Y1719), 65p (Y1722), £1 (Y1725)) . . . . 16·00 ☐

Presentation Pack (P.O. Pack No. 58) (contains 37p (Y1698), 42p (Y1709), 47p (Y1716), 68p (Y1723) . . . . 7·50 ☐

Presentation Pack (P.O. Pack No. 62) (contains £1·50 (Y1726), £2 (Y1727), £3 (Y1728), £5 (Y1729)) . . . . 23·00 ☐

Presentation Pack (P.O. Pack No. 67) (contains 7p (No. Y1673), 1st (1668), 35p (Y1694), 39p (Y1703), 40p (Y1705), 43p (Y1712), Worldwide postcard (2357a) . . . . 6·00 ☐

Presentation Pack (P.O. Pack No. 71) (contains 1p (Y1667), 2p (Y1668), 5p (Y1670), 9p (Y1675), 10p (Y1676), 20p (Y1682), 35p (Y1695), 40p (Y1705), 42p (Y1709), 46p (Y1716), 47p (Y1717), 50p (Y1719), 68p (Y1723), £1 (Y1725), 2nd (2039), 1st (2295), Worldwide postcard (2357a), Europe (2358), Worldwide (2359) . . . . . . 11·50 ☐

Presentation Pack (P.O. Pack No. 72) (contains 37p (Y1699), 44p (Y1714), 49p (Y1718), 72p (Y1724) . . . . 3·50 ☐

For P.O. Pack No. 37 see below No. 1977.
For P.O. Pack No. 74 see below No. 2657.

First Day Covers

26 Oct. 1993	19*p*, 25*p*, 29*p*, 36*p*, 38*p*, 41*p* (*Nos.* Y1677, Y1683, Y1687, Y1696, Y1700, Y1706)	6·00 ☐
9 Aug. 1994	60*p* (*No.* Y1758)	4·00 ☐
22 Aug. 1995	£1 (*No.* Y1725)	3·50 ☐
25 June 1996	20*p*, 26*p*, 31*p*, 37*p*, 39*p*, 43*p*, 63*p* (*Nos.* Y1680, Y1685, Y1689, Y1697, Y1702, Y1710, Y1720)	8·00 ☐
9 Mar. 1999	£1·50, £2, £3, £5 (*Nos.* Y1800/3)	27·00 ☐
20 Apr. 1999	7*p*, 38*p*, 44*p*, 64*p* (*Nos.* Y1672, Y1701, Y1713, Y1721)	5·00 ☐
25 Apr. 2000	8*p*, 33*p*, 40*p*, 41*p*, 45*p*, 65*p* (*Nos.* Y1674, Y1690, Y1704, Y1708, Y1715, Y1722)	5·00 ☐
4 July 2002	37*p*, 42*p*, 47*p*, 68*p*, (*Nos.* Y1698, Y1709, Y1716, Y1723)	4·00 ☐

6 May 2003	34p (No. Y1691)	1·20		☐	
1 July 2003	£1·50, £2, £3, £5 (Nos. Y1726/9) .	21·00		☐	
1 April 2004	7p, 35p, 39p, 40p, 43p, World-wide postcard (Nos. Y1673, Y1694, Y1703, Y1705, Y1712, 2357a)	9·00		☐	
5 April 2005	9p, 35p, 46p (Nos. Y1675, Y1695, Y1716)	2·20		☐	
28 March 2006	37p, 44p, 49p, 72p (Nos. Y1699, Y1714, Y1718, Y1724)	4·25		☐	

Nos. Y1725/9 are printed in Iriodin ink which gives a shiny effect to the solid part of the background behind the Queen's head.

Nos. Y1693 and Y1707 were only issued in coils and Nos. Y1676a, Y1678, Y1681, Y1701a, Y1711a, Y1743 and Y1748/59 only in booklets.

No. Y1750 exists with the phosphor band at the left or right of the stamp, but Nos. Y1678 and Y1681 exist with band at right only.

> For self-adhesive versions of the 42p and 68p see Nos. 2297/8.

1094 'Family Group' (bronze sculpture) (Henry Moore)

1095 'Kew Gardens' (lithograph) (Edward Bawden)

1096 'St Francis and the Birds' (Stanley Spencer)

1097 'Still Life: Odyssey I' (Ben Nicholson)

Europa. Contemporary Art

1993 (11 MAY) Phosphorised paper. Perf 14 × 14½

1767	**1094**	24p multicoloured	60	20	☐	☐	
1768	**1095**	28p multicoloured	90	1·00	☐	☐	
1769	**1096**	33p multicoloured	1·25	1·40	☐	☐	
1770	**1097**	39p multicoloured	1·75	1·75	☐	☐	
		Set of 4	4·00	4·00	☐	☐	
		First Day Cover		4·50		☐	
		Presentation Pack	4·50		☐		
		PHQ Cards (set of 4)	4·00	7·00	☐	☐	
		Set of 4 Gutter Pairs	10·00		☐		

1098 Emperor Claudius (from gold coin)

1099 Emperor Hadrian (bronze head)

1100 Goddess Roma (from gemstone)

1101 Christ (Hinton St Mary mosaic)

Roman Britain

1993 (15 JUNE) Phosphorised paper with two phosphor bands. Perf 14 × 14½

1771	**1098**	24p multicoloured	60	20	☐	☐	
1772	**1099**	28p multicoloured	90	1·00	☐	☐	
1773	**1100**	33p multicoloured	1·30	1·50	☐	☐	
1774	**1101**	39p multicoloured	1·50	1·60	☐	☐	
		Set of 4	4·00	4·00	☐	☐	
		First Day Cover		4·00		☐	
		Presentation Pack	4·50		☐		
		PHQ Cards (set of 4)	4·25	7·00	☐	☐	
		Set of 4 Gutter Pairs	10·00		☐		

1102 Midland Maid and other Narrow Boats, Grand Junction Canal

1103 Yorkshire Maid and other Humber Keels, Stainforth and Keadby Canal

1104 Valley Princess and other Horse-drawn Barges, Brecknock and Abergavenny Canal

1105 Steam Barges including Pride of Scotland and and Fishing Boats, Crinan Canal

Inland Waterways

1993 (20 July) Two phosphor bands. Perf 14½ × 14

1775	1102	24p multicoloured	50	20	☐	☐
1776	1103	28p multicoloured	1·00	1·00	☐	☐
1777	1104	33p multicoloured	1·25	1·25	☐	☐
1778	1105	39p multicoloured	1·50	1·40	☐	☐
		Set of 4	3·75	3·50		☐
		First Day Cover		3·75		☐
		Presentation Pack	4·50		☐	
		PHQ Cards (set of 4)	4·25	7·00	☐	☐
		Set of 4 Gutter Pairs	9·00		☐	

Nos. 1775/8 commemorate the bicentenaries of the Acts of Parliament authorising the canals depicted.

1106   Horse Chestnut

1107   Blackberry

1108   Hazel

1109   Rowan

1110   Pear

The Four Seasons. Autumn. Fruits and Leaves

1993 (14 Sept.) One phosphor band (18p) or phosphorised paper (others)

1779	1106	18p multicoloured	50	20	☐	☐
1780	1107	24p multicoloured	75	20	☐	☐
1781	1108	28p multicoloured	1·10	1·25	☐	☐
1782	1109	33p multicoloured	1·40	1·50	☐	☐
1783	1110	39p multicoloured	1·50	1·50	☐	☐
		Set of 5	4·75	4·50	☐	☐
		First Day Cover		4·50		☐
		Presentation Pack	4·75		☐	
		PHQ Cards (set of 5)	4·50	7·00	☐	☐
		Set of 5 Gutter Pairs	10·50		☐	

SHERLOCK HOLMES & DR. WATSON "THE REIGATE SQUIRE"

1111   *The Reigate Squire*

SHERLOCK HOLMES & SIR HENRY "THE HOUND OF THE BASKERVILLES"

1112   *The Hound of the Baskervilles*

SHERLOCK HOLMES & LESTRADE "THE SIX NAPOLEONS"

1113   *The Six Napoleons*

SHERLOCK HOLMES & MYCROFT "THE GREEK INTERPRETER"

1114   *The Greek Interpreter*

SHERLOCK HOLMES & MORIARTY "THE FINAL PROBLEM"

1115   *The Final Problem*

T 1111/15 were printed together, *se-tenant,* in horizontal strips of 5 throughout the sheet.

Sherlock Holmes. Centenary of the Publication of The Final Problem

1993 (12 Oct.) Phosphorised paper. Perf 14 × 14½

1784	1111	24p multicoloured	50	40	☐	☐
		a. Horiz strip of 5. Nos.				
		1784/8	5·00	5·25	☐	☐
1785	1112	24p multicoloured	50	40	☐	☐
1786	1113	24p multicoloured	50	40	☐	☐
1787	1114	24p multicoloured	50	40	☐	☐
1788	1115	24p multicoloured	50	40	☐	☐
		Set of 5	5·00	5·25		☐
		First Day Cover		5·50		☐
		Presentation Pack	5·00		☐	
		PHQ Cards (set of 5)	4·50	8·00	☐	☐
		Gutter Strip of 10	11·00		☐	

1116

Self-adhesive Booklet Stamp

1993 (19 Oct.) *Litho Walsall. Two phosphor bands. Die-cut perf 14 × 15 (with one elliptical hole on each vertical side)*

1789	**1116** (1st) orange-red	. . . . .	1·25	1·40	□	□
	First Day Cover	. . . .		4·50		□
	Presentation Pack (booklet pane of 20)	. . . .	20·00		□	
	PHQ Card	. . . .	4·00	8·00	□	□

For similar 2nd and 1st designs printed in photogravure by Enschedé see Nos. 1976/7.

1117 Bob Cratchit and Tiny Tim

1118 Mr and Mrs Fezziwig

1119 Scrooge

1120 The Prize Turkey

1121 Mr Scrooge's Nephew

Christmas. 150th Anniversary of Publication of A Christmas Carol

1993 (9 Nov.) *One phosphor band* (19p) *or phosphorised paper (others)*

1790	**1117**	19p multicoloured	. . . .	60	15	□ □
1791	**1118**	25p multicoloured	. . . .	90	15	□ □
1792	**1119**	30p multicoloured	. . . .	1·25	1·50	□ □
1793	**1120**	35p multicoloured	. . . .	1·40	1·60	□ □
1794	**1121**	41p multicoloured	. . . .	1·40	1·60	□ □
		Set of 5	. . . .	4·50	4·50	□ □
		First Day Cover	. . . .		5·00	□
		Presentation Pack	. . . .	5·00		□
		PHQ Cards (set of 5)	. . . . . .	4·50	8·00	□ □
		Set of 5 Gutter Pairs	. . . . . .	11·00		□

Collectors Pack 1993

1993 (9 Nov.) *Comprises Nos.* 1639/43, 1654/7, 1659/63, 1767/88 *and* 1790/4

CP1794a	Collectors Pack	. . . . . .	45·00	□

Post Office Yearbook

1993 (9 Nov.) *Comprises Nos.* 1639/43, 1654/7, 1659/63, 1767/88 *and* 1790/4 *in hardback book with slip case*

YB1794a	Yearbook	. . . .	65·00	□

1122 Class 5 No. 44957 and Class B1 No. 61342 on West Highland Line

1123 Class A1 No. 60149 *Amadis* at Kings Cross

1124 Class 4 No. 43000 on Turntable at Blyth North

1125 Class 4 No. 42455 near Wigan Central

1126 Class Castle No. 7002 *Devizes Castle* on Bridge crossing Worcester and Birmingham Canal

The Age of Steam. Railway Photographs by Colin Gifford

1994 (18 Jan.) *One phosphor band* (19p) *or phosphorised paper with two bands* (others). *Perf* 14½

1795	**1122**	19p deep blue-green, grey-black and black	55	25 □ □
1796	**1123**	25p slate-lilac, grey-black and black	90	95 □ □
1797	**1124**	30p lake-brown, grey-black and black . . .	1·40	1·50 □ □
1798	**1125**	35p deep claret, grey-black and black . . .	1·75	1·80 □ □
1799	**1126**	41p indigo, grey-black and black	1·80	1·90 □ □
		Set of 5	6·00	6·00 □ □
		First Day Cover		6·00 □
		Presentation Pack	5·75	□
		PHQ Cards (set of 5)	5·75	11·00 □ □
		Set of 5 Gutter Pairs	12·00	□

1127 Dan Dare and the Mekon

1128 The Three Bears

1129 Rupert Bear

1130 Alice (*Alice in Wonderland*)

1131 Noggin and the Ice Dragon

1132 Peter Rabbit posting Letter

1133 Red Riding Hood and Wolf

1134 Orlando the Marmalade Cat

1135 Biggles

1136 Paddington Bear on Station

T 1127/36 were printed together, *se-tenant,* in booklet panes of 10 stamps and 20 half stamp-size labels.

Greeting Stamps. 'Messages'

1994 (1 Feb.) *Two phosphor bands. Perf* 15 × 14 (*with one elliptical hole on each vertical side*)

1800	**1127**	(1st) multicoloured	50	40 □ □
		a. Booklet pane. Nos. 1800/9	13·00	12·00 □ □
1801	**1128**	(1st) multicoloured	50	40 □ □
1802	**1129**	(1st) multicoloured	50	40 □ □
1803	**1130**	(1st) gold, bistre-yellow and black	50	40 □ □
1804	**1131**	(1st) multicoloured	50	40 □ □
1805	**1132**	(1st) multicoloured	50	40 □ □
1806	**1133**	(1st) multicoloured	50	40 □ □
1807	**1134**	(1st) multicoloured	50	40 □ □
1808	**1135**	(1st) multicoloured	50	40 □ □
1809	**1136**	(1st) multicoloured	50	40 □ □
		Set of 10	13·00	12·00 □ □
		First Day Cover		12·00 □
		Presentation Pack	18·00	□
		PHQ Cards (set of 10)	16·00	28·00 □ □

1137 Castell Y Waun (Chirk Castle), Clwyd, Wales

1138 Ben Arkle, Sutherland, Scotland

1139 Mourne Mountains, County Down, Northern Ireland

1140 Dersingham, Norfolk, England

1141 Dolwyddelan, Gwynedd, Wales

25th Anniversary of Investiture of the Prince of Wales. Paintings by Prince Charles

1994 (1 MAR.) *One phosphor band* (19p) *or phosphorised paper* (*others*)

1810	**1137**	19p multicoloured	. . . .	55	20 □ □
1811	**1138**	25p multicoloured	. . . .	1·00	20 □ □
1812	**1139**	30p multicoloured	. . . .	1·10	1·50 □ □
1813	**1140**	35p multicoloured	. . . .	1·40	1·75 □ □
1814	**1141**	41p multicoloured	. . . .	1·50	1·75 □ □
		Set of 5	. . . .	5·00	5·00 □ □
		First Day Cover	. . . .		5·00 □
		Presentation Pack	. . . .	5·00	□
		PHQ Cards (set of 5)	. . . . .	5·75	11·50 □ □
		Set of 5 Gutter Pairs	. . . . . .	11·00	□

1142 Bather at Blackpool

1143 'Where's my Little Lad?'

1144 'Wish You were Here!'

1145 Punch and Judy Show

1146 'The Tower Crane' Machine

Centenary of Picture Postcards

1994 (12 APR.) *One side band* (19p) *or two phosphor bands* (*others*). *Perf* 14 × 14½

1815	**1142**	19p multicoloured	. . . .	60	20 □ □
1816	**1143**	25p multicoloured	. . . .	90	20 □ □
1817	**1144**	30p multicoloured	. . . .	1·10	1·50 □ □
1818	**1145**	35p multicoloured	. . . .	1·40	1·75 □ □
1819	**1146**	41p multicoloured	. . . .	1·50	1·75 □ □
		Set of 5	. . . .	5·00	5·00 □ □
		First Day Cover	. . . .		5·00 □
		Presentation Pack	. . . .	5·00	□
		PHQ Cards (set of 5)	. . . . .	5·75	11·50 □ □
		Set of 5 Gutter Pairs	. . . . . .	11·00	□

1147 British Lion and French Cockerel over Tunnel

1148 Symbolic Hands over Train

Nos. 1820/1 and 1822/3 were printed together, *se-tenant*, in horizontal pairs throughout the sheets.

Opening of Channel Tunnel

1994 (3 MAY) *Phosphorised paper. Perf* 14 × 14½

1820	**1147**	25p multicoloured	. . . .	50	40 □ □
		a. Horiz pair. Nos. 1820/1		1·75	2·00 □ □
1821	**1148**	25p multicoloured	. . . .	50	40 □ □
1822	**1147**	41p multicoloured	. . . .	60	50 □ □
		a. Horiz pair. Nos. 1822/3		3·25	2·50 □ □
1823	**1148**	41p multicoloured	. . . .	60	50 □ □
		Set of 4	. . . .	4·50	4·50 □ □
		First Day Cover	. . . .		5·25 □
		Presentation Pack	. . . .	5·00	□
		Souvenir Book	. . . .	50·00	□
		PHQ Cards (set of 4)	. . . . .	5·75	9·00 □ □

Stamps in similar designs were also issued by France and these are included in the Souvenir Book.

1149 Groundcrew replacing Smoke Canisters on Douglas Boston of 88 Sqn

1150 H.M.S. *Warspite* (battleship) shelling Enemy Positions

1154 The Old Course, St Andrews

1155 The 18th Hole, Muirfield

1151 Commandos landing on Gold Beach

1152 Infantry regrouping on Sword Beach

1156 The 15th Hole ('Luckyslap'), Carnoustie

1157 The 8th Hole ('The Postage Stamp'), Royal Troon

1153 Tank and Infantry advancing, Ouistreham

Nos. 1824/8 were printed together, *se-tenant*, in horizontal strips of 5 throughout the sheet.

50th Anniversary of D-Day

1994 (6 JUNE) *Two phosphor bands. Perf 14½ × 14*

1824	1149	25p multicoloured	50	40	☐	☐
		a. Horiz strip of 5. Nos.				
		1824/8	4·25	5·00	☐	☐
1825	1150	25p multicoloured	50	40	☐	☐
1826	1151	25p multicoloured	50	40	☐	☐
1827	1152	25p multicoloured	50	40	☐	☐
1828	1153	25p multicoloured	50	40	☐	☐
		Set of 5	4·25	5·00	☐	☐
		First Day Cover		5·50		☐
		Presentation Pack	5·50		☐	
		PHQ Cards (*set of* 5)	5·00	11·50	☐	☐
		Gutter Block of 10	11·00		☐	

1158 The 9th Hole, Turnberry

Scottish Golf Courses

1994 (5 JULY) *One phosphor band* (19p) *or phosphorised paper* (*others*). *Perf* 14½ × 14

1829	1154	19p multicoloured	50	20	☐	☐
1830	1155	25p multicoloured	75	20	☐	☐
1831	1156	30p multicoloured	1·10	1·40	☐	☐
1832	1157	35p multicoloured	1·25	1·40	☐	☐
1833	1158	41p multicoloured	1·40	1·40	☐	☐
		Set of 5	4·50	4·25	☐	☐
		First Day Cover		4·75		☐
		Presentation Pack	4·75		☐	
		PHQ Cards (*set of* 5)	5·75	11·50	☐	☐
		Set of 5 Gutter Pairs	11·50		☐	

Nos. 1829/33 commemorate the 250th anniversary of golf's first set of rules produced by the Honourable Company of Edinburgh Golfers.

1159   Royal Welsh Show, Llanelwedd

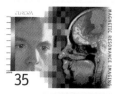

1160   All England Tennis Championships, Wimbledon

1161   Cowes Week

1162   Test Match, Lord's

1163   Braemar Gathering

The Four Seasons. Summertime. Events
1994 (2 Aug.) *One phosphor band* (19p) *or phosphorised paper* (*others*)

1834	**1159**	19p multicoloured	50	20	□	□
1835	**1160**	25p multicoloured	75	20	□	□
1836	**1161**	30p multicoloured	1·10	1·25	□	□
1837	**1162**	35p multicoloured	1·25	1·60	□	□
1838	**1163**	41p multicoloured	1·40	1·60	□	□
		Set of 5	4·50	4·25	□	□
		First Day Cover		4·75		□
		Presentation Pack	4·75		□	
		PHQ Cards (set of 5)	5·75	11·50	□	□
		Set of 5 Gutter Pairs	11·50		□	

1164   Ultrasonic Imaging

1165   Scanning Electron Microscopy

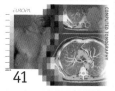

1166   Magnetic Resonance Imaging

1167   Computed Tomography

Europa. Medical Discoveries
1994 (27 Sept.) *Phosphorised paper. Perf* 14 × 14½

1839	**1164**	25p multicoloured	75	25	□	□
1840	**1165**	30p multicoloured	1·00	1·25	□	□
1841	**1166**	35p multicoloured	1·50	1·75	□	□
1842	**1167**	41p multicoloured	1·75	1·75	□	□
		Set of 4	4·50	4·50	□	□
		First Day Cover		4·75		□
		Presentation Pack	4·75		□	
		PHQ Cards (set of 4)	5·75	10·00	□	□
		Set of 4 Gutter Pairs	11·00		□	

1168   Virgin Mary and Joseph

1169   Three Wise Men

1170   Virgin and Child

1171   Shepherds

1172   Angels

111

Christmas. Children's Nativity Plays

1994 (1 Nov.) *One phosphor band* (19p) *or phosphorised paper* (*others*)

1843	**1168**	19p multicoloured	50	15 ☐ ☐
1844	**1169**	25p multicoloured	75	15 ☐ ☐
1845	**1170**	30p multicoloured	1·00	1·50 ☐ ☐
1846	**1171**	35p multicoloured	1·25	1·50 ☐ ☐
1847	**1172**	41p multicoloured	1·50	1·75 ☐ ☐
		Set of 5	4·50	4·75 ☐ ☐
		First Day Cover		4·75 ☐
		Presentation Pack	4·75	☐
		PHQ Cards (set of 5)	5·75	11·50 ☐ ☐
		Set of 5 Gutter Pairs	10·50	☐

Collectors Pack 1994

1994 (14 Nov.) *Comprises Nos. 1795/1847*

CP1847*a* Collectors Pack . . . . 55·00 ☐

Post Office Yearbook

1994 (14 Nov.) *Comprises Nos. 1795/9 and 1810/47 in hardback book with slip case*

YB1847*a* Yearbook . . . . 55·00 ☐

Cats

1995 (17 Jan.) *One phosphor band* (19p) *or two phosphor bands* (*others*). *Perf* 14½ × 14

1848	**1173**	19p multicoloured	75	20 ☐ ☐
1849	**1174**	25p multicoloured	75	25 ☐ ☐
1850	**1175**	30p multicoloured	1·00	1·50 ☐ ☐
1851	**1176**	35p multicoloured	1·25	1·50 ☐ ☐
1852	**1177**	41p multicoloured	1·50	1·50 ☐ ☐
		Set of 5	4·75	4·75 ☐ ☐
		First Day Cover		4·75 ☐
		Presentation Pack	5·50	☐
		PHQ Cards (set of 5)	6·00	11·50 ☐ ☐
		Set of 5 Gutter Pairs	11·00	☐

1178　Dandelions

1179　Sweet Chestnut Leaves

1180　Garlic Leaves

1181　Hazel Leaves

1173　Sophie (black cat)

1174　Puskas (Siamese) and Tigger (tabby)

1182　Spring Grass

1175　Chloe (ginger cat)

1176　Kikko (tortoiseshell) and Rosie (Abyssinian)

The Four Seasons. Springtime. Plant Sculptures by Andy Goldsworthy

1995 (14 Mar.) *One phosphor band* (19p) *or two phosphor bands* (*others*)

1853	**1178**	19p multicoloured	75	15 ☐ ☐
1854	**1179**	25p multicoloured	75	15 ☐ ☐
1855	**1180**	30p multicoloured	1·00	1·50 ☐ ☐
1856	**1181**	35p multicoloured	1·25	1·50 ☐ ☐
1857	**1182**	41p multicoloured	1·50	1·75 ☐ ☐
		Set of 5	4·75	4·75 ☐ ☐
		First Day Cover		4·75 ☐
		Presentation Pack	5·00	☐
		PHQ Cards (set of 5)	6·00	11·50 ☐ ☐
		Set of 5 Gutter Pairs	11·50	☐

1177　Fred (black and white cat)

1183 'La Danse a la Campagne' (Renoir)

1184 'Troilus and Criseyde' (Peter Brookes)

1185 'The Kiss' (Rodin)

1186 'Girls on the Town' (Beryl Cook)

1187 'Jazz' (Andrew Mockett)

1188 'Girls performing a Kathal Dance' (Aurangzeb period)

1189 'Alice Keppel with her Daughter' (Alice Hughes)

1190 'Children Playing' (L. S. Lowry)

1191 'Circus Clowns' (Emily Firmin and Justin Mitchell)

1192 Decoration from 'All the Love Poems of Shakespeare' (Eric Gill)

T **1183/92** were printed together, *se-tenant,* in booklet panes of 10 stamps and 20 half stamp-size labels.

Greetings Stamp. 'Greetings in Art'

1995 (21 Mar.) *Two phosphor bands. Perf* $14\frac{1}{2} \times 14$ (*with one elliptical hole on each vertical side*)

1858	**1183**	(1st) multicoloured	50	40	□	□
		a. Booklet pane. Nos.				
		1858/67	11·50	11·00	□	□
1859	**1184**	(1st) multicoloured	50	40	□	□
1860	**1185**	(1st) multicoloured	50	40	□	□
1861	**1186**	(1st) multicoloured	50	40	□	□
1862	**1187**	(1st) multicoloured	50	40	□	□
1863	**1188**	(1st) multicoloured	50	40	□	□
1864	**1189**	(1st) purple-brown and silver	50	40	□	□
1865	**1190**	(1st) multicoloured	50	40	□	□
1866	**1191**	(1st) multicoloured	50	40	□	□
1867	**1192**	(1st) black, greenish yellow and silver . .	50	40	□	□
	Set of 10	. . . .	11·50	11·00	□	□
	First Day Cover	. . . .		11·50		□
	Presentation Pack	. . . .	12·00		□	
	PHQ Cards (set of 10)	. . . . . .	16·00	28·00	□	□

The National Trust
Celebrating 100 Years 19

1193 Fireplace Decoration, Attingham Park, Shropshire

The National Trust
Protecting Land 25

1194 Oak Seedling

The National Trust
Conserving Art 30

1195 Carved Table Leg, Attingham Park

The National Trust
Saving Coast 35

1196 St David's Head, Dyfed, Wales

The National Trust
Repairing Buildings 41

1197 Elizabethan Window, Little Moreton Hall, Cheshire

Centenary of The National Trust

1995 (11 APR.) *One phosphor band* (19p), *two phosphor bands* (25p, 35p) *or phosphorised paper* (30p, 41p)

1868	**1193**	19p multicoloured	60	20 □ □
1869	**1194**	25p multicoloured	80	20 □ □
1870	**1195**	30p multicoloured	1·00	1·50 □ □
1871	**1196**	35p multicoloured	1·25	1·50 □ □
1872	**1197**	41p multicoloured	1·40	1·75 □ □
		Set of 5	4·50	4·75 □ □
		First Day Cover		4·75 □
		Presentation Pack	4·75	□
		PHQ Cards (set of 5)	6·00	11·50 □ □
		Set of 5 Gutter Pairs	11·00	□

1198 British Troops and French Civilians celebrating

1199 Symbolic Hands and Red Cross

1200 St Paul's Cathedral and Searchlights

1201 Symbolic Hand releasing Peace Dove

1202 Symbolic Hands

For full information on all future British issues, collectors should write to Royal Mail, Freepost EH3647, 21 South Gyle Crescent, Edinburgh EH12 9PE.

Europa. Peace and Freedom

1995 (2 MAY) *One phosphor band* (Nos. 1873/4) *or two phosphor bands* (others). Perf $14\frac{1}{2} \times 14$

1873	**1198**	19p silver, bistre-brown and grey-black . . .	70	40 □ □
1874	**1199**	19p multicoloured	70	40 □ □
1875	**1200**	25p silver, blue and grey-black	1·00	1·00 □ □
1876	**1201**	25p multicoloured	1·00	1·00 □ □
1877	**1202**	30p multicoloured	1·25	2·25 □ □
		Set of 5	4·25	4·25 □ □
		First Day Cover		4·75 □
		Presentation Pack	5·00	□
		PHQ Cards (set of 5)	6·00	11·50 □ □
		Set of 5 Gutter Pairs	10·50	□

Nos. 1873 and 1875 commemorate the 50th anniversary of the end of the Second World War, No. 1874 the 125th anniversary of the British Red Cross Society and Nos. 1876/7 the 50th anniversary of the United Nations.

Nos. 1876/7 include the 'EUROPA' emblem.

For No. 1875 with the face value expressed as '1st' see No. **MS**2547.

1203 The Time Machine

1204 The First Men in the Moon

1205 The War of the Worlds

1206 The Shape of Things to Come

Science Fiction. Novels by H. G. Wells

1995 (6 JUNE) *Two phosphor bands. Perf* $14\frac{1}{2} \times 14$

1878	**1203**	25p multicoloured	75	25 □ □
1879	**1204**	30p multicoloured	1·25	1·50 □ □
1880	**1205**	35p multicoloured	1·25	1·60 □ □
1881	**1206**	41p multicoloured	1·50	1·60 □ □
		Set of 4	4·25	4·50 □ □
		First Day Cover		4·75 □
		Presentation Pack	5·00	□
		PHQ Cards (set of 4)	6·00	11·50 □ □
		Set of 4 Gutter Pairs	10·00	□

Nos. 1878/81 commemorate the centenary of publication of Wells's *The Time Machine*.

1207 The Swan, 1595

1208 The Rose, 1592

1212 Sir Rowland Hill and Uniform Penny Postage Petition

1213 Hill and Penny Black

1209 The Globe, 1599

1210 The Hope, 1613

1214 Guglielmo Marconi and Early Wireless

1215 Marconi and Sinking of *Titanic* (liner)

1211 The Globe, 1614

T **1207/11** were printed together, *se-tenant*, in horizontal strips of 5 throughout the sheet, the backgrounds forming a composite design.

Reconstruction of Shakespeare's Globe Theatre

1995 (8 Aug.) Two phosphor bands. Perf 14½

1882	**1207**	25p multicoloured	50	40	□	□
		a. Horiz strip of 5. Nos. 1882/6	4·50	4·75	□	□
1883	**1208**	25p multicoloured	50	40	□	□
1884	**1209**	25p multicoloured	50	40	□	□
1885	**1210**	25p multicoloured	50	40	□	□
1886	**1211**	25p multicoloured	50	40	□	□
		Set of 5	4·50	4·75	□	□
		First Day Cover		5·50		□
		Presentation Pack	5·00		□	
		PHQ Cards (set of 5)	6·00	11·50	□	□
		Gutter Strip of 10	10·50		□	

Pioneers of Communications

1995 (5 Sept.) One phosphor band (19p) or phosphorised paper (others). Perf 14½ × 14

1887	**1212**	19p silver, red and black	75	30	□	□
1888	**1213**	25p silver, brown and black	1·00	50	□	□
1889	**1214**	41p silver, grey-green and black	1·50	1·75	□	□
1890	**1215**	60p silver, deep ultra-marine and black . .	1·75	2·25	□	□
		Set of 4	4·50	4·50	□	□
		First Day Cover		4·75		□
		Presentation Pack	5·00		□	
		PHQ Cards (set of 4)	5·75	11·50	□	□
		Set of 4 Gutter Pairs	11·00		□	

Nos. 1887/8 mark the birth bicentenary of Sir Rowland Hill and Nos. 1889/90 the centenary of the first radio transmissions.

1216 Harold Wagstaff

1217 Gus Risman

JIM SULLIVAN
RUGBY LEAGUE 1895-1995

BILLY BATTEN
RUGBY LEAGUE 1895-1995

1218 Jim Sullivan

1219 Billy Batten

BRIAN BEVAN
RUGBY LEAGUE 1895-1995

1220 Brian Bevan

Centenary of Rugby League

1995 (3 Oct.) *One phosphor band* (19p) *or two phosphor bands* (*others*). *Perf* 14 × 14½

1891	**1216**	19p multicoloured	75	25	□	□
1892	**1217**	25p multicoloured	75	30	□	□
1893	**1218**	30p multicoloured	1·00	1·50	□	□
1894	**1219**	35p multicoloured	1·00	1·60	□	□
1895	**1220**	41p multicoloured	1·50	1·60	□	□
		Set of 5	4·75	4·75	□	
		First Day Cover		4·75		□
		Presentation Pack	5·50		□	
		PHQ Cards (set of 5)	6·00	11·50	□	□
		Set of 5 Gutter Pairs	11·00		□	

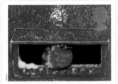

1221 European Robin in Mouth of Pillar Box

1222 European Robin on Railings and Holly

1223 European Robin on Snow-covered Milk Bottles

1224 European Robin on Road Sign

1225 European Robin on Door Knob and Christmas Wreath

Christmas. Christmas Robins

1995 (30 Oct.) *One phosphor band* (19p) *or two phosphor bands* (*others*)

1896	**1221**	19p multicoloured	60	20	□	□
1897	**1222**	25p multicoloured	85	30	□	□
1898	**1223**	30p multicoloured	1·25	1·50	□	□
1899	**1224**	41p multicoloured	1·60	1·75	□	□
1900	**1225**	60p multicoloured	1·75	1·90	□	□
		Set of 5	5·50	5·50	□	□
		First Day Cover		5·50		□
		Presentation Pack	5·75		□	
		PHQ Cards (set of 5)	6·00	11·50	□	□
		Set of 5 Gutter Pairs	12·00		□	

The 19p value was re-issued on 3 October 2000 in sheets of 20 each with *se-tenant* label, in connection with 'customised' stamps available from the Philatelic Bureau. The labels show either Christmas greetings or a personal photograph.

Collectors Pack 1995

1995 (30 Oct.) *Comprises Nos. 1848/1900*
CP1900*a* Collectors Pack . . . . 55·00 □

Post Office Yearbook

1995 (30 Oct.) *Comprises Nos. 1848/57 and 1868/1900 in hardback book with slip case*
YB1900*a* Yearbook . . . . 55·00 □

ROBERT BURNS 1759-1796

ROBERT BURNS 1759-1796

1226 Opening Lines of 'To a Mouse' and Fieldmouse

1227 'O my Luve's like a red, red rose' and Wild Rose

ROBERT BURNS 1759-1796

ROBERT BURNS 1759-1796

1228 'Scots, wha hae wi Wallace bled' and Sir William Wallace

1229 'Auld Lang Syne' and Highland Dancers

Death Bicentenary of Robert Burns (*Scottish poet*)

1996 (25 Jan.) *One phosphor band* (19p) *or two phosphor bands* (*others*). *Perf* 14½

1901	**1226**	19p cream, bistre-brown and black	75	25 □ □
1902	**1227**	25p multicoloured	1·00	30 □ □
1903	**1228**	41p multicoloured	1·50	2·00 □ □
1904	**1229**	60p multicoloured	1·75	2·50 □ □
		Set of 4	4·50	4·50 □ □
		First Day Cover		4·75 □
		Presentation Pack	5·00	□
		PHQ Cards (*set of 4*)	6·00	11·50 □ □
		Set of 4 Gutter Pairs	10·50	□

1230	'MORE! LOVE' (Mel Calman)	1231	'Sincerely' (Charles Barsotti)
1232	'Do you have something for the HUMAN CONDITION?' (Mel Calman)	1233	'MENTAL FLOSS' (Leo Cullum)
1234	'4.55 P.M.' (Charles Barsotti)	1235	'Dear lottery prize winner (Larry)
1236	'I'm writing to you because...' (Mel Calman)	1237	'FETCH THIS, FETCH THAT' (Charles Barsotti)

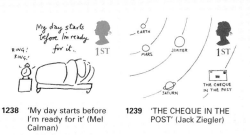

1238	'My day starts before I'm ready for it' (Mel Calman)	1239	'THE CHEQUE IN THE POST' (Jack Ziegler)

T **1230/9** were printed together, *se-tenant,* in booklet panes of 10 stamps and 20 half stamp-size labels.

Greetings Stamps. Cartoons

1996 (26 Feb.–11 Nov.) *'All-over' phosphor. Perf* 14½ × 14 (*with one elliptical hole on each vertical side*)

1905	**1230**	(1st) black and bright mauve	50	40 □ □
		a. Booklet pane. Nos. 1905/14	10·00	11·00 □ □
		p. Two phosphor bands	70	50 □ □
		pa. Booklet pane. Nos. 1905p/14p (11 Nov.)	37·00	36·00 □ □
1906	**1231**	(1st) black and blue-green	50	40 □ □
		p. Two phosphor bands	70	50 □ □
1907	**1232**	(1st) black and new blue	50	40 □ □
		p. Two phosphor bands	70	50 □ □
1908	**1233**	(1st) black and bright violet	50	40 □ □
		p. Two phosphor bands	70	50 □ □
1909	**1234**	(1st) black and vermilion	50	40 □ □
		p. Two phosphor bands	70	50 □ □
1910	**1235**	(1st) black and new blue	50	40 □ □
		p. Two phosphor bands	70	50 □ □
1911	**1236**	(1st) black and vermilion	50	40 □ □
		p. Two phosphor bands	70	50 □ □
1912	**1237**	(1st) black and bright violet	50	40 □ □
		p. Two phosphor bands	70	50 □ □
1913	**1238**	(1st) black and blue-green	50	40 □ □
		p. Two phosphor bands	70	50 □ □
1914	**1239**	(1st) black and bright mauve	50	40 □ □
		p. Two phosphor bands	70	50 □ □
		Set of 10 (*Nos. 1905/14*)	10·00	11·00 □ □
		Set of 10 (*Nos. 1905p/14p*)	37·00	36·00 □ □
		First Day Cover (*Nos. 1905/14*)		11·00 □
		Presentation Pack (*Nos. 1905/14*)	16·00	□
		PHQ Cards (*set of 10*)	16·00	28·00 □ □

Nos. 1905/14 were re-issued on 18 December 2001 in sheets of 10, each stamp with a *se-tenant* label showing cartoon titles. They were again issued on 29 July 2003 in sheets of 20 containing two of each design, each stamp accompanied by a half stamp size label showing a crossword grid or personal photograph. Such sheets are perforated without elliptical holes.

For full information on all future British issues, collectors should write to Royal Mail, Freepost EH3647, 21 South Gyle Crescent, Edinburgh EH12 9PE.

1240 'Muscovy Duck'

1241 'Lapwing'

1242 'White-fronted Goose'

1243 'Bittern'

1244 'Whooper Swan'

50th Anniversary of the Wildfowl and Wetlands Trust. Bird Paintings by C. F. Tunnicliffe

1996 (12 MAR.) *One phosphor band* (19p) *or phosphorised paper* (others). *Perf* 14 × 14½

1915	**1240**	19p multicoloured	70	25	☐	☐
1916	**1241**	25p multicoloured	90	30	☐	☐
1917	**1242**	30p multicoloured	1·00	1·25	☐	☐
1918	**1243**	35p multicoloured	1·10	1·50	☐	☐
1919	**1244**	41p multicoloured	1·50	1·60	☐	☐
	Set of 5		4·75	4·50	☐	☐
	First Day Cover			5·75		☐
	Presentation Pack		5·00			☐
	PHQ Cards (set of 5)		6·00	11·50	☐	☐
	Set of 5 Gutter Pairs		10·50			☐

1245 The Odeon, Harrogate

1247 Old Cinema Ticket

1248 Pathé News Still

1249 Cinema Sign, The Odeon, Manchester

Centenary of Cinema

1996 (16 APR.) *One phosphor band* (19p) *or two phosphor bands* (others). *Perf* 14 × 14½

1920	**1245**	19p multicoloured	50	25	☐	☐
1921	**1246**	25p multicoloured	70	30	☐	☐
1922	**1247**	30p multicoloured	1·00	1·75	☐	☐
1923	**1248**	35p black, red and silver	1·25	2·00	☐	☐
1924	**1249**	41p multicoloured	1·50	2·25	☐	☐
	Set of 5		4·75	4·75	☐	☐
	First Day Cover			5·75		☐
	Presentation Pack		5·50			☐
	PHQ Cards (set of 5)		6·00	11·50	☐	☐
	Set of 5 Gutter Pairs		11·00			☐

1246 Laurence Olivier and Vivien Leigh in *Lady Hamilton* (film)

1250 Dixie Dean

1251 Bobby Moore

1252 Duncan Edwards

1253 Billy Wright

1254 Danny Blanchflower

European Football Championship

1996 (14 MAY) *One phosphor band* (19p) *or two phosphor bands* (*others*). *Perf* 14½ × 14

1925	**1250**	19p multicoloured	50	20	☐	☐
1926	**1251**	25p multicoloured	75	20	☐	☐
1927	**1252**	35p multicoloured	1·25	1·75	☐	☐
1928	**1253**	41p multicoloured	1·50	1·75	☐	☐
1929	**1254**	60p multicoloured	1·75	2·00	☐	☐
		Set of 5	5·50	5·75	☐	☐
		First Day Cover		5·75		☐
		Presentation Pack	5·75			☐
		PHQ Cards (set of 5)	6·00	11·50	☐	☐
		Set of 5 Gutter Pairs	12·00			☐

1255 Athlete on Starting Blocks

1256 Throwing the Javelin

1257 Basketball

1258 Swimming

1259 Athlete celebrating and Olympic Rings

T **1255/9** were printed together, *se-tenant*, in horizontal strips of 5 throughout the sheet.

Olympic and Paralympic Games, Atlanta

1996 (9 JULY) *Two phosphor bands. Perf* 14½ × 14

1930	**1255**	26p multicoloured	50	40	☐	☐
		a. Horiz strip of 5. Nos.				
		1930/4	4·50	4·50	☐	☐
1931	**1256**	26p multicoloured	50	40	☐	☐
1932	**1257**	26p multicoloured	50	40	☐	☐
1933	**1258**	26p multicoloured	50	40	☐	☐
1934	**1259**	26p multicoloured	50	40	☐	☐
		Set of 5	4·50	4·50	☐	☐
		First Day Cover		5·00		☐
		Presentation Pack	4·50			☐
		PHQ Cards (set of 5)	6·00	11·50	☐	☐
		Gutter Strip of 10	11·00			☐

For these designs with the face value expressed as '1st' see **MS2554**.

1260 Prof. Dorothy Hodgkin (scientist)

1261 Dame Margot Fonteyn (ballerina)

1262 Dame Elisabeth Frink (sculptress)

1263 Dame Daphne du Maurier (novelist)

1264 Dame Marea Hartman (sports administrator)

Europa. Famous Women

1996 (6 AUG.) *One phosphor band* (20p) *or two phosphor bands* (*others*). *Perf* 14½

1935	**1260**	20p dull blue-green, brownish grey and black	60	25	☐	☐
1936	**1261**	26p dull mauve, brownish grey and black . . .	75	25	☐	☐

1937	**1262**	31p bronze, brownish grey and black . . .	1·10	1·10	☐	☐
1938	**1263**	37p silver, brownish grey and black	1·25	1·40	☐	☐
1939	**1264**	43p gold, brownish grey and black	1·50	1·50	☐	☐
		Set of 5	4·75	4·50	☐	☐
		First Day Cover		5·00		☐
		Presentation Pack	4·75		☐	
		PHQ Cards (set of 5)	6·00	11·50	☐	☐
		Set of 5 Gutter Pairs	12·00		☐	

Nos. 1936/7 include the 'EUROPA' emblem.

1265 *Muffin the Mule*

1266 *Sooty*

1267 *Stingray*

1268 *The Clangers*

1269 *Dangermouse*

50th Anniversary of Children's Television

1996 (3 SEPT.)–**97** *One phosphor band* (20p) *or two phosphor bands* (*others*). *Perf* $14\frac{1}{2} \times 14$

1940	**1265**	20p multicoloured	55	20	☐	☐
		a. Perf 15 × 14 (23.9.97)	2·00	2·00	☐	☐
1941	**1266**	26p multicoloured	80	20	☐	☐
1942	**1267**	31p multicoloured	1·00	1·50	☐	☐
1943	**1268**	37p multicoloured	1·40	1·75	☐	☐
1944	**1269**	43p multicoloured	1·60	2·00	☐	☐
		Set of 5	4·75	4·75	☐	☐
		First Day Cover		4·75		☐
		Presentation Pack	4·75		☐	
		PHQ Cards (set of 5)	6·00	11·50	☐	☐
		Set of 5 Gutter Pairs	10·50		☐	

No. 1940a comes from stamp booklets.

1270 Triumph TR3

1271 MG TD

1272 Austin-Healey 100

1273 Jaguar XK120

1274 Morgan Plus 4

Classic Sports Cars

1996 (1 OCT.) *One phosphor band* (20p) *or two phosphor bands* (*others*). *Perf* $14\frac{1}{2}$

1945	**1270**	20p multicoloured	55	20	☐	☐
1946	**1271**	26p multicoloured	1·10	20	☐	☐
1947	**1272**	37p multicoloured	1·40	1·90	☐	☐
1948	**1273**	43p multicoloured	1·60	1·90	☐	☐
1949	**1274**	63p multicoloured	1·75	2·00	☐	☐
		Set of 5	5·75	6·00	☐	☐
		First Day Cover		6·00		☐
		Presentation Pack	6·00		☐	
		PHQ Cards (set of 5)	6·00	11·50	☐	☐
		Set of 5 Gutter Pairs	13·00		☐	

1275 The Three Kings

1276 The Annunciation

1277 The Journey to
Bethlehem

1278 The Nativity

1279 The Shepherds

Christmas

1996 (28 OCT.) *One phosphor band* (2nd) *or two phosphor bands* (*others*)

1950	**1275**	(2nd) multicoloured . . .	75	20	☐	☐
1951	**1276**	(1st) multicoloured . . .	1·00	35	☐	☐
1952	**1277**	31p multicoloured . . .	1·25	1·75	☐	☐
1953	**1278**	43p multicoloured . . .	1·25	1·75	☐	☐
1954	**1279**	63p multicoloured . . .	1·50	2·00	☐	☐
		Set of 5	5·50	5·50	☐	☐
		First Day Cover		6·00		☐
		Presentation Pack	5·75		☐	
		PHQ Cards (set of 5)	6·00	11·50	☐	☐
		Set of 5 Gutter Pairs	13·00		☐	

Collectors Pack 1996

1996 (28 OCT.) *Comprises Nos.* 1901/4 *and* 1915/54
CP1954*a* Collectors Pack . . . . 55·00 ☐

Post Office Yearbook

1996 (28 OCT.) *Comprises Nos.* 1901/4 *and* 1915/54 *in hardback book with slip case*
YB1954*a* Yearbook . . . . 60·00 ☐

1280 Gentiana acaulis
(Georg Ehret)

1281 Magnolia grandiflora
(Ehret)

1282 Camellia japonica
(Alfred Chandler)

1283 Tulipa
(Ehret)

1284 Fuchsia 'Princess of
Wales' (Augusta Withers)

1285 Tulipa gesneriana
(Ehret)

1286 Guzmania splendens
(Charlotte Sowerby)

1287 Iris latifolia
(Ehret)

1288 Hippeastrum rutilum
(Pierre-Joseph Redoute)

1289 Passiflora coerulea
(Ehret)

T **1280**/9 were printed together, *se-tenant,* in booklet panes of 10 stamps and 20 half stamp-size labels.

Greeting Stamps. 19th-century Flower Paintings

1997 (6 JAN.) *Two phosphor bands. Perf* 14½ × 14 (*with one elliptical hole on each vertical side*)

1955	**1280**	(1st) multicoloured	50	40	☐	☐
		a. Booklet pane. Nos.				
		1955/64	11·00	11·00	☐	☐
1956	**1281**	(1st) multicoloured	50	40	☐	☐
1957	**1282**	(1st) multicoloured	50	40	☐	☐
1958	**1283**	(1st) multicoloured	50	40	☐	☐
1959	**1284**	(1st) multicoloured	50	40	☐	☐
1960	**1285**	(1st) multicoloured	50	40	☐	☐
1961	**1286**	(1st) multicoloured	50	40	☐	☐
1962	**1287**	(1st) multicoloured	50	40	☐	☐

1963	**1288**	(1st) multicoloured	50	40	□	□
1964	**1289**	(1st) multicoloured	50	40	□	□
		Set of 10	11·00	11·00	□	□
		First Day Cover		11·50		□
		Presentation Pack	16·00		□	
		PHQ Cards (set of 10)	16·00	28·00	□	□

Nos. 1955/64 were re-issued on 21 January 2003 in *se-tenant* sheets of 20, each accompanied by a label showing flowers or personal photograph. Such sheets are perforated without elliptical holes.

For Nos. 1955, 1958 and 1962 perf 15 × 14 see Nos. 2463/5.

1290 'King Henry VIII'

1291 'Catherine of Aragon' **1292** 'Anne Boleyn'

1293 'Jane Seymour' **1294** 'Anne of Cleves'

1295 'Catherine Howard' **1296** 'Catherine Parr'

T **1290/6** were printed together, *se-tenant,* in horizontal strips of 6 throughout the sheet.

450th Death Anniversary of King Henry VIII

1997 (21 Jan.) *Two phosphor bands. Perf* 15 (*No.* 1965) *or* 14 × 15 (*others*)

1965	**1290**	26p multicoloured	50	40	□	□
1966	**1291**	26p multicoloured	50	40	□	□
		a. Horiz strip of 6. Nos.				
		1966/71	8·00	8·50	□	□
1967	**1292**	26p multicoloured	50	40	□	□
1968	**1293**	26p multicoloured	50	40	□	□
1969	**1294**	26p multicoloured	50	40	□	□
1970	**1295**	26p multicoloured	50	40	□	□
1971	**1296**	26p multicoloured	50	40	□	□
		Set of 7	8·00	8·50	□	□
		First Day Cover		9·50		□
		Presentation Pack	10·00		□	
		PHQ Cards (set of 7)	10·00	18·00	□	□
		Gutter Pair and Gutter Block of 12	17·00		□	

1297 St Columba in Boat **1298** St Columba on Iona

1299 St Augustine with King Ethelbert **1300** St Augustine with Model of Cathedral

Religious Anniversaries

1997 (11 Mar.) *Two phosphor bands. Perf* 14½

1972	**1297**	26p multicoloured	75	35	□	□
1973	**1298**	37p multicoloured	1·10	1·50	□	□
1974	**1299**	43p multicoloured	1·50	1·50	□	□
1975	**1300**	63p multicoloured	2·00	2·10	□	□
		Set of 4	4·75	5·00	□	□
		First Day Cover		5·75		□
		Presentation Pack	5·25		□	
		PHQ Cards (set of 4)	5·75	11·50	□	□
		Set of 4 Gutter Pairs	11·50		□	

Nos. 1972/3 commemorate the 1400th death anniversary of St Columba and Nos. 1974/5 the 1400th anniversary of the arrival of St Augustine of Canterbury in Kent.

| | 1301 | | 1302 | | |

Self-adhesive Coil Stamps

1997 (18 Mar.) *Photo Enschedé. One centre phosphor band (2nd) or two phosphor bands (1st). Perf* 14 × 15 *die-cut (with one elliptical hole on each vertical side)*

1976	**1301**	(2nd) bright blue	2·75	2·50	☐	☐
1977	**1302**	(1st) bright orange-red .	2·75	2·75	☐	☐
	Set of 2	. . . .	4·50	5·25	☐	☐
	First Day Cover		5·50		☐
	Presentation Pack	6·50			☐

Nos. 1976/7, which were priced at 20p and 26p, were each sold in rolls of 100 with the stamps separate on the backing paper.

> Machin stamps printed in gold were issued on 21 April 1997 for the Royal Golden Wedding. These are listed as definitives under Nos. 1668 (1st) and Y1686 26p.

1303 *Dracula*

1304 *Frankenstein*

1305 *Dr Jekyll and Mr Hyde*

1306 *The Hound of the Baskervilles*

> **Minimum Price.** The minimum price quoted is 10p. This represents a handling charge rather than a basis for valuing common stamps. Where the actual value of a stamp is less than 10p this may be apparent when set prices are shown, particularly for sets including a number of 10p stamps. It therefore follows that in valuing common stamps the 10p catalogue price should not be reckoned automatically since it covers a variation in real scarcity.

Europa. Tales and Legends. Horror Stories

1997 (13 May) *Two phosphor bands. Perf* 14 × 15

1980	**1303**	26p multicoloured	1·00	40	☐	☐
1981	**1304**	31p multicoloured	1·10	1·50	☐	☐
1982	**1305**	37p multicoloured	1·30	1·75	☐	☐
1983	**1306**	43p multicoloured	2·00	1·95	☐	☐
	Set of 4	. . . .	5·00	5·50	☐	☐
	First Day Cover		5·50		☐
	Presentation Pack	5·25			☐
	PHQ Cards (set of 4)	5·75	11·50	☐	☐
	Set of 4 Gutter Pairs	12·00			☐

Nos. 1980/3 commemorate the birth bicentenary of Mary Shelley (creator of Frankenstein) with the 26p and 31p values incorporating the 'EUROPA' emblem.

1307 Reginald Mitchell and Supermarine Spitfire MkIIA

1308 Roy Chadwick and Avro Lancaster MkI

1309 Ronald Bishop and De Havilland Mosquito B MkXVI

1310 George Carter and Gloster Meteor T Mk7

1311 Sir Sidney Camm and Hawker Hunter FGA Mk9

British Aircraft Designers

1997 (10 June) *One phosphor band (20p) or two phosphor bands (others)*

1984	**1307**	20p multicoloured	75	40	☐	☐
1985	**1308**	26p multicoloured	1·10	1·25	☐	☐
1986	**1309**	37p multicoloured	1·40	1·25	☐	☐
1987	**1310**	43p multicoloured	1·50	1·60	☐	☐
1988	**1311**	63p multicoloured	2·00	2·00	☐	☐
	Set of 5	. . . .	6·00	6·50	☐	☐
	First Day Cover		6·50		☐
	Presentation Pack	6·50			☐
	PHQ Cards	6·00	13·00	☐	☐
	Set of 5 Gutter Pairs	15·00			☐

1312 Carriage Horse
and Coachman

1313 Lifeguards Horse
and Trooper

1314 Household Cavalry
Drum Horse and
Drummer

1315 Duke of Edinburgh's
Horse and Groom

'All The Queen's Horses'. 50th Anniv of the British Horse Society

1997 (8 JULY) *One phosphor band (20p) or two phosphor bands (others). Perf* 14½

1989	1312	20p multicoloured	. . . .	80	45	□	□
1990	1313	26p multicoloured	. . . .	1·10	1·50	□	□
1991	1314	43p multicoloured	. . . .	1·50	1·50	□	□
1992	1315	63p multicoloured	. . . .	2·00	2·00	□	□
		Set of 4	. . . .	5·00	5·25	□	□
		First Day Cover	. . . .		5·75		□
		Presentation Pack	. . . .	5·50		□	
		PHQ Cards (set of 4)	. . . . . .	5·75	11·50	□	□
		Set of 4 Gutter Pairs	. . . . . .	12·00		□	

CASTLE

Harrison printing (Nos. 1611/14)

CASTLE

Enschedé printing (Nos. 1993/6)

Differences between Harrison and Enschedé printings:
Harrison – 'C' has top serif and tail of letter points to right.
'A' has flat top. 'S' has top and bottom serifs.
Enschedé – 'C' has no top serif and tail of letter points
upwards. 'A' has pointed top. 'S' has no serifs.

1997 (29 JULY) *Designs as Nos. 1611/14 with Queen's head in silhouette as T* **1044**, *but re-engraved as above. Perf* 15 × 14 (*with one elliptical hole on each vertical side*).

1993	880	£1·50 deep claret and gold†	12·00	6·00	□	□
1994	881	£2 indigo and gold†	. . .	14·00	2·25	□	□

1995	1044	£3 violet and gold†	. . .	30·00	3·50	□	□
1996	882	£5 deep brown and gold†	36·00	10·00	□	□
		Set of 4	. . . .	75·00	18·00	□	□
		Set of 4 Gutter Pairs	. . . . . .	£140		□	
		Presentation Pack (P.O Pack No.				
		40)	. . . .	£150		□	

† The Queen's head on these stamps is printed in optically variable ink which changes colour from gold to green when viewed from different angles.

1316 Haroldswick,
Shetland

1317 Painswick,
Gloucestershire

1318 Beddgelert, Gwynedd

1319 Ballyroney, County Down

Sub-Post Offices

1997 (12 AUG.) *One phosphor band (20p) or two phosphor bands (others). Perf* 14½

1997	1316	20p multicoloured	. . . .	75	50	□	□
1998	1317	26p multicoloured	. . . .	1·00	1·00	□	□
1999	1318	43p multicoloured	. . . .	1·50	1·50	□	□
2000	1319	63p multicoloured	. . . .	2·25	2·25	□	□
		Set of 4	. . . .	5·50	5·00	□	□
		First Day Cover	. . . .		5·75		□
		Presentation Pack	. . . .	5·00		□	
		PHQ Cards (set of 4)	. . . . . .	5·75	11·50	□	□
		Set of 4 Gutter Pairs	. . . . . .	12·00		□	

Nos. 1997/2000 also mark the centenary of the National Federation of Sub-Postmasters.

Enid Blyton's *Noddy*

Enid Blyton's *Famous Five*

1320 Noddy

1321 Famous Five

Enid Blyton's *Secret Seven*

1322 Secret Seven

Enid Blyton's *Faraway Tree*

1323 Faraway Tree

Enid Blyton's *Malory Towers*

1324 Malory Towers

Birth Centenary of Enid Blyton (children's author)

1997 (9 SEPT.) *One phosphor band* (20p) *or two phosphor bands* (*others*). Perf 14 × 14½

2001	**1320**	20p multicoloured	. . . .	50	45	☐	☐
2002	**1321**	26p multicoloured	. . . .	1·00	1·25	☐	☐
2003	**1322**	37p multicoloured	. . . .	1·25	1·25	☐	☐
2004	**1323**	43p multicoloured	. . . .	1·50	2·00	☐	☐
2005	**1324**	63p multicoloured	. . . .	1·75	2·00	☐	☐
		Set of 5	. . . .	5·50	6·00	☐	☐
		First Day Cover	. . . .		6·00		☐
		Presentation Pack	. . . .	5·75		☐	
		PHQ Cards (set of 5)	. . . . . .	6·00	13·00	☐	☐
		Set of 5 Gutter Pairs	. . . . . .	12·00		☐	

1325 Children and Father Christmas pulling Cracker

1326 Father Christmas with Traditional Cracker

1327 Father Christmas riding Cracker

1328 Father Christmas on Snowball

1329 Father Christmas and Chimney

Christmas. 150th Anniversary of the Christmas Cracker

1997 (27 OCT.) *One phosphor band* (2nd) *or two phosphor bands* (*others*)

2006	**1325**	(2nd) multicoloured	. . . .	75	20	☐	☐
2007	**1326**	(1st) multicoloured	. . . .	90	30	☐	☐
2008	**1327**	31p multicoloured	. . . .	1·00	1·50	☐	☐
2009	**1328**	43p multicoloured	. . . .	1·25	1·75	☐	☐
2010	**1329**	63p multicoloured	. . . .	1·60	2·00	☐	☐
		Set of 5	. . . .	5·50	5·00	☐	☐
		First Day Cover	. . . .		6·00		☐
		Presentation Pack	. . . .	5·75		☐	
		PHQ Cards (set of 5)	. . . . . .	6·00	13·00	☐	☐
		Set of 5 Gutter Pairs	. . . . . .	12·00		☐	

The 1st value was re-issued on 3 October 2000, in sheets of 10 in photogravure, each stamp with a *se-tenant* label, in connection with 'customised' service available from the Philatelic Bureau. On 1 October 2002 in sheet size of 20 in lithography the 1st value was again issued but perforated 14½ × 14. The labels show either Christmas greetings or a personal photograph.

1330 Wedding Photograph, 1947

1331 Queen Elizabeth II and Prince Philip, 1997

Royal Golden Wedding

1997 (13 NOV.) *One phosphor band* (20p) *or two phosphor bands* (*others*). Perf 15

2011	**1330**	20p gold, yellow-brown and grey-black	. . .	85	45	☐	☐
2012	**1331**	26p multicoloured		1·10	70	☐	☐
2013	**1330**	43p gold, bluish green and grey-black	. . .	1·90	2·25	☐	☐
2014	**1331**	63p multicoloured	. . . .	2·50	3·00	☐	☐
		Set of 4	. . . .	5·75	5·75	☐	☐
		First Day Cover	. . . .		8·25		☐
		Presentation Pack	. . . .	6·25		☐	
		Souvenir Book (contains Nos. 1668, 1989/92 and 2011/14)	. .	50·00		☐	
		PHQ Cards (set of 4)	. . . . . .	5·75	11·50	☐	☐
		Set of 4 Gutter Pairs	. . . . . .	12·00		☐	

Collectors Pack 1997

1997 (13 Nov.) *Comprises Nos. 1965/75, 1980/92 and 1997/2014*
CP2014a Collectors Pack . . . . 65·00 ☐

Post Office Yearbook

1997 (13 Nov.) *Comprises Nos. 1965/75, 1980/92 and 1997/2014 in hardback book with slip case*
YB2014a Yearbook . . . . 65·00 ☐

20 **ENDANGERED SPECIES**
Common dormouse
Muscardinus avellanarius

1332 Common Doormouse

26 **ENDANGERED SPECIES**
Lady's slipper orchid
Cypripedium calceolus

1333 Lady's Slipper Orchid

31 **ENDANGERED SPECIES**
Song thrush
Turdus philomelos

1334 Song Thrush

37 **ENDANGERED SPECIES**
Shining ram's-horn snail
Segmentina nitida

1335 Shining Ram's-horn Snail

43 **ENDANGERED SPECIES**
Mole cricket
Gryllotalpa gryllotalpa

1336 Mole Cricket

63 **ENDANGERED SPECIES**
Devil's bolete
Boletus satanas

1337 Devil's Bolete

Endangered Species

1998 (20 Jan.) *One side phosphor band* (20p) *or two phosphor bands* (others). *Perf* 14 × 14½

2015	**1332**	20p multicoloured	. . . .	60	40	☐ ☐
2016	**1333**	26p multicoloured	. . . .	75	40	☐ ☐
2017	**1334**	31p multicoloured	. . . .	1·00	2·00	☐ ☐
2018	**1335**	37p multicoloured	. . . .	1·25	1·25	☐ ☐

2019	**1336**	43p multicoloured	. . . .	1·40	1·75	☐ ☐
2020	**1337**	63p multicoloured	. . . .	1·90	2·25	☐ ☐
		Set of 6		6·25	6·50	☐ ☐
		First Day Cover	. . . .		6·50	☐
		Presentation Pack	. . . .	6·75		☐
		PHQ Cards (Set of 6)	. . . .	6·00	14·00	☐ ☐
		Set of 6 Gutter Pairs	. . . .	15·00		☐

1338 Diana, Princess of Wales (photo by Lord Snowdon)

1339 At British Lung Foundation Function, April 1997 (photo by John Stillwell)

1340 Wearing Tiara, 1991 (photo by Lord Snowdon)

1341 On Visit to Birmingham, October 1995 (photo by Tim Graham)

1342 In Evening Dress, 1987 (photo by Terence Donovan)

T **1338/42** were printed together, *se-tenant,* in horizontal strips of 5 throughout the sheet.

Diana, Princess of Wales Commemoration

1998 (3 Feb.) *Two phosphor bands*

2021	**1338**	26p multicoloured	. . . .	50	40	☐ ☐
		a. Horiz strip of 5. Nos.				
		2021/5	. . . .	4·50	4·50	☐ ☐
2022	**1339**	26p multicoloured	. . . .	50	40	☐ ☐
2023	**1340**	26p multicoloured	. . . .	50	40	☐ ☐

2024	**1341**	26p multicoloured	50	40 ☐	☐
2025	**1342**	26p multicoloured	50	40 ☐	☐
		Set of 5	4·50	4·50 ☐	☐
		First Day Cover		5·50	☐
		Presentation Pack	16·00		☐
		Presentation Pack (Welsh) . . .	£150		☐
		Gutter Strip of 10	10·00		☐

1343 Lion of England and Griffin of Edward III **1344** Falcon of Plantagenet and Bull of Clarence

1345 Lion of Mortimer and Yale of Beaufort **1346** Greyhound of Richmond and Dragon of Wales

1347 Unicorn of Scotland and Horse of Hanover

T **1343/7** were printed together, *se-tenant,* in horizontal strips of 5 throughout the sheet.

650th Anniversary of the Order of the Garter. The Queen's Beasts

1998 (24 FEB.) *Two phosphor bands*

2026	**1343**	26p multicoloured	90	90 ☐	☐
		a. Horiz strip of 5. Nos. 2026/30	4·50	4·50 ☐	☐
2027	**1344**	26p multicoloured	90	90 ☐	☐
2028	**1345**	26p multicoloured	90	90 ☐	☐
2029	**1346**	26p multicoloured	90	90 ☐	☐
2030	**1347**	26p multicoloured	90	90 ☐	☐
		Set of 5	4·00	4·00 ☐	☐
		First Day Cover		5·25	☐
		Presentation Pack	5·00		☐
		PHQ Cards (set of 5)	6·00	13·00 ☐	☐
		Gutter Block of 10	10·00		☐

The phosphor bands on Nos. 2026/30 are only half the height of the stamps and do not cover the silver parts of the designs.

1348

Booklet Stamps

1998 (10 MAR.) *Design as T* **157** *(issued 1952–54), but with face values in decimal currency as T* **1348**. *One side phosphor band (20p) or two phosphor bands (others). Perf 14 (with one elliptical hole on each vertical side)*

2031	**1348**	20p light green	70	75 ☐	☐
2032		26p red-brown	90	95 ☐	☐
2033		37p light purple	2·75	2·75 ☐	☐
		Set of 3	4·00	4·00 ☐	☐

For further Wilding designs see Nos. 2258/9, **MS**2326, **MS**2367 and 2378/80.

1349 St John's Point Lighthouse, County Down

1350 Smalls Lighthouse, Pembrokeshire

1351 Needles Rock Lighthouse, Isle of Wight, c 1900

1352 Bell Rock Lighthouse, Arbroath, mid-19th-century

1353 Eddystone Lighthouse, Plymouth, 1698

Lighthouses

1998 (24 MAR.) *One side phosphor band (20p) or two phosphor bands (others). Perf 14½ × 14*

2034	**1349**	20p multicoloured	50	40	☐	☐
2035	**1350**	26p multicoloured	75	50	☐	☐
2036	**1351**	37p multicoloured	1·10	1·50	☐	☐
2037	**1352**	43p multicoloured	1·50	1·75	☐	☐
2038	**1353**	63p multicoloured	2·10	2·50	☐	☐
		Set of 5	5·50	6·00	☐	☐
		First Day Cover		6·00		☐
		Presentation Pack	6·00		☐	
		PHQ Cards (set of 5)	6·00	13·00	☐	☐
		Set of 5 Gutter Pairs	13·50		☐	

Nos. 2034/8 commemorate the 300th anniversary of the first Eddystone Lighthouse and the final year of manned light-houses.

Self-adhesive stamps

1998 (6 APR.) *Photo Enschedé, Questa or Walsall. Designs as T **913/14**. One centre phosphor band (2nd) or two phosphor bands (1st). Perf 15 × 14 die-cut (with one elliptical hole on each vertical side)*

2039	(2nd) bright blue	30	35	☐	☐
	b. Perf 14½ × 14 die-cut	£150		☐	☐
2040	(1st) bright orange-red	40	45	☐	☐
	b. Perf 14½ × 14 die-cut	£150		☐	☐
	Set of 2	70	80	☐	☐

Nos. 2039/40 were initially priced at 20p and 26p, and were available in coils of 200 (Enschedé), sheets of 100 (Enschedé, Questa or Walsall) or self-adhesive booklets (Questa or Walsall). See also Nos. 2295/8.

1354 Tommy Cooper

1355 Eric Morecambe

1356 Joyce Grenfell

1357 Les Dawson

1358 Peter Cook

Comedians

1998 (23 APR.) *One phosphor band (20p) or two phosphor bands (others). Perf 14½ × 14*

2041	**1354**	20p multicoloured	50	50	☐	☐
2042	**1355**	26p multicoloured	75	85	☐	☐
2043	**1356**	37p multicoloured	1·25	1·25	☐	☐
2044	**1357**	43p multicoloured	1·50	1·50	☐	☐
2045	**1358**	63p multicoloured	1·75	2·10	☐	☐
		Set of 5	5·25	5·50	☐	☐
		First Day Cover		6·00		☐
		Presentation Pack	6·00		☐	
		PHQ Cards (set of 5)	6·00	13·00	☐	☐
		Set of 5 Gutter Pairs	13·50		☐	

1359 Hands forming Heart

1360 Adult and Child holding Hands

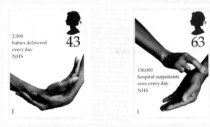

1361 Hands forming Cradle   **1362** Hands taking Pulse

50th Anniversary of National Health Service

1998 (23 JUNE) *One side phosphor band (20p) or two phosphor bands (others). Perf 14 × 14½*

2046	**1359**	20p multicoloured	50	50	☐	☐
2047	**1360**	26p multicoloured	90	90	☐	☐
2048	**1361**	43p multicoloured	1·50	1·50	☐	☐
2049	**1362**	63p multicoloured	2·10	2·10	☐	☐
		Set of 4	4·50	4·50	☐	☐
		First Day Cover		5·75		☐
		Presentation Pack	5·50		☐	
		PHQ Cards (set of 4)	5·75	11·50	☐	☐
		Set of 4 Gutter Pairs	11·00		☐	

For full information on all future British issues, collectors should write to Royal Mail, Freepost EH3647, 21 South Gyle Crescent, Edinburgh EH12 9PE.

1363 *The Hobbit
(J. R. R. Tolkien)*

1364 *The Lion, The Witch
and the Wardrobe
(C. S. Lewis)*

1365 *The Phoenix and the
Carpet (E. Nesbit)*

1366 *The Borrowers
(Mary Norton)*

1367 *Through the Looking
Glass (Lewis Carroll)*

Famous Children's Fantasy Novels

1998 (21 July) *One phosphor band* (20p) *or two phosphor
bands* (others)

2050	**1363**	20p multicoloured	50	45	☐	☐
2051	**1364**	26p multicoloured	75	55	☐	☐
2052	**1365**	37p multicoloured	1·25	1·50	☐	☐
2053	**1366**	43p multicoloured	1·50	1·50	☐	☐
2054	**1367**	63p multicoloured	2·10	2·00	☐	☐
		Set of 5	5·75	5·75	☐	☐
		First Day Cover		5·75		☐
		Presentation Pack	6·00		☐	
		PHQ Cards (set of 5)	6·00	13·00	☐	☐
		Set of 5 Gutter Pairs	13·00		☐	

Nos. 2050/4 commemorate the birth centenary of C. S. Lewis
and the death centenary of Lewis Carroll.

1368 Woman in Yellow
Feathered Costume

1369 Woman in Blue
Costume and Headdress

1370 Group of Children in
White and Gold Robes

1371 Child in 'Tree' Costume

Europa. Festivals. Notting Hill Carnival

1998 (25 Aug.) *One centre phosphor band* (20p) *or two
phosphor bands* (others). *Perf* 14 × 14½

2055	**1368**	20p multicoloured	75	45	☐	☐
2056	**1369**	26p multicoloured	95	55	☐	☐
2057	**1370**	43p multicoloured	1·50	2·00	☐	☐
2058	**1371**	63p multicoloured	2·00	2·75	☐	☐
		Set of 4	4·75	4·75	☐	☐
		First Day Cover		5·75		☐
		Presentation Pack	5·25		☐	
		PHQ Cards (set of 4)	5·75	11·50	☐	☐
		Set of 4 Gutter Pairs	12·50		☐	

Nos. 2055/6 include the 'EUROPA' emblem.

1372 Sir Malcolm Campbell's
Bluebird, 1925

1373 Sir Henry Segrave's
Sunbeam, 1926

1374 John G. Parry Thomas's
Babs, 1926

1375 John R. Cobb's
Railton Mobil Special, 1947

1376 Donald Campbell's
Bluebird CN7, 1964

British Land Speed Record Holders

1998 (29 Sept.–13 Oct.) *One phosphor band* (20p) *or two phosphor bands* (others). *Perf* 15 × 14

2059	**1372**	20p multicoloured (centre band)	50	25	☐	☐
		a. Perf 14½ × 13½ (side band) (13 Oct.) . . .	1·40	1·20	☐	☐
2060	**1373**	26p multicoloured	75	30	☐	☐
2061	**1374**	30p multicoloured	1·25	1·50	☐	☐
2062	**1375**	43p multicoloured	1·50	1·60	☐	☐
2063	**1376**	63p multicoloured	2·00	2·40	☐	☐
		Set of 5	5·50	5·50		☐
		First Day Cover		6·00		☐
		Presentation Pack	6·25		☐	
		PHQ Cards (set of 5)	6·00	13·00	☐	☐
		Set of 5 Gutter Pairs	13·00		☐	

No. 2059a, which occurs with the phosphor band at the left or right of the stamp, comes from stamp booklets. There are minor differences of design between No. 2059 and No. 2059a, which also omits the copyright symbol and date.

Nos. 2059/63 commemorate the 50th death anniversary of Sir Malcolm Campbell.

1377 Angel with Hands raised in Blessing

1378 Angel praying

1379 Angel playing Flute

1380 Angel playing Lute

1381 Angel praying

Christmas. Angels

1998 (2 Nov.) *One phosphor band* (20p) *or two phosphor bands* (others)

2064	**1377**	20p multicoloured	50	50	☐	☐
2065	**1378**	26p multicoloured	75	60	☐	☐
2066	**1379**	30p multicoloured	1·25	1·50	☐	☐
2067	**1380**	43p multicoloured	1·50	1·60	☐	☐
2068	**1381**	63p multicoloured	2·00	2·25	☐	☐
		Set of 5	5·75	5·75	☐	☐
		First Day Cover		6·00		☐
		Presentation Pack	6·50		☐	
		PHQ Cards (set of 5)	6·00	13·00	☐	☐
		Set of 5 Gutter Pairs	13·00		☐	

Collectors Pack 1998

1998 (2 Nov.) *Comprises Nos.* 2015/30, 2034/8 *and* 2041/68

CP2068a	*Collectors Pack*	95·00		☐

Post Office Yearbook

1998 (2 Nov.) *Comprises Nos.* 2015/30, 2034/8 *and* 2041/68 *in hardback book with slip case*

YB2068a	*Yearbook*	85·00		☐

1382 Greenwich Meridian and Clock (John Harrison's chronometer)

1383 Industrial Worker and Blast Furnace (James Watt's discovery of steam power)

1384 Early Photos of Leaves (Henry Fox-Talbot's photographic experiments)

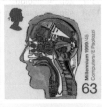

1385 Computer inside Human Head (Alan Turing's work on computers)

Millennium Series. The Inventors' Tale

1999 (12 Jan.–21 Sept.) *One centre phosphor band* (20p) *or two phosphor bands* (others). *Perf* 14 × 14½

2069	**1382**	20p multicoloured	75	70	☐	☐
2070	**1383**	26p multicoloured	95	1·00	☐	☐
2071	**1384**	43p multicoloured	1·50	1·60	☐	☐
2072	**1385**	63p multicoloured	2·25	2·40	☐	☐
		a. Perf 13½ × 14 (21 Sept.)	3·50	3·50	☐	☐
		Set of 4	5·25	5·25	☐	☐
		First Day Cover		14·00		☐
		Presentation Pack	7·50		☐	
		PHQ Cards (set of 4)	8·50	13·00	☐	☐
		Set of 4 Gutter Pairs	13·00		☐	

No. 2072a comes from stamp booklets.

1386 Airliner hugging Globe (International air travel)

1387 Woman on Bicycle (Development of the bicycle)

1388 Victorian Railway Station (Growth of public transport)

1389 Captain Cook and Maori (Captain James Cook's voyages)

Millennium Series. The Travellers' Tale

1999 (2 Feb.) *One centre phosphor band* (20p) *or two phosphor bands* (*others*)*. Perf* 14 × 14½

2073	**1386**	20p multicoloured	75	70	☐	☐
2074	**1387**	26p multicoloured	95	1·00	☐	☐
2075	**1388**	43p grey-black, stone and bronze	1·50	1·60	☐	☐
2076	**1389**	63p multicoloured	2·25	2·40	☐	☐
		Set of 4	5·25	5·25	☐	☐
		First Day Cover		8·00	☐	
		Presentation Pack	7·50		☐	
		PHQ Cards (set of 4)	8·50	13·00	☐	☐
		Set of 4 Gutter Pairs	13·00		☐	

1390

1999 (16 Feb.) (*a*) *Embossed and litho Walsall. Self-adhesive. Die-cut perf* 14 × 15

2077 **1390** (1st) grey (face value) (Queen's head in colourless relief) (phosphor background around head) . . . . . 3·00 2·25 ☐ ☐

(*b*) *Recess Enschedé. Perf* 14 × 14½

2078 **1390** (1st) grey-black (2 phosphor bands) . . . . 3·00 2·25 ☐ ☐

(*c*) *Typo Harrison. Perf* 14 × 15

2079 **1390** (1st) black (2 phosphor bands) . . . . 3·00 2·25 ☐ ☐

Set of 3 . . . . 8·00 6·00 ☐ ☐

Nos. 2077/9 were only issued in £7·54 stamp booklets.

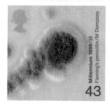

1391 Vaccinating Child (pattern in cow markings) (Jenner's development of smallpox vaccine)

1392 Patient on Trolley (nursing care)

1393 Penicillin Mould (Fleming's discovery of penicillin)

1394 Sculpture of Test-tube Baby (development of in vitro fertilization)

Millennium Series. The Patients' Tale

1999 (2 Mar.) *One centre phosphor band* (20p) *or two phosphor bands* (*others*)*. Perf* 13½ × 14

2080	**1391**	20p multicoloured	75	70	☐	☐
2081	**1392**	26p multicoloured	95	1·00	☐	☐
2082	**1393**	43p multicoloured	1·50	1·60	☐	☐
2083	**1394**	63p multicoloured	2·25	2·40	☐	☐
		Set of 4	5·25	5·25	☐	☐
		First Day Cover		8·00	☐	
		Presentation Pack	7·50		☐	
		PHQ Cards (set of 4)	8·50	13·00	☐	☐
		Set of 4 Gutter Pairs	13·00		☐	

Minimum Price. The minimum price quoted is 10p. This represents a handling charge rather than a basis for valuing common stamps. Where the actual value of a stamp is less than 10p this may be apparent when set prices are shown, particularly for sets including a number of 10p stamps. It therefore follows that in valuing common stamps the 10p catalogue price should not be reckoned automatically since it covers a variation in real scarcity.

1395 Dove and Norman Settler (medieval migration to Scotland)

1396 Pilgrim Fathers and Red Indian (17th-century migration to America)

1397 Sailing Ship and Aspects of Settlement (19th-century migration to Australia)

1398 Hummingbird and Superimposed Stylised Face (20th-century migration to Great Britain)

Millennium Series. The Settlers' Tale

1999 (6 APR.) *One centre phosphor band* (20p) *or two phosphor bands* (*others*). *Perf* 14 × 14½

2084	1395	20p multicoloured	. . . .	75	70 □ □
2085	1396	26p multicoloured	. . . .	95	1·00 □ □
2086	1397	43p multicoloured	. . . .	2·00	1·75 □ □
2087	1398	63p multicoloured	. . . .	3·00	3·00 □ □
		Set of 4	. . . .	5·75	5·75 □ □
		First Day Cover	. . . .		8·00 □
		Presentation Pack	. . . .	7·50	□
		PHQ Cards (set of 4)	. . . . .	8·50	13·00 □ □
		Set of 4 Gutter Pairs	. . . . . .	13·00	□

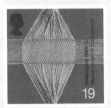

1399 Woven Threads (woollen industry)

1400 Salts Mill, Saltaire (worsted cloth industry)

1401 Hull on Slipway (shipbuilding)

1402 Lloyd's Building (City of London finance centre)

Millennium Series. The Workers' Tale

1999 (4 MAY) *One centre phosphor band* (19p) *or two phosphor bands* (*others*). *Perf* 14 × 14½

2088	1399	19p multicoloured	. . . .	75	70 □ □
2089	1400	26p multicoloured	. . . .	95	1·00 □ □
2090	1401	44p multicoloured	. . . .	1·75	1·60 □ □
2091	1402	64p multicoloured	. . . .	2·25	2·40 □ □
		Set of 4	. . . .	5·25	5·25 □ □
		First Day Cover	. . . .		8·00 □
		Presentation Pack	. . . .	7·50	□
		PHQ Cards (set of 4)	. . . . .	8·50	13·00 □ □
		Set of 4 Gutter Pairs	. . . . . .	13·00	□

1403 Freddie Mercury (lead singer of Queen) ('Popular Music')

1404 Bobby Moore with World Cup, 1966 ('Sport')

1405 Dalek from *Dr Who* (science-fiction series) ('Television')

1406 Charlie Chaplin (film star) ('Cinema')

Millennium Series. The Entertainers' Tale

1999 (1 JUNE) *One centre phosphor band* (19p) *or two phosphor bands* (*others*). *Perf* 14 × 14½

2092	1403	19p multicoloured	. . . .	75	70 □ □
2093	1404	26p multicoloured	. . . .	95	1·00 □ □

2094	**1405**	44p multicoloured	. . . .	1·50	1·60	☐	☐
2095	**1406**	64p multicoloured		2·25	2·40	☐	☐
		Set of 4	. . . .	5·25	5·25	☐	☐
		First Day Cover			8·00		☐
		Presentation Pack	. . . . .	7·50		☐	
		PHQ Cards (*set of 4*)	. . . . .	8·50	13·00	☐	☐
		Set of 4 Gutter Pairs	. . . . .	13·00		☐	

1407 Prince Edward and Miss Sophie Rhys-Jones **1408**
(from photos by John Swannell)

Royal Wedding

1999 (15 June) *Two phosphor bands*

2096	**1407**	26p multicoloured	. . . .	85	85	☐	☐
2097	**1408**	64p multicoloured	. . . .	2·50	2·50	☐	☐
		Set of 2	. . . .	3·00	3·00	☐	☐
		First Day Cover	. . . .		4·75		☐
		Presentation Pack	. . . .	4·00			☐
		PHQ Cards (*set of 2*)	. . . . .	8·50	6·75	☐	☐
		Set of 2 Gutter Pairs	. . . . .	7·00			☐

1409 Suffragette behind Prison Window ('Equal Rights for Women')   **1410** Water Tap ('Right to Health')

1411 Generations of School Children ('Right to Education')   **1412** 'MAGNA CARTA' ('Human Rights')

Millennium Series. The Citizens' Tale

1999 (6 July) *One centre phosphor band* (19p) *or two phosphor bands* (*others*). *Perf* 14 × 14½

2098	**1409**	19p multicoloured	. . . .	75	70	☐	☐
2099	**1410**	26p multicoloured		95	1·00	☐	☐

2100	**1411**	44p multicoloured	. . . .	1·75	1·60	☐	☐
2101	**1412**	64p multicoloured		2·50	2·40	☐	☐
		Set of 4	. . . .	5·75	5·25	☐	☐
		First Day Cover			8·00		☐
		Presentation Pack	. . . . .	7·50		☐	
		PHQ Cards (*set of 4*)	. . . . .	8·50	13·00	☐	☐
		Set of 4 Gutter Pairs	. . . . .	13·00		☐	

1413 Molecular Structures ('DNA decoding')   **1414** Galapagos Finch and Fossilized Skeleton ('Darwin's theory of evolution')

1415 Rotation of Polarized Light by Magnetism (Faraday's work on electricity)   **1416** Saturn (development of astronomical telescopes)

Millennium Series. The Scientists' Tale

1999 (3 Aug.–21 Sept.) *One centre phosphor band* (19p) *or two phosphor bands* (*others*). *Perf* 13½ × 14 (19p, 64p) *or* 14 × 14½ (26p, 44p)

2102	**1413**	19p multicoloured	. . . .	75	70	☐	☐
2103	**1414**	26p multicoloured	. . . .	1·50	1·00	☐	☐
		b. Perf 14½ × 14 (21 Sept.)	. . . .	3·00	3·00	☐	☐
2104	**1415**	44p multicoloured	. . . .	1·50	1·60	☐	☐
		a. Perf 14½ × 14 (21 Sept.)	. . . .	2·75	2·75	☐	☐
2105	**1416**	64p multicoloured	. . . .	2·25	2·40	☐	☐
		Set of 4	. . . .	5·25	5·25	☐	☐
		First Day Cover	. . . .		8·00		☐
		Presentation Pack	. . . .	7·50		☐	
		PHQ Cards (*set of 4*)	. . . . .	8·50	13·00	☐	☐
		Set of 4 Gutter Pairs	. . . . .	13·00		☐	

Nos. 2103*b* and 2104*a* come from stamp booklets.

For full information on all future British issues, collectors should write to Royal Mail, Freepost EH3647, 21 South Gyle Crescent, Edinburgh EH12 9PE.

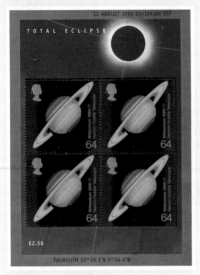

1416a

Solar Eclipse

1999 (11 Aug.) *Sheet 89 × 121 mm. Two phosphor bands. Perf 14 × 14½*

MS2106	1416a	64p × 4 multicoloured	21·00	21·00	☐	☐
		First Day Cover		22·00		☐

1417 Upland Landscape (Strip farming)

1418 Horse-drawn Rotary Seed Drill (Mechanical farming)

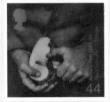

1419 Man peeling Potato (Food imports)

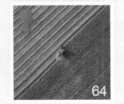

1420 Aerial View of Combine Harvester (Satellite agriculture)

Millennium Series. The Farmers' Tale

1999 (7 Sept.) *One centre phosphor band (19p) or two phosphor bands (others). Perf 14 × 14½*

2107	1417	19p multicoloured	75	70	☐	☐
2108	1418	26p multicoloured	95	1·00	☐	☐
2109	1419	44p multicoloured	2·00	1·60	☐	☐
2110	1420	64p multicoloured	2·50	2·40	☐	☐
		Set of 4	5·75	5·25	☐	☐
		First Day Cover		8·00		☐
		Presentation Pack	7·50		☐	
		PHQ Cards (set of 4)	8·50	13·00	☐	☐
		Set of 4 Gutter Pairs	13·00		☐	

No. 2107 includes the 'EUROPA' emblem.

1421 Robert the Bruce (Battle of Bannockburn, 1314)

1422 Cavalier and Horse (English Civil War)

1423 War Graves Cemetery, The Somme (World Wars)

1424 Soldiers with Boy (Peace-keeping)

Millennium Series. The Soldiers' Tale

1999 (5 Oct.) *One centre phosphor band (19p) or two phosphor bands (others). Perf 14 × 14½*

2111	1421	19p black, stone and				
		silver	75	70	☐	☐
2112	1422	26p multicoloured	95	1·00	☐	☐
2113	1423	44p grey-black, black and				
		silver	2·00	1·60	☐	☐
2114	1424	64p multicoloured	2·50	2·40	☐	☐
		Set of 4	5·75	5·25	☐	☐
		First Day Cover		8·00		☐
		Presentation Pack	7·50		☐	
		PHQ Cards (set of 4)	8·50	13·00	☐	☐
		Set of 4 Gutter Pairs	13·00		☐	

For full information on all future British issues, collectors should write to Royal Mail, Freepost EH3647, 21 South Gyle Crescent, Edinburgh EH12 9PE.

1425 'Hark the herald angels sing', and Hymnbook (John Wesley)

1426 King James I and Bible (Authorised Version of Bible)

1431 'World of Literature' (Lisa Milroy)

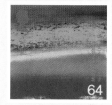

1432 'New Worlds' (Sir Howard Hodgkin)

Millennium Series. The Artists' Tale

1999 (7 DEC.) *One centre phosphor band* (19p) *or two phosphor bands* (others). *Perf* 14 × 14½

2119	**1429**	19p multicoloured	. . . .	75	70 □ □
2120	**1430**	26p multicoloured	. . . .	95	1·00 □ □
2121	**1431**	44p multicoloured	. . . .	1·50	1·60 □ □
2122	**1432**	64p multicoloured	. . . .	2·25	2·40 □ □
		Set of 4	. . . .	5·25	5·25 □ □
		First Day Cover	. . . .		8·00 □
		Presentation Pack	. . . . . .	7·50	□
		PHQ Cards (set of 4)	. . . . .	8·50	13·00 □ □
		Set of 4 Gutter Pairs	. . . . . .	13·00	□

1427 St Andrews Cathedral, Fife ('Pilgrimage')

1428 Nativity ('First Christmas')

Millennium Series. The Christians' Tale

1999 (2 NOV.) *One centre phosphor band* (19p) *or two phosphor bands* (others). *Perf* 14 × 14½

2115	**1425**	19p multicoloured	. . . .	75	70 □ □
2116	**1426**	26p multicoloured	. . . .	95	1·00 □ □
2117	**1427**	44p multicoloured	. . . .	1·50	1·60 □ □
2118	**1428**	64p multicoloured	. . . .	2·25	2·40 □ □
		Set of 4	. . . .	5·25	5·25 □ □
		First Day Cover	. . . .		8·00 □
		Presentation Pack	. . . .	7·50	□
		PHQ Cards (set of 4)	. . . . .	8·50	13·00 □ □
		Set of 4 Gutter Pairs	. . . . . .	13·00	□

Collectors Pack 1999

1999 (7 DEC.) *Comprises Nos.* 2069/76, 2080/105 *and* 2107/22

CP2122*a* Collectors Pack . . . . . £135 □

Post Office Yearbook

1999 (7 DEC.) *Comprises Nos.* 2069/76, 2080/105 *and* 2107/22 *in hardback book with slip case*

YB2122*a* Yearbook . . . . £135 □

1429 'World of the Stage' (Allen Jones)

1430 'World of Music' (Bridget Riley)

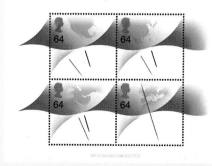

1433*a*

Millennium Series. 'Millennium Timekeeper'

1999 (14 DEC.) *Sheet* 120 × 89 *mm. Multicoloured. Two phosphor bands. Perf* 14 × 14½

MS2123 **1433a** 64p Clock face and map
of North America; 64p Clock face
and map of Asia; 64p Clock face
and map of Middle East; 64p Clock

face and map of Europe	26·00	26·00	□	□
First Day Cover		26·00		□
Presentation Pack	30·00		□	
PHQ Cards (set of 5)	14·00	32·00	□	□

No. **MS**2123 also exists overprinted 'EARLS COURT, LONDON 22–28 MAY 2000 THE STAMP SHOW 2000' from Exhibition Premium Passes, costing £10, available from 1 March 2000.

1437   Queen Elizabeth II

New Millennium

2000 (6 JAN.) *Photo De La Rue, Questa or Walsall* (No. 2124); *Questa or Walsall* (No. 2124d). *Two phosphor bands. Perf* 15 × 14 (*with one elliptical hole on each vertical side*)

2124 **1437** (1st) olive-brown	1·00	1·00	□	□
d. Perf 14	1·00	1·00	□	□
First Day Cover		3·00		□
Presentation Pack	6·00		□	
PHQ Card (23 May)	5·00	16·00	□	□

No. 2124 comes from sheets or stamp booklets and No. 2124d from booklets only.

1438   Barn Owl (World Owl
Trust, Muncaster)

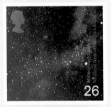

1439   Night Sky (National
Space Science
Centre, Leicester)

1440   River Goyt and Textile
Mills (Torrs Walkway,
New Mills)

1441   Cape Gannets
(Seabird Centre,
North Berwick)

Millennium Projects (1st series). 'Above and Beyond'

2000 (18 JAN.–26 MAY) *One centre phosphor band* (19p) *or two phosphor bands* (others). *Perf* 14 × 14½ (1st, 44p) *or* 13½ × 14 (*others*)

2125	**1438**	19p multicoloured . .	1·25	70	□	□
2126	**1439**	26p multicoloured . .	95	1·00	□	□
2126a		(1st) multicoloured				
		(26 May)	5·25	4·50	□	□
2127	**1440**	44p multicoloured . .	1·50	1·75	□	□
2128	**1441**	64p multicoloured . .	2·50	2·50	□	□
		Set of 4 (ex No. 2126a)	5·75	5·75	□	□
		First Day Cover		8·00		□
		Presentation Pack	6·50		□	
		PHQ Cards (set of 4)	8·50	13·00	□	□
		Set of 4 Gutter Pairs	15·00		□	

No. 2126a was only issued in £2·70 and £6·83 stamp booklets.

1442   Millennium Beacon
(Beacons across
the Land)

1443   Garratt Steam
Locomotive No. 143
pulling Train
(Rheilffordd Eryri,
Welsh Highland
Railway)

1444   Lightning (Dynamic
Earth Centre,
Edinburgh)

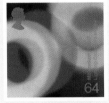

1445   Multicoloured Lights
(Lighting Croydon's
Skyline)

Millennium Projects (2nd series). 'Fire and Light'

2000 (1 FEB.) *One centre phosphor band* (19p) *or two phosphor bands* (others). *Perf* 14 × 14½

2129	**1442**	19p multicoloured	75	70	□	□
2130	**1443**	26p multicoloured	1·25	1·00	□	□
2131	**1444**	44p multicoloured	1·50	1·50	□	□
2132	**1445**	64p multicoloured	2·25	2·50	□	□
		Set of 4	5·50	5·50	□	□
		First Day Cover		8·00		□
		Presentation Pack	6·50		□	
		PHQ Cards (set of 4)	8·50	13·00	□	□
		Set of 4 Gutter Pairs	15·00		□	

1446 Queen Victoria and Queen Elizabeth II

2000 (15 Feb.) *Design T* **929**, *but redrawn with* '1st' *face value as* T **1446**. *Two phosphor bands. Perf* 14 (*with one elliptical hole on each vertical side*)

2133 **1446** (1st) brownish black
and cream . . . . . 1·50   1·25 □ □

No. 2133 was only issued in stamp booklets.

1451 Reed Beds, River Braid (ECOS, Ballymena)

1452 South American Leaf-cutter Ants ('Web of Life' Exhibition, London Zoo)

1447 Beach Pebbles (Turning the Tide, Durham Coast)

1448 Frog's Legs and Water Lilies (National Pondlife Centre, Merseyside)

1453 Solar Sensors (Earth Centre, Doncaster)

1454 Hydroponic Leaves (Project SUZY, Teesside)

Millennium Projects (4th series). 'Life and Earth'
2000 (4 Apr.) *One centre phosphor band* (2nd) *or two phosphor bands* (*others*). *Perf* 14 × 14½

2138	**1451**	(2nd) multicoloured . . .	75	70	□	□
2139	**1452**	(1st) multicoloured . . .	1·25	1·00	□	□
2140	**1453**	44p multicoloured . . .	1·50	1·50	□	□
2141	**1454**	64p multicoloured . . .	2·25	1·50	□	□
	Set of 4		5·50	5·50	□	□
	First Day Cover			8·00		
	Presentation Pack		6·50		□	
	PHQ Cards (set of 4)		8·50	13·00	□	□
	Set of 4 Gutter Pairs		15·00		□	

1449 Cliff Boardwalk (Parc Arfordirol, Llanelli Coast)

1450 Reflections in Water (Portsmouth Harbour Development)

Millennium Projects (3rd series). 'Water and Coast'
2000 (7 Mar.) *One centre phosphor band* (19p) *or two phosphor bands* (*others*). *Perf* 14 × 14½

2134	**1447**	19p multicoloured	75	70	□	□
2135	**1448**	26p multicoloured	1·25	1·00	□	□
2136	**1449**	44p black, grey and silver	1·50	1·50	□	□
2137	**1450**	64p multicoloured	2·25	2·50	□	□
	Set of 4		5·50	5·50	□	□
	First Day Cover			8·00		
	Presentation Pack		6·50		□	
	PHQ Cards (set of 4)		8·50	13·00	□	□
	Set of 4 Gutter Pairs		15·00		□	

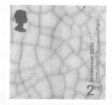

1455 Pottery Glaze (Ceramica Museum, Stoke-on-Trent)

1456 Bankside Galleries (Tate Modern, London)

1457 Road Marking (Cycle
Network Artworks)

1458 People of Salford
(Lowry Centre, Salford)

Millennium Projects (5th series). 'Art and Craft'

2000 (2 MAY) One centre phosphor band (2nd) or two phosphor bands (others). Perf 14 × 14½

2142	**1455**	(2nd) multicoloured . . .	75	70	☐	☐
2143	**1456**	(1st) multicoloured . . .	1·25	1·00	☐	☐
2144	**1457**	45p multicoloured . . .	1·50	1·50	☐	☐
2145	**1458**	65p multicoloured . . .	2·25	2·50	☐	☐
	Set of 4	. . . .	5·50	5·50	☐	☐
	First Day Cover	. . . .		8·00		☐
	Presentation Pack	. . . .	7·50		☐	
	PHQ Cards (set of 4)	. . . . . .	8·50	13·00	☐	☐
	Set of 4 Gutter Pairs	. . . . . .	15·00		☐	

'Stamp Show 2000' International Stamp Exhibition, London.
Jeffrey Matthews Colour Palette

2000 (22 MAY) Sheet, 124 × 70 mm, containing stamps as T **367** with two labels. Phosphorised paper. Perf 15 × 14 (with one elliptical hole on each vertical side)

MS2146 4p new blue; 5p dull red-brown;
6p yellow-olive; 10p dull orange;
31p dp mauve; 39p brt magenta;
64p turq-green; £1 bluish violet   24·00   24·00 ☐ ☐

First Day Cover . . . .   24·00   ☐

Exhibition Card (wallet, sold at £4.99, containing one mint sheet and one cancelled on postcard) . . . . 75·00   ☐

The £1 value is printed in Iriodin ink which gives a shiny effect to the solid part of the background behind the Queen's head.

1459

'Stamp Show 2000' International Stamp Exhibition, London.
'Her Majesty's Stamps'

2000 (23 MAY) Sheet 121 × 89 mm. Phosphorised paper. Perf 15 × 14 (with one elliptical hole on each vertical side of stamps as T **1437**)

MS2147 **1459** (1st) olive-brown (Type
1437) × 4; £1 slate-green (as Type
163) . . . . 21·00   21·00 ☐ ☐

First Day Cover . . . .   22·00   ☐

Presentation Pack . . . . £100   ☐

PHQ Cards (set of 2) . . . . . . 16·00   28·00 ☐ ☐

The £1 value is an adaptation of the 1953 Coronation 1s. 3d. stamp. It is shown on one of the PHQ cards with the other depicting the complete miniature sheet.

See also No. 2380 for T **163** from £7·46 stamp booklet.

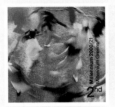

1460 Children playing
(Millennium Greens
Project)

1461 Millennium Bridge,
Gateshead

1462 Daisies (Mile End
Park, London)

1463 African Hut and
Thatched Cottage
('On the Meridian
Line' Project)

Millennium Projects (6th series). 'People and Places'

2000 (6 JUNE) One centre phosphor band (2nd) or two phosphor bands (others). Perf 14 × 14½

2148	**1460**	(2nd) multicoloured . . .	75	70	☐	☐
2149	**1461**	(1st) multicoloured . . .	1·25	1·00	☐	☐
2150	**1462**	45p multicoloured . . .	1·50	1·50	☐	☐
2151	**1463**	65p multicoloured . . .	2·25	2·50	☐	☐
	Set of 4	. . . .	5·50	5·50	☐	☐
	First Day Cover	. . . .		8·00		☐
	Presentation Pack	. . . .	7·50		☐	
	PHQ Cards (set of 4)	. . . . . .	8·50	13·00	☐	☐
	Set of 4 Gutter Pairs	. . . . . .	15·00		☐	

1464 Raising the Stone (Strangford Stone, Killyleagh)

1465 Horse's Hooves (Trans Pennine Trail, Derbyshire)

1470 Sycamore Seeds (Millennium Seed Bank, Wakehurst Place, Surrey)

1471 Forest, Doire Dach ('Forest for Scotland')

Millennium Projects (8th series). 'Tree and Leaf'

2000 (1 AUG.) *One centre phosphor band* (2nd) *or two phosphor bands* (others). *Perf* 14 × 14½

2156	**1468**	(2nd) multicoloured . . .	75	70	☐	☐
2157	**1469**	(1st) multicoloured . . .	1·25	1·00	☐	☐
2158	**1470**	45p multicoloured . . .	1·50	1·60	☐	☐
2159	**1471**	65p multicoloured . . .	2·50	2·50	☐	☐
	Set of 4		5·50	5·50	☐	☐
	First Day Cover			8·00		☐
	Presentation Pack		7·50		☐	
	PHQ Cards (*set of 4*)		8·50	13·00	☐	☐
	Set of 4 Gutter Pairs		15·00		☐	

1466 Cyclist (Kingdom of Fife Cycle Ways, Scotland)

1467 Bluebell Wood (Groundwork's 'Changing Places' Project)

Millennium Projects (7th series). 'Stone and Soil'

2000 (4 JULY) *One centre phosphor band* (2nd) *or two phosphor bands* (others). *Perf* 14 × 14½

2152	**1464**	(2nd) brownish black, grey-black and silver	75	70	☐	☐
2153	**1465**	(1st) multicoloured . . .	1·25	1·00	☐	☐
2154	**1466**	45p multicoloured . . .	1·50	1·75	☐	☐
2155	**1467**	65p multicoloured . . .	2·50	2·50	☐	☐
	Set of 4		5·50	5·75	☐	☐
	First Day Cover			8·00		☐
	Presentation Pack		7·50		☐	
	PHQ Cards (*set of 4*)		8·50	13·00	☐	☐
	Set of 4 Gutter Pairs		15·00		☐	

1472 Queen Elizabeth the Queen Mother

1468 Tree Roots ('Yews for the Millennium' Project)

1469 Sunflower ('Eden' Project, St. Austell)

1472a Royal Family on Queen Mother's 100th Birthday (from photo by J. Swannell)

Queen Elizabeth the Queen Mother's 100th Birthday

2000 (4 Aug.) *Phosphorised paper plus two phosphor bands. Perf 14½*

2160	**1472**	27p multicoloured . . .	2·50	2·75	☐	☐

MS2161 121 × 89 mm. **1472a** 27p Queen Elizabeth II; 27p Prince William; 27p Queen Elizabeth the Queen Mother; 27p Prince Charles ... 11·00 11·00 ☐ ☐

First Day Cover (**MS**2161)	. . . .		12·00	☐
Presentation Pack (**MS**2161)	. .	28·00		☐
PHQ Cards (set of 5)	. . . .	11·00	24·00	☐ ☐

No. 2160 was only issued in stamp booklets and in No. **MS**2161.

The complete miniature sheet is shown on one of the PHQ cards with the others depicting individual stamps.

1473 Head of *Gigantiops destructor* (Ant) (Wildscreen at Bristol)

1474 Gathering Water Lilies on Broads (Norfolk and Norwich Project)

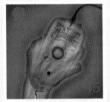

1475 X-ray of Hand holding Computer Mouse (Millennium Point, Birmingham)

1476 Tartan Wool Holder (Scottish Cultural Resources Access Network)

Millennium Projects (9th series). 'Mind and Matter'

2000 (5 Sept.) *One centre phosphor band (2nd) or two phosphor bands (others). Perf 14 × 14½*

2162	**1473**	(2nd) multicoloured . . .	75	70	☐	☐
2163	**1474**	(1st) multicoloured . . .	1·25	1·00	☐	☐
2164	**1475**	45p multicoloured . . .	1·50	1·75	☐	☐
2165	**1476**	65p multicoloured . . .	2·25	2·50	☐	☐
		Set of 4	5·50	5·75	☐	☐
		First Day Cover		8·00		☐
		Presentation Pack	7·50			☐
		PHQ Cards (set of 4)	8·50	13·00	☐	☐
		Set of 4 Gutter Pairs	15·00			☐

1477 Acrobatic Performers (Millennium Dome)

1478 Football Players (Hampden Park, Glasgow)

1479 Bather (Bath Spa Project)

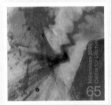

1480 Hen's Egg under Magnification (Centre for Life, Newcastle)

Millennium Projects (10th series). 'Body and Bone'

2000 (3 Oct.) *One centre phosphor band (2nd) or two phosphor bands (others). Perf 14 × 14½ (2nd) or 13½ × 14 (others).*

2166	**1477**	(2nd) black, slate-blue and silver	75	70	☐	☐
2167	**1478**	(1st) multicoloured . . .	1·25	1·00	☐	☐
2168	**1479**	45p multicoloured . . .	1·50	1·50	☐	☐
2169	**1480**	65p multicoloured . . .	2·25	2·50	☐	☐
		Set of 4	5·50	5·75	☐	☐
		First Day Cover		8·00		☐
		Presentation Pack	7·50			☐
		PHQ Cards (set of 4)	8·50	13·00	☐	☐
		Set of 4 Gutter Pairs	15·00			☐

1481 Virgin and Child Stained Glass Window, St. Edmundsbury Cathedral (Suffolk Cathedral Millennium Project)

1482 Floodlit Church of St. Peter and St. Paul, Overstowey (Church Floodlighting Trust)

1483 12th-cent. Latin Gradual (St. Patrick Centre, Downpatrick)

1484 Chapter House Ceiling, York Minster (York Millennium Mystery Plays)

Millennium Projects (11th series). 'Spirit and Faith'

2000 (7 Nov.) *One centre phosphor band* (2nd) *or two phosphor bands* (others). *Perf* 14 × 14½

2170	**1481**	(2nd) multicoloured . . .	75	70	□	□
2171	**1482**	(1st) multicoloured . . .	1·25	1·00	□	□
2172	**1483**	45p multicoloured . . .	1·50	1·50	□	□
2173	**1484**	65p multicoloured . . .	2·25	2·50	□	□
	Set of 4	. . . .	5·50	5·50	□	□
	First Day Cover	. . . .		8·00		□
	Presentation Pack	. . . .	7·50		□	
	PHQ Cards (set of 4)	. . . . . .	8·50	13·00	□	□
	Set of 4 Gutter Pairs	. . . . . .	15·00		□	

Post Office Yearbook

2000 (7 Nov.) *Comprises Nos.* **MS**2125/6, 2127/32, 2134/45, 2148/59 *and* **MS**2161/81 *in hardback book with slip case*

YB2181a   Yearbook   . . . .   £120   □

The last two issues in the Millennium Projects Series were supplied for insertion into the above at a later date.

1485 Church Bells (Ringing in the Millennium)

1486 Eye (Year of the Artist)

1487 Top of Harp (Canolfan Mileniwm, Cardiff)

1488 Figure within Latticework (TS2K Creative Enterprise Centres, London)

Millennium Projects (12th series). 'Sound and Vision'

2000 (5 Dec.) *One centre phosphor band* (2nd) *or two phosphor bands* (others). *Perf* 14 × 14½

2174	**1485**	(2nd) multicoloured . . .	75	70	□	□
2175	**1486**	(1st) multicoloured . . .	1·25	1·00	□	□
2176	**1487**	45p multicoloured . . .	1·50	1·50	□	□
2177	**1488**	65p multicoloured . . .	2·25	2·50	□	□
	Set of 4	. . . .	5·50	5·50	□	□
	First Day Cover	. . . .		8·00		□
	Presentation Pack	. . . .	7·50		□	
	PHQ Cards (set of 4)	. . . . . .	8·50	13·00	□	□
	Set of 4 Gutter Pairs	. . . . . .	15·00		□	

Collectors Pack 2000

2000 (5 Dec.) *Comprises Nos.* **MS**2125/6, 2127/32, 2134/45, 2148/59 *and* **MS**2161/81

CP2181a   Collectors Pack   . . . .   £120   □

1489 'Flower' ('Nurture Children')

1490 'Tiger' ('Listen to Children')

1491 'Owl' ('Teach Children')

1492 'Butterfly' ('Ensure Children's Freedom')

New Millennium. Rights of the Child. Face Paintings

2001 (16 Jan.) *One centre phosphor band* (2nd) *or two phosphor bands* (others). *Perf* 14 × 14½

2178	**1489**	(2nd) multicoloured . . .	75	75	□	□
2179	**1490**	(1st) multicoloured . . .	1·00	1·10	□	□
2180	**1491**	45p multicoloured . . .	1·60	1·75	□	□
2181	**1492**	65p multicoloured . . .	2·40	2·50	□	□
	Set of 4	. . . .	5·75	5·75	□	□
	First Day Cover	. . . .		7·50		□
	Presentation Pack	. . . .	7·50		□	
	PHQ Cards (set of 4)	. . . . . .	8·50	13·00	□	□
	Set of 4 Gutter Pairs	. . . . . .	14·00		□	

1493 'Love'

1494 'THANKS'

1495 'abc' (New Baby)

1496 'WELCOME'

1497 'Cheers'

'Occasions' Greetings Stamps

2001 (6 FEB.) *Two phosphor bands. Perf* 14½ × 14

2182	**1493**	(1st) multicoloured	. . . .	1·10	1·10 ☐	☐
2183	**1494**	(1st) multicoloured	. . . .	1·10	1·10 ☐	☐
2184	**1495**	(1st) multicoloured	. . . .	1·10	1·10 ☐	☐
2185	**1496**	(1st) multicoloured	. . . .	1·10	1·10 ☐	☐
2186	**1497**	(1st) multicoloured	. . . .	1·10	1·10 ☐	☐
		Set of 5	. . . .	5·00	5·00 ☐	☐
		First Day Cover	. . . .		6·50	☐
		Presentation Pack (13 Feb.)	. . .	6·50		☐
		PHQ Cards (set of 5)	. . . . . .	8·50	13·00 ☐	☐
		Set of 5 Gutter Pairs	. . . . .	13·00		☐

The silver-grey backgrounds are printed in Iriodin ink which gives a shiny effect.

Further packs of Nos. 2182/6 were sold from 3 July 2001. These comprised the listed stamps in blocks of ten (from sheets) with an insert describing the occasion (*Price* £10 *per pack*).

Nos. 2182/6 were printed in photogravure. They were subsequently re-issued on 1 May, as sheets of 20, printed in lithography instead of photogravure with each stamp accompanied by a half stamp-size label showing either postal symbols or a personal photograph.

1498 Dog and Owner on Bench

1499 Dog in Bath

1500 Boxer at Dog Show

1501 Cat in Handbag

1502 Cat on Gate

1503 Dog in Car

1504 Cat at Window

1505 Dog behind Fence

1506 Cat watching Bird

1507 Cat in Washbasin

T **1498/1507** were printed together in sheetlets of 10 (5 × 2), with the surplus self-adhesive paper around each stamp retained. The booklet pane has vertical roulettes between rows 2/3 and 4/5.

Cats and Dogs

2001 (13 FEB.) *Self-adhesive. Two phosphor bands. Die-cut perf* 15 × 14

2187	**1498**	(1st) black, grey and silver	60	50 ☐	☐
		a. Sheetlet. Nos. 2187/96	15·00	12·00 ☐	☐
		b. Booklet pane. Nos. 2187/96 *plus* Nos. 2040 × 2	15·00		☐
2188	**1499**	(1st) black, grey and silver	60	50 ☐	☐
2189	**1500**	(1st) black, grey and silver	60	50 ☐	☐
2190	**1501**	(1st) black, grey and silver	60	50 ☐	☐
2191	**1502**	(1st) black, grey and silver	60	50 ☐	☐
2192	**1503**	(1st) black, grey and silver	60	50 ☐	☐
2193	**1504**	(1st) black, grey and silver	60	50 ☐	☐
2194	**1505**	(1st) black, grey and silver	60	50 ☐	☐
2195	**1506**	(1st) black, grey and silver	60	50 ☐	☐
2196	**1507**	(1st) black, grey and silver	60	50 ☐	☐
		Set of 10	15·00	12·00 ☐	☐
		First Day Cover		15·00	☐
		Presentation Pack	20·00		☐
		PHQ Cards (set of 10)	14·00	30·00 ☐	☐

1508 'RAIN'

1509 'FAIR'

1510 'STORMY'

1511 'VERY DRY'

Nos. 2197/200 show the four quadrants of a barometer dial which are combined on the miniature sheet.

The Weather

2001 (13 Mar.) *One side phosphor band* (19p) *or two phosphor bands (others). Perf* 14½

2197	**1508**	19p multicoloured	. . . .	70	75 □ □
2198	**1509**	27p multicoloured	. . . .	85	1·00 □ □
2199	**1510**	45p multicoloured	. . . .	1·50	1·50 □ □
2200	**1511**	65p multicoloured	. . . .	2·40	2·50 □ □
		Set of 4	. . . .	5·00	5·50 □ □
		First Day Cover	. . . .		7·00 □
		Presentation Pack	. . . .	12·50	□
		Set of 4 Gutter Pairs	. . . . . .	14·00	□
MS2201	105 × 105 mm. Nos. 2197/200			13·00	13·00 □ □
		First Day Cover	. . . .		15·00 □
		PHQ Cards (set of 5)	. . . . . .	8·50	16·00 □ □

The reddish violet on both the 27p and the miniature sheet is printed in thermochromic ink which changes from reddish violet to light blue when exposed to heat.

The PHQ cards depict the four values and the miniature sheet.

1512 *Vanguard* Class Submarine, 1992

1513 *Swiftsure* Class Submarine, 1973

1514 *Unity* Class Submarine, 1939

1515 'Holland' Type Submarine, 1901

1516 White Ensign

1517 Union Jack

1518 Jolly Roger flown by H.M.S. *Proteus* (submarine)

1519 Flag of Chief of Defence Staff

Centenary of Royal Navy Submarine Service

2001 (10 Apr.–22 Oct.) *One centre phosphor band* (2nd) *or two phosphor bands (others). (a) Submarines. PVA gum. Perf* 15 × 14

2202	**1512**	(2nd) multicoloured	. . . .	70	75 □ □
		a. Perf 15½ × 15 (22 Oct.)		3·75	3·00 □ □
2203	**1513**	(1st) multicoloured	. . . .	85	90 □ □
		a. Perf 15½ × 15 (22 Oct.)		3·75	3·00 □ □
2204	**1514**	45p multicoloured	. . . .	1·75	1·60 □ □
		a. Perf 15½ × 15 (22 Oct.)		3·75	3·00 □ □
2205	**1515**	65p multicoloured	. . . .	2·40	2·50 □ □
		a. Perf 15½ × 15 (22 Oct.)		3·75	3·00 □ □
		Set of 4	. . . .	5·25	5·25 □ □
		First Day Cover	. . . .		7·50 □
		Presentation Pack	. . . .	7·50	□
		PHQ Cards (set of 4)	. . . . . .	8·50	14·00 □ □
		Set of 4 Gutter Pairs	. . . . . .	13·50	□

(b) Flags. Sheet 92 × 97 *mm. PVA gum. Perf* 14½

MS2206	**1516**	(1st) multicoloured;		
	1517	(1st) multicoloured; **1518**		
		(1st) multicoloured; **1519** (1st)		
		multicoloured (22 Oct.)	. . . .	9·00	9·00 □ □
		First Day Cover	. . . .		11·00 □
		Presentation Pack	. . . .	12·00	□
		PHQ Cards (set of 5)	. . . . . .	5·00	12·00 □ □

(c) Self-adhesive. Die-cut perf $15\frac{1}{2} \times 14$ (No. 2207)

or $14\frac{1}{2}$ (others)

2207	**1513**	(1st) multicoloured (17 Apr.)	40·00	37·00	☐	☐
2208	**1516**	(1st) multicoloured (22 Oct.)	12·00	12·00	☐	☐
2209	**1518**	(1st) multicoloured (22 Oct.)	12·00	12·00	☐	☐

Nos. 2202*a*/5*a* only come from stamp booklets.

The five PHQ cards depict the four designs and the complete miniature sheet.

Nos. 2207/9 only come from two different £1.62 booklets.

Type **1516** was re-issued on 21 June 2005 in sheets of 20, printed in lithography instead of photogravure, with half stamp-size *se-tenant* labels showing signal flags.

Designs as Type **1517** were issued on 27 July 2004 in sheets of 20 printed in lithography instead of photogravure with each vertical row of stamps alternated with half stamp-size labels.

1520 Leyland X2 Open-top, London General B Type, Leyland Titan TD1 and AEC Regent 1	**1521** AEC Regent 1, Daimler COG5, Utility Guy Arab Mk II and AEC Regent III RT Type

1522 AEC Regent III RT Type, Bristol KSW5G Open-top, AEC Routemaster and Bristol Lodekka FSF6G	**1523** Bristol Lodekka FSF6G, Leyland Titan PD3/4, Leyland Atlantean PDR1/1 and Daimler Fleetline CRG6LX-33

1524 Daimler Fleetline CRG6LX-33, MCW Metrobus DR102/43, Leyland Olympian ONLXB/1R and Dennis Trident

T **1520/4** were printed together, *se-tenant*, in horizontal strips of 5 throughout the sheet. The illustrations of the first bus on No. 2210 and the last bus on No. 2214 continue onto the sheet margins.

150th Anniversary of First Double-decker Bus

2001 (15 MAY) *'All-over' phosphor.* Perf $14\frac{1}{2} \times 14$

2210	**1520**	(1st) multicoloured ...	60	50	☐	☐
		a. Horiz strip of 5. Nos.				
		2210/14	5·25	5·50	☐	☐
2211	**1521**	(1st) multicoloured ...	60	50	☐	☐
2212	**1522**	(1st) multicoloured ...	60	50	☐	☐
2213	**1523**	(1st) multicoloured ...	60	50	☐	☐
2214	**1524**	(1st) multicoloured ...	60	50	☐	☐
		Set of 5	5·25	5·50	☐	☐
		First Day Cover		6·50		☐
		Presentation Pack	8·00		☐	
		PHQ Cards (set of 5)	8·50	24·00	☐	☐
		Gutter Strip of 10	12·00		☐	
MS2215		120 × 105 mm. Nos. 2210/14	9·75	9·75	☐	☐
		First Day Cover		15·00		☐

In No. **MS**2215 the illustrations of the AEC Regent III RT Type and the Daimler Fleetline CRG6LX-33 appear twice.

1525 Toque Hat by Pip Hackett	**1526** Butterfly Hat by Dai Rees

1527 Top Hat by Stephen Jones	**1528** Spiral Hat by Philip Treacy

Fashion Hats

2001 (19 JUNE) *'All-over' phosphor.* Perf $14\frac{1}{2}$

2216	**1525**	(1st) multicoloured ...	85	90	☐	☐
2217	**1526**	(E) multicoloured ...	1·10	1·25	☐	☐
2218	**1527**	45p multicoloured ...	1·60	1·60	☐	☐
2219	**1528**	65p multicoloured ...	2·50	2·50	☐	☐
		Set of 4	5·50	5·50	☐	☐
		First Day Cover		7·25		☐
		Presentation Pack	7·50		☐	
		PHQ Cards (set of 4)	8·50	14·00	☐	☐
		Set of 4 Gutter Pairs	13·00		☐	

1529 Common Frog

1530 Great Diving Beetle

1531 Three-spined Stickleback

1532 Southern Hawker Dragonfly

Europa. Pond Life

2001 (10 July) *Two phosphor bands*

2220	**1529**	(1st) multicoloured . . .	1·00	1·00 □	□
2221	**1530**	(E) multicoloured . . .	1·25	1·25 □	□
2222	**1531**	45p multicoloured . . .	1·50	1·50 □	□
2223	**1532**	65p multicoloured . . .	2·00	2·25 □	□
		Set of 4	5·50	5·75 □	□
		First Day Cover		11·00	□
		Presentation Pack	7·50		□
		PHQ Cards (*set of* 4)	8·50	14·00 □	□
		Set of 4 *Gutter Pairs*	15·00		□

The 1st and E values incorporate the 'EUROPA' emblem.
The bluish silver on all four values is in Iriodin ink and was used as a background for those parts of the design below the water line.

1533 Policeman

1534 Clown

1535 Mr. Punch

1536 Judy

1537 Beadle

1538 Crocodile

Nos. 2224/9 were printed together, *se-tenant*, in horizontal strips of 6 throughout the sheet.

Punch and Judy Show Puppets

2001 (4 Sept.) *Two phosphor bands*. (*a*) *PVA gum*. *Perf* 14 × 15

2224	**1533**	(1st) multicoloured . . .	60	50 □	□
		a. *Horiz strip of* 6.			
		Nos. 2224/9	5·50	5·50 □	□
2225	**1534**	(1st) multicoloured . . .	60	50 □	□
2226	**1535**	(1st) multicoloured . . .	60	50 □	□
2227	**1536**	(1st) multicoloured . . .	60	50 □	□
2228	**1537**	(1st) multicoloured . . .	60	50 □	□
2229	**1538**	(1st) multicoloured . . .	60	50 □	□
		Set of 6	5·50	5·50 □	□
		First Day Cover		7·00	□
		Presentation Pack	7·00		□
		PHQ Cards (*set of* 6)	8·50	18·00 □	□
		Gutter Block of 12	13·00		□

(*b*) *Self-adhesive. Die-cut perf* 14 × 15½

2230	**1535**	(1st) multicoloured . . .	15·00	15·00 □	□
2231	**1536**	(1st) multicoloured . . .	15·00	15·00 □	□

Nos. 2230/1 were only issued in £1.62 stamp booklets.

For full information on all future British issues, collectors should write to Royal Mail, Freepost EH3647, 21 South Gyle Crescent, Edinburgh EH12 9PE.

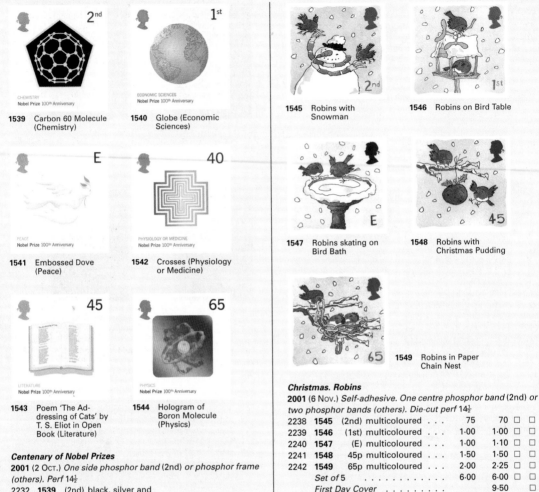

1539 Carbon 60 Molecule (Chemistry)

1540 Globe (Economic Sciences)

1541 Embossed Dove (Peace)

1542 Crosses (Physiology or Medicine)

1543 Poem 'The Addressing of Cats' by T. S. Eliot in Open Book (Literature)

1544 Hologram of Boron Molecule (Physics)

Centenary of Nobel Prizes

2001 (2 Oct.) *One side phosphor band* (2nd) *or phosphor frame (others). Perf* 14½

2232	**1539**	(2nd) black, silver and grey-black	75	65	□	□
2233	**1540**	(1st) multicoloured . . .	1·00	90	□	□
2234	**1541**	(E) black, silver and bright green	1·00	1·25	□	□
2235	**1542**	40p multicoloured . . .	1·25	1·25	□	□
2236	**1543**	45p multicoloured . . .	1·50	1·75	□	□
2237	**1544**	65p black and silver . .	2·25	2·50	□	□
	Set of 6	. . . .	7·50	7·50	□	□
	First Day Cover	. . . .		9·50		□
	Presentation Pack	. . . . . .	10·00		□	
	PHQ Cards (set of 6)	. . . . .	10·00	18·00	□	□
	Set of 6 Gutter Pairs	. . . . .	16·00		□	

The grey-black on No. 2232 is printed in thermochromic ink which temporarily changes to pale grey when exposed to heat. The centre of No. 2235 is coated with a eucalyptus scent.

1545 Robins with Snowman

1546 Robins on Bird Table

1547 Robins skating on Bird Bath

1548 Robins with Christmas Pudding

1549 Robins in Paper Chain Nest

Christmas. Robins

2001 (6 Nov.) *Self-adhesive. One centre phosphor band* (2nd) *or two phosphor bands* (others). *Die-cut perf* 14½

2238	**1545**	(2nd) multicoloured . . .	75	70	□	□
2239	**1546**	(1st) multicoloured . . .	1·00	1·00	□	□
2240	**1547**	(E) multicoloured . . .	1·00	1·10	□	□
2241	**1548**	45p multicoloured . . .	1·50	1·50	□	□
2242	**1549**	65p multicoloured . . .	2·00	2·25	□	□
	Set of 5	. . . .	6·00	6·00	□	□
	First Day Cover	. . . .		9·50		□
	Presentation Pack	. . . . . .	8·00		□	
	PHQ Cards (set of 5)	. . . . .	11·00	16·00	□	□

The 1st value was re-issued on 30 September 2003, in sheets of 20, in lithography instead of photogravure, each stamp *se-tenant* with a Christmas label or a personal photograph. The sheet contained die-cut perforated stamps and labels.

The 2nd and 1st class stamps were issued again on 1 November 2005 in sheets of 20 containing ten 1st class and ten 2nd class stamps, each stamp accompanied by a *se-tenant* label showing a snowman.

Collectors Pack 2001

2001 (6 Nov.) *Comprises Nos.* 2178/2200, 2202/**MS**2206, 2210/14, 2216/29 *and* 2232/42

CP2242a	Collectors Pack	. . . .	£120	□

Post Office Yearbook

2001 (6 Nov.) *Comprises Nos. 2178/96,* **MS**2201/6, **MS**2215/29 *and 2232/42 in hardback book with slip case*

YB2242a   Yearbook . . . .   £110   ☐

1550   'How the Whale got his Throat'

1551   'How the Camel got his Hump'

1552   'How the Rhinoceros got his Skin'

1553   'How the Leopard got his Spots'

1554   'The Elephant's Child'

1555   'The Sing-Song of Old Man Kangaroo'

1556   'The Beginning of the Armadillos'

1557   'The Crab that played with the Sea'

1558   'The Cat that walked by Himself'

1559   'The Butterfly that stamped'

T **1550/9** were printed together in sheetlets of 10 (5×2), with the surplus self-adhesive paper around each stamp retained.

Centenary of Publication of Rudyard Kipling's Just So Stories

2002 (15 JAN.) *Self-adhesive. Two phosphor bands. Die-cut perf 15 × 14*

2243	**1550**	(1st) multicoloured	. . . .	50	45	☐	☐
		a. Sheetlet. Nos. 2243/					
		52	. . . .	10·00	10·00	☐	☐
2244	**1551**	(1st) multicoloured	. . . .	50	45	☐	☐
2245	**1552**	(1st) multicoloured	. . . .	50	45	☐	☐
2246	**1553**	(1st) multicoloured	. . . .	50	45	☐	☐
2247	**1554**	(1st) multicoloured	. . . .	50	45	☐	☐
2248	**1555**	(1st) multicoloured	. . . .	50	45	☐	☐
2249	**1556**	(1st) multicoloured	. . . .	50	45	☐	☐
2250	**1557**	(1st) multicoloured	. . . .	50	45	☐	☐
2251	**1558**	(1st) multicoloured	. . . .	50	45	☐	☐
2252	**1559**	(1st) multicoloured	. . . .	50	45	☐	☐
	Set of 10	. . . .		10·00	10·00	☐	☐
	First Day Cover	. . . .			11·00		☐
	Presentation Pack	. . . .		15·00		☐	
	PHQ Cards (set of 10)	. . . . . .		8·50	28·00	☐	☐

1560   Queen Elizabeth II, 1952 (Dorothy Wilding)

1561   Queen Elizabeth II, 1968 (Cecil Beaton)

1562   Queen Elizabeth II, 1978 (Lord Snowdon)

1563   Queen Elizabeth II, 1984 (Yousef Karsh)

1564   Queen Elizabeth II, 1996 (Tim Graham)

1565

Golden Jubilee. Studio portraits of Queen Elizabeth II by photographers named

2002 (6 Feb.) *One centre phosphor band* (2nd) *or two phosphor bands* (others). W **1565**. *Perf* $14\frac{1}{2} \times 14$

2253	**1560**	(2nd) multicoloured	. . . .	75	55	□	□
2254	**1561**	(1st) multicoloured	. . . .	1·00	80	□	□
2255	**1562**	(E) multicoloured	. . . .	1·25	1·25	□	□
2256	**1563**	45p multicoloured	. . . .	1·50	1·50	□	□
2257	**1564**	65p multicoloured	. . . .	2·25	2·50	□	□
		Set of 5	. . . .	6·00	6·50	□	□
		First Day Cover	. . . .		9·00		□
		Presentation Pack	. . . .	7·50		□	
		PHQ Cards (set of 5)	. . . . . .	4·50	14·00	□	□
		Set of 5 Gutter Pairs		16·00		□	

Stamps from sheets had the watermark sideways: those from stamp booklets had the watermark upright.

1566

Booklet Stamps

2002 (6 Feb.) *Designs as* 1952-54 *issue, but with service indicator as T* **1566**. *One centre phosphor band* (2nd) *or two phosphor bands* (1st). W **1565**. *Uncoated paper. Perf* 15×14 (*with one elliptical hole on each vertical side*)

2258	**1566**	(2nd) carmine-red	. . . . .	1·20	1·00	□	□
2259	**154**	(1st) green	. . . .	1·25	1·25	□	□
		Set of 2	. . . .	2·40	2·25	□	□

Nos. 2258/9 were only issued in £7·29 stamp booklets.
See also Nos. 2031/3, **MS**2326, **MS**2367 and 2378/80.

1567 Rabbits ('a new baby')

1568 'LOVE'

1569 Aircraft Sky-writing 'hello'

1570 Bear pulling Potted Topiary Tree (Moving Home)

1571 Flowers ('best wishes')

'Occasions' Greetings Stamps

2002 (5 Mar.) 03 *Two phosphor bands.* (a) *Litho. PVA gum.* Perf 15×14

2260	**1567**	(1st) multicoloured	. . . .	1·00	1·00	□	□
2261	**1568**	(1st) multicoloured	. . . .	1·00	1·00	□	□
2262	**1569**	(1st) multicoloured	. . . .	1·00	1·00	□	□
2263	**1570**	(1st) multicoloured	. . . .	1·00	1·00	□	□
2264	**1571**	(1st) multicoloured	. . . .	1·00	1·00	□	□
		Set of 5	. . . .	4·75	4·75	□	□
		First Day Cover	. . . .		6·75		□
		Presentation Pack	. . . .	6·00		□	
		PHQ Cards (set of 5)	. . . . . .	4·50	14·00	□	□
		Set of 5 Gutter Pairs	. . . .	10·00		□	

(b) *Photo. Self-adhesive. Die-cut perf* 15×14

2264a	**1569**	(1st) multicoloured (4.3.03)	5·50	5·50	

Nos. 2260/4 were re-issued on 23 April 2002 in sheets of 20 perforated $14\frac{1}{2} \times 14$, either of one design or *se-tenant*, with each stamp accompanied by a half stamp-size label showing either greetings or a personal photograph.

No. 2262 was also issued in sheets of 20 with *se-tenant* labels in connection with the Hong Kong Stamp Expo on 30 January 2004. It was issued in sheets of 20 perforated $14\frac{1}{2} \times 14$ with *se-tenant* labels on 21 April 2005 for Pacific Explorer 2005 World Stamp Expo, on 25 May 2006 for Washington 2006 International Stamp Exhibition, and on 14 November 2006 for Belgica 2006 International Stamp Exhibition.

No. 2264a was only issued in £1·62 stamp booklets in which the surplus self-adhesive paper around each stamp was removed.

1572 Studland Bay, Dorset

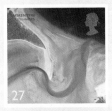

1573 Luskentyre, South Harris

1574 Cliffs, Dover, Kent

1575 Padstow Harbour, Cornwall

1576 Broadstairs, Kent

1577 St. Abb's Head, Scottish Borders

1578 Dunster Beach, Somerset

1579 Newquay Beach, Cornwall

1580 Portrush, County Antrim

1581 Sand-spit, Conwy

T **1572/81** were printed together, *se-tenant*, in blocks of 10 (5 × 2) throughout the sheet.

British Coastlines

2002 (19 MAR.) *Two phosphor bands. Perf* 14½

2265	**1572**	27p multicoloured	60	50	☐	☐
		a. Block of 10.				
		Nos. 2265/74	8·75	8·75	☐	☐
2266	**1573**	27p multicoloured	60	50	☐	☐
2267	**1574**	27p multicoloured	60	50	☐	☐
2268	**1575**	27p multicoloured	60	50	☐	☐
2269	**1576**	27p multicoloured	60	50	☐	☐
2270	**1577**	27p multicoloured	60	50	☐	☐
2271	**1578**	27p multicoloured	60	50	☐	☐
2272	**1579**	27p multicoloured	60	50	☐	☐
2273	**1580**	27p multicoloured	60	50	☐	☐
2274	**1581**	27p multicoloured	60	50	☐	☐
		Set of 10	8·75	8·75	☐	☐
		First Day Cover		11·50	☐	
		Presentation Pack	10·50		☐	
		PHQ Cards (set of 10)	9·25	28·00	☐	☐
		Gutter Block of 20	18·00		☐	

1582 Slack Wire Act

1583 Lion Tamer

1584 Trick Tri-cyclists

1585 Krazy Kar

1586 Equestrienne

Europa. Circus

2002 (10 APR.) *One centre phosphor band* (2nd) *or two phosphor bands* (others). *Perf* 14½

2275	**1582**	(2nd) multicoloured	50	60	☐	☐
2276	**1583**	(1st) multicoloured	75	85	☐	☐
2277	**1584**	(E) multicoloured	1·00	1·25	☐	☐
2278	**1585**	45p multicoloured	1·75	1·50	☐	☐
2279	**1586**	65p multicoloured	2·75	2·25	☐	☐
		Set of 5	6·00	6·00	☐	☐
		First Day Cover		8·00	☐	
		Presentation Pack	7·50		☐	
		PHQ Cards (set of 5)	4·50	14·00	☐	☐
		Set of 5 *Gutter Pairs*	14·00		☐	

The 1st and E values incorporate the "EUROPA" emblem.

Due to the funeral of the Queen Mother, the actual issue of Nos. 2275/9 was delayed from 9 April which is the date that appears on first day covers.

1587 Queen Elizabeth the Queen Mother

Queen Elizabeth the Queen Mother Commemoration

2002 (25 APR.) *Vert designs as T 955/8 with changed face values and showing both the Queen's head and frame in black as in T 1587. Two phosphor bands. Perf 14 × 15*

2280	**1587**	(1st) multicoloured	. . . .	1·00	85	☐	☐
2281	**956**	(E) black and indigo	. .	1·25	1·10	☐	☐
2282	**957**	45p multicoloured	. . . .	1·50	1·50	☐	☐
2283	**958**	65p black, stone and sepia		2·00	2·25	☐	☐
	Set of 4	. . . .		5·50	5·50	☐	☐
	First Day Cover	. . . .			8·00		☐
	Presentation Pack	. . . .		7·00		☐	
	Set of 4 Gutter Pairs	. . . . . .		14·00		☐	

50th Anniversary of Passenger Jet Aviation. Airliners

2002 (2 MAY) *One centre phosphor band (2nd) or two phosphor bands (others). Perf 14½. (a) Photo De La Rue. PVA gum*

2284	**1588**	(2nd) multicoloured	. . . .	75	55	☐	☐
2285	**1589**	(1st) multicoloured	. . . .	1·00	80	☐	☐
2286	**1590**	(E) multicoloured	. . . .	1·25	1·25	☐	☐
2287	**1591**	45p multicoloured	. . . .	1·50	1·50	☐	☐
2288	**1592**	65p multicoloured	. . . .	2·00	2·25	☐	☐
	Set of 5	. . . .		6·00	6·00	☐	☐
	First Day Cover	. . . .			8·00		☐
	Presentation Pack	. . . .		7·50		☐	
	Set of 5 Gutter Pairs	. . . . . .		14·00		☐	
MS2289	120 × 105 mm. Nos. 2284/8	.		9·00	9·00	☐	☐
	First Day Cover	. . . .			12·00	☐	
	PHQ Cards (set of 6)	. . . . . .		5·25	15·00	☐	☐

(b) Photo Questa. Self-adhesive

2290	**1589**	(1st) multicoloured	. . . .	6·50	6·50	☐	☐

The complete miniature sheet is shown on one of the PHQ cards with the others depicting individual stamps.

No. 2290 was only issued in £1.62 stamp booklets.

1588 Airbus A340-600 (2002)

1589 Concorde (1976)

1590 Trident (1964)

1591 VC 10 (1964)

1592 Comet (1952)

1593 Crowned Lion with Shield of St. George

1594 Top Left Quarter of English Flag, and Football

1595 Top Right Quarter of English Flag, and Football

1596 Bottom Left Quarter of English Flag, and Football

1597 Bottom Right Quarter of English Flag, and Football

World Cup Football Championship, Japan and Korea

2002 (21 May) *Two phosphor bands. Perf* $14\frac{1}{2} \times 14$ (*a*) *PVA gum*

2291	**1593**	(1st) deep turquoise-blue, scarlet-vermilion and silver	2·50	2·50	□	□

MS2292 145 × 74 mm. No. 2291; **1594** (1st) multicoloured; **1595** (1st) multi-coloured; **1596** (1st) multicoloured;

1597 (1st) multicoloured	5·50	5·75	□	□
First Day Cover (**MS**2292) . . .		9·00		□
Presentation Pack (**MS**2292) . .	6·25			□
PHQ Cards (*set of* 6)	5·25	12·00	□	□
Gutter Pair (*No.* 2291)	12·00			□

(*b*) *Self-adhesive. Die-cut perf* 15 × 14

2293	**1594**	(1st) multicoloured	4·50	4·50	□	□
2294	**1595**	(1st) multicoloured	4·50	4·50	□	□

The complete miniature sheet is shown on one of the PHQ cards with the others depicting individual stamps from **MS**2292 and No. 2291.

Nos. 2293/4 were only issued in £1.62 stamp booklets.

Stamps as Type **1597** were also issued in sheets of 20, *se-tenant* with half stamp-sized labels, printed in lithography instead of photogravure. The labels show either match scenes or personal photographs.

Self-adhesive Stamps

2002 (5 June–4 July) *Self-adhesive. Photo Questa, Walsall or Enschedé* (*No.* 2295) *or Walsall* (*others*). *Two phosphor bands. Perf* 15 × 14 *die-cut* (*with one elliptical hole on each vertical side*)

2295	**914**	(1st) gold	1·00	1·00	□	□
2296	**1093a**	(E) deep blue (4 July) . . .	1·25	1·25	□	□
2297	**367a**	42p deep olive-grey (4 July)	1·25	1·25	□	□
2298		68p grey-brown (4 July) .	2·00	2·00	□	□
	Set of 4	. . . .	5·00	5·00	□	□
	PHQ Card (*No.* 2295)	45	2·00	□	□

Further printings of No. 2295 in sheets of 100 appeared on 4 July 2002 produced by Enschedé and on 18 March 2003 printed by Walsall.

1598 Swimming

1599 Running

1600 Cycling

1601 Long Jumping

1602 Wheelchair Racing

17th Commonwealth Games, Manchester

2002 (16 July) *One side phosphor band* (2nd) *or two phosphor bands* (*others*). *Perf* $14\frac{1}{2}$

2299	**1598**	(2nd) multicoloured	75	55	□	□
2300	**1599**	(1st) multicoloured	1·00	80	□	□
2301	**1600**	(E) multicoloured	1·25	1·25	□	□
2302	**1601**	47p multicoloured	1·50	1·50	□	□
2303	**1602**	68p multicoloured	2·00	2·25	□	□
	Set of 5	. . . .	6·00	6·00	□	□
	First Day Cover		8·00		□
	Presentation Pack	7·50			□
	PHQ Cards (*set of* 5)	4·75	15·00	□	□
	Set of 5 *Gutter Pairs*	14·00			□

1603 Tinkerbell

1604 Wendy, John and Michael Darling in front of Big Ben

1605 Crocodile and Alarm Clock

1606 Captain Hook

1607 Peter Pan

150th Anniversary of Great Ormond Street Children's Hospital. Peter Pan by Sir James Barrie

2002 (20 Aug.) *One centre phosphor band* (2nd) *or two phosphor bands* (others). *Perf* 15 × 14

2304	**1603**	(2nd) multicoloured	. . . .	75	55	☐	☐
2305	**1604**	(1st) multicoloured	. . . .	1·00	80	☐	☐
2306	**1605**	(E) multicoloured	. . . .	1·25	1·25	☐	☐
2307	**1606**	47p multicoloured	. . . .	1·50	1·50	☐	☐
2308	**1607**	68p multicoloured	. . . .	2·00	2·25	☐	☐
	Set of 5	. . . .		6·00	6·00	☐	☐
	First Day Cover	. . . .			8·00		☐
	Presentation Pack	. . . . . .		7·50		☐	
	PHQ Cards (set of 5)	. . . . . .		4·75	15·00	☐	☐
	Set of 5 Gutter Pairs	. . . . . .		14·00		☐	

1608 Millennium Bridge, 2001

1609 Tower Bridge, 1894

1610 Westminster Bridge, 1864

1611 'Blackfriars Bridge, c1800' (William Marlow)

1612 'London Bridge, c1670' (Wenceslaus Hollar)

Bridges of London

2002 (10 Sept.) *One centre phosphor band* (2nd) *or two phosphor bands* (others). (a) *Litho. PVA gum. Perf* 15 × 14

2309	**1608**	(2nd) multicoloured	. . . .	75	55	☐	☐
2310	**1609**	(1st) multicoloured	. . . .	1·00	80	☐	☐
2311	**1610**	(E) multicoloured	. . . .	1·25	1·25	☐	☐
2312	**1611**	47p multicoloured	. . . .	1·50	1·50	☐	☐
2313	**1612**	68p multicoloured	. . . .	2·00	2·25	☐	☐
	Set of 5	. . . .		6·50	6·00	☐	☐
	First Day Cover	. . . .			9·00		☐
	Presentation Pack	. . . .		8·00		☐	
	PHQ Cards (set of 5)	. . . . .		4·00	9·00	☐	☐
	Set of 5 Gutter Pairs	. . . . . .		15·00		☐	

(b) *Photo. Self-adhesive. Die-cut perf* 14½ × 14

2314	**1609**	(1st) multicoloured	. . . .	6·00	6·00	☐	☐

No. 2314 was only issued in £1.62 stamp booklets.

1613 Galaxies and Nebula

Astronomy

2002 (24 Sept.) *Sheet* 120 × 89 *mm. Multicoloured. Two phosphor bands. Perf* 14½ × 14

MS2315	**1613**	(1st) Planetary nebula in Aquila; (1st) Seyfert 2 galaxy in Pegasus; (1st) Planetary nebula in Norma; (1st) Seyfert 2 galaxy in Circinus	. . . .	5·25	5·25	☐	☐
	First Day Cover	. . . .			5·75		☐
	Presentation Pack	. . . .		5·50		☐	
	PHQ Cards (set of 5)	. . . . .		4·75	18·00	☐	☐

The five PHQ cards depict the four designs and the complete miniature sheet.

1614 Green Pillar Box, 1857

1615 Horizontal Aperture Box, 1874

1616 Air Mail Box, 1934

1617 Double Aperture Box, 1939

1618 Modern Style Box, 1980

1619 Blue Spruce Star

1620 Holly

1621 Ivy

1622 Mistletoe

1623 Pine Cone

150th Anniversary of the First Pillar Box

2002 (8 Oct.) *One centre phosphor band* (2nd) *or two phosphor bands* (*others*)*. Perf* 14 × 14½

2316	**1614**	(2nd)	multicoloured	. . . .	75	55 □ □
2317	**1615**	(1st)	multicoloured	. . . .	1·00	80 □ □
2318	**1616**	(E)	multicoloured	. . . .	1·25	1·25 □ □
2319	**1617**	47p	multicoloured	. . . .	1·50	1·50 □ □
2320	**1618**	68p	multicoloured	. . . .	2·00	2·25 □ □
	Set of 5		. . . .		6·00	6·00 □ □
	First Day Cover		. . . .			8·50 □
	Presentation Pack		. . . .		7·50	□
	PHQ Cards (*set of* 5)		. . . . .		4·75	16·00 □ □
	Set of 5 *Gutter Pairs*		. . . . . .		14·00	□

Christmas

2002 (5 Nov.) *Self-adhesive. One centre phosphor band* (2nd) *or two phosphor bands* (*others*)*. Die-cut perf* 14½ × 14

2321	**1619**	(2nd)	multicoloured	. . .	75	55 □ □
2322	**1620**	(1st)	multicoloured	. . . .	1·00	80 □ □
2323	**1621**	(E)	multicoloured	. . . .	1·25	1·25 □ □
2324	**1622**	47p	multicoloured	. . . .	1·50	1·50 □ □
2325	**1623**	68p	multicoloured	. . . .	2·00	2·25 □ □
	Set of 5		. . . .		6·00	6·00 □ □
	First Day Cover		. . . .			8·50 □
	Presentation Pack		. . . .		7·50	□
	PHQ Cards (*set of* 5)		. . . . . .		4·75	16·00 □ □

Collectors Pack 2002

2002 (5 Nov.) *Comprises Nos.* 2243/57, 2260/4, 2265/88, 2291/2, 2299/313 *and* **MS**2315/25

CP2325*a*	*Collectors Pack*	. . . .	£100	□

Post Office Yearbook

2002 (5 Nov.) *Comprises Nos.* 2243/57, 2260/4, 2265/88, 2291//2, 2299/313 *and* **MS**2315/25 *in hardback book with slip case*

YB2325*a*	*Yearbook*	. . . .	95·00	□

50th Anniversary of Wilding Definitives (1st issue)

2002 (5 DEC.) *Sheet, 124 × 70 mm, containing designs as T **154/5** and **157/60** (1952–54 issue), but with values in decimal currency as T **1348** or with service indicator as T **1566**, printed on pale cream. One centre phosphor band (2nd) or two phosphor bands (others). W **1565**. Perf 15 × 14 (with one elliptical hole on each vertical side)*

MS2326 1p orange-red; 2p ultramarine; 5p red-brown; (2nd) carmine-red; (1st) green; 33p brown; 37p magenta; 47p bistre-brown; 50p green and label showing national emblems	10·00	10·00	□	□
First Day Cover		10·00		□
Presentation Pack	£100		□	
PHQ Cards (set of 5)	3·00	12·00	□	□

The PHQ cards depict the (2nd), (1st), 33p, 37p and 47p stamps.

See also No. **MS**2367.

1624 Barn Owl landing

1625 Barn Owl with folded Wings and Legs down

1626 Barn Owl with extended Wings and Legs down

1627 Barn Owl in Flight with Wings lowered

1628 Barn Owl in Flight with Wings raised

1629 Kestrel with Wings folded

1630 Kestrel with Wings fully extended upwards

1631 Kestrel with Wings horizontal

1632 Kestrel with Wings partly extended downwards

1633 Kestrel with Wings fully extended downwards

T **1624/33** were printed together, *se-tenant*, in blocks of 10 (5 × 2) throughout the sheet.

Birds of Prey

2003 (14 JAN.) *Phosphor background. Perf 14½*

2327	**1624**	(1st) multicoloured	70	80	□	□
		a. Block of 10.				
		Nos. 2327/36	9·00	8·75	□	□
2328	**1625**	(1st) multicoloured	70	80	□	□
2329	**1626**	(1st) multicoloured	70	80	□	□
2330	**1627**	(1st) multicoloured	70	80	□	□
2331	**1628**	(1st) multicoloured	70	80	□	□
2332	**1629**	(1st) multicoloured	70	80	□	□
2333	**1630**	(1st) multicoloured	70	80	□	□
2334	**1631**	(1st) multicoloured	70	80	□	□
2335	**1632**	(1st) multicoloured	70	80	□	□
2336	**1633**	(1st) multicoloured	70	80	□	□
		Set of 10	9·00	8·75	□	□
		First Day Cover		11·00		□
		Presentation Pack	12·00		□	
		PHQ Cards (set of 10)	9·25	28·00	□	□
		Gutter Block of 20	24·00		□	

1634 'Gold star, See me, Playtime'

1635 '1♥U, XXXX, S.W.A.L.K.'

1636 'Angel, Poppet, Little terror'

1637 'Yes, No, Maybe'

1638 'Oops!, Sorry, Will try harder'

1639 'I did it!, You did it!, We did it!'

T **2337/42** were printed together, *se-tenant*, in blocks of 6 (3 × 2) throughout the sheet.

'Occasions' Greetings Stamps

2003 (4 Feb.) *Two phosphor bands. Perf 14½ × 14*

2337	**1634**	(1st) lemon and new blue	60	50	□	□
		a. Block of 6. Nos. 2337/42	5·50	5·50	□	□
2338	**1635**	(1st) red and deep ultramarine	60	50	□	□
2339	**1636**	(1st) purple and bright yellow-green	60	50	□	□
2340	**1637**	(1st) bright yellow-green and red	60	50	□	□
2341	**1638**	(1st) deep ultramarine and lemon	60	50	□	□
2342	**1639**	(1st) new blue and purple	60	50	□	□
		Set of 6	5·50	5·50	□	□
		First Day Cover		9·00		□
		Presentation Pack	7·00		□	
		PHQ Cards (set of 6)	5·25	18·00	□	□
		Gutter Block of 12	7·00		□	

Nos. 2337/42 were also available in *se-tenant* sheets of 20 containing four examples of Nos. 2338 and 2340 and three of each of the others. The stamps are accompanied by half stamp-size printed labels or a personal photograph.

1640 Completing the Genome Jigsaw

1641 Ape with Moustache and Scientist

1642 DNA Snakes and Ladders

1643 'Animal Scientists'

1644 Genome Crystal Ball

50th Anniversary of Discovery of DNA

2003 (25 Feb.) *One centre phosphor band* (2nd) *or two phosphor bands* (others). *Perf 14½*

2343	**1640**	(2nd) multicoloured	1·00	55	□	□
2344	**1641**	(1st) multicoloured	1·00	80	□	□
2345	**1642**	(E) multicoloured	1·25	1·25	□	□
2346	**1643**	47p multicoloured	1·50	1·50	□	□
2347	**1644**	68p multicoloured	2·00	2·25	□	□
		Set of 5	6·50	6·00	□	□
		First Day Cover		10·00		□
		Presentation Pack	8·00		□	
		PHQ Cards (set of 5)	4·75	18·00	□	□
		Set of 5 Gutter Pairs	15·00		□	

1645 Strawberry

1646 Potato

1647 Apple

1648 Red Pepper

1649 Pear

1650 Orange

1651 Tomato

1652 Lemon

1653 Cabbage

1654 Aubergine

T **1645/54** were printed together in sheets of 10 with the surplus self-adhesive paper around each stamp retained. The stamp pane is accompanied by a similar-sized pane of self-adhesive labels showing ears, eyes, mouths, hats etc which are intended for the adornment of fruit and vegetables depicted. This pane is separated from the stamps by a line of roulettes.

Fruit and Vegetables

2003 (25 Mar.) *Self-adhesive. Two phosphor bands. Perf* $14\frac{1}{2}$ × 14 *die-cut (without teeth around protruding tops or bottoms of the designs)*

2348	**1645**	(1st) multicoloured	. . . .	70	50 □	□
		a. *Sheetlet. Nos.* 2348/57				
		and pane of				
		decorative labels . .	10·00	9·00 □	□
2349	**1646**	(1st) multicoloured	. . . .	70	50 □	□
2350	**1647**	(1st) multicoloured	. . . .	70	50 □	□
2351	**1648**	(1st) multicoloured	. . . .	70	50 □	□
2352	**1649**	(1st) multicoloured	. . . .	70	50 □	□
2353	**1650**	(1st) multicoloured	. . . .	70	50 □	□
2354	**1651**	(1st) multicoloured	. . . .	70	50 □	□
2355	**1652**	(1st) multicoloured	. . . .	70	50 □	□
2356	**1653**	(1st) multicoloured	. . . .	70	50 □	□
2357	**1654**	(1st) multicoloured	. . . .	70	50 □	□
		Set of 10	10·00	9·00 □	□
		First Day Cover		12·00	□
		Presentation Pack	65·00		□
		PHQ Cards (*set of* 10)	9·25	12·00 □	□

Nos. 2348/57 were re-issued on 7th March 2006 in sheets of 20 containing two of each of the ten designs, each stamp accompanied by a *se-tenant* speech bubble label. These sheets were printed in lithography instead of photogravure, and have stickers showing eyes, hats, etc in the sheet margin.

1655

Overseas Booklet Stamps

2003 (27 Mar.)–**2004** *Self-adhesive. Two phosphor bands. Perf* 15 × 14 *die-cut with one elliptical hole on each vertical side*

2357*a*		(Worldwide postcard)			
		grey-black, rosine			
		and ultramarine . . .	65	70 □	□
2358	**1655**	(Europe) new blue and			
		rosine	80	85 □	□
2359		(Worldwide) rosine and			
		new blue	1·60	1·70 □	□
		First Day Cover (*Nos.* 2358/9) .		5·25	□
		Presentation Pack (*Nos.* 2358/9)	3·00		□
		PHQ Card (*No.* 2358)	45	2·00 □	□

Nos. 2358/9 were intended to pay postage on mail up to 40 grams to either Europe (52p) or to foreign destinations outside Europe (£1.12). No. 2359*a* was intended to pay postcard rate to foreign destinations (43p).

Operationally they were only available in separate booklets of 4, initially sold at £2.08, £4.48 and £1.72, with the surplus self-adhesive paper around each stamp removed. Single examples of the stamps were available from philatelic outlets as sets of two or in presentation packs.

For first day cover and presentation pack for No. 2357*a* see below Nos. Y1667/1803.

1656 Amy Johnson (pilot) and Biplane

1657 Members of 1953 Everest Team

1658 Freya Stark (traveller and writer) and Desert

1659 Ernest Shackleton (Antarctic explorer) and Wreck of *Endurance*

1660 Francis Chichester (yachtsman) and *Gipsy Moth IV*

1661 Robert Falcon Scott (Antarctic explorer) and Norwegian Expedition at the Pole

Extreme Endeavours (British Explorers)

2003 (29 APR.) *One centre phosphor band* (2nd) *or two phosphor bands* (others). (*a*) *Photo Questa. PVA gum. Perf* 15 × 14½

2360	**1656**	2nd) multicoloured	. . . .	50	50 □ □
2361	**1657**	(1st) multicoloured	. . . .	75	75 □ □
2362	**1658**	(E) multicoloured	. . . .	1·25	1·50 □ □
2363	**1659**	42p multicoloured	. . . .	1·25	1·75 □ □
2364	**1660**	47p multicoloured	. . . .	1·50	2·00 □ □
2365	**1661**	68p multicoloured	. . . .	2·00	2·50 □ □
		Set of 6	. . . .	7·00	7·75 □ □
		First Day Cover	. . . .		12·00 □
		Presentation Pack	. . . .	9·00	□
		PHQ Cards (set of 6)	. . . . . .	3·25	12·00 □ □
		Set of 6 Gutter Pairs	. . . . . .	16·00	□

(*b*) *Photo De La Rue. Self-adhesive. Die-cut perf* 14½

2366	**1657**	(1st) multicoloured	. . . .	3·00	3·00 □ □

The phosphor bands on Nos. 2361/5 are at the centre and right of each stamp.

No. 2366 was only issued in £1.62 stamp booklets in which the surplus self-adhesive paper around each stamp was removed.

50th Anniversary of Wilding Definitives (2nd issue)

2003 (20 MAY) *Sheet, 124 × 70 mm, containing designs as T **155/8** and **160** (1952–54 issue), but with values in decimal currency as T **1348** or with service indicator as T **1566**, printed on pale cream. One centre phosphor band* (20p) *or two phosphor bands* (others). *W* **1565**. *P* 15 × 14 (*with one elliptical hole on each vertical side*).

MS2367	4p deep lilac; 8p ultramarine; 10p reddish purple; 20p bright green; 28p bronze-green; 34p brown-purple; (E) chestnut; 42p Prussian blue; 68p grey-blue and label showing national emblems	10·50	11·25 □ □
	First Day Cover		13·00 □
	Presentation Pack	18·00	□

1662 Guardsmen in Coronation Procession

1663 East End Children reading Coronation Party Poster

1664 Queen Elizabeth II in Coronation Chair with Bishops of Durham and Bath & Wells

1665 Children in Plymouth working on Royal Montage

1666 Queen Elizabeth II in Coronation Robes (photograph by Cecil Beaton)

1667 Children's Race at East End Street Party

1668 Coronation Coach passing through Marble Arch

1669 Children in Fancy Dress

1670 Coronation Coach outside Buckingham Palace

1671 Children eating at London Street Party

T **1662/71** were printed together, *se-tenant*, in blocks of 10 (5 × 2) throughout sheets of 60

50th Anniversary of Coronation

2003 (2 June) W **1565**. *Two phosphor bands. Perf* 14½ × 14

2368	**1662**	(1st) multicoloured	45	50	□	□
		a. Block of 10.				
		Nos. 2368/77	8·75	8·75	□	□
2369	**1663**	(1st) black and gold	45	50	□	□
2370	**1664**	(1st) multicoloured	45	50	□	□
2371	**1665**	(1st) black and gold	45	50	□	□
2372	**1666**	(1st) multicoloured	45	50	□	□
2373	**1667**	(1st) black and gold	45	50	□	□
2374	**1668**	(1st) multicoloured	45	50	□	□
2375	**1669**	(1st) black and gold	45	50	□	□

2376	**1670**	(1st) multicoloured	45	50	□	□
2377	**1671**	(1st) black and gold	45	50	□	□
		Set of 10	8·75	8·75	□	□
		First Day Cover		12·00		□
		Presentation Pack	25·00			□
		PHQ Cards (set of 10)	3·75	12·00	□	□
		Gutter Block of 20	20·00			□

No. 2372 does not show the Queen's head in gold as do the other nine designs.

50th Anniversary of Coronation. Booklet Stamps

2003 (2 June) *Designs as T* **160** (*Wilding definitive of 1952*) *and* **163** (*Coronation commemorative of 1953*), *but with values in decimal currency as T* **1348**. *W* **1565**. *Two phosphor bands. P* 15 × 14 (*with one elliptical hole on each vertical side for Nos. 2378/9*)

2378	**160**	47p bistre-brown	5·00	2·50	□	□
2379		68p grey-blue	5·00	2·50	□	□
2380	**163**	£1 deep yellow-green . . .	50·00	45·00	□	□
		Set of 3	55·00	45·00	□	□

Nos. 2378/80 were only available in £7.46 stamp booklets. Stamps as Nos. 2378/9, but on pale cream, were also included in the Wilding miniature sheets, Nos. **MS**2326 or **MS**2367. A £1 design as No. 2380, but on phosphorised paper, was previously included in the "Stamp Show 2000" miniature sheet, No. **MS**2147.

1672 Prince William in September 2001 (Brendan Beirne)

1673 Prince William in September 2000 (Tim Graham)

1674 Prince William in September 2001 (Camera Press)

1675 Prince William in September 2001 (Tim Graham)

21st Birthday of Prince William of Wales

2003 (17 June) *Phosphor backgrounds. Perf* 14½

2381	**1672**	28p multicoloured	1·00	50	□	□
2382	**1673**	(E) dull mauve, grey-black and light green . . .	1·25	1·50	□	□

2383	**1674**	47p multicoloured	1·75	2·00	□	□
2384	**1675**	68p sage-green, black and				
		bright green	2·50	2·50	□	□
		Set of 4	6·00	6·00	□	□
		First Day Cover		10·00		□
		Presentation Pack	25·00		□	
		PHQ Cards (set of 4)	2·50	10·00	□	□
		Set of 4 Gutter Pairs	13·00		□	

1676 Loch Assynt,
Sutherland

1677 Ben More, Isle of Mull

1678 Rothiemurchus,
Cairngorms

1679 Dalveen Pass, Lowther
Hills

1680 Glenfinnan Viaduct,
Lochaber

1681 Papa Little, Shetland
Islands

A British Journey: Scotland
2003 (15 JULY) *One centre phosphor band* (2nd) *or two
phosphor bands* (others). *Perf* 14½. (a) *PVA gum*

2385	**1676**	(2nd) multicoloured	50	35	□	□
2386	**1677**	(1st) multicoloured	75	50	□	□
2387	**1678**	(E) multicoloured	1·25	1·25	□	□

2388	**1679**	42p multicoloured	1·25	1·50	□	□
2389	**1680**	47p multicoloured	1·50	2·00	□	□
2390	**1681**	68p multicoloured	2·00	2·50	□	□
		Set of 6	7·00	7·75	□	□
		First Day Cover		11·00		□
		Presentation Pack	9·50		□	
		PHQ Cards (set of 6)	2·25	11·00	□	□
		Set of 6 Gutter Pairs	16·00		□	

(b) Self-adhesive. Die-cut perf 14½

2391	**1677**	(1st) multicoloured . . .	6·00	6·00	□	□

No. 2391 was only issued in £1.68 stamp booklets in which
the surplus self-adhesive paper around each stamp was
removed.

1682 'The Station'
(Andrew Davidson)

1683 'Black Swan'
(Stanley Chew)

1684 'The Cross Keys'
(George Mackenney)

1685 'The Mayflower'
(Ralph Ellis)

1686 'The Barley Sheaf' (Joy Cooper)

Europa. British Pub Signs
2003 (12 AUG.) *Two phosphor bands. Perf* 14 × 14½

2392	**1682**	(1st) multicoloured	75	50	□	□
2393	**1683**	(E) multicoloured	2·00	2·00	□	□
2394	**1684**	42p multicoloured	1·50	1·50	□	□
2395	**1685**	47p multicoloured	1·75	2·00	□	□

2396 **1686**	68p multicoloured	. . . .	2·00	2·25	□	□
	Set of 5	. . . .	7·50	7·75	□	□
	First Day Cover	. . . .		11·00		□
	Presentation Pack	. . . .	9·00			□
	PHQ Cards (set of 5)	. . . . . .	2·75	11·00	□	□
	Set of 5 Gutter Pairs	. . . . . .	17·00			□

The 1st and E values incorporate the "EUROPA" emblem.

MECCANO
Constructor Biplane c 1931

WELLS-BRIMTOY
Clockwork Double-decker Omnibus c 1938

1687 Meccano Constructor Biplane, *c.* 1931

1688 Wells-Brimtoy Clockwork Double-decker Omnibus, *c.* 1938

HORNBY
M1 Clockwork Locomotive and Tender c 1948

DINKY TOYS
Ford Zephyr c 1956

1689 Hornby M1 Clockwork Locomotive and Tender, *c.* 1948

1690 Dinky Toys Ford Zephyr, *c.* 1956

METTOY
Friction Drive
Space Ship Eagle c 1960

1691 Mettoy Friction Drive Space Ship Eagle, *c.* 1960

Classic Transport Toys

2003 (18 SEPT.) *Two phosphor bands.* (*a*) *Photo Enschedé. PVA gum. Perf* 14½ × 14

2397 **1687**	(1st) multicoloured	. . . .	75	50	□	□
2398 **1688**	(E) multicoloured	. . . .	1·25	1·25	□	□
2399 **1689**	42p multicoloured	. . . .	1·50	1·50	□	□
2400 **1690**	47p multicoloured	. . . .	1·75	1·75	□	□
2401 **1691**	68p multicoloured	. . . .	2·00	2·50	□	□
	Set of 5	. . . .	7·00	7·25	□	□
	First Day Cover	. . . .		10·00		□
	Presentation Pack	. . . .	9·00			□
	PHQ Cards (set of 6)	. . . . . .	2·75	10·00	□	□
	Set of 5 Gutter Pairs	. . . . . .	16·00			□
MS2402	115 × 105 mm. Nos. 2397/401		7·00	8·25	□	□
	First Day Cover	. . . .		14·00		□

(*b*) *Photo DLR. Self-adhesive. Die-cut perf* 14½ × 14

2403 **1687**	(1st) multicoloured	. . . .	6·00	6·00	□	□

The complete miniature sheet is shown on one of the PHQ cards with the others depicting individual stamps.

No. 2403 was only issued in £1.68 stamp booklets in which the surplus self-adhesive paper around each stamp was removed.

1692 Coffin of Denytenamun, Egyptian, *c.* 900BC

1693 Alexander the Great, Greek, *c.* 200BC

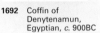
1694 Sutton Hoo Helmet, Anglo-Saxon, *c.* AD600

1695 Sculpture of Parvati, South Indian, *c.* AD1550

1696 Mask of Xiuhtecuhtli, Mixtec-Aztec, *c.* AD1500

1697 Hoa Hakananai'a, Easter Island, *c.* AD1000

250th Anniversary of the British Museum

2003 (7 Oct.) *One side phosphor band* (2nd), *two phosphor bands* ((1st), (E), 47*p*) *or phosphor background at left and band at right* (42*p*, 68*p*). *Perf* 14 × 14½

2404	**1692**	(2nd) multicoloured	. . . .	50	35 □ □
2405	**1693**	(1st) multicoloured	. . . .	75	50 □ □
2406	**1694**	(E) multicoloured	. . . .	1·25	1·25 □ □
2407	**1695**	42p multicoloured	. . . .	1·25	1·50 □ □
2408	**1696**	47p multicoloured	. . . .	1·50	2·00 □ □
2409	**1697**	68p multicoloured	. . . .	2·00	2·75 □ □
	Set of 6	. . . .		7·00	7·75 □ □
	First Day Cover	. . . .			11·00 □
	Presentation Pack	. . . . . .		9·00	□
	PHQ Cards (set of 6)	. . . . . .		2·75	11·00 □ □
	Set of 6 *Gutter Pairs*	. . . . . .		16·00	□

1698 Ice Spiral

1699 Icicle Star

1700 Wall of Ice Blocks

1701 Ice Ball

1702 Ice Hole

1703 Snow Pyramids

Christmas. Ice Sculptures by Andy Goldsworthy

2003 (4 Nov.) *Self-adhesive. One side phosphor band* (2nd), *'all-over' phosphor* (1st) *or two bands* (others). *Die-cut perf* 14½ × 14

2410	**1698**	(2nd) multicoloured	. . .	75	35 □ □
2411	**1699**	(1st) multicoloured	. . . .	1·25	50 □ □
2412	**1700**	(E) multicoloured	. . . .	1·50	1·50 □ □
2413	**1701**	53p multicoloured	. . . .	1·75	1·75 □ □
2414	**1702**	68p multicoloured	. . . .	2·00	2·00 □ □
2415	**1703**	£1.12 multicoloured	. . . .	2·00	2·00 □ □
	Set of 6	. . . .		9·00	9·00 □ □
	First Day Cover	. . . .			12·50 □
	Presentation Pack	. . . . . .		12·00	□
	PHQ Cards (set of 6)	. . . . . .		4·00	12·50 □ □

The 2nd and 1st class were also issued in separate sheets of 20, each stamp printed in lithography instead of photogravure and accompanied by a half stamp-size *se-tenant* label showing either animals, ice sculptures or a personal photograph.

Collectors Pack 2003

2003 (4 Nov.) *Comprises Nos.* 2327/57, 2360/5, 2368/77, 2381/90, 2392/401 *and* 2404/15

CP2415a *Collectors Pack* . . . . £100 □

Post Office Yearbook

2003 (4 Nov.) *Comprises Nos.* 2327/57, 2360/5, 2368/77, 2381/90, 2392/401 *and* 2404/15

YB2415a *Yearbook* . . . . £100 □

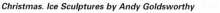

1704 Rugby Scenes

England's Victory in Rugby World Cup Championship, Australia

2003 (19 Dec.) *Sheet* 115 × 85 *mm. Multicoloured. Two phosphor bands. Perf* 14

MS2416 **1704** (1st) England flags and fans; (1st) England team standing in circle before match; 68p World Cup trophy; 68p Victorious England players after match . . 6·00 10·00 □ □
First Day Cover . . . . 12·00 □
Presentation Pack . . . . 16·00 □

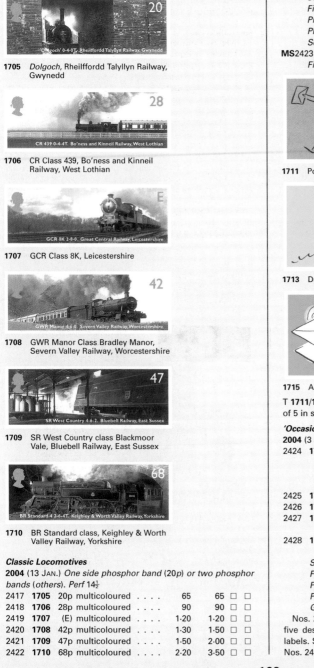

1705 *Dolgoch*, Rheilfffordd Talyllyn Railway, Gwynedd

1706 CR Class 439, Bo'ness and Kinneil Railway, West Lothian

1707 GCR Class 8K, Leicestershire

1708 GWR Manor Class Bradley Manor, Severn Valley Railway, Worcestershire

1709 SR West Country class Blackmoor Vale, Bluebell Railway, East Sussex

1710 BR Standard class, Keighley & Worth Valley Railway, Yorkshire

Classic Locomotives

2004 (13 Jan.) *One side phosphor band* (20p) *or two phosphor bands* (*others*). *Perf* 14½

2417	**1705**	20p multicoloured	65	65	□	□
2418	**1706**	28p multicoloured	90	90	□	□
2419	**1707**	(E) multicoloured	1·20	1·20	□	□
2420	**1708**	42p multicoloured	1·30	1·50	□	□
2421	**1709**	47p multicoloured	1·50	2·00	□	□
2422	**1710**	68p multicoloured	2·20	3·50	□	□

Set of 6	7·00	8·50	□	□
First Day Cover		12·00		□
Presentation Pack	35·00		□	
PHQ Cards (set of 6)	5·75	12·00	□	□
Set of 6 Gutter Pairs	15·00		□	
MS2423 190 × 67 mm. Nos. 2417/22 .	35·00	35·00	□	□
First Day Cover		35·00		□

1711 Postman

1712 Face

1713 Duck

1714 Baby

1715 Aircraft

T **1711/15** were printed together, *se-tenant*, as horizontal strips of 5 in sheets of 25 (5 × 5).

'Occasions' Greetings Stamps

2004 (3 Feb.) *Two phosphor bands. Perf* 14½ × 14

2424	**1711**	(1st) bright mauve and black	50	50	□	□
		a. Horiz strip of 5. Nos. 2424/8	5·00	5·00	□	□
2425	**1712**	(1st) magenta and black . .	50	50	□	□
2426	**1713**	(1st) lemon and black . .	50	50	□	□
2427	**1714**	(1st) pale turquoise-green and black . .	50	50	□	□
2428	**1715**	(1st) bright new blue and black	50	50	□	□

Set of 5	5·00	5·00	□	□
First Day Cover		8·00		□
Presentation Pack	6·25		□	
PHQ Cards (set of 5)	4·75	12·00	□	□
Gutter Block of 10	11·00		□	

Nos. 2424/8 were also issued in sheets of 20 containing the five designs *se-tenant* with half stamp-size printed message labels. Similar sheets containing either Nos. 2424 and 2428 or Nos. 2425/7 came with personal photographs on the labels.

1716 Map showing Middle Earth

1717 Forest of Lothlórien in Spring

1718 Dust-jacket for *The Fellowship of the Ring*

1719 Rivendell

1720 The Hall at Bag End

1721 Orthanc

1722 Doors of Durin

1723 Barad-dûr

1724 Minas Tirith

1725 Fangorn Forest

T **1716/25** were printed together, *se-tenant*, in blocks of 10 (5 × 2) throughout the sheet.

***50th Anniversary of Publication of* The Fellowship of the Ring *and* The Two Towers *by J. R. R. Tolkien**

2004 (26 FEB.) *Two phosphor bands. Perf* 14½

2429	**1716**	(1st) multicoloured	. . . .	50	50	□	□
		a. *Block of* 10. Nos.					
		2429/38	. . . .	9·00	10·00	□	□
2430	**1717**	(1st) multicoloured	. . .	50	50	□	□
2431	**1718**	(1st) multicoloured	. . .	50	50	□	□
2432	**1719**	(1st) multicoloured	. . .	50	50	□	□
2433	**1720**	(1st) multicoloured	. . .	50	50	□	□
2434	**1721**	(1st) multicoloured	. . .	50	50	□	□
2435	**1722**	(1st) multicoloured	. . .	50	50	□	□
2436	**1723**	(1st) multicoloured	. . .	50	50	□	□
2437	**1724**	(1st) multicoloured	. . .	50	50	□	□
2438	**1725**	(1st) multicoloured	. . .	50	50	□	□
		Set of 10	. . . .	9·00	10·00	□	□
		First Day Cover	. . . .		10·00		□
		Presentation Pack	. . . .	30·00		□	
		PHQ Cards (set of 10)	. . . . . .	9·75	15·00	□	□
		Gutter Block of 20	. . . .	19·00		□	

1726 Ely Island, Lower Lough Erne

1727 Giant's Causeway, Antrim Coast

1728 Slemish, Antrim Mountains

1729 Banns Road, Mourne Mountains

1730 Glenelly Valley, Sperrins

1731 Islandmore, Strangford Lough

A British Journey: Northern Ireland

2004 (16 Mar.) *One side phosphor band* (2nd) *or two phosphor bands* (others). *Perf* 14½ (a) *PVA gum*

2439	**1726**	(2nd) multicoloured . . .	65	65	□	□
2440	**1727**	(1st) multicoloured	90	90	□	□
2441	**1728**	(E) multicoloured	1·20	1·20	□	□
2442	**1729**	42p multicoloured	1·30	1·30	□	□
2443	**1730**	47p multicoloured	1·50	1·50	□	□
2444	**1731**	68p multicoloured	2·20	2·20	□	□
		Set of 6	7·75	7·75	□	□
		First Day Cover		12·50		□
		Presentation Pack	14·00		□	
		PHQ Cards (set of 6)	5·75	14·00	□	□
		Set of 6 Gutter Pairs	16·00		□	

(b) *Self-adhesive. Die-cut perf* 14½

2445	**1727**	(1st) multicoloured . . .	6·00	6·00	□	□

No. 2445 was only issued in £1.68 stamp booklets in which the surplus self-adhesive paper around each stamp was removed.

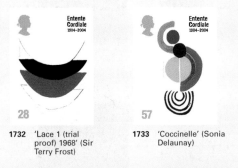

1732 'Lace 1 (trial proof) 1968' (Sir Terry Frost)

1733 'Coccinelle' (Sonia Delaunay)

Centenary of the Entente Cordiale. Contemporary Paintings

2004 (6 Apr.) *Two phosphor bands. Perf* 14 × 14½

2446	**1732**	28p grey, black and rosine	1·00	85	□	□
2447	**1733**	57p multicoloured	2·25	2·00	□	□
		Set of 2	3·00	2·75	□	□
		First Day Cover		4·50		□
		Presentation Pack	35·00		□	
		Presentation Pack (UK and French stamps)	35·00		□	
		PHQ Cards (set of 2)	1·90	5·00	□	□
		Set of 2 Gutter Pairs	7·00		□	
		Set of 2 Traffic Light Gutter Blocks of 4	15·00		□	

Stamps in similar designs were issued by France and these are included in the joint Presentation Pack.

1734 'RMS *Queen Mary 2*, 2004' (Edward D. Walker)

1735 'SS *Canberra* 1961' (David Cobb)

1736 'RMS *Queen Mary* 1936' (Charles Pears)

1737 'RMS *Mauretania*, 1907' (Thomas Henry)

1738 'SS *City of New York*, 1888' (Raphael Monleaon y Torres)

1739 'PS *Great Western*, 1838' (Joseph Walter)

Ocean Liners

2004 (13 Apr.) *Two phosphor bands.* (a) *PVA gum. Perf* 14½ × 14

2448	**1734**	(1st) multicoloured . . .	90	90	□	□
2449	**1735**	(E) multicoloured . . .	1·30	1·30	□	□
2450	**1736**	42p multicoloured . . .	1·30	1·30	□	□
2451	**1737**	47p multicoloured . . .	1·50	1·50	□	□
2452	**1738**	57p multicoloured . . .	1·80	1·80	□	□
2453	**1739**	68p multicoloured . . .	2·20	2·20	□	□
		Set of 6	9·00	9·00	□	□
		First Day Cover		10·00		□
		Presentation Pack	11·00		□	
		PHQ Cards (set of 7)	6·75	15·00	□	□
		Set of 6 Gutter Pairs	20·00		□	
MS2454	114 × 104 mm. Nos. 2448/53		18·00	18·00	□	□
	First Day Cover			18·00		□

(b) *Self-adhesive. Die-cut perf* 14½ × 14

2455	**1734**	(1st) multicoloured . . .	6·00	6·00	□	□

Nos. 2448/55 commemorate the introduction to service of the Queen Mary 2.

No. 2455 was only issued in £1.68 stamp booklets in which the surplus self-adhesive paper around each stamp was removed.

The complete miniature sheet is shown on one of the PHQ cards with the others depicting individual stamps.

1740 Dianthus Allwoodii Group

1741 Dahlia 'Garden Princess'

1742 Clematis 'Arabella'

1743 Miltonia 'French Lake'

1744 Lilium 'Lemon Pixie'

1745 Delphinium 'Clifford Sky'

Bicentenary of the Royal Horticultural Society (1st issue)

2004 (25 May) *One side phosphor band (2nd) or 'all-over' phosphor (others). Perf 14½*

2456	**1740**	(2nd) multicoloured	. . .	70	70 □ □
2457	**1741**	(1st) multicoloured	. . .	90	90 □ □
2458	**1742**	(E) multicoloured	. . .	1·30	1·30 □ □
2459	**1743**	42p multicoloured	. . .	2·00	2·00 □ □
2460	**1744**	47p multicoloured	. . .	2·50	2·50 □ □
2461	**1745**	68p multicoloured	. . .	3·50	3·50 □ □
		Set of 6		10·00	10·00 □ □
		First Day Cover			12·00 □
		Presentation Pack		11·00	□
		PHQ Cards (set of 7)		6·75	12·00 □ □
		Set of 6 Gutter Pairs		16·00	□
MS2462		115 × 105 mm. Nos. 2456/61		12·00	12·00 □ □
		First Day Cover			15·00 □

The complete miniature sheet is shown on one of the PHQ cards with the others depicting individual stamps.

The 1st class stamp was also issued in sheets of 20, printed in lithography instead of photogravure, each stamp accompanied by a *se-tenant* stamp-size label.

Bicentenary of the Royal Horticultural Society (2nd issue).
Booklet stamps

2004 (25 May) *Designs as Nos. 1955, 1958 and 1962 (1997 Greeting Stamps 19th-century Flower Paintings). Two phosphor bands. Perf 15 × 14 (with one elliptical hole on each vertical side)*

2463	**1280**	(1st) multicoloured	. . .	5·00	5·00 □ □
2464	**1283**	(1st) multicoloured	. . .	1·00	1·00 □ □
2465	**1287**	(1st) multicoloured	. . .	5·00	5·00 □ □
		Set of 3		10·00	10·00 □ □

On Nos. 2463/5 the phosphor bands appear at the left and the centre of each stamp.

Nos. 2463/5 were only available in £7.23 stamp booklets.

1746 Barmouth Bridge

1747 Hyddgen, Plynlimon

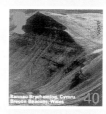

1748 Brecon Beacons

1749 Pen-pych, Rhondda Valley

1750 Rhewl, Dee Valley

1751 Marloes Sands

A British Journey: Wales

2004 (15 June) *One centre phosphor band* (2nd), 'all-over' phosphor (1st) *or two phosphor bands* (others). (a) *PVA gum.* Perf 14½

2466	**1746**	(2nd) multicoloured . . .	70	70	☐	☐
2467	**1747**	(1st) multicoloured . . .	90	90	☐	☐
2468	**1748**	40p multicoloured . . .	1·75	1·50	☐	☐
2469	**1749**	43p multicoloured . . .	2·00	2·00	☐	☐
2470	**1750**	47p multicoloured . . .	2·50	3·00	☐	☐
2471	**1751**	68p multicoloured . . .	3·50	4·00	☐	☐
		Set of 6	10·00	10·00	☐	☐
		First Day Cover		11·00		☐
		Presentation Pack	11·00		☐	
		PHQ Cards (set of 6)	5·75	12·00	☐	☐
		Set of 6 Gutter Pairs	22·00		☐	

(b) *Self-adhesive. Die-cut perf* 14½

2472	**1747**	(1st) multicoloured . . .	8·00	8·00	☐	☐

The 1st and 40p values include the 'EUROPA' emblem.

No. 2472 was only issued in £1.68 stamp booklets in which the surplus self-adhesive paper around each stamp was removed.

250th Anniversary of the Royal Society of Arts

2004 (10 Aug.) *Two phosphor bands. Perf* 14

2473	**1752**	(1st) multicoloured . . .	95	95	☐	☐
2474	**1753**	40p multicoloured . . .	1·30	1·30	☐	☐
2475	**1754**	43p multicoloured . . .	1·40	1·40	☐	☐
2476	**1755**	47p multicoloured . . .	1·50	1·50	☐	☐
2477	**1756**	57p silver, vermilion and black	2·20	2·20	☐	☐
2478	**1757**	68p silver, vermilion and black	3·00	3·00	☐	☐
		Set of 6	10·00	10·00	☐	☐
		First Day Cover		12·00		☐
		Presentation Pack	11·00		☐	
		PHQ Cards (set of 6)	5·75	12·00	☐	☐
		Set of 6 Gutter Pairs	22·00		☐	

1752 Sir Rowland Hill Award

1753 William Shipley (Founder of Royal Society of Arts)

1754 'RSA' as Typewriter Keys and Shorthand

1755 Chimney Sweep

1756 'Gill Typeface'

1757 'Zero Waste'

1758 Pine Marten

1759 Roe Deer

1760 Badger

1761 Yellow-necked Mouse

1762 Wild Cat

1763 Red Squirrel

1764 Stoat

1765 Natterer's Bat

1768 Pte. McNamara, 5th Dragoon Guards, Heavy Brigade Charge, Battle of Balaklava

1769 Piper Muir, 42nd Regt of Foot, Amphibious Assault on Kerch

1766 Mole

1767 Fox

1770 Sgt. Maj. Edwards, Scots Fusilier Guards, Gallant Action, Battle of Inkerman

1771 Sgt. Powell, 1st Regt of Foot Guards, Battles of Alma and Inkerman

T **1758/67** were printed together, *se-tenant*, in blocks of 10 (5 × 2) throughout the sheet.

Woodland Animals

2004 (16 Sept.) *Two phosphor bands.* P 14½

2479	**1758**	(1st) multicoloured	. . .	60	50 ☐ ☐
		a. Block of 10. Nos.			
		2479/88	. . . .	10·00	10·00 ☐ ☐
2480	**1759**	(1st) multicoloured	. . .	60	50 ☐ ☐
2481	**1760**	(1st) multicoloured	. . .	60	50 ☐ ☐
2482	**1761**	(1st) multicoloured	. . .	60	50 ☐ ☐
2483	**1762**	(1st) multicoloured	. . .	60	50 ☐ ☐
2484	**1763**	(1st) multicoloured	. . .	60	50 ☐ ☐
2485	**1764**	(1st) multicoloured	. . .	60	50 ☐ ☐
2486	**1765**	(1st) multicoloured	. . .	60	50 ☐ ☐
2487	**1766**	(1st) multicoloured	. . .	60	50 ☐ ☐
2488	**1767**	(1st) multicoloured	. . .	60	50 ☐ ☐
		Set of 10	. . . .	10·00	10·00 ☐ ☐
		First Day Cover	. . . . . .		12·00 ☐
		Presentation Pack	. . . . . .	12·00	☐
		PHQ Cards (set of 10)	. . . . .	9·75	16·00 ☐ ☐
		Gutter Block of 20	. . . .	22·00	☐

1772 Sgt. Maj. Poole, Royal Sappers and Miners, Defensive Line, Battle of Inkerman

1773 Sgt. Glasgow, Royal Artillery, Gun Battery besieged Sevastopol

150th Anniversary of the Crimean War

2004 (12 Oct.) *One centre phosphor band* (2nd) *or two phosphor bands* (others). *Perf* 14

2489	**1768**	(2nd) multicoloured . . .	70	70 □ □
2490	**1769**	(1st) multicoloured . . .	90	90 □ □
2491	**1770**	40p multicoloured . . .	2·00	2·00 □ □
2492	**1771**	57p multicoloured . . .	2·50	2·50 □ □
2493	**1772**	68p multicoloured . . .	2·75	3·00 □ □
2494	**1773**	£1·12 multicoloured . . .	4·50	5·00 □ □
		Set of 6	12·00	12·00 □ □
		First Day Cover		13·50 □
		Presentation Pack	12·50	□
		PHQ Cards (set of 6)	5·75	14·00 □ □
		Set of 6 Gutter Pairs	25·00	□
		Set of 6 Traffic Light Pairs . . .	30·00	□

Nos. 2489/94 show 'Crimean Heroes' photographs taken in 1856.

1774 Father Christmas on Snowy Roof	**1775** Celebrating the Sunrise

1776 On Roof in Gale	**1777** With Umbrella in Rain

1778 In Fog on Edge of Roof with Torch	**1779** Sheltering from Hailstorm behind Chimney

Christmas

2004 (2 Nov.) *One centre phosphor band* (2nd) *or two phosphor bands* (others). *Perf* 14½ × 14. (*a*) *Self-adhesive*.

2495	**1774**	(2nd) multicoloured . . .	70	70 □ □
2496	**1775**	(1st) multicoloured . . .	90	90 □ □
2497	**1776**	40p multicoloured . . .	1·30	1·30 □ □
2498	**1777**	57p multicoloured . . .	1·80	1·80 □ □
2499	**1778**	68p multicoloured . . .	2·20	2·20 □ □
2500	**1779**	£1·12 multicoloured . . .	3·75	3·75 □ □
		Set of 6	11·00	12·00 □ □
		First Day Cover		13·50 □
		Presentation Pack	12·50	□
		PHQ Cards (set of 7)	6·75	14·00 □ □

(b) PVA gum

MS2501	115 × 105 mm. As Nos.		
	2495/500	11·00	11·00 □ □
	First Day Cover		13·50 □

The seven PHQ cards depict the six individual stamps and the miniature sheet.

The 2nd and 1st class stamps were also issued in sheets of 20 printed in lithography instead of photogravure containing ten 1st class and ten 2nd class stamps, each stamp accompanied by a *se-tenant* stamp-size label showing Father Christmas. Separate sheets of either 20 1st or 20 2nd class were available with personal photographs.

Collectors Pack 2004

2004 (2 Nov.) *Comprises Nos. 2417/22, 2424/44, 2446/53, 2456/61, 2466/71 and 2473/2500*
CP2500*a* Collectors Pack . . . . 80·00 □

Post Office Yearbook

2004 (2 Nov.) *Comprises Nos. 2417/22, 2424/44, 2446/53, 2456/61, 2466/71 and 2473/2500*
YB2500*a* Yearbook . . . . £110 □

1780 British Saddleback Pigs	**1781** Khaki Campbell Ducks

1782 Suffolk Horses	**1783** Dairy Shorthorn Cattle

1784 Border Collie Dog

1785 Light Sussex Chicks

1786 Suffolk Sheep

1787 Bagot Goat

1788 Norfolk Black Turkeys

1789 Embden Geese

T **1780/9** were printed together, *se-tenant*, in blocks of 10 (5 × 2) throughout the sheet.

Farm Animals

2005 (11 JAN.) *Two phosphor bands. Perf 14½*

2502	**1780**	(1st) multicoloured	. . .	50	60	☐ ☐
		a. Block of 10. Nos.				
		2502/11	. . . . . .	10·00	12·00	☐ ☐
2503	**1781**	(1st) multicoloured	. . . .	50	60	☐ ☐
2504	**1782**	(1st) multicoloured	. . . .	50	60	☐ ☐
2505	**1783**	(1st) multicoloured	. . . .	50	60	☐ ☐
2506	**1784**	(1st) multicoloured	. . . .	50	60	☐ ☐
2507	**1785**	(1st) multicoloured	. . . .	50	60	☐ ☐
2508	**1786**	(1st) multicoloured	. . . .	50	60	☐ ☐
2509	**1787**	(1st) multicoloured	. . . .	50	60	☐ ☐
2510	**1788**	(1st) multicoloured	. . . .	50	60	☐ ☐
2511	**1789**	(1st) multicoloured	. . . .	50	60	☐ ☐
		Set of 10	. . . .	10·00	12·00	☐ ☐
		First Day Cover	. . . .		12·00	☐
		Presentation Pack	. . . .	13·00		☐
		PHQ Cards (set of 10)	. . . . . .	7·25	14·00	☐ ☐
		Gutter Block of 20	. . . .	20·00		☐

Nos. 2502/11 were also issued in sheets of 20, printed in lithography instead of photogravure, containing two of each of the ten designs, arranged in vertical strips of five alternated with printed labels.

1790 Old Harry Rocks, Studland Bay

1791 Wheal Coates, St. Agnes

1792 Start Point, Start Bay

1793 Horton Down, Wiltshire

1794 Chiselcombe, Exmoor

1795 St. James's Stone, Lundy

A British Journey. South West England

2005 (8 FEB.) *One centre phosphor band* (2nd) *or two phosphor bands* (*others*). *Perf 14½*

2512	**1790**	(2nd) multicoloured	. . . .	50	50	☐ ☐
2513	**1791**	(1st) multicoloured	. . . .	50	75	☐ ☐
2514	**1792**	40p multicoloured	. . . .	1·50	1·75	☐ ☐
2515	**1793**	43p multicoloured	. . . .	1·75	2·00	☐ ☐
2516	**1794**	57p multicoloured	. . .	2·50	2·50	☐ ☐
2517	**1795**	68p multicoloured	. . .	3·50	3·00	☐ ☐
		Set of 6	. . . .	10·00	10·00	☐ ☐
		First Day Cover	. . . .		12·00	☐
		Presentation Pack	. . . .	11·00		☐
		PHQ Cards (set of 6)	. . . . . .	4·25	10·00	☐ ☐
		Set of 6 Gutter Pairs	. . . . . .	21·00		☐

1796 'Mr Rochester'

1797 'Come to Me'

1798 'In the Comfort of her Bonnet'

1799 'La Ligne des Rats'

1800 'Refectory'

1801 'Inspection'

150th Death Anniversary of Charlotte Brontë. Illustrations of Scenes from Jane Eyre by Paula Rego

2005 (24 FEB.) *One centre phosphor band* (2nd) *or two phosphor bands* (others). *Perf* 14 × 14½

2518	1796	(2nd multicoloured		30	35	☐ ☐
2519	1797	(1st) multicoloured		40	45	☐ ☐
2520	1798	40p multicoloured		1·00	1·50	☐ ☐
2521	1799	57p silver, brownish grey				
		and black		2·50	2·50	☐ ☐
2522	1800	68p multicoloured		3·00	3·00	☐ ☐
2523	1801	£1.12 silver, brownish grey				
		and black		3·50	3·50	☐ ☐
	Set of 6			10·00	11·00	☐ ☐
	First Day Cover				12·00	☐
	Presentation Pack			10·00		☐
	PHQ Cards (set of 6)			11·00	15·00	☐ ☐
	Set of 6 Gutter Pairs			21·00		☐
	Set of 6 Traffic Light gutter					
	blocks of four			42·00		☐ ☐
MS2524 114 × 105 mm. Nos. 2518/23				10·00	10·00	☐ ☐
	First Day Cover				12·00	☐ ☐

The complete miniature sheet is shown on one of the PHQ cards with the others depicting individual stamps.

1802 Spinning Coin   **1803** Rabbit out of Hat Trick

1804 Knotted Scarf Trick   **1805** Card Trick

1806 Pyramid under Fez Trick

Centenary of the Magic Circle

2005 (15 MAR.) *Two phosphor bands. Perf* 14½ × 14

2525	1802	(1st) multicoloured . . .	65	45	☐ ☐
2526	1803	40p multicoloured	1·00	65	☐ ☐
2527	1804	47p multicoloured	2·50	2·75	☐ ☐
2528	1805	68p multicoloured	3·00	3·00	☐ ☐
2529	1806	£1.12 multicoloured	3·50	3·50	☐ ☐
	Set of 5		10·00	10·00	☐ ☐
	First Day Cover			11·75	☐
	Presentation Pack		10·00		☐
	PHQ Cards (set of 5)		5·00	12·00	☐ ☐
	Set of 5 Gutter Pairs		21·00		☐

Nos. 2525/9 are each printed with instructions for the illusion or trick on the stamp.

No. 2525 can be rubbed with a coin to reveal the 'head' or 'tail' of a coin. The two versions, which appear identical before rubbing, are printed in alternate rows of the sheet, indicated by the letters H and T in the side margins of the sheet.

No. 2525 was also issued in sheets of 20 with *se-tenant* labels showing magic tricks, printed in lithography instead of photogravure.

Nos. 2526 and 2528 each show optical illusions.

The spotted scarf on No. 2527 and the fezzes on No. 2529 are printed in thermochromic inks which fade temporarily when exposed to heat, making the pyramid under the centre fez visible.

50th Anniversary of First Castles Definitives

2005 (22 MAR.) *Sheet* 127 × 73 mm, *containing horiz designs as T* **166/9** (*Castles definitive of 1955-58*) *but with values in decimal currency, printed on pale cream. 'All-over' phosphor. Perf* 11 × 11½.

MS2530 166 50p brownish-black; 169 50p black; 167 £1 dull				
vermilion; 168 £1 royal blue		10·00	10·00	☐ ☐
	First Day Cover			12·00	☐
	Presentation Pack		12·00		☐
	PHQ Cards (set of 5)		2·20	12·00	☐ ☐

1807 Prince Charles and Mrs Camilla Parker Bowles

Royal Wedding

2005 (9 APR.) *Sheet* 85 × 115 *mm. Multicoloured. 'All-over' phosphor. Perf* 13½ × 14

MS2531 1807 30p × 2 Prince Charles and Mrs Camilla Parker Bowles laughing; 68p × 2 Prince Charles and Mrs Camilla Parker Bowles smiling into camera . 6·00 6·00 ☐ ☐
First Day Cover . . . . 10·00 ☐
Presentation Pack . . . . 6·50 ☐

1808 Hadrian's Wall, England

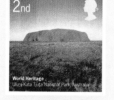

1809 Uluru-Kata Tjuta National Park, Australia

1810 Stonehenge, England

1811 Wet Tropics of Queensland, Australia

1812 Blenheim Palace, England

1813 Greater Blue Mountains Area, Australia

1814 Heart of Neolithic Orkney, Scotland

1815 Purnululu National Park, Australia

Nos. 2532/3, 2534/5, 2536/7 and 2538/9 were each printed together, *se-tenant*, in horizontal pairs.

World Heritage Sites

2005 (21 APR.) *One side phosphor band (2nd) or two phosphor bands (others). Perf* 14½

2532	**1808**	(2nd) multicoloured	30	35	☐	☐
		a. Horiz pair. Nos.				
		2532/3	1·00	1·00	☐	☐
2533	**1809**	(2nd) multicoloured	30	35	☐	☐
2534	**1810**	(1st) multicoloured	45	45	☐	☐
		a. Horiz pair. Nos.				
		2534/5	2·00	1·50	☐	☐
2535	**1811**	(1st) multicoloured	45	45	☐	☐
2536	**1812**	47p multicoloured	60	60	☐	☐
		a. Horiz pair. Nos.				
		2536/7	3·00	3·50	☐	☐
2537	**1813**	47p multicoloured	60	60	☐	☐
2538	**1814**	68p multicoloured	90	90	☐	☐
		a. Horiz pair. Nos.				
		2538/9	5·00	5·00	☐	☐
2539	**1815**	68p multicoloured	90	90	☐	☐
		Set of 8	11·00	11·00	☐	☐
		First Day Cover		12·00		☐
		Presentation Pack	12·00		☐	
		Presentation Pack (UK and Australian stamps)	11·00		☐	
		PHQ Cards (set of 8)	5·00	12·00	☐	☐
		Set of 8 Gutter Pairs	23·00		☐	

Stamps in these designs were also issued by Australia and these are included in the joint Presentation Pack.

1816 Ensign of the Scots Guards, 2002

1817 Queen taking the salute as Colonel-in-Chief of the Grenadier Guards, 1983

1818 Trumpeter of the Household Cavalry, 2004

1819 Welsh Guardsman, 1990s

1820 Queen riding side-saddle, 1972

1821 Queen and Duke of Edinburgh in Carriage, 2004

Trooping the Colour

2005 (7 June) *One phosphor band* (2nd), *two phosphor bands* (*others*). *Perf* 14½

2540	**1816**	(2nd) multicoloured	. . . .	70	80 □ □
2541	**1817**	(1st) multicoloured	. . .	75	90 □ □
2542	**1818**	42p multicoloured	. . . .	1·00	1·20 □ □
2543	**1819**	60p multicoloured	. . . .	2·00	2·00 □ □
2544	**1820**	68p multicoloured	. . . .	2·50	2·50 □ □
2545	**1821**	£1.12 multicoloured	. . . .	3·50	3·50 □ □
		Set of 6		10·00	10·00 □ □
		First Day Cover			12·00 □
		Presentation Pack		11·00	□
		PHQ Cards (*set of* 6)		5·00	12·00 □ □
		Set of 6 *Gutter Pairs*		21·00	□
MS2546		115 × 105 *mm. Nos.* 2540/5 .		11·00	11·00 □ □
		First Day Cover			12·00 □

1822

60th Anniversary of End of the Second World War

2005 (5 July) *Sheet* 115 × 105 *mm containing design as* T **1200** (1995 *Peace and Freedom*) *but with service indicator and No.* 1664*b* × 5. *Two phosphor bands. Perf* 15 × 14 (*with one elliptical hole on each vert side*) (1664*b*) *or* 14½ × 14 (*other*)

MS2547	**1822**	(1st) gold × 5; (1st) silver, blue and grey-black	6·00	6·00 □ □
		First Day Cover		8·00 □

1991 **Norton F.1** road version of a race winner

1969 **BSA Rocket 3** early three cylinder 'superbike'

1823 Norton F.1, Road Version of Race Winner (1991)

1824 BSA Rocket 3, Early Three Cylinder 'Superbike' (1969)

1949 **Vincent Black Shadow** fastest standard motorcycle

1938 **Triumph Speed Twin** two cylinder innovation

1825 Vincent Black Shadow, Fastest Standard Motorcycle (1949)

1826 Triumph Speed Twin, Two Cylinder Innovation (1938)

60

68

1930 **Brough Superior** bespoke luxury motorcycle

1914 **Royal Enfield** small engined motor bicycle

| 1827 | Brough Superior, Bespoke Luxury Motorcycle (1930) | 1828 | Royal Enfield, Small Engined Motor Bicycle (1914) |

Motorcycles

2005 (19 JULY) *Two phosphor bands. Perf* 14 × 14½

2548	**1823**	(1st) multicoloured	. . . .	75	80	☐	☐
2549	**1824**	40p multicoloured	. . . .	90	1·00	☐	☐
2550	**1825**	42p multicoloured	. . . .	1·25	1·00	☐	☐
2551	**1826**	47p multicoloured	. . . .	1·75	2·00	☐	☐
2552	**1827**	60p multicoloured	. . . .	2·50	2·50	☐	☐
2553	**1828**	68p multicoloured	. . . .	3·00	3·00	☐	☐
	Set of 6	. . . .		9·00	9·00	☐	☐
	First Day Cover	. . . .			12·00		☐
	Presentation Pack	. . . . . .		15·00		☐	
	PHQ Cards (set of 6)	. . . . .		5·00	11·00	☐	☐
	Set of 6 Gutter Pairs	. . . . . .		19·00		☐	

1829

London's Successful Bid for Olympic Games, 2012

2005 (5 AUG.) *Sheet* 115 × 105 *mm containing designs as* T **1255/9**, *but with service indicator. Multicoloured. Two phosphor bands. Perf* 14½

MS2554 **1829** (1st) Athlete celebrating
× 2; (1st) Throwing the javelin;
(1st) Swimming; (1st) Athlete on
starting blocks; (1st) Basketball 6·00 6·00 ☐ ☐
First Day Cover . . . . 8·00 ☐
Presentation Pack . . . . 8·00 ☐

Stamps from **MS**2554 are all inscribed 'London 2012—Host City' and have imprint date '2005'. The design as Type **1259** omits the Olympic rings.

| 1830 | African Woman eating Rice | 1831 | Indian Woman drinking Tea |

| 1832 | Boy eating Sushi | 1833 | Woman eating Pasta |

| 1834 | Woman eating Chips | 1835 | Teenage Boy eating Apple |

Europa. Gastronomy. Changing Tastes in Britain

2005 (23 AUG.) *One side phosphor band* (2nd) *or two phosphor bands* (others). *Perf* 14½

2555	**1830**	(2nd) multicoloured	. . .	60	70	☐	☐
2556	**1831**	(1st) multicoloured	. . . .	90	1·00	☐	☐
2557	**1832**	42p multicoloured	. . .	1·30	1·40	☐	☐
2558	**1833**	47p multicoloured	. . .	1·50	1·60	☐	☐
2559	**1834**	60p multicoloured	. . .	2·00	1·90	☐	☐
2560	**1835**	68p multicoloured	. . . .	2·50	2·20	☐	☐
	Set of 6	. . . .		8·00	8·00	☐	☐
	First Day Cover	. . . .			10·00		☐
	Presentation Pack	. . . .		9·00		☐	
	PHQ Cards (set of 6)	. . . . .		5·00	10·00	☐	☐
	Set of 6 Gutter Pairs	. . . . . .		17·00		☐	

The 1st and 42p values include the 'EUROPA' emblem.

1836 *Inspector Morse*

1837 *Emmerdale*

1838 *Rising Damp*

1839 *The Avengers*

1840 *The South Bank Show*

1841 *Who Wants to be a Millionaire*

50th Anniversary of Independent Television. Classic ITV Programmes

2005 (15 Sept.) *One side phosphor band (2nd) or two phosphor bands (others). Perf* 14½ × 14.

2561	**1836**	(2nd) multicoloured	60	70	□	□
2562	**1837**	(1st) multicoloured	90	1·00	□	□
2563	**1838**	42p multicoloured	1·30	1·40	□	□
2564	**1839**	47p multicoloured	1·40	1·50	□	□
2565	**1840**	60p multicoloured	2·00	1·90	□	□
2566	**1841**	68p multicoloured	2·20	2·20	□	□
	Set of 6		8·00	8·00	□	□
	First Day Cover			11·00		□
	Presentation Pack		9·00		□	
	PHQ Cards (set of 6)		5·00	10·00	□	□
	Set of 6 *Gutter Pairs*		17·00		□	

The 1st class stamps were also issued in sheets of 20 with each stamp accompanied by a half stamp-size *se-tenant* label.

1842 *Guzmania splendens (Charlotte Sowerby)*

Nos. 2567/72 were printed together, *se-tenant*, in booklet panes of 6 in which the surplus self-adhesive paper around each stamp was removed.

'Smilers' Booklet stamps (1st series)

2005 (4 Oct.) *Designs as Types* **992**, **1221**, **1286**, **1517** *and* **1568/9** *but smaller*, 20 × 23 *mm, and inscribed* 1st *as T* **1842**. *Self-adhesive. Two phosphor bands. Die-cut perf* 15 × 14½.

2567	**1842**	(1st) multicoloured	60	60	□	□
		a. Booklet pane. Nos. 2567/72	5·00		□	
2568	**1569**	(1st) multicoloured	60	60	□	□
2569	**1568**	(1st) multicoloured	60	60	□	□
2570	**1517**	(1st) multicoloured	60	60	□	□
2571	**992**	(1st) multicoloured	60	60	□	□
2572	**1221**	(1st) multicoloured	60	60	□	□
	Set of 6		5·00	6·00	□	□
	First Day Cover			6·75		□

Nos. 2567/72 were re-issued on 4 July 2006 in sheets of 20 with *se-tenant* labels, printed in lithography instead of photogravure.

THE ASHES ENGLAND WINNERS 2005

1843 Cricket Scenes

England's Ashes Victory

2005 (6 Oct.) *Sheet* 115 × 90 *mm. Multicoloured. Two phosphor bands. Perf* 14½ × 14.

MS2573 **1843** (1st) England team with Ashes trophy; (1st) Kevin Pieterson, Michael Vaughan and Andrew Flintoff on opening day of First Test, Lords; 68p Michael Vaughan, Third Test, Old Trafford; 68p Second Test

Edgbaston	6·00	6·00	□	□
First Day Cover		10·00		□
Presentation Pack	8·00		□	

1844 *Entrepreante* with dismasted British *Belle Isle*

1845 Nelson wounded on Deck of HMS *Victory*

1846 British Cutter *Entreprenae* attempting to rescue Crew of burning French *Achille*

1847 Cutter and HMS *Pickle* (schooner)

1848 British Fleet attacking in Two Columns

1849 Franco/Spanish Fleet putting to Sea from Cadiz

Nos. 2574/5, 2576/7 and 2578/9 were each printed together, *se-tenant*, in horizontal pairs throughout the sheets, each pair forming a composite design.

Bicentenary of the Battle of Trafalgar (1st issue). Scenes from 'Panorama of the Battle of Trafalgar' by William Heath

2005 (18 Oct.) *Two phosphor bands. Perf* 15 × 14½

2574	**1844**	(1st) multicoloured	45	45	☐	☐
		a. *Horiz pair. Nos.*				
		2574/5	1·75	2·00	☐	☐
2575	**1845**	(1st) multicoloured	45	45	☐	☐
2576	**1846**	42p multicoloured	65	65	☐	☐
		a. *Horiz. pair. Nos.*				
		2576/7	2·50	2·75	☐	☐
2577	**1847**	42p multicoloured	65	65	☐	☐
2578	**1848**	68p multicoloured	90	90	☐	☐
		a. *Horiz. pair. Nos.*				
		2578/9	4·00	4·40	☐	☐
2579	**1849**	68p multicoloured	90	90	☐	☐
		Set of 6	8·00	9·00	☐	☐
		First Day Cover		11·00		☐
		Presentation Pack	10·00		☐	
		PHQ Cards (*set of* 7)	5·00	10·00	☐	☐
		Set of 3 *Gutter Strips of* 4 . . .	17·00		☐	
MS2580		190 × 68 mm. Nos. 2574/9 .	8·00	10·00	☐	☐
		First Day Cover		11·00		☐

The phosphor bands are at just left of centre and at right of each stamp.

The seven PHQ cards depict the six individual stamps and the miniature sheet.

Bicentenary of the Battle of Trafalgar (2nd issue). Booklet stamp.

2005 (18 Oct.) *Design as Type* **1516** (*White Ensign from* 2001 *Submarine Centenary*). *Two phosphor bands. Perf* 14½.

2581	**1516**	(1st) multicoloured . . .	1·25	1·25	☐	☐

No. 2581 was only available in £7.26 stamp booklets.

1850 Black Madonna and Child from Haiti

1851 'Madonna and Child' (Marianne Stokes)

1852 'The Virgin Mary with the Infant Christ'

1853 Choctaw Virgin Mother and Child (Fr. John Giuliani)

1854 'Madonna and the Infant Jesus' (from India)

1855 'Come let us adore Him' (Dianne Tchumut)

Christmas. Madonna and Child Paintings

2005 (1 Nov.) *One side phosphor band* (2nd) *or two phosphor bands* (others). *Perf* 14½ × 14

(a) Self-adhesive

2582	**1850**	(2nd) multicoloured	60	70	☐	☐
2583	**1851**	(1st) multicoloured	90	1·00	☐	☐
2584	**1852**	42p multicoloured	1·30	1·40	☐	☐
2585	**1853**	60p multicoloured	1·80	1·90	☐	☐
2586	**1854**	68p multicoloured	2·00	2·20	☐	☐
2587	**1855**	£1.12 multicoloured	3·40	3·60	☐	☐
	Set of 6	. . . .	9·50	10·00	☐	☐
	First Day Cover	. . . .		11·00		☐
	Presentation Pack	. . . .	11·00		☐	
	PHQ Cards (set of 7)	. . . . . .	4·00	9·00	☐	☐

(b) PVA gum

MS2588 115 × 102 mm. As Nos.

2582/7	. . . .	9·50	10·00	☐	☐
First Day Cover	. . . .		11·00		☐

The seven PHQ cards depict the six individual stamps and the miniature sheet.

Collectors Pack

2005 (1 Nov.) *Comprises Nos.* 2502/23, 2525/9, **MS**2531/45, 2548/53, 2555/66, 2574/9 and 2582/7

CP2587a	Collectors Pack	. . . .	80·00	☐

Post Office Yearbook

2005 (1 Nov.) *Comprises Nos.* 2502/23, 2525/9, **MS**2531/45, 2548/53, 2555/66, 2574/9 and 2582/7

YB2587a	Yearbook	. . . .	90·00	☐

Miniature Sheet Collection

2005 (1 Nov.) *Comprises Nos.* **MS**2524, **MS**2530/1, **MS**2546/7, **MS**2554, **MS**2580 and **MS**2588

MS2588a	Miniature Sheet Collection	50·00	☐

1856 The Tale of Mr. Jeremy Fisher (Beatrix Potter)

1857 Kipper (Mick Inkpen)

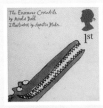

1858 The Enormous Crocodile (Roald Dahl)

1859 More About Paddington (Michael Bond)

1860 Comic Adventures of Boots (Satoshi Kitamura)

1861 Alice's Adventures in Wonderland (Lewis Carroll)

1862 The Very Hungry Caterpillar (Eric Carle)

1863 Maisy's ABC (Lucy Cousins)

Nos. 2589/90, 2591/2, 2593/4 and 2595/6 were printed together, *se-tenant*, in horizontal pairs in sheets of 30.

Animal Tales

2006 (10 JAN.) *One side phosphor band* (2nd) *or two phosphor bands* (others). *Perf* 14½

2589	**1856**	(2nd) multicoloured . . .	30	35	☐	☐
		a. Horiz pair. Nos.				
		2589/90	60	70	☐	☐
2590	**1857**	(2nd) multicoloured	30	35	☐	☐
2591	**1858**	(1st) multicoloured	45	50	☐	☐
		a. Horiz pair. Nos.				
		2591/2	1·50	1·50	☐	☐
2592	**1859**	(1st) multicoloured	45	50	☐	☐
2593	**1860**	42p multicoloured	65	70	☐	☐
		a. Horiz pair. Nos.				
		2593/4	2·50	2·75	☐	☐
2594	**1861**	42p multicoloured	65	70	☐	☐

2595	**1862**	68p multicoloured	80	1·00	☐	☐
		a. Horiz pair. Nos.				
		2595/6	4·00	4·25	☐	☐
2596	**1863**	68p multicoloured	80	1·00	☐	☐
		Set of 8	7·25	7·50	☐	☐
		First Day Cover		7·75		☐
		Presentation Pack	8·50		☐	
		PHQ Cards (set of 8)	4·50	9·00	☐	☐
		Set of 4 Gutter Blocks of 4 . . .	15·00		☐	
		Set of 4 Traffic Light Gutter				
		Blocks of 8	20·00		☐	

No. 2595 contains two die-cut holes.

A design as No. 2592 but self-adhesive was also issued in sheets of 20 with each stamp accompanied by a *se-tenant* label.

1864 Carding Mill Valley, Shropshire

1865 Beachy Head, Sussex

1866 St. Paul's Cathedral, London

1867 Brancaster, Norfolk

1868 Derwent Edge, Peak District

1869 Robin Hood's Bay, Yorkshire

1870 Buttermere, Lake District

1871 Chipping Campden, Cotswolds

1872 St. Boniface Down, Isle of Wight

1873 Chamberlain Square, Birmingham

Nos. 2597/606 were printed together, *se-tenant*, in blocks of ten (5 × 2) throughout the sheets of 30.

A British Journey: England

2006 (7 FEB.) *Two phosphor bands. Perf* 14½

2597	**1864**	(1st) multicoloured	45	50	☐	☐
		a. Block of 10. Nos.				
		2597/606	6·75	7·00	☐	☐
2598	**1865**	(1st) multicoloured	45	50	☐	☐
2599	**1866**	(1st) multicoloured	45	50	☐	☐
2600	**1867**	(1st) multicoloured	45	50	☐	☐
2601	**1868**	(1st) multicoloured	45	50	☐	☐
2602	**1869**	(1st) multicoloured	45	50	☐	☐
2603	**1870**	(1st) multicoloured	45	50	☐	☐
2604	**1871**	(1st) multicoloured	45	50	☐	☐
2605	**1872**	(1st) multicoloured	45	50	☐	☐
2606	**1873**	(1st) multicoloured	45	50	☐	☐
		Set of 10	6·75	7·00	☐	☐
		First Day Cover		7·25		☐
		Presentation Pack	7·75		☐	
		PHQ Cards (set of 10)	5·75	9·50	☐	☐
		Gutter Block of 20	9·25		☐	

1874 Royal Albert Bridge

1875 Box Tunnel

1876 Paddington Station

1877 *Great Eastern* (paddle steamer)

1878 Clifton Suspension Bridge Design

1879 Maidenhead Bridge

Birth Bicentenary of Isambard Kingdom Brunel (engineer) (1st issue)

2006 (23 FEB.) *Phosphor-coated paper (42p) or two phosphor bands (others). Perf* 14 × 13½

2607	**1874**	(1st) multicoloured	. . . .	45	50 □ □
2608	**1875**	40p multicoloured	. . . .	75	75 □ □
2609	**1876**	42p multicoloured	. . . .	1·00	1·00 □ □
2610	**1877**	47p multicoloured	. . . .	1·00	1·00 □ □
2611	**1878**	60p multicoloured	. . . .	1·50	1·75 · □
2612	**1879**	68p multicoloured	. . . .	2·00	2·25 □ □
		Set of 6	. . . .	6·50	6·75 □ □
		First Day Cover	. . . .		7·00 □
		Presentation Pack	. . . .	7·50	□
		PHQ Cards (set of 7)	. . . . . .	4·00	8·00 □ □
		Set of 6 Gutter Pairs	. . . . . .	14·00	□

MS2613 190 × 65 mm. Nos. 2607/12 . 6·50 6·75 □ □
  First Day Cover . . . . 7·00 □

The phosphor bands on Nos. 2607/8 and 2610/12 are at just left of centre and at right of each stamp.

The complete miniature sheet is shown on one of the PHQ cards with the others depicting individual stamps.

Birth Bicentenary of Isambard Kingdom Brunel (engineer) (2nd issue). Booklet stamp

2006 (23 FEB.) *Design as Type* **1739** (*PS* Great Western *from* 2004 *Ocean Liners*). *Two phosphor bands. Perf* 14½ × 14
2614 **1739** 68p multicoloured . . . . 1·60 1·60 □ □
  No. 2614 was only available in £7.40 stamp booklets.

1880 Sabre-tooth Cat   **1881** Giant Deer

1882 Woolly Rhino   **1883** Woolly Mammoth

1884 Cave Bear

Ice Age Animals

2006 (21 MAR.) *Two phosphor bands. Perf* 14½

2615	**1880**	(1st) black and silver	. . .	45	50 □ □
2616	**1881**	42p black and silver	. . .	75	70 □ □
2617	**1882**	47p black and silver	. . .	1·75	2·00 □ □
2618	**1883**	68p black and silver	. . .	2·00	2·25 □ □
2619	**1884**	£1.12 black and silver	. . .	2·25	2·50 □ □

Set of 5	6·75	7·00 □ □	
First Day Cover		7·25 □	
Presentation Pack	7·75	□	
PHQ Cards (set of 5)	2·75	6·00 □ □	
Set of 5 Gutter Pairs	14·00	□	

1885 On *Britannia*, 1972

1886 At Royal Windsor Horse Show, 1985

1887 At Heathrow Airport, 2001

1888 As Young Princess Elizabeth with Duchess of York, 1931

1889 At State Banquet, Ottawa, 1951

1890 Queen Elizabeth II in 1960

1891 As Princess Elizabeth, 1940

1892 With Duke of Edinburgh, 1951

Nos. 2620/1, 2622/3, 2624/5 and 2626/7 were each printed together, *se-tenant*, in horizontal pairs in sheets of 30.

80th Birthday of Queen Elizabeth II

2006 (18 APR.) *One centre phosphor band* (2nd) *or two phosphor bands* (others). *Perf* 14½

2620	**1885**	(2nd) black, turquoise-green and grey . . .	35	40 □ □	
		a. Horiz pair. Nos. 2620/1	70	80 □ □	
2621	**1886**	(2nd) black, turquoise-green and grey . . .	35	40 □ □	
2622	**1887**	(1st) black, turquoise-green and grey . . .	45	50 □ □	
		a. Horiz pair. Nos. 2622/3	1·50	1·75 □ □	
2623	**1888**	(1st) black, turquoise-green and grey . . .	45	50 □ □	
2624	**1889**	44p black, turquoise-green and grey . . .	65	70 □ □	
		a. Horiz pair. Nos. 2624/5	2·00	2·50 □ □	
2625	**1890**	44p black, turquoise-green and grey . . .	65	70 □ □	
2626	**1891**	72p black, turquoise-green and grey . . .	1·10	1·20 □ □	
		a. Horiz pair. Nos. 2626/7	4·00	4·50 □ □	
2627	**1892**	72p black, turquoise-green and grey . . .	1·10	1·20 □ □	
	Set of 8		7·75	8·00 □ □	
	First Day Cover			8·25 □	
	Presentation Pack		8·75	□	
	PHQ Cards (set of 8)		4·50	9·00 □ □	
	Set of 4 Gutter Strips of 4 . . .		16·00	□	

1893 England (1966)

1894 Italy (1934, 1938, 1982)

1895 Argentina (1978, 1986)

1896 Germany (1954, 1974, 1990)

64　　　　　　　**72**

1897　France (1998)

1898　Brazil (1958, 1962, 1970, 1994, 2002)

World Cup Football Championship, Germany. World Cup Winners

2006 (6 JUNE) *Two phosphor bands. Perf* 14½

2628	**1893**	(1st) multicoloured	45	50	☐	☐
2629	**1894**	42p multicoloured	65	70	☐	☐
2630	**1895**	44p multicoloured	1·00	1·00	☐	☐
2631	**1896**	50p multicoloured	1·50	1·50	☐	☐
2632	**1897**	64p multicoloured	1·75	2·00	☐	☐
2633	**1898**	72p multicoloured	2·00	2·25	☐	☐
		Set of 6	6·75	7·00	☐	☐
		First Day Cover		7·25		☐
		Presentation Pack	8·00		☐	
		PHQ Cards (*set of 6*)	4·00	9·00	☐	☐
		Set of 6 Gutter Pairs	14·00		☐	

The 1st class stamp was also issued in sheets of 20 with each stamp accompanied by a *se-tenant* label showing scenes from the 1966 World Cup final.

1899　30 St. Mary Axe, London

1900　Maggie's Centre, Dundee

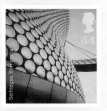

1901　Selfridges, Birmingham

1902　Downland Gridshell, Chichester

64　　　　　　　**72**

1903　An Turas, Isle of Tiree

1904　The Deep, Hull

Modern Architecture

2006 (20 JUNE). *Two phosphor bands. Perf* 14½

2634	**1899**	(1st) multicoloured	45	50	☐	☐
2635	**1900**	42p multicoloured	65	70	☐	☐
2636	**1901**	44p multicoloured	1·00	1·00	☐	☐
2637	**1902**	50p multicoloured	1·50	1·50	☐	☐
2638	**1903**	64p multicoloured	1·75	2·00	☐	☐
2639	**1904**	72p multicoloured	2·00	2·25	☐	☐
		Set of 6	6·75	7·00	☐	☐
		First Day Cover		7·25		☐
		Presentation Pack	8·00		☐	
		PHQ Cards (*set of 6*)	4·00	9·00	☐	☐
		Set of 6 Gutter Pairs	14·00		☐	

1905　'Sir Winston Churchill' (Walter Sickert)

1906　'Sir Joshua Reynolds' (self-portrait)

1907　'T. S. Eliot' (Patrick Heron)

1908　'Emmeline Pankhurst' (Georgina Agnes Brackenbury)

1909 Virginia Woolf (photo by George Charles Beresford)

1910 Bust of Sir Walter Scott (Sir Francis Leggatt Chantry)

1911 'Mary Seacole' (Albert Charles Challen)

1912 'William Shakespeare' (attrib to John Taylor)

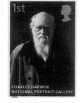

1913 'Dame Cicely Saunders' (Catherine Goodman)

1914 'Charles Darwin' (John Collier)

Nos. 2640/9 were printed together, *se-tenant*, in blocks of ten (5 × 2) in sheets of 30.

150th Anniversary of National Portrait Gallery, London

2006 (18 July) *Two phosphor bands. Perf* 14½

2640	**1905**	(1st) multicoloured	45	50	☐	☐
		a. Block of 10. *Nos.*				
		2640/9	7·25	7·50	☐	☐
2641	**1906**	(1st) multicoloured	45	50	☐	☐
2642	**1907**	(1st) multicoloured	45	50	☐	☐
2643	**1908**	(1st) multicoloured	45	50	☐	☐
2644	**1909**	(1st) multicoloured	45	50	☐	☐
2645	**1910**	(1st) multicoloured	45	50	☐	☐
2646	**1911**	(1st) multicoloured	45	50	☐	☐
2647	**1912**	(1st) multicoloured	45	50	☐	☐
2648	**1913**	(1st) multicoloured	45	50	☐	☐
2649	**1914**	(1st) multicoloured	45	50	☐	☐
		Set of 10	7·25	7·50	☐	☐
		First Day Cover		7·75		☐
		Presentation Pack	8·25		☐	
		PHQ Cards (set of 10)	6·75	11·00	☐	☐
		Gutter Block of 20	15·00		☐	
		Traffic Light Gutter Block of 20 .	20·00		☐	

1915 1916

'Pricing in Proportion'

2006 (1 Aug–12 Sept.) *Perf* 15 × 14 *(with one elliptical hole on each vertical side)*. (*a*) *PVA gum. Photo De La Rue*. (i) *As T* **1915**

2650	(2nd) bright blue (1 centre band)	50	40	☐	☐
2651	(1st) gold (2 bands) . . .	75	50	☐	☐

(ii) *As T* **1916**.

2652	(2nd Large) bright blue (2 bands)	1·00	60	☐	☐
2653	(1st Large) gold (2 bands) . . .	1·50	70	☐	☐

(*b*) *Self-adhesive. Photo Walsall.* (i) *As T* **1915**

2654	(2nd) bright blue (1 centre band) (12 Sept) . . .	50	40	☐	☐
2655	(1st) gold (2 bands) (12 Sept)	75	50	☐	☐

(ii) *As T* **1916**.

2656	(2nd Large) bright blue (2 bands) (15 Aug)	55	60	☐	☐
2657	(1st Large) gold (2 bands) (15 Aug)	65	70	☐	☐
	First Day Cover (Nos. Y1676*b/c*, 2650/3)		5·00		☐
	Presentation Pack	4·75		☐	

No. 2654 was issued in booklets of twelve sold at £2.76.

No. 2655 was available in booklets of six or twelve, sold at £1.92 or £3.84.

Nos. 2656/7 were issued in separate booklets of four, sold at £1.48 or £1.76.

All these booklets had the surplus self-adhesive paper around each stamp removed.

1917

70th Anniversary of the Year of Three Kings
2006 (31 Aug.) *Sheet 127 × 72 mm containing No. Y1728. Multicoloured. Two phosphor bands. Perf 15 × 14 (with one elliptical hole on each vertical side).*

MS2658 **1917** £3 deep mauve	. . . .	6·75	7·00 □ □
First Day Cover	. . . .		7·50 □

1918   Corporal Agansing Rai

1919   Boy Seaman Jack Cornwell

1920   Midshipman Charles Lucas

1921   Captain Noel Chavasse

1922   Captain Albert Ball

1923   Captain Charles Upham

Nos. 2659/60, 2661/2 and 2663/4 were each printed together, se-tenant, in horizontal pairs in sheets of 30.

150th Anniversary of the Victoria Cross (1st issue)
2006 (21 Sept.) *One side phosphor band. Perf 14½ × 14*

2659	**1918**	(1st) multicoloured	. . . .	45	50 □ □
		a. Horiz pair. Nos.			
		2659/60	. . . . . .	1·00	1·00 □ □
2660	**1919**	(1st) multicoloured	. . . .	45	50 □ □
2661	**1920**	64p multicoloured	. . .	75	75 □ □
		a. Horiz pair. Nos.			
		2661/2	. . . .	2·50	2·50 □ □
2662	**1921**	64p multicoloured	. . . .	75	75 □ □
2663	**1922**	72p multicoloured	. . . .	1·00	1·00 □ □
		a. Horiz pair. Nos.			
		2663/4	. . . .	4·00	4·50 □ □
2664	**1923**	72p multicoloured	. . . .	1·00	1·00 □ □
		Set of 6	. . . .	7·50	8·00 □ □
		First Day Cover	. . . .		8·25 □
		Presentation Pack	. . . . . .	8·75	□
		Set of 3 Gutter Strips of 4	. . .	16·00	□

MS2665 190 × 67 mm. No. 2666 and as Nos. 2659/64 but 'all-over'

phosphor	. . . .	8·00	8·50 □ □
First Day Cover	. . . .		8·75 □
PHQ Cards *(set of 7)*	. . . . . .	4·50	8·50 □ □

The seven PHQ cards depict the six individual stamps and the miniature sheet.

150th Anniversary of the Victoria Cross (2nd issue). Booklet stamp

2006 (21 Sept.) *Design as No.* 1517 (1990 *Gallantry Awards*). *'All-over' phosphor. Perf 14*

2666 **959** 20p multicoloured . . . . 50 55 ☐ ☐

No. 2666 was only issued in No. **MS**2663 and in £7.44 stamp booklets.

1924 Sitar Player and Dancer

1925 Reggae Bass Guitarist and African Drummer

1926 Fiddler and Harpist

1927 Sax Player and Blues Guitarist

1928 Maraca Player and Salsa Dancers

Europa. Integration. Sounds of Britain

2006 (3 Oct.) *'All-over' phosphor. Perf 14½*

2667	**1924**	(1st) multicoloured	45	50	☐	☐
2668	**1925**	42p multicoloured	1·00	1·00	☐	☐
2669	**1926**	50p multicoloured	1·25	1·25	☐	☐
2670	**1927**	72p multicoloured	1·75	1·75	☐	☐
2671	**1928**	£1.19 multicoloured	2·50	3·00	☐	☐
	Set of 5	6·75	7·00	☐	☐
	First Day Cover		7·25	☐	☐
	Presentation Pack	8·00		☐
	PHQ Cards (*set of 5*)	3·75	7·50	☐	☐
	Set of 5 Gutter Pairs	14·00		☐

The 1st class and 50p values include the 'EUROPA' emblem.

1929 'New Baby' (Alison Carmichael)

1930 'Best Wishes' (Alan Kitching)

1931 'THANK YOU' (Alan Kitching)

1932 Balloons (Ivan Chermayeff)

1933 Firework (Kam Tang)

1934 Champagne, Flowers and Butterflies (Olaf Hajek)

Nos. 2672/7 were printed together, *se-tenant*, in booklet panes of 6 in which the surplus self-adhesive paper around each stamp was removed.

'Smilers' Booklet stamps (2nd series). Occasions

2006 (17 Oct.) *Self-adhesive. Two phosphor bands. Die-cut perf 15 × 14½*

2672	**1929**	(1st) chrome-yellow . . .	45	50	☐	☐
		a. Booklet pane. Nos.			
		2672/7	2·50		☐
2673	**1930**	(1st) turquoise-blue . . .	45	50	☐	☐
2674	**1931**	(1st) scarlet-vermilion,			
		rosine and yellow . .	45	50	☐	☐
2675	**1932**	(1st) multicoloured	45	50	☐	☐
2676	**1933**	(1st) multicoloured	45	50	☐	☐
2677	**1934**	(1st) multicoloured	45	50	☐	☐
	Set of 6	2·50	3·00	☐	☐
	First Day Cover		4·00	☐
	Presentation Pack	3·75		☐
	PHQ Cards	2·75		☐

Nos. 2672/7 were also issued in sheets of 20 with *se-tenant* labels, printed in lithography instead of photogravure.

1935 Snowman

1936 Father Christmas

1937 Snowman

1938 Father Christmas

1939 Reindeer

1940 Christmas Tree

Christmas

2006 (7 Nov.) One centre phosphor band (2nd) or two phosphor bands (others). Perf 15 × 14. (a) Self-adhesive

2678	**1935**	(2nd) multicoloured	35	40	□	□
		a. Booklet pane. No.				
		2678 × 12	4·00		□	
2679	**1936**	(1st) multicoloured	45	50	□	□
		a. Booklet pane. No.				
		2679 × 12	5·25		□	
2680	**1937**	(2nd Large) multicoloured	55	60	□	□
2681	**1938**	(1st Large) multicoloured	65	70	□	□
2682	**1939**	72p multicoloured	1·10	1·20	□	□
2683	**1940**	£1.19 multicoloured	1·80	1·90	□	□
		Set of 6	4·75	5·00	□	□
		First Day Cover		6·50		□
		Presentation Pack	5·75		□	
		PHQ Cards (set of 7)	3·00	5·50	□	□

(b) PVA gum

MS2684 115 × 102 mm. As Nos.

2678/83	. . . .	4·75	5·00	□	□
First Day Cover	. . . .		6·50		□

The seven PHQ cards depict the six individual stamps and the miniature sheet.

The 2nd and 1st class stamps were also issued in sheets of 20 printed in lithography instead of photogravure containing ten 1st class and ten 2nd class stamps, each stamp accompanied by a se-tenant label. Separate sheets of 20 1st or 20 2nd class were available with personal photographs.

1941

'Lest We Forget' (1st issue). 90th Anniversary of the Battle of the Somme

2006 (9 Nov.) Sheet 124 × 71 mm containing new stamp and designs as Nos. EN13, W105, S116 and NI101. Two phosphor bands. Perf 14½ (1st) or 15 × 14 (72p).

MS2685 **1941** (1st) Poppies on barbed wire stems; 72p × 4 As Nos.					
EN13, W105, S116 and NI101 .	4·75	5·00	□	□
First Day Cover		6·25		□
Presentation Pack	5·50		□	

No. **MS**2685 (including the Northern Ireland stamp) is printed in gravure.

The 1st class stamp was also issued in sheets of 20 with se-tenant labels showing war memorials, printed in lithography instead of photogravure.

Collectors Pack

2006 (9 Nov.) Comprises Nos. 2589/612, 2615/49, 2659/64, 2667/71, 2678/83 and **MS**2685

CP2685a Collectors Pack	55·00	□

Post Office Yearbook

2006 (9 Nov.) Comprises Nos. 2589/612, 2615/49, 2659/64, 2667/71, 2678/83 and **MS**2685

YB2685a Yearbook	65·00	□

Miniature Sheet Collection

2006 (30 Nov.) Comprises Nos. **MS**2613, **MS**2658, **MS**2665, **MS**2684/5 and **MS**S121 . . . .

MS2685a Miniature Sheet Collection .	36·00	□

REGIONAL ISSUES

PERFORATION AND WATERMARK. All the following Regional stamps are perforated 15 × 14, unless otherwise stated.
For listing of First Day Covers see pages 173/5.

1 England

EN **1**   Three Lions

EN **2**   Crowned Lion with Shield of St. George

EN **3**   Oak Tree

EN **4**   Tudor Rose

2001 (23 Apr.)–**02** *Printed in photogravure by De La Rue or Questa (Nos.* EN1/2*), De La Rue (others). One centre phosphor band (2nd) or two phosphor bands (others). Perf* 15 × 14 *(with one elliptical hole on each vertical side)*

EN1	EN **1**	(2nd) slate-green and silver	60	60	□	□
EN2	EN **2**	(1st) lake-brown and silver	90	90	□	□
EN3	EN **3**	(E) olive-green and silver	1·00	1·00	□	□
EN4	EN **4**	65p deep reddish lilac and silver	3·00	3·00	□	□
EN5		68p deep reddish lilac and silver	2·00	2·00	□	□
	Presentation Pack (P.O. Pack No. 54)					
	(*Nos.* EN1/4)	7·00		□		
	PHQ Cards (set of 4) (*Nos.* EN1/4)	2·00	10·00	□	□	

Nos. EN1/3 were initially sold at 19p, 27p and 36p, the latter representing the basic European airmail rate.

Combined Presentation Packs for England, Northern Ireland, Scotland and Wales

Presentation Pack (P.O. Pack No. 59) (*contains* 68p *from England, Northern Ireland, Scotland and Wales* (*Nos.* EN5, NI93, S99, W88))	9·00		□
Presentation Pack (P.O. Pack No. 68) (*contains* 40p *from England, Northern Ireland, Scotland and Wales* (*Nos.* EN9, NI97, S112, W101))	6·25		□
Presentation Pack (P.O. Pack No. 70) (*contains* 42p *from England, Northern Ireland, Scotland and Wales* (*Nos.* EN10, NI98, S113, W102)) .	6·00		□
Presentation Pack (P.O. Pack No. 73) (*contains* 44p *and* 72p *from England, Northern Ireland, Scotland and Wales* (*Nos.* EN11, EN13, NI99, NI101, S114, S116, W103 *and* W105))	7·50		□

2003 (14 Oct.)–**06**. *As Nos.* EN1/3 *and* EN5 *but with white borders. Printed in photogravure by Walsall or De La Rue (2nd), 40p, 42p) or De La Rue (others). One centre phosphor band (2nd) or two phosphor bands (others). Perf* 15 × 14 *(with one elliptical hole on each vertical side).*

EN6	EN **1**	(2nd) slate-green and silver	75	60	□	□
EN7	EN **2**	(1st) lake-brown and silver	80	75	□	□
EN8	EN **3**	(E) olive-green and silver	1·20	1·00	□	□
EN9		40p olive-green and silver	1·25	1·25	□	□
EN10		42p olive-green and silver	1·00	1·00	□	□
EN11		44p olive-green and silver	80	75	□	□
EN12	EN **4**	68p deep reddish lilac and silver	2·00	1·75	□	□
EN13		72p deep reddish lilac and silver	1·30	1·20	□	□
	Presentation Pack (P.O. Pack No. 63) (*Nos.* EN6/8, EN12) . . .	5·00		□	
	PHQ Cards (set of 4) (*Nos.* EN6/8, EN12)	2·00	6·00	□	□

Nos. EN6/8 were initially sold at 20p, 28p and 38p, the latter representing the basic European airmail rate.

2 Northern Ireland

N **1**    N **2**    N **3**    N **4**

1958–67 *Wmk* **179**

NI1	N **1**	3d lilac	15	10	☐	☐
		p. One centre phosphor band	15	15	☐	☐
NI2		4d blue	15	15	☐	☐
		p. Two phosphor bands	15	15	☐	☐
NI3	N **2**	6d purple	20	25	☐	☐
NI4		9d bronze-green (2 phosphor bands) . .	30	70	☐	☐
NI5	N **3**	1s 3d green	30	70	☐	☐
NI6		1s 6d blue (2 phosphor bands)	30	70	☐	☐

1968–69 *One centre phosphor band* (Nos. NI8/9) *or two phosphor bands* (others). *No wmk*

NI7	N **1**	4d blue	15	15	☐	☐
NI8		4d sepia	15	15	☐	☐
NI9		4d vermilion	20	20	☐	☐
NI10		5d blue	20	20	☐	☐
NI11	N **3**	1s 6d blue	2·25	2·50	☐	☐
		Presentation Pack (comprises Nos. NI1p, NI4/6, NI8/10) . . .	3·50		☐	

Decimal Currency

1971–91 Type N **4**. *No wmk*

(a) Printed in photogravure with phosphor bands

NI12	2½p magenta (1 centre band) .	70	45	☐	☐
NI13	3p ultramarine (2 bands) . . .	30	25	☐	☐
NI14	3p ultramarine (1 centre band)	20	15	☐	☐
NI15	3½p olive-grey (2 bands)	20	25	☐	☐
NI16	3½p olive-grey (1 centre band)	20	25	☐	☐
NI17	4½p grey-blue (2 bands)	30	25	☐	☐
NI18	5p violet (2 bands)	1·00	1·00	☐	☐
NI19	5½p violet (2 bands)	20	20	☐	☐
NI20	5½p violet (1 centre band) . . .	20	25	☐	☐
NI21	6½p blue (1 centre band) . . .	20	20	☐	☐
NI22	7p brown (1 centre band) . .	35	25	☐	☐
NI23	7½p chestnut (2 bands)	1·50	1·50	☐	☐
NI24	8p rosine (2 bands)	35	35	☐	☐
NI25	8½p yellow-green (2 bands) . .	35	40	☐	☐
NI26	9p violet (2 bands)	40	40	☐	☐
NI27	10p orange-brown (2 bands) .	40	50	☐	☐
NI28	10p orange-brown (1 centre band)	50	50	☐	☐
NI29	10½p blue (2 bands)	40	50	☐	☐
NI30	11p scarlet (2 bands)	50	50	☐	☐

(b) Printed in photogravure on phosphorised paper

NI31	12p yellowish green	50	50	☐	☐
NI32	13½p purple-brown	60	70	☐	☐
NI33	15p ultramarine	60	70	☐	☐

(c) Printed in lithography. Perf 14 (11½p, 12½p, 14p (No. NI38), 15½p, 16p, 18p, (No. NI45), 19½p, 20½p, 22p (No. NI53), 26p (No. NI60), 28p (No. NI62)) or 15 × 14 (others)

NI34	11½p drab (1 side band)	85	85	☐	☐
NI35	12p bright emerald (1 side band)	70	80	☐	☐
NI36	12½p light emerald (1 side band)	60	60	☐	☐
	a. Perf 15 × 14	5·25	5·25	☐	☐
NI37	13p pale chestnut (1 side band)	80	50	☐	☐
NI38	14p grey-blue (phosphorised paper)	75	75	☐	☐
NI39	14p deep blue (1 centre band)	75	60	☐	☐
NI40	15p bright blue (1 centre band)	90	60	☐	☐
NI41	15½p pale violet (phosphorised paper)	80	80	☐	☐
NI42	16p drab (phosphorised paper)	1·00	1·00	☐	☐
	a. Perf 15 × 14	8·25	8·50	☐	☐
NI43	17p grey-blue (phosphorised paper)	90	95	☐	☐
NI44	17p deep blue (1 centre band)	1·00	80	☐	☐
NI45	18p deep violet (phosphorised paper)	1·00	1·00	☐	☐
NI46	18p olive-grey (phosphorised paper)	1·00	90	☐	☐
NI47	18p bright green (1 centre band)	1·00	95	☐	☐
	a. Perf 14	2·50	2·50	☐	☐
NI48	18p bright green (1 side band)	2·25	2·25	☐	☐
NI49	19p bright orange-red (phosphorised paper) . . .	1·00	1·00	☐	☐
NI50	19½p olive-grey (phosphorised paper)	1·50	1·75	☐	☐
NI51	20p brownish black (phosphorised paper) . . .	1·00	80	☐	☐
NI52	20½p ultramarine (phosphorised paper)	4·50	4·25	☐	☐
NI53	22p blue (phosphorised paper)	1·10	1·10	☐	☐
NI54	22p yellow-green (phosphorised paper)	1·10	1·10	☐	☐
NI55	22p bright orange-red (phosphorised paper) . . .	1·25	90	☐	☐
NI56	23p bright green (phosphorised paper)	1·25	1·10	☐	☐
NI57	24p Indian red (phosphorised paper)	1·25	1·25	☐	☐
NI58	24p chestnut (phosphorised paper)	1·10	90	☐	☐
NI59	24p chestnut (2 bands)	2·25	2·50	☐	☐
NI60	26p rosine (phosphorised paper)	1·25	1·25	☐	☐
	a. Perf 15 × 14	3·00	3·25	☐	☐
NI61	26p drab (phosphorised paper)	1·75	1·75	☐	☐
NI62	28p deep violet-blue (phosphorised paper) . . .	1·50	1·50	☐	☐
	a. Perf 15 × 14	1·25	1·25	☐	☐

NI63	28p deep bluish grey (phosphorised paper) . . .	1·50	1·50	□	□
NI64Ea	31p bright purple (phosphorised paper) . . .	1·90	1·75	□	□
NI65	32p greenish blue (phosphorised paper) . . .	1·75	1·75	□	□
NI66	34p deep bluish grey (phosphorised paper) . . .	1·75	1·75	□	□
NI67	37p rosine (phosphorised paper)	2·00	2·50	□	□
NI68	39p bright mauve (phosphorised paper) . . .	2·00	2·25	□	□

Nos. NI48 and NI59 were only issued in stamp booklets.

Presentation Pack (*P.O. Pack No. 29*) (*contains* 2½p (NI12), 3p (NI13), 5p (NI18), 7½p (NI23)) . . . . 3·50 □

Presentation Pack (*P.O. Pack No. 61*) (*contains* 3p (NI14), 3½p (NI15), 5½p (NI19), 8p (NI24) *later with* 4½p (NI17) *added*) . 2·25 □

Presentation Pack (*P.O. Pack No. 84*) (*contains* 6½p (NI21), 8½p (NI25), 10p (NI27), 11p (NI30)) 2·00 □

Presentation Pack (*P.O. Pack No. 129d*) (*contains* 7p (NI22), 9p (NI26), 10½p (NI29), 11½p (NI31), 12p (NI31), 13½p (NI32), 14p (NI38), 15p (NI33), 18p (NI45), 22p (NI53)) . . . . . . 9·00 □

Presentation Pack (*P.O. Pack No. 4*) (*contains* 10p (NI28), 12½p (NI36), 16p (NI42), 20½p (NI52), 26p (NI60), 28p (NI62)) . . . . 17·00 □

Presentation Pack (*P.O. Pack No. 8*) (*contains* 10p (NI28), 13p (NI37), 16p (NI42a), 17p (NI43), 22p (NI54), 26p (NI60), 28p (NI62), 31p (NI64)) . . . . 18·00 □

Presentation Pack (*P.O. Pack No. 12*) (*contains* 12p (NI35), 13p (NI37), 17p (NI43), 18p (NI46), 22p (NI54), 26p (NI60a), 28p (NI62a), 31p (NI64)) . . . . 17·00 □

Combined Presentation Packs for Northern Ireland, Scotland and Wales

Presentation Pack (*P.O. Pack No. 17*) (*contains* 14p, 19p, 23p, 32p *from Northern Ireland, Scotland and Wales* (*Nos.* NI39, NI49, NI56, NI65, S54, S62, S67, S77, W40, W50, W57, W66)) . . . . 17·00 □

Presentation Pack (*P.O. Pack No. 20*) (*contains* 15p, 20p, 24p, 34p *from Northern Ireland, Scotland and Wales* (*Nos.* NI40, NI5I, NI57, NI66, S56, S64, S69, S78, W41, W52, W58, W67)) . . . . 16·00 □

Presentation Pack (*P.O. Pack No. 23*) (*contains* 17p, 22p, 26p, 37p *from Northern Ireland, Scotland and Wales* (*Nos.* NI44, NI55, NI6I, NI67, S58, S66, S73, S79, W45, W56, W62, W68)) . . . . 16·00 □

Presentation Pack (*P.O. Pack No. 26*) (*contains* 18p, 24p, 28p, 39p *from Northern Ireland, Scotland and Wales* (*Nos.* NI47, NI58, NI63, NI68, S60, S70, S75, S80, W48, W59, W64, W69)) . . . . 16·00 □

1993 (7 Dec.)–**2000** (*a*) *Printed in lithography by Questa. Perf* 15 × 14 (*with one elliptical hole on each vertical side*)

NI69	N **4**	19p bistre (1 centre band)	90	80	□	□
NI70		19p bistre (1 side band) . .	1·25	1·75	□	□
NI71		20p bright green (1 centre band)	1·50	1·50	□	□
NI72		25p red (2 bands)	75	75	□	□
NI73		26p red-brown (2 bands) .	1·75	1·75	□	□
NI74		30p deep olive-grey (2 bands)	1·25	1·25	□	□
NI75		37p bright mauve (2 bands)	2·75	3·00	□	
NI76		41p grey-brown (2 bands)	1·50	1·75	□	□
NI77		63p light emerald (2 bands)	4·75	5·00	□	□

(*b*) *Printed in photogravure by Walsall* (19p, 20p, 26p (*No.* NI81b), 38p, 40p, 63p, 64p, 65p), *Harrison or Walsall* (26p (*No.* NI81), 37p). *Perf* 14 (*No.* NI80) *or* 15 × 14 (*others*) (*both with one elliptical hole on each vertical side*)

NI78	N **4**	19p bistre (1 centre band)	2·50	2·00	□	□
NI79		20p bright green (1 centre band)	90	80	□	□
NI80		20p bright green (1 side band)	3·00	3·00	□	□
NI81		26p chestnut (2 bands) . .	1·25	1·00	□	□
		b. Perf 14	3·00	3·00	□	□
NI82		37p bright mauve (2 bands)	2·25	2·25	□	□
NI83		38p ultramarine (2 bands)	8·00	8·00	□	□
NI84		40p deep azure (2 bands)	2·50	2·50	□	□
NI85		63p light emerald (2 bands)	5·00	5·00	□	□
NI86		64p turquoise-green (2 bands)	9·00	9·00	□	□
NI87		65p greenish blue (2 bands)	2·75	3·00	□	□

Nos. NI70, NI80 and NI81*b* were only issued in stamp booklets. No. NI70 exists with the phosphor band at the left or right of the stamp.

Presentation Pack (*P.O. Pack No. 47*) (*contains* 19p, 26p, 38p, 64p (*Nos.* NI78, NI81, NI83 NI86))	14·00	☐
Presentation Pack (*P.O. Pack No. 52*) (*contains* 1st, 40p, 65p) (*Nos.* NI84, NI87, NI88*b*) . .	10·00	☐

Combined Presentation Packs for Northern Ireland, Scotland and Wales

Presentation Pack (*P.O. Pack No. 31*) (*contains* 19p, 25p, 30p, 41p *from Northern Ireland, Scotland and Wales* (*Nos.* NI69, NI72, NI74, NI76, S81, S84, S86, S88, W70, W73, W75, W77))	16·00	☐
Presentation Pack (*P.O. Pack No. 36*) (*contains* 20p, 26p, 37p, 63p *from Northern Ireland, Scotland and Wales* (*Nos.* NI71, NI73, NI75, NI77, S83, S85, S87, S89, W72, W74 W76, W78))	26·00	☐
Presentation Pack (*P.O. Pack No. 42*) (*contains* 20p (1 *centre band*), 26p, 37p, 63p *from Northern Ireland, Scotland and Wales* (*Nos.* NI79, NI81/2, NI85, S90/3, W79/82))	24·00	☐

N 5

2000 (15 FEB.–25 APR.) *Type* N **4** *redrawn with* '1st' *face value as Type* N **5**. *Two phosphor bands. Perf* 14 (*with one elliptical hole on each vertical side*)

NI88	N **5**	(1st) bright orange-red . .	2·75	2·75	☐	☐
		b. Perf 15 ×14 (25 Apr.)	9·00	8·00	☐	☐

No. NI88 was only issued in stamp booklets. No. NI88*b* was issued in sheets on 25 April.

N 6 Basalt Columns, Giant's Causeway

N 7 Aerial View of Patchwork Fields

N 8 Linen Pattern

N 9 Vase Pattern from Belleek

2001 (6 MAR.)–**02** *Printed in lithography by De La Rue* (68p), *De La Rue or Walsall* (E), *Walsall or Enschedé* (2nd) *or Walsall* (*others*). *One centre phosphor band* (2nd) *or two phosphor bands* (*others*). *Perf* 15 × 14 (*with one elliptical hole on each vertical side*)

NI89	N **6**	(2nd) black, new blue, bright magenta and greenish yellow . . .	60	60	☐	☐
NI90	N **7**	(1st) black, new blue and greenish yellow . . .	1·00	1·00	☐	☐
NI91	N **8**	(E) black, new blue and pale orange	1·25	1·25	☐	☐
NI92	N **9**	65p black, bright magenta and greenish yellow	2·75	2·75	☐	☐
NI93		68p black, bright magenta and greenish yellow	2·75	2·75	☐	☐
Presentation Pack (*P.O. Pack No.* 53) (*Nos.* NI89/92)			7·00		☐	
PHQ Cards (*set of 4*) (*Nos.* NI89/92)			2·00	10·00	☐	☐

Nos. NI89, NI90 and NI91 were initially sold at 19p, 27p and 36p, the latter representing the basic European airmail rate.

For combined presentation packs for all four Regions, see under England.

2003 (14 OCT.)–**06**. *As Nos.* NI89/91 *and* NI93 *but with white borders. Printed in lithography by Walsall* (NI98) *or De La Rue* (*others*). *One centre phosphor band* (2nd) *or two phosphor bands* (*others*). *Perf* 15 × 14 (*with one elliptical hole on each vertical side*)

NI94	N **6**	(2nd) black, new blue, bright magenta and greenish yellow	70	60	☐	☐
NI95	N **7**	(1st) black, new blue and greenish yellow . .	80	75	☐	☐
NI96	N **8**	(E) black and new blue	1·20	1·20	☐	☐
NI97		40p black and new blue	1·25	1·25	☐	☐
NI98		42p black, new blue and orange-yellow . . .	1·25	1·25	☐	☐
		a. Black, new blue and greenish yellow . .	65	70	☐	☐
NI99		44p black, new blue and greenish yellow . .	75	70	☐	☐
NI100	N **9**	68p black, bright magenta and greenish yellow . .	2·75	2·75	☐	☐

| NI101 | | 72p black, greyish black, bright magenta and greenish yellow .. | 1·30 | 1·20 | ☐ | ☐ |

Presentation Pack (P.O. Pack No.
  66) (Nos. NI94/6, NI100) . . . 6·00   ☐
PHQ Cards (set of 4) (Nos.
  NI94/6, NI100) . . . . 2·00 10·00 ☐ ☐

Nos. NI94/6 were initially sold at 20p, 28p and 38p, the latter representing the basic European airmail rate.

No. NI98 (Walsall printing) appears bluish grey and No. NI98a (De La Rue printing) appears olive-grey.

3 Scotland

S 1   S 2   S 3   S 4

1958–67 Wmk 179

S1	S 1	3d lilac	15	15	☐	☐
		p. Two phosphor bands	13·00	2·75	☐	☐
		pa. One side band . . .	20	25	☐	☐
		pb. One centre band . .	15	15	☐	☐
S2		4d blue	15	15	☐	☐
		p. Two phosphor bands	15	15	☐	☐
S3	S 2	6d purple	20	15	☐	☐
		p. Two phosphor bands	20	20	☐	☐
S4		9d bronze-green (2 phosphor bands) . .	35	40	☐	☐
S5	S 3	1s 3d green	40	40	☐	☐
		p. Two phosphor bands	40	40	☐	☐
S6		1s 6d blue (2 phosphor bands)	45	50	☐	☐

No. S1pa exists with the phosphor band at the left or right of the stamp.

1967–70 One centre phosphor band (Nos. S7, S9/10) or two phosphor bands (others). No wmk

S7	S 1	3d lilac	10	15	☐	☐
S8		4d blue	10	15	☐	☐
S9		4d sepia	10	10	☐	☐
S10		4d vermilion	10	10	☐	☐
S11		5d blue	20	10	☐	☐
S12	S 2	9d bronze-green	6·00	6·00	☐	☐
S13	S 3	1s 6d blue	1·75	1·50	☐	☐

Presentation Pack (containing
  Nos. S3, S5p, S7, S9/13) . . . 8·00   ☐

Decimal Currency
1971–93 Type S 4. No wmk
(a) Printed in photogravure by Harrison and Sons with phosphor bands. Perf 15 × 14

S14	2½p magenta (1 centre band) .	25	20	☐	☐
S15	3p ultramarine (2 bands) . . .	35	15	☐	☐
S16	3p ultramarine (1 centre band)	15	15	☐	☐
S17	3½p olive-grey (2 bands)	20	25	☐	☐
S18	3½p olive-grey (1 centre band)	20	25	☐	☐
S19	4½p grey-blue (2 bands)	30	25	☐	☐
S20	5p violet (2 bands)	1·00	1·25	☐	☐
S21	5½p violet (2 bands)	20	20	☐	☐
S22	5½p violet (1 centre band) . . .	20	25	☐	☐
S23	6½p blue (1 centre band)	20	20	☐	☐
S24	7p brown (1 centre band) . .	30	30	☐	☐
S25	7½p chestnut (2 bands)	1·25	1·25	☐	☐
S26	8p rosine (2 bands)	45	40	☐	☐

S27	8½p yellow-green (2 bands) ..	40	40 □ □
S28	9p violet (2 bands)	40	40 □ □
S29	10p orange-brown (2 bands) .	45	50 □ □
S30	10p orange-brown (1 centre band)	40	50 □ □
S31	10½p blue (2 bands)	45	50 □ □
S32	11p scarlet (2 bands)	50	50 □ □

(b) *Printed in photogravure by Harrison and Sons on phosphorised paper. Perf 15 × 14*

S33	12p yellowish green	50	50 □ □
S34	13½p purple-brown	70	80 □ □
S35	15p ultramarine	60	70 □ □

(c) *Printed in lithography by John Waddington. One side phosphor band (11½p, 12p, 12½p, 13p) or phosphorised paper (others). Perf 14*

S36	11½p drab	80	80 □ □
S37	12p bright emerald	2·00	2·00 □ □
S38	12½p light emerald	60	70 □ □
S39	13p pale chestnut	75	75 □ □
S40	14p grey-blue	75	75 □ □
S41	15½p pale violet	80	80 □ □
S42	16p drab	80	85 □ □
S43Ea	17p grey-blue	1·75	1·50 □ □
S44	18p deep violet	80	80 □ □
S45	19½p olive-grey	1·75	1·75 □ □
S46	20½p ultramarine	3·50	3·50 □ □
S47	22p blue	1·00	1·00 □ □
S48	22p yellow-green	4·25	4·25 □ □
S49	26p rosine	1·25	1·25 □ □
S50	28p deep violet-blue	1·25	1·25 □ □
S51	31p bright purple	2·50	2·50 □ □

(d) *Printed in lithography by Questa. Perf 15 × 14*

S52	12p bright emerald (1 side band)	2·00	2·25 □ □
S53	13p pale chestnut (1 side band)	70	75 □ □
S54	14p deep blue (1 centre band)	60	70 □ □
S55	14p deep blue (1 side band) ..	80	90 □ □
S56	15p bright blue (1 centre band)	70	70 □ □
S57	17p grey-blue (phosphorised paper)	4·00	4·00 □ □
S58	17p deep blue (1 centre band)	1·00	1·10 □ □
S59	18p olive-grey (phosphorised paper)	1·10	85 □ □
S60	18p bright green (1 centre band)	1·25	90 □ □
	a. *Perf* 14	1·00	1·00 □ □
S61	18p bright green (1 side band)	2·75	3·00 □ □
S62	19p bright orange-red (phosphorised paper) ...	70	70 □ □
S63	19p bright orange-red (2 bands)	2·25	2·00 □ □
S64	20p brownish black (phosphorised paper) ...	95	95 □ □
S65	22p yellow-green (phosphorised paper)	1·25	1·50 □ □
S66	22p bright orange-red (phosphorised paper) ...	1·25	90 □ □

S67	23p bright green (phosphorised paper)	1·25	1·10 □ □
S68	23p bright green (2 bands) ..	14·00	14·00 □ □
S69	24p Indian red (phosphorised paper)	1·25	1·25 □ □
S70	24p chestnut (phosphorised paper)	1·40	1·25 □ □
	a. *Perf* 14	3·00	3·25 □ □
S71	24p chestnut (2 bands)	2·75	3·00 □ □
S72	26p rosine (phosphorised paper)	3·75	4·00 □ □
S73	26p drab (phosphorised paper)	1·25	1·25 □ □
S74	28p deep violet-blue (phosphorised paper) ...	1·25	1·25 □ □
S75	28p deep bluish grey (phosphorised paper) ...	1·25	1·50 □ □
	a. *Perf* 14	6·50	6·75 □ □
S76	31p bright purple (phosphorised paper)	2·25	2·25 □ □
S77	32p greenish blue (phosphorised paper) ...	1·75	2·00 □ □
S78	34p deep bluish grey (phosphorised paper) ...	1·75	1·75 □ □
S79	37p rosine (phosphorised paper)	2·00	2·25 □ □
S80	39p bright mauve (phosphorised paper)	2·00	2·25 □ □
	a. *Perf* 14	4·50	4·75 □ □

Nos. S55, S61, S63, S68 and S71 were only issued in stamp booklets.

Presentation Pack (P.O. Pack No. 27) (contains 2½p *(S14),* 3p *(S15),* 5p *(S20),* 7½p *(S25))* ..	3·50	□
Presentation Pack (P.O. Pack No. 62) (contains 3p *(S16),* 3½p *(S17),* 5½p *(S21),* 8p *(S26), later with* 4½p *(S19) added)* .	2·50	□
Presentation Pack (P.O. Pack No. 85) (contains 6½p *(S23),* 8½p *(S27),* 10p *(S29),* 11p *(S32))*	2·00	□
Presentation Pack (P.O. Pack No. 129b) (contains 7p *(S24),* 9p *(S28),* 10½p *(S31),* 11½p *(S36),* 12p *(S33),* 13½p *(S34),* 14p *(S40),* 15p *(S35),* 18p *(S44),* 22p *(S47))*	9·00	□
Presentation Pack (P.O. Pack No. 2) (contains 10p *(S30),* 12½p *(S38),* 16p *(S42),* 20½p *(S46),* 26p *(S49),* 28p *(S50))*	17·00	□
Presentation Pack (P.O. Pack No. 6) (contains 10p *(S30),* 13p *(S39),* 16p *(S42),* 17p *(S43),* 22p *(S48),* 26p *(S49),* 28p *(S50),* 31p *(S51))*	17·00	□

Presentation Pack (*P.O. Pack No.*
10) (*contains* 12p (S52), 13p
(S53), 17p (S57), 18p (S59),
22p (S65), 26p (S72), 28p (S74),
31p (S76)) . . . . 20·00 □

For combined packs containing values from all three Regions see under Northern Ireland.

1993 (7 DEC.)–**98** (*a*) *Printed in lithography by Questa. Perf 15 × 14* (*with one elliptical hole on each vertical side*)

S81	S 4	19p bistre (1 centre band)	80	70 □ □
S82		19p bistre (1 side band) .	3·00	3·25 □ □
S83		20p bright green (1 centre band)	1·50	1·50 □ □
S84		25p red (2 bands)	1·10	1·00 □ □
S85		26p red-brown (2 bands)	1·75	2·00 □ □
S86		30p deep olive-grey (2 bands)	1·25	1·25 □ □
S87		37p bright mauve (2 bands)	2·75	3·00 □ □
S88		41p grey-brown (2 bands)	1·75	2·00 □ □
S89		63p light emerald (2 bands)	4·00	4·25 □ □

(*b*) *Printed in photogravure by Walsall* (20p, 26p (*No.* S91a), 63p), Harrison or Walsall (26p (*No.* S91), 37p). *Perf 14* (*No.* S90a) *or 15 × 14* (*others*) (*both with one elliptical hole on each vertical side*)

S90	S 4	20p bright green (1 centre band)	1·00	60 □ □
S90a		20p bright green (1 side band)	3·00	3·00 □ □
S91		26p chestnut (2 bands) .	1·00	1·00 □ □
		a. *Perf* 14	3·00	3·00 □ □
S92		37p bright mauve (2 bands)	1·50	1·50 □ □
S93		63p light emerald (2 bands)	4·00	4·00 □ □

Nos. S82, S90a and S91a were only issued in stamp booklets. For combined presentation packs for all three Regions, see under Northern Ireland.

S 5   Scottish Flag

S 6   Scottish Lion

S 7   Thistle

S 8   Tartan

1999 (8 JUNE)–**2002** *Printed in photogravure by De La Rue* (68p), De La Rue, Questa or Walsall (2nd, 1st) *or Walsall* (*others*). *One centre phosphor band* (2nd) *or two phosphor bands* (*others*). *Perf 15 × 14* (*with one elliptical hole on each vertical side*)

S94	S 5	(2nd) new blue, blue and silver	30	35 □ □
S95	S 6	(1st) greenish yellow, deep rose-red, rose-red and silver	40	45 □ □
S96	S 7	(E) bright lilac, deep lilac and silver	1·75	1·75 □ □
S97	S 8	64p greenish yellow, bright magenta, new blue, grey-black and silver	9·00	8·50 □ □
S98		65p greenish yellow, bright magenta, new blue, grey-black and silver	3·00	3·25 □ □
S99		68p greenish yellow, bright magenta, new blue, grey-black and silver	3·25	3·25 □ □

Presentation Pack (*P.O. Pack No.* 45) (*contains* 2nd, 1st, E, 64p) (*Nos.* S94/7)) . . . . . 14·00 □

Presentation Pack (*P.O. Pack No.* 50) (*contains* 65p) (*No.* S98)) 9·00 □

Presentation Pack (*P.O. Pack No.* 55) (*contains* 2nd, 1st, E, 65p) (*Nos.* S94/6, S98) . . . . 6·00 □

PHQ Cards (*Nos.* S94/7) . . . . 2·00 10·00 □ □

Nos. S94, S95 and S96 were initially sold at 19p, 26p and 30p, the latter representing the basic European airmail rate.

For combined presentation packs for all four Regions, see under England.

S 9

2000 (15 FEB.) *Type S **4** redrawn with '1st' face value as Type S **9**. Two phosphor bands. Perf 14* (*with one elliptical hole on each vertical side*)

S108	S 9	(1st) bright orange-red . .	3·00	3·25 □ □

No. S108 was only issued in stamp booklets.

2003 (14 OCT.)–**06**. *As Nos. S94/6 and S99 but with white borders. Printed in photogravure by Walsall or De La Rue* (42p) *or De La Rue* (*others*). *One centre phosphor band* (2nd) *or two phosphor bands* (*others*). *Perf 15 × 14* (*with one elliptical hole on each vertical side*).

S109	S 5	(2nd) new blue, blue and silver	60	50 □ □
S110	S 6	(1st) rose-red, greenish yellow, deep rose-red and silver	80	75 □ □
S111	S 7	(E) bright lilac, deep lilac and silver	1·00	1·00 □ □

S112	40p bright lilac, deep lilac and silver	1·25	1·25	☐	☐
S113	42p bright lilac, deep lilac and silver	1·20	1·20	☐	☐
S114	44p bright lilac, deep lilac and silver	65	70	☐	☐
S115 **S 8**	68p bright magenta, greenish yellow, new blue, grey-black and silver	2·00	2·00	☐	☐
S116	72p bright magenta, greenish yellow, new blue, grey-black and silver	1·10	1·20	☐	☐
	Presentation Pack (P.O. Pack No. 64) (Nos. S109/11, S115) . . .	5·00		☐	
	PHQ Cards (set of 4) (Nos. S109/11, S115)	2·00	6·00	☐	☐

Nos. S109/11 were initially sold at 20p, 28p and 38p, the latter representing the basic European airmail rate.

Opening of New Scottish Parliament Building

2004 (5 Oct.) Sheet 123 × 70 mm. Printed in photogravure by De La Rue. One centre phosphor band (2nd) or two phosphor bands (others). Perf 15 × 14 (with one elliptical hole on each vertical side).

MSS120	Nos. S109, S110 × 2 and S112 × 2	6·00	6·00	☐	☐
	First Day Cover		7·25		☐

S 10

Celebrating Scotland

2006 (30 Nov.) Sheet 124 × 71 mm. Printed in photogravure by De La Rue. Two phosphor bands. Perf 15 × 14 (with one elliptical hole on each vertical side) (1st) or 14 × 14 (72p).

MSS121	(1st) As No. S110; (1st) Scottish Flag; 72p St. Andrew; 72p Edinburgh Castle	3·00	3·25	☐	☐
	First Day Cover		4·25		☐
	Presentation Pack	4·00		☐	
	PHQ Cards (set of 5)	2·25	5·50	☐	☐

For full information on all future British issues, collectors should write to Royal Mail, Freepost EH3647, 21 South Gyle Crescent, Edinburgh EH12 9PE.

4 Wales

W **1**   W **2**   W **3**

1958–67 Wmk **179**

W1	W **1**	3d lilac	15	15	☐	☐
		p. One centre phosphor band	20	15	☐	☐
W2		4d blue	20	15	☐	☐
		p. Two phosphor bands	20	15	☐	☐
W3	W **2**	6d purple	35	30	☐	☐
W4		9d bronze-green (2 phosphor bands) . .	40	35	☐	☐
W5	W **3**	1s 3d green	40	40	☐	☐
W6		1s 6d blue (2 phosphor bands)	40	40	☐	☐

1967–69 One centre phosphor band (Nos. W7, W9/10) or two phosphor bands (others). No wmk

W7	W **1**	3d lilac	10	15	☐	☐
W8		4d blue	10	15	☐	☐
W9		4d sepia	15	15	☐	☐
W10		4d vermilion	15	15	☐	☐
W11		5d blue	15	15	☐	☐
W12	W **3**	1s 6d blue	3·50	3·50	☐	☐
		Presentation Pack (comprises Nos. W4, W6/7, W9/11)	4·00		☐	

W **4** With 'p'   W **5** Without 'p'

Decimal Currency
1971–92 Type W **4**. No wmk

(a) Printed in photogravure with phosphor bands

W13	2½p magenta (1 centre band) .	20	20	☐	☐
W14	3p ultramarine (2 bands) . . .	25	20	☐	☐
W15	3p ultramarine (1 centre band)	25	25	☐	☐
W16	3½p olive-grey (2 bands)	20	30	☐	☐
W17	3½p olive-grey (1 centre band)	20	30	☐	☐
W18	4½p grey-blue (2 bands)	30	30	☐	☐
W19	5p violet (2 bands)	1·25	1·25	☐	☐
W20	5½p violet (2 bands)	25	30	☐	☐
W21	5½p violet (1 centre band) . . .	25	30	☐	☐
W22	6½p blue (1 centre band)	20	20	☐	☐
W23	7p brown (1 centre band) . .	25	25	☐	☐
W24	7½p chestnut (2 bands)	1·75	1·75	☐	☐

W25	8p rosine (2 bands)	30	35 ☐ ☐
W26	8½p yellow-green (2 bands) . .	30	35 ☐ ☐
W27	9p violet (2 bands)	40	40 ☐ ☐
W28	10p orange-brown (2 bands) . .	40	40 ☐ ☐
W29	10p orange-brown (1 centre band)	40	40 ☐ ☐
W30	10½p blue (2 bands)	45	45 ☐ ☐
W31	11p scarlet (2 bands)	45	45 ☐ ☐

(b) Printed in photogravure on phosphorised paper

W32	12p yellow-green	50	50 ☐ ☐
W33	13½p purple-brown	60	70 ☐ ☐
W34	15p ultramarine	60	70 ☐ ☐

(c) Printed in lithography. Perf 14 (11½p, 12½p, 14p (*No.* W39), 15½p. 16p, 18p (*No.* W46), 19½p, 20½p, 22p (*No.* W54), 26p (*No.* W61), 28p (*No.* W63)) *or* 15 × 14 (*others*)

W35	11½p drab (1 side band)	90	80 ☐ ☐
W36	12p bright emerald (1 side band)	2·00	2·00 ☐ ☐
W37	12½p light emerald (1 side band)	70	70 ☐ ☐
	a. Perf 15 × 14	4·75	4·25 ☐ ☐
W38	13p pale chestnut (1 side band)	60	60 ☐ ☐
W39	14p grey-blue (phosphorised paper)	70	70 ☐ ☐
W40	14p deep blue (1 centre band)	75	75 ☐ ☐
W41	15p bright blue (1 centre band)	80	75 ☐ ☐
W42	15½p pale violet (phosphorised paper)	75	75 ☐ ☐
W43	16p drab (phosphorised paper)	1·75	1·75 ☐ ☐
	a. Perf 15 × 14	1·75	1·75 ☐ ☐
W44	17p grey-blue (phosphorised paper)	70	80 ☐ ☐
W45	17p deep blue (1 centre band)	90	80 ☐ ☐
W46	18p deep violet (phosphorised paper)	1·00	95 ☐ ☐
W47	18p olive-grey (phosphorised paper)	95	90 ☐ ☐
W48	18p bright green (1 centre band)	75	75 ☐ ☐
	b. Perf 14	5·25	5·25 ☐ ☐
W49	18p bright green (1 side band)	2·00	2·00 ☐ ☐
W50	19p bright orange-red (phosphorised paper) . . .	1·00	80 ☐ ☐
W51	19½p olive-grey (phosphorised paper)	1·75	2·00 ☐ ☐
W52	20p brownish black (phosphorised paper)	90	90 ☐ ☐
W53	20½p ultramarine (phosphorised paper)	3·75	3·75 ☐ ☐
W54	22p blue (phosphorised paper)	1·10	1·10 ☐ ☐
W55	22p yellow-green (phosphorised paper)	95	1·10 ☐ ☐
W56	22p bright orange-red (phosphorised paper) . . .	1·00	1·10 ☐ ☐
W57	23p bright green (phosphorised paper)	1·00	1·10 ☐ ☐
W58	24p Indian red (phosphorised paper)	1·25	1·25 ☐ ☐

W59	24p chestnut (phosphorised paper)	75	75 ☐ ☐
	b. Perf 14	4·75	5·25 ☐ ☐
W60	24p chestnut (2 bands)	1·25	1·50 ☐ ☐
W61	26p rosine (phosphorised paper)	1·10	1·10 ☐ ☐
	a. Perf 15 × 14	5·75	6·00 ☐ ☐
W62	26p drap (phosphorised paper)	1·75	1·75 ☐ ☐
W63	28p deep violet-blue (phosphorised paper)	1·50	1·50 ☐ ☐
	a. Perf 15 × 14	1·50	1·50 ☐ ☐
W64	28p deep bluish grey (phosphorised paper) . . .	1·50	1·50 ☐ ☐
W65	31p bright purple (phosphorised paper)	1·75	1·75 ☐ ☐
W66	32p greenish blue (phosphorised paper)	1·75	1·75 ☐ ☐
W67	34p deep bluish grey (phosphorised paper) . . .	1·75	1·75 ☐ ☐
W68	37p rosine (phosphorised paper)	2·25	2·25 ☐ ☐
W69	39p bright mauve (phosphorised paper)	2·25	2·25 ☐ ☐

Nos. W49 and W60 were only issued in stamp booklets. The former exists with the phosphor band at the left or right of the stamp.

Presentation Pack (*P.O. Pack No. 28*) (*contains* 2½p (W13), 3p (W14), 5p (W19), 7½p (W24)) . 3·50 ☐

Presentation Pack (*P.O. Pack No. 63*) (*contains* 3p (W15), 3½p (W16), 5½p (W20), 8p (W25), *later with* 4½p (W18) *added*) . 2·50 ☐

Presentation Pack (*P.O. Pack No. 86*) (*contains* 6½p (W22), 8½p (W26), 10p (W28), 11p (W31)) 2·00 ☐

Presentation Pack (*P.O. Pack No. 129c*) (*contains* 7p (W23), 9p (W27), 10½p (W30), 11½p (W35), 12p (W32), 13½p (W33), 14p (W39), 15p (W34), 18p (W46), 22p (W54)) . . . . . 9·00 ☐

Presentation Pack (*P.O. Pack No. 3*) (*contains* 10p (W29), 12½p (W37), 16p (W43), 20½p (W53), 26p (W61), 28p (W63)) . . . . 17·00 ☐

Presentation Pack (*P.O. Pack No. 7*) (*contains* 10p (W29), 13p (W38), 16p (W43a), 17p (W44), 22p (W55), 26p (W61), 28p (W63), 31p (W65)) . . . . 17·00 ☐

Presentation Pack (*P.O. Pack No. 11*) (*contains* 12p (W36), 13p (W38), 17p (W44), 18p (W47), 22p (W55), 26p (W61a), 28p (W63a), 31p (W65)) . . . . . . 17·00 ☐

For combined packs containing values from all three Regions see under Northern Ireland.

1993 (7 Dec.)–**96** *Printed in lithography by Questa. Perf* 15 × 14 (*with one elliptical hole on each vertical side*)

W70	**W 4**	19p bistre (1 centre band)	80	70 ☐ ☐
W71		19p bistre (1 side band) .	3·75	4·00 ☐ ☐
W72		20p bright green (1 centre band)	1·75	2·00 ☐ ☐
W73		25p red (2 bands)	1·25	1·00 ☐ ☐
W74		26p red-brown (2 bands)	2·00	2·25 ☐ ☐
W75		30p deep olive-grey (2 bands)	1·25	1·25 ☐ ☐
W76		37p bright mauve (2 bands)	2·75	3·00 ☐ ☐
W77		41p grey-brown (2 bands)	2·00	2·00 ☐ ☐
W78		63p light emerald (2 bands)	4·50	4·75 ☐ ☐

No. W71 was only issued in stamp booklets.

For combined presentation packs for all three Regions see under Northern Ireland.

1997 (1 July)–**98** *Printed in photogravure by Walsall* (20p, 26p (*No.* W80a), 63p), *Harrison or Walsall* (26p (*No.* W80), 37p) *Perf* 14 (*No.* W79a) *or* 15 × 14 (*both with one elliptical hole on each vertical side*)

W79	**W 5**	20p bright green (1 centre band)	80	80 ☐ ☐
W79a		20p bright green (1 side band)	2·25	2·00 ☐ ☐
W80		26p chestnut (2 bands) .	1·00	1·00 ☐ ☐
		a. *Perf* 14	2·75	2·75 ☐ ☐
W81		37p bright mauve (2 bands)	2·75	2·75 ☐ ☐
W82		63p light emerald (2 bands)	4·00	4·50 ☐ ☐

Presentation Pack (*P.O. Pack No.* 39) (*Nos.* W79 *and* W80/2) . . 17·00   ☐

Nos. W79a and W80a were only issued in stamp booklets.

W **6**   Leek

W **7**   Welsh Dragon

W **8**   Daffodil

W **9**   Prince of Wales Feathers

1999 (8 June)–**2002** *Printed in photogravure by De La Rue* (68p), *Walsall or De La Rue* (1st), (2nd), (*No.* W83) *or Walsall* (*others*). *One phosphor band* (2nd) *or two phosphor bands* (*others*). *Perf* 14 (*No.* W83a) *or* 15 × 14 (*others*) (*both with one elliptical hole on each vertical side*)

W83	**W 6**	(2nd) orange-brown, yellow-orange and black (1 centre band) . . .	60	50 ☐ ☐
W83a		(2nd) orange-brown, yellow-orange and black (1 side band)	3·75	4·00 ☐ ☐
W84	**W 7**	(1st) blue-green, greenish yellow, silver and black	1·00	60 ☐ ☐
W85	**W 8**	(E) greenish blue, deep greenish blue and grey-black	1·50	1·50 ☐ ☐
W86	**W 9**	64p violet, gold, silver and black	9·00	9·00 ☐ ☐
W87		65p violet, gold, silver and black	3·00	3·25 ☐ ☐
W88		68p violet, gold, silver and black	2·75	2·75 ☐ ☐

Presentation Pack (*P.O. Pack No.* 46) (*contains* 2nd, 1st, E, 64p) (*Nos.* W83, W84/6)) . . . . 14·00   ☐

Presentation Pack (*P.O. Pack No.* 51) (*contains* 65p) (No. W87)) . . . 8·00   ☐

Presentation Pack (*P.O. Pack No.* 56) (*contains* 2nd, 1st, E, 65p) (*Nos.* W83, W84/5, W87)) . . . 8·00   ☐

PHQ Cards (*Nos.* W83, W84/6) . 2·00   10·00 ☐ ☐

Nos. W83, W84 and W85 were initially sold at 19p, 26p and 30p, the latter representing the basic European airmail rate.

No. W83a was only issued in stamp booklets.

For combined presentation packs for all four Regions, see under England.

W **10**

2000 (15 Feb.) *Type* W **4** *redrawn with* '1af/st' *face value as Type* W **10**. *Two phosphor bands. Perf* 14 (*with one elliptical hole on each vertical side*)

W97	**W 10**	(1st) bright orange-red .	3·00	2·75 ☐ ☐

No. W97 was only issued in stamp booklets.

2003 (14 Oct.)–**06.** *As Nos.* W83, W84/5 *and* W88, *but with white borders. Printed in photogravure by Walsall or De La Rue (42p) or De La Rue (others). One centre phosphor band (2nd) or two phosphor bands (others). Perf* 15×14 *(with one elliptical hole on each vertical side).*

W98	W **6**	(2nd) orange-brown, deep orange-brown and black	80	75	☐	☐
W99	W **7**	(1st) blue-green, greenish yellow, silver and black	80	75	☐	☐
W100	W **8**	(E) greenish blue, deep greenish blue and grey-black	1·00	1·00	☐	☐
W101		40p greenish blue, deep greenish blue and grey-black	1·25	1·25	☐	☐
W102		42p greenish blue, deep greenish blue and grey-black	1·20	1·20	☐	☐
W103		44p greenish blue, deep greenish blue and grey-black	80	70	☐	☐
W104	W **9**	68p violet, gold, silver and black	2·00	2·00	☐	☐
W105		72p violet, gold, silver and black	1·40	1·20	☐	☐
		Presentation Pack (*P.O. Pack No.* 65) (*Nos.* W98/100, W104) . .	5·00		☐	
		PHQ Cards (*set of* 4) (*Nos.* W98/100, W104)	2·00	6·00	☐	☐

Nos. W98/100 were initially sold at 20p, 28p and 38p, the latter representing the basic European airmail rate.

Opening of New Welsh Assembly Building, Cardiff

2006 (1 Mar.) *Sheet* 123 × 70 mm. *Printed in photogravure by De La Rue. One centre phosphor band (2nd) or two phosphor bands (others). Perf* 15 × 14 *(with one elliptical hole on each vertical side).*

MSW109	Nos. W98, W99 × 2 and W103 × 2	4·00	4·00	☐	☐
	First Day Cover		6·00		☐

ISLE OF MAN

Regional Issues

1   **2**   **3**

1958–67 *Wmk* 179. *Perf* 15 × 14

1	**1**	2½d red	50	1·25	☐	☐
2	**2**	3d lilac	50	20	☐	☐
		p. *One centre phosphor band*	20	50	☐	☐
3		4d blue	1·50	1·50	☐	☐
		p. *Two phosphor bands* . .	20	30	☐	☐

1968–69 *One centre phosphor band (Nos. 5/6) or two phosphor bands (others). No wmk*

4	**2**	4d blue	25	30	☐	☐
5		4d sepia	25	40	☐	☐
6		4d vermilion	45	75	☐	☐
7		5d blue	45	75	☐	☐

Decimal Currency

1971 (7 July) *One centre phosphor band (2½p) or two phosphor bands (others). No wmk*

8	**3**	2½p magenta	20	15	☐	☐
9		3p ultramarine	20	15	☐	☐
10		5p violet	40	60	☐	☐
11		7½p chestnut	40	75	☐	☐
		Presentation Pack	2·75		☐	

For comprehensive listings of the Independent Administration issues of the Isle of Man, see Stanley Gibbons *Collect Channel Islands and Isle of Man Stamps*.

CHANNEL ISLANDS

1 General Issue

C **1**   Gathering Vraic   C **2**   Islanders gathering Vraic

Third Anniversary of Liberation

1948 (10 May) *Wmk Type* **127.** *Perf* 15 × 14

C1	C **1**	1d red	25	30	☐	☐
C2	C **2**	2½d blue	25	30	☐	☐
		First Day Cover		35·00		☐

2 Guernsey

(a) War Occupation Issues

Stamps issued under British authority during the German Occupation.

| 1 | 2 | 3 |

1941–44 *Rouletted.* (*a*) *White paper. No wmk*

1f	**1**	½d green	3·00	2·00 □ □
2		1d red	2·25	1·25 □ □
3a		2½d blue	6·00	5·00 □ □

(b) Bluish French bank-note paper. Wmk loops

4	**1**	½d green	27·00	21·00 □ □
5		1d red	14·00	21·00 □ □

(b) Regional Issues

1958–67 *Wmk* **179**. *Perf* 15 × 14

6	**2**	2½d red	35	40 □ □
7	**3**	3d lilac	30	30 □ □
		p. One centre phosphor band	15	20 □ □
8		4d blue	25	30 □ □
		p. Two phosphor bands . .	15	20 □ □

1968–69 *One centre phosphor band* (*Nos.* 10/11) *or two phosphor bands* (*others*). *No wmk*

9	**3**	4d blue	10	20 □ □
10		4d sepia	10	15 □ □
11		4d vermilion	20	25 □ □
12		5d blue	20	30 □ □

For comprehensive listings of the Independent Postal Administration issues of Guernsey, see Stanley Gibbons *Collect Channel Islands and Isle of Man Stamps.*

3 Jersey

(a) War Occupation Issues

Stamps issued under British authority during the German Occupation.

| 1 | 2 Old Jersey Farm | 3 Portelet Bay |

| 4 Corbière Lighthouse | 5 Elizabeth Castle |

| 6 Mont Orgueil Castle | 7 Gathering Vraic (seaweed) |

1941–42 *White paper. No wmk Perf* 11

1	**1**	½d green	5·25	3·75 □ □
2		1d red	6·25	3·50 □ □

1943 *No wmk Perf* 13½

3	**2**	½d green	9·75	10·00 □ □
4	**3**	1d red	2·25	50 □ □
5	**4**	1½d brown	7·00	5·75 □ □
6	**5**	2d orange	6·50	2·00 □ □
7a	**6**	2½d blue	1·00	1·75 □ □
8	**7**	3d violet	1·25	2·75 □ □
		Set of 6	22·00	21·00 □ □

(b) Regional Issues

| 8 | 9 |

1958–67 *Wmk* **179**. *Perf* 15 × 14

9	**8**	2½d red	30	45 □ □
10	**9**	3d lilac	30	25 □ □
		p. One centre phosphor band	15	15 □ □
11		4d blue	25	30 □ □
		p. Two phosphor bands . .	15	25 □ □

1968–69 *One centre phosphor band* (4*d values*) *or two phosphor bands* (5*d*). *No wmk*

12	**9**	4d sepia	15	25 □ □
13		4d vermilion	15	25 □ □
14		5d blue	15	50 □ □

For comprehensive listings of the Independent Postal Adminstration issues of Jersey, see Stanley Gibbons *Collect Channel Islands and Isle of Man Stamps.*

REGIONAL FIRST DAY COVERS

PRICES for First Day Covers listed below are for stamps, as indicated, used on illustrated envelopes and postmarked with operational cancellations (before 1964) or with special First Day of Issue cancellations (1964 onwards). First Day postmarks of 8 June 1964 and 7 February 1966 were of the machine cancellation 'envelope' type.

£sd Issues

18 Aug. 1958	Guernsey 3d (No. 7)	20·00	☐
	Isle of Man 3d (No. 2)	32·00	☐
	Jersey 3d (No. 10)	20·00	☐
	Northern Ireland 3d (No. NI1)	30·00	☐
	Scotland 3d (No. S1)	17·00	☐
	Wales 3d (No. W1)	12·00	☐
29 Sept. 1958	Northern Ireland 6d, 1s 3d (Nos. NI3, NI5)	35·00	☐
	Scotland 6d, 1s 3d (Nos. S3, S5)	25·00	☐
	Wales 6d, 1s 3d (Nos. W3, W5)	25·00	☐
8 June 1964	Guernsey $2\frac{1}{2}$d (No. 6)	30·00	☐
	Isle of Man $2\frac{1}{2}$d (No. 1)	45·00	☐
	Jersey $2\frac{1}{2}$d (No. 9)	30·00	☐
7 Feb. 1966	Guernsey 4d (No. 8)	8·00	☐
	Isle of Man 4d (No. 3)	15·00	☐
	Jersey 4d (No. 11)	10·00	☐
	Northern Ireland 4d (No. NI2)	7·00	☐
	Scotland 4d (No. S2)	7·00	☐
	Wales 4d (No. W2)	7·00	☐
1 March 1967	Northern Ireland 9d, 1s 6d (Nos. NI4, NI6)	4·00	☐
	Scotland 9d, 1s 6d (Nos. S4, S6)	6·00	☐
	Wales 9d, 1s 6d (Nos. W4, W6)	4·00	☐
4 Sept. 1968	Guernsey 4d, 5d (Nos. 10, 12)	3·00	☐
	Isle of Man 4d, 5d (Nos. 5, 7)	4·00	☐
	Jersey 4d, 5d (Nos. 12, 14)	3·00	☐
	Northern Ireland 4d, 5d (Nos. NI8, NI10)	3·00	☐
	Scotland 4d, 5d (Nos. S9, S11)	3·00	☐
	Wales 4d, 5d (Nos. W9, W11)	3·00	☐

Decimal Issues

7 July 1971	Isle of Man $2\frac{1}{2}$p, 3p, 5p, $7\frac{1}{2}$p (Nos. 8/11)	3·00	☐
	Northern Ireland $2\frac{1}{2}$p, 3p, 5p, $7\frac{1}{2}$p (Nos. NI12/13, NI18, NI23)	3·50	☐
	Scotland $2\frac{1}{2}$p, 3p, 5p, $7\frac{1}{2}$p (Nos. S14/15, S20, S25)	3·00	☐
	Wales $2\frac{1}{2}$p, 3p, 5p, $7\frac{1}{2}$p (Nos. W13/14, W19, W24)	3·00	☐
23 Jan. 1974	Northern Ireland 3p, $3\frac{1}{2}$p, $5\frac{1}{2}$p, 8p (Nos. NI14/15, NI19, NI24)	2·40	☐
	Scotland 3p, $3\frac{1}{2}$p, $5\frac{1}{2}$p, 8p (Nos. S16/17, S21, S26)	2·50	☐
	Wales 3p, $3\frac{1}{2}$p, $5\frac{1}{2}$p, 8p (Nos. W15/16, W20, W25)	2·50	☐
6 Nov. 1974	Northern Ireland $4\frac{1}{2}$p (No. NI17)	1·50	☐
	Scotland $4\frac{1}{2}$p (No. S19)	1·50	☐
	Wales $4\frac{1}{2}$p (No. W18)	1·50	☐
14 Jan. 1976	Northern Ireland $6\frac{1}{2}$p, $8\frac{1}{2}$p (Nos. NI21, NI25)	1·50	☐
	Scotland $6\frac{1}{2}$p, $8\frac{1}{2}$p (Nos. S23, S27)	1·50	☐
	Wales $6\frac{1}{2}$p, $8\frac{1}{2}$p (Nos. W22, W26)	1·50	☐
20 Oct. 1976	Northern Ireland 10p, 11p (Nos. NI27, NI30)	1·75	☐
	Scotland 10p, 11p (Nos. S29, S32)	1·50	☐
	Wales 10p, 11p (Nos. W28, W31)	1·50	☐
18 Jan. 1978	Northern Ireland 7p, 9p, $10\frac{1}{2}$p (Nos. NI22, NI26, NI29)	1·75	☐
	Scotland 7p, 9p, $10\frac{1}{2}$p (Nos. S24, S28, S31)	1·75	☐
	Wales 7p, 9p, $10\frac{1}{2}$p (Nos. W23, W27, W30)	1·75	☐
23 July 1980	Northern Ireland 12p, $13\frac{1}{2}$p, 15p (Nos. NI31/3)	3·00	☐
	Scotland 12p, $13\frac{1}{2}$p, 15p (Nos. S33/5)	2·75	☐
	Wales 12p, $13\frac{1}{2}$p, 15p (Nos. W32/4)	3·00	☐
8 April 1981	Northern Ireland $11\frac{1}{2}$p, 14p, 18p, 22p (Nos. NI34, NI38, NI45, NI53)	2·50	☐
	Scotland $11\frac{1}{2}$p, 14p, 18p, 22p (Nos. S36, S40, S44, S47)	2·50	☐
	Wales $11\frac{1}{2}$p, 14p, 18p, 22p (Nos. W35, W39, W46, W54)	2·50	☐
24 Feb. 1982	Northern Ireland $12\frac{1}{2}$p, $15\frac{1}{2}$p, $19\frac{1}{2}$p, 26p (Nos. NI36, NI41, NI50, NI60)	4·00	☐
	Scotland $12\frac{1}{2}$p, $15\frac{1}{2}$p, $19\frac{1}{2}$p, 26p (Nos. S38, S41, S45, S49)	3·50	☐
	Wales $12\frac{1}{2}$p, $15\frac{1}{2}$p, $19\frac{1}{2}$p, 26p (Nos. W37, W42, W51, W61)	3·50	☐
27 April 1983	Northern Ireland 16p, $20\frac{1}{2}$p, 28p (Nos. NI42, NI52, NI62)	4·00	☐
	Scotland 16p, $20\frac{1}{2}$p, 28p (Nos. S42, S46, S50)	4·00	☐
	Wales 16p, $20\frac{1}{2}$p, 28p (Nos. W43, W53, W63)	3·50	☐
23 Oct. 1984	Northern Ireland 13p, 17p, 22p, 31p (Nos. NI37, NI43, NI54, NI64)	4·75	☐
	Scotland 13p, 17p, 22p, 31p (Nos. S39, S43, S48, S51)	4·00	☐
	Wales 13p, 17p, 22p, 31p (Nos. W38, W44, W55, W65)	4·25	☐

7 Jan. 1986	*Northern Ireland* 12*p* (*No.* NI35)	2·00	☐
	Scotland 12*p* (*No.* S37)	2·00	☐
	Wales 12*p* (*No.* W36)	2·00	☐
6 Jan. 1987	*Northern Ireland* 18*p* (*No.* NI46)	2·00	☐
	Scotland 18*p* (*No.* S59)	1·80	☐
	Wales 18*p* (*No.* W47)	2·00	☐
8 Nov. 1988	*Northern Ireland* 14*p*, 19*p*, 23*p*, 32*p* (*Nos.* NI39, NI49, NI56, NI65)	4·25	☐
	Scotland 14*p*, 19*p*, 23*p*, 32*p* (*Nos.* S54, S62, S67, S77)	4·25	☐
	Wales 14*p*, 19*p*, 23*p*, 32*p* (*Nos.* W40, W50, W57, W66)	4·50	☐
28 Nov. 1989	*Northern Ireland* 15*p*, 20*p*, 24*p*, 34*p* (*Nos.* NI40, NI51, NI57, NI66)	5·00	☐
	Scotland 15*p*, 20*p*, 24*p*, 34*p* (*Nos.* S56, S64, S69, S78) . . .	5·00	☐
	Wales 15*p*, 20*p*, 24*p*, 34*p* (*Nos.* W41, W52, W58, W67)	5·00	☐
4 Dec. 1990	*Northern Ireland* 17*p*, 22*p*, 26*p*, 37*p* (*Nos.* NI44, NI55, NI61, NI67)	5·00	☐
	Scotland 17*p*, 22*p*, 26*p*, 37*p* (*Nos.* S58, S66, S73, S79) . . .	5·00	☐
	Wales 17*p*, 22*p*, 26*p*, 37*p* (*Nos.* W45, W56, W62, W68)	5·00	☐
3 Dec. 1991	*Northern Ireland* 18*p*, 24*p*, 28*p*, 39*p* (*Nos.* NI47, NI58, NI63, NI68)	5·50	☐
	Scotland 18*p*, 24*p*, 28*p*, 39*p* (*Nos.* S60, S70, S75, S80) . . .	5·50	☐
	Wales 18*p*, 24*p*, 28*p*, 39*p* (*Nos.* W48, W59, W64, W69)	5·50	☐
7 Dec 1993	*Northern Ireland* 19*p*, 25*p*, 30*p*, 41*p* (*Nos.* NI69, NI72, NI74, NI76)	6·00	☐
	Scotland 19*p*, 25*p*, 30*p*, 41*p* (*Nos.* S81, S84, S86, S88) . . .	6·00	☐
	Wales 19*p*, 25*p*, 30*p*, 41*p* (*Nos.* W70, W73, W75, W77)	6·00	☐
23 July 1996	*Northern Ireland* 20*p* (1 *centre band*), 26*p*, 37*p*, 63*p* (*Nos.* NI71, NI73, NI75, NI77)	8·75	☐
	Scotland 20*p* (1 *centre band*), 26*p*, 37*p*, 63*p* (*Nos.* S83, S85, S87, S89)	8·75	☐
	Wales 20*p*, 26*p*, 37*p*, 63*p* (*Nos.* W72, W74, W76, W78)	7·00	☐
1 July 1997	*Wales* 20*p* (1 *centre band*), 26*p*, 37*p*, 63*p* (*Nos.* W79 and W80/2)	6·00	☐
8 June 1999	*Northern Ireland* 38*p*, 64*p* (*Nos.* NI83, NI86)	4·00	☐
	Scotland 2nd, 1st, E, 64*p* (*Nos* S94/7)	6·00	☐
	Wales 2nd, 1st, E, 64*p* (*Nos.* W83, W84/6)	6·00	☐
25 Apr 2000	*Northern Ireland* 1st, 40*p*, 65*p* (*Nos.* NI84, NI87, NI88*b*)	7·00	☐
	Scotland 65*p* (*No.* S98)	3·00	☐
	Wales 65*p* (*No.* W87)	3·00	☐
6 Mar 2001	*Northern Ireland* 2nd, 1st, E, 65*p* (*Nos.* NI89/92)	4·50	☐
23 Apr 2001	*England* 2nd, 1st, E, 65*p* (*Nos.* EN1/4)	3·25	☐
4 July 2002	*England* 68*p* (*No.* EN5)	1·75	☐
	Northern Ireland 68*p* (*No.* NI93)	2·50	☐
	Scotland 68*p* (*No.* S99)	1·75	☐
	Wales 68*p* (*No.* W88)	1·75	☐
14 Oct 2003	*England* 2nd, 1st, E, 68*p* (*Nos.* EN6/8, EN11)	3·25	☐
	Northern Ireland 2nd, 1st, E, 68*p* (*Nos.* NI94/6, NI99)	3·25	☐
	Scotland 2nd, 1st, E, 68*p* (*Nos.* S109/11, S114)	3·25	☐
	Wales 2nd, 1st, E, 68*p* (*Nos.* W98/100, W103)	3·25	☐
11 May 2004	*England* 40*p* (*No.* EN9)	2·75	☐
	Northern Ireland 40*p* (*No.* NI97)	2·75	☐
	Scotland 40*p* (*No.* S112)	2·75	☐
	Wales 40*p* (*No.* W101)	2·75	☐
5 Apr 2005	*England* 42*p* (*No.* EN11)	1·40	☐
	Northern Ireland 42*p* (*No.* NI98)	1·40	☐
	Scotland 42*p* (*No.* S113)	1·40	☐
	Wales 42*p* (*No.* W102)	1·40	☐
28 Mar 2006	*England* 44*p*, 72*p* (*Nos.* EN11, EN13)	2·75	☐
	Northern Ireland 44*p*, 72*p* (*Nos.* NI99, NI101)	2·75	☐
	Scotland 44*p*, 72*p* (*Nos.* S114, S116)	2·75	☐
	Wales 44*p*, 72*p* (*Nos.* W103, W105)	2·75	☐

POSTAGE DUE STAMPS

PERFORATION. All postage due stamps to No. D101 are perf 14 × 15.

D **1**    D **2**

1914–22 *Wmk Type* **100** (*Royal Cypher* ('*Simple*')) *sideways*

D1	D **1**	½d green	. . . .	50	25	☐	☐
D2		1d red	. . . .	50	25	☐	☐
D3		1½d brown	. . . .	48·00	20·00	☐	☐
D4		2d black	. . . .	50	25	☐	☐
D5		3d violet	. . . .	5·00	75	☐	☐
D6		4d green	. . . .	18·00	5·00	☐	☐
D7		5d brown	. . . .	7·00	3·50	☐	☐
D8		1s blue	. . . .	40·00	5·00	☐	☐
	Set of 8			£100	32·00	☐	☐

1924–31 *Wmk Type* **111** (*Block* G v R) *sideways*

D10	D **1**	½d green	. . . .	1·25	75	☐	☐
D11		1d red	. . . .	60	25	☐	☐
D12		1½d brown	. . . .	47·00	22·00	☐	☐
D13		2d black	. . . .	1·00	25	☐	☐
D14		3d violet	. . . .	1·50	25	☐	☐
D15		4d green	. . . .	15·00	4·25	☐	☐
D16		5d brown	. . . .	65·00	45·00	☐	☐
D17		1s blue	. . . .	8·50	50	☐	☐
D18	D **2**	2s 6d purple/*yellow*	. . . .	85·00	1·75	☐	☐
	Set of 9			£200	60·00	☐	☐

1936–37 *Wmk Type* **125** (E 8 R) *sideways*

D19	D **1**	½d green	. . . .	12·00	10·50	☐	☐
D20		1d red	. . . .	2·00	1·75	☐	☐
D21		2d black	. . . .	12·00	12·00	☐	☐
D22		3d violet	. . . .	2·00	2·00	☐	☐
D23		4d green	. . . .	40·00	34·00	☐	☐
D24*a*		5d brown	. . . .	28·00	28·00	☐	☐
D25		1s blue	. . . .	11·00	8·50	☐	☐
D26	D **2**	2s 6d purple/*yellow*	. . . .	£320	12·00	☐	☐
	Set of 8			£390	90·00	☐	☐

1937–38 *Wmk Type* **127** (G vi R) *sideways*

D27	D **1**	½d green	. . . .	13·00	8·75	☐	☐
D28		1d red	. . . .	3·00	50	☐	☐
D29		2d black	. . . .	2·75	30	☐	☐
D30		3d violet	. . . .	10·50	30	☐	☐
D31		4d green	. . . .	£110	10·00	☐	☐
D32		5d brown	. . . .	16·50	75	☐	☐
D33		1s blue	. . . .	78·00	75	☐	☐
D34	D **2**	2s 6d purple/*yellow*	. . .	85·00	1·25	☐	☐
	Set of 8			£260	18·00	☐	☐

1951–52 *Colours changed and new value* (1½*d*) *Wmk Type* **127** (G vi R) *sideways*

D35	D **1**	½d orange	. . . .	3·50	3·50	☐	☐
D36		1d blue	. . . .	1·50	75	☐	☐
D37		1½d green	. . . .	2·00	2·00	☐	☐
D38		4d blue	. . . .	50·00	22·00	☐	☐
D39		1s brown	. . . .	28·00	5·25	☐	☐
	Set of 5		. . . .	75·00	28·00	☐	☐

1954–55 *Wmk Type* **153** (*Mult Tudor Crown and* E 2 R) *sideways*

D40	D **1**	½d orange	. . . .	7·00	5·25	☐	☐
D41		2d black	. . . .	26·00	18·00	☐	☐
D42		3d violet	. . . .	62·00	52·00	☐	☐
D43		4d blue	. . . .	26·00	26·00	☐	☐
D44		5d brown	. . . .	20·00	15·50	☐	☐
D45	D **2**	2s 6d purple/*yellow*	. . .	£135	5·75	☐	☐
	Set of 6		. . . .	£225	£100	☐	☐

1955–57 *Wmk Type* **165** (*Mult St Edward's Crown and* E 2 R) *sideways*

D46	D **1**	½d orange	. . . .	2·75	3·25	☐	☐
D47		1d blue	. . . .	5·00	1·50	☐	☐
D48		1½d green	. . . .	8·50	7·00	☐	☐
D49		2d black	. . . .	45·00	3·50	☐	☐
D50		3d violet	. . . .	6·00	1·50	☐	☐
D51		4d blue	. . . .	25·00	6·00	☐	☐
D52		5d brown	. . . .	26·00	20·00	☐	☐
D53		1s brown	. . . .	65·00	2·25	☐	☐
D54	D **2**	2s 6d purple/*yellow*	. . .	£200	8·25	☐	☐
D55		5s red/*yellow*	. . . . .	£150	32·00	☐	☐
	Set of 10		. . . .	£425	65·00	☐	☐

1959–63 *Wmk Type* **179** (*Mult St Edward's Crown*) *sideways*

D56	D **1**	½d orange	. . . .	15	1·25	☐	☐
D57		1d blue	. . . .	15	50	☐	☐
D58		1½d green	. . . .	2·50	2·50	☐	☐
D59		2d black	. . . .	1·10	50	☐	☐
D60		3d violet	. . . .	30	30	☐	☐
D61		4d blue	. . . .	30	30	☐	☐
D62		5d brown	. . . .	45	60	☐	☐
D63		6d purple	. . . .	50	30	☐	☐
D64		1s brown	. . . .	90	30	☐	☐
D65	D **2**	2s 6d purple/*yellow*	. . .	3·00	50	☐	☐
D66		5s red/*yellow*	. . . . .	8·25	1·00	☐	☐
D67		10s blue/*yellow*	. . . . .	11·50	5·75	☐	☐
D68		£1 black/*yellow*	. . . . .	45·00	8·25	☐	☐
	Set of 13		. . . .	68·00	20·00	☐	☐

1968–69 *Design size* 22½ × 19 *mm. No wmk*

D69	D **1**	2d black	. . . .	75	1·00	☐	☐
D70		3d violet	. . . .	1·00	1·00	☐	☐
D71		4d blue	. . . .	1·00	1·00	☐	☐
D72		5d orange-brown	. . . .	8·00	11·00	☐	☐
D73		6d purple	. . . .	2·25	1·75	☐	☐
D74		1s brown	. . . .	4·00	2·50	☐	☐
	Set of 6		. . . .	16·50	20·00	☐	☐

1968–69 *Design size* 21½ × 17½ *mm. No wmk*

D75	D **1**	4d blue	. . . .	7·00	6·75	☐	☐
D76		8d red	. . . .	50	1·00	☐	☐

D 3

D 4

Decimal Currency
1970–77 No wmk

D77	D 3	½p turquoise-blue ...	15	2·50	□	□
D78		1p reddish purple ...	15	15	□	□
D79		2p myrtle-green	20	15	□	□
D80		3p ultramarine	20	15	□	□
D81		4p yellow-brown	25	15	□	□
D82		5p violet	25	15	□	□
D83		7p red-brown	35	1·00	□	□
D84	D 4	10p red	30	30	□	□
D85		11p green	50	1·00	□	□
D86		20p brown	60	25	□	□
D87		50p ultramarine	2·00	1·25	□	□
D88		£1 black	4·00	1·00	□	□
D89		£5 orange-yellow and black	36·00	1·50	□	□
		Set of 13	40·00	7·75	□	□
		Presentation Pack (P.O. Pack No. 36) (Nos. D77/82, D84, D86/8)	20·00		□	
		Presentation Pack (P.O. Pack No. 93) (Nos. D77/88)	10·00		□	

D 5

D 6

D 7

1982 No wmk

D90	D 5	1p lake	10	30	□	□
D91		2p bright blue	30	30	□	□
D92		3p deep mauve	15	30	□	□
D93		4p deep blue	15	25	□	□
D94		5p sepia	20	25	□	□
D95	D 6	10p light brown	30	40	□	□
D96		20p olive-green	50	60	□	□
D97		25p deep greenish blue .	80	90	□	□
D98		50p grey-black	1·75	1·75	□	□
D99		£1 red	3·25	1·25	□	□
D100		£2 turquoise-blue ...	7·00	4·25	□	□
D101		£5 dull orange	14·00	2·25	□	□
		Set of 12	24·00	10·00	□	□
		Set of 12 Gutter Pairs	48·00		□	
		Presentation Pack	48·00		□	

1994 (15 Feb.) *Perf* 15 × 14 (*with one elliptical hole on each vertical side*)

D102	D 7	1p red, yellow and black	10	75	□	□
D103		2p magenta, purple and black	10	75	□	□
D104		5p yellow, red-brown and black	15	50	□	□
D105		10p yellow, emerald and black	30	75	□	□
D106		20p blue-green, violet and black	75	1·50	□	□
D107		25p cerise, rosine and black	1·50	2·00	□	□
D108		£1 violet, magenta and black	7·00	10·00	□	□
D109		£1.20 greenish blue, blue-green and black	8·00	12·00	□	□
D110		£5 greenish black, blue-green and black	30·00	20·00	□	□
		Set of 9	45·00	45·00	□	□
		First Day Cover		22·00		□
		Presentation Pack	60·00		□	

ROYAL MAIL POSTAGE LABELS

These imperforate labels were issued as an experiment by the Post Office. Special microprocessor-controlled machines were installed at post offices in Cambridge, London, Shirley (Southampton) and Windsor to provide an after-hours sales service to the public. The machines printed and dispensed the labels according to the coins inserted and the buttons operated by the customer. Values were initially available in $\frac{1}{2}$p steps to 16p and in addition, the labels were sold at philatelic counters in two packs containing either 3 values ($3\frac{1}{2}$, $12\frac{1}{2}$, 16p) or 32 values ($\frac{1}{2}$p to 16p).

From 28 August 1984 the machines were adjusted to provide values up to 17p. After 31 December 1984 labels including $\frac{1}{2}$p values were withdrawn. The machines were taken out of service on 30 April 1985.

Machine postage-paid impression in red on phosphorised paper with grey-green background design. No watermark. imperforate.

1984 (1 MAY–28 AUG.)

Set of 32 ($\frac{1}{2}$p to 16p)	15·00	22·00 □ □
Set of 3 ($3\frac{1}{2}$p, $12\frac{1}{2}$p, 16p)	2·50	3·00 □ □
Set of 3 on First Day Cover		
(1 May)		6·50 □
Set of 2 ($16\frac{1}{2}$p, 17p) (28 August)	4·00	3·00 □ □

OFFICIAL STAMPS

Various stamps of Queen Victoria and King Edward VII overprinted in Black.

I.R. OFFICIAL (O 1)	I. R. OFFICIAL (O 2)	O.W. OFFICIAL (O 3)
ARMY OFFICIAL (O 4)	ARMY OFFICIAL (O 5)	GOVᵀ PARCEL8 (O 7)

1 Inland Revenue

Overprinted with Types O 1 or O 2 (5s, 10s, £1)

1882–1901 *Queen Victoria*

O 2	52	$\frac{1}{2}$d green	65·00	25·00 □ □
O 5		$\frac{1}{2}$d blue	65·00	22·00 □ □
O13	71	$\frac{1}{2}$d vermilion	8·00	3·00 □ □
O17		$\frac{1}{2}$d green	10·00	6·00 □ □
O 3	57	1d lilac (Die II)	4·00	2·00 □ □
O 6	64	$2\frac{1}{2}$d lilac	£300	£100 □ □
O14	74	$2\frac{1}{2}$d purple on blue	£100	10·00 □ □
O 4	43	6d grey (Plate 18)	£400	85·00 □ □
O18	79	6d purple on red	£300	80·00 □ □
O 7	65	1s green	£4000	£1200 □ □
O15	82	1s green	£550	£175 □ □
O19		1s green and red	£2400	£850 □ □
O 9	59	5s red	£3500	£1200 □ □
O10	60	10s blue	£5000	£1750 □ □
O11	61	£1 brown (Wmk Crowns) . .	£35000	£18000 □ □
O12		£1 brown (Wmk Orbs) . .	£55000	£25000 □ □
O16		£1 green	£7500	£1750 □ □

1902–04 *King Edward VII*

O20	83	$\frac{1}{2}$d blue-green	22·00	3·00 □ □
O21		1d red	15·00	2·00 □ □
O22	86	$2\frac{1}{2}$d blue	£700	£175 □ □
O23	83	6d purple	£135000	£80000 □ □
O24	93	1s green and red	£2250	£500 □ □
O25	95	5s red	£10000	£6000 □ □
O26	96	10s blue	£55000	£25000 □ □
O27	97	£1 green	£37000	£18000 □ □

2 Office of Works

Overprinted with Type O 3

1896–1902 *Queen Victoria*

O31	71	$\frac{1}{2}$d vermilion	£200	£100 □ □
O32		$\frac{1}{2}$d green	£300	£150 □ □
O33	57	1d lilac (Die II)	£350	£100 □ □
O34	78	5d dull purple and blue .	£2000	£750 □ □
O35	81	10d dull purple and red . .	£3500	£1000 □ □

1902–03 *King Edward VII*

O36	83	$\frac{1}{2}$d blue-green	£500	£150 □ □
O37		1d red	£500	£150 □ □
O38	85	2d green and red	£1500	£375 □ □
O39	86	$2\frac{1}{2}$d blue	£2000	£550 □ □
O40	92	10d purple and red	£20000	£4750 □ □

3 Army

Overprinted with Types O 4 (½d, 1d) or O 5 (2½d, 6d)

1896–1901 *Queen Victoria*

O41	71	½d vermilion	3·50	1·50	□	□
O42		½d green	4·00	7·00	□	□
O43	57	1d lilac (Die II)	3·50	2·50	□	□
O44	74	2½d purple on blue	30·00	20·00	□	□
O45	79	6d purple on red	75·00	40·00	□	□

Overprinted with Type O 4

1902 *King Edward VII*

O48	83	½d blue-green	5·00	2·00	□	□
O49		1d red	5·00	2·00	□	□
O50		6d purple	£150	70·00	□	□

4 Government Parcels

Overprinted with Type O 7

1883–1900 *Queen Victoria*

O69	57	1d lilac (Die II)	70·00	15·00	□	□
O61	62	1½d lilac	£300	60·00	□	□
O65	72	1½d purple and green . . .	80·00	7·00	□	□
O70	73	2d green and red	£150	20·00	□	□
O71	77	4½d green and red	£250	£180	□	□
O62	63	6d green	£1750	£750	□	□
O66	79	6d purple on red	£150	30·00	□	□
O63	64	9d green	£1500	£600	□	□
O67	80	9d purple and blue	£225	40·00	□	□
O64	44	1s brown (Plate 13)	£850	£200	□	□
O64c		1s brown (Plate 14)	£1800	£300	□	□
O68	82	1s green	£400	£175	□	□
O72		1s green and red	£425	£160	□	□

1902 *King Edward VII*

O74	83	1d red	30·00	12·00	□	□
O75	85	2d green and red	£140	35·00	□	□
O76	83	6d purple	£240	35·00	□	□
O77	91	9d purple and blue	£480	£150	□	□
O78	93	1s green and red	£800	£225	□	□

5 Board of Education

Overprinted with Type O 8

1902 *Queen Victoria*

O81	78	5d dull purple and blue .	£2000	£550	□	□
O82	82	1s green and red	£5500	£3500	□	□

1902–04 *King Edward VII*

O83	83	½d blue-green	£150	35·00	□	□
O84		1d red	£150	35·00	□	□
O85	86	2½d blue	£3000	£250	□	□
O86	89	5d purple and blue	£15000	£4000	□	□
O87	93	1s green and red	£75000		□	

6 Royal Household

Overprinted with Type O 9

1902 *King Edward VII*

O91	83	½d blue-green	£350	£180	□	□
O92		1d red	£300	£150	□	□

7 Admiralty

Overprinted with Type O 10

1903 *King Edward Vii*

O101	83	½d blue-green	25·00	12·00	□	□
O102		1d red	15·00	6·00	□	□
O103	84	1½d purple and green . . .	£225	£110	□	□
O104	85	2d green and red	£250	£125	□	□
O105	86	2½d blue	£375	£110	□	□
O106	87	3d purple on yellow . . .	£300	£120	□	□

PHILATELIC, NUMISMATIC AND PHILATELIC MEDALLIC COVERS

On 2 June 1993 Royal Mail and the Royal Mint prepared a commemorative cover to celebrate the 40th anniversary of the Coronation of Her Majesty The Queen. The cover bore the Royal Mint's Coronation Anniversary Crown and the £10 'Britannia' stamp, issued on 2 March 1993 (No. 1658).

On 1 March 1994 a similar cover was produced for the 25th Anniversary of the Investiture of HRH The Prince of Wales. The cover bore the set of five stamps issued on that date (Nos. 1810/14), showing paintings by Prince Charles, and a commemorative medal struck by the Royal Mint.

So began a series of Philatelic Numismatic Covers (PNC) and Philatelic Medallic Covers (PMC) produced by Royal Mail and the Royal Mint.

This listing comprises only those jointly produced covers sold by the Philatelic Bureau. Privately sponsored covers incorporating coins or medals including those sponsored by the Royal Mint alone, are outside its scope.

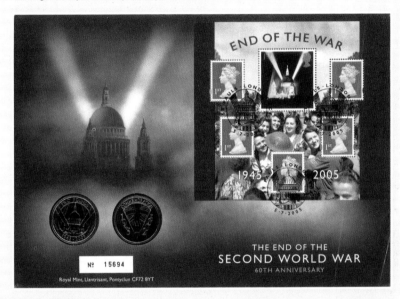

No.	Date	Issue	Stamps	Coin/Medal	Price
RMC1	2.6.93	*Coronation 40th Anniv*	1658	£5 Coin	28·00
RMC2	1.3.94	*Prince of Wales Investiture 25th Anniv*	1810/14	Medal	22·00
RMC3	27.7.94	*Bank of England 300th Anniv*	1666×4 +label	£2 Coin	20·00
RMC4	20.5.95	*R. J. Mitchell Birth Cent*	1666×4+label	Medal	20·00
RMC5	15.8.95	*End of Second World War 50th Anniv*	1873, 1875	£2 Coin	20·00
RMC6	29.10.95	*William Wyon Birth Bicent*	Y1707	Medal	20·00
RMC7	21.4.96	*Queen's 70th Birthday*	1666×4+label	£5 Coin	24·00
RMC8	14.5.96	*European Football Championship*	1925/9	£2 Coin	20·00
RMC9	1.10./3.11.96	*Classic Sports Cars*	1945/9	Medal	20·00
RMC10	28.1.97	*King Henry VIII 450th Death Anniv*	1965/71	£1 Coin	20·00
RMC11	30.6.97	*Transfer of Hong Kong to Chinese Rule*	1666×4+label	Hong Kong $5 Coin	20·00
RMC12	23.8.97	*British Aircraft Designers*	1984/8	£2 Coin	20·00
RMC13	20.11.97	*Royal Golden Wedding*	2011/14	£5 Coin	24·00
RMC14	24.2.98	*Order of the Garter 650th Anniv*	2026/30	£1 Coin	20·00
RMC15	5.7.98	*NHS 50th Anniv*	2046/9	50p Coin	20·00
RMC16	25.8.98	*Notting Hill Carnival*	2055/8	50p Coin	20·00
RMC17	14.11.98	*HRH Prince of Wales 50th Birthday*	1666×4+label	£5 Coin	24·00
RMC18	12.5.99	*Berlin Airlift 50th Anniv*	1666×4+label	Medal	20·00
RMC19	1.7.99	*New Scottish Parliament Building*	S94/7	£1 Coin	20·00
RMC20	1.10.99	*Rugby World Cup, Wales*	1664a×4+label	£2 Coin	20·00
RMC21	31.12.99	*Millennium*	**MS**2123	£5 Coin	34·00
RMC22	4.4.00	*National Botanic Garden of Wales*	2124×4+label	£1 Coin	20·00

RMC23	14.8.00	150 *Years of Public Libraries*	2116, 2121, 2100	50p Coin	20·00
RMC24	4.8.00	*Queen Mother's 100th Birthday*	**MS**2161	£5 Coin	24·00
RMC25	1.1.01	Archers *Radio Programme* 50th *Anniv*	2107/8, 2110	Medal	20·00
RMC26	24.5.01	*RN Submarine Service Cent*	2202/5	Medal	20·00
RMC27	20.6.01	*Queen Victoria Death Cent*	2133+label	£5 Coin	24·00
RMC28	2.10.01	*Northern Ireland*	NI89/92	£1 Coin	20·00
RMC29	6.02	*Golden Jubilee*	2253/7	£5 Coin	24·00
RMC29a	6.2.02	*Golden Jubilee*	2258/9	£5 Coin and £5 note	28·00
RMC30	31.5.02	*World Cup Football, Japan & Korea*	5×1st from **MS**2292	£1 Coin	20·00
RMC31	16.7.02	*17th Commonwealth Games, Manchester*	2299/303	4×£2 Coins	30·00
RMC32	11.12.02	*Queen Mother Commemoration*	2280/3	£5 Coin	24·00
RMC33	25.2.03	*Discovery of DNA 50th Anniv*	2343/7	£2 Coin	21·00
RMC34	2.6.03	*Coronation 50th Anniv*	2368/77	£5 Coin	24·00
RMC35	27.8.03	*Extreme Endeavours*	2360/5	£1 Coin	20·00
RMC36	7.10.03	*British Museum 250th Anniv*	2404/9	Medal	20·00
RMC37	13.1.04	*Classic Locomotives*	2417/22	£2 Coin	21·00
RMC38	6.4.04	*Entente Cordiale Cent*	2446/7 + France 50c, 75c	£5 Coin	25·00
RMC39	13.4.04	*Ocean Liners*	2448/53	Medal	22·00
RMC40	25.5.04	*RHS Bicentenary*	2456/61	Medal	21·00
RMC41	30.11.04	*Scotland Definitive*	S109/10, S112/13	£1 Coin	20·00
RMC42	24.2.05	*Charlotte Brontë 150th Death Anniv*	2518/23	50p Coin	20·00
RMC43	1.3.05	*Wales Definitive*	W98/9, W101/2	£1 Coin	20·00
RMC44	21.4.05	*World Heritage Sites*	2532/5+Australia 2×50c. & 2×$1	50p Coin + Australia 50c.	24·00
RMC45	5.7.05	*End of the War 60th Anniv*	**MS**2547	Medal and £2 Coin	24·00
RMC46	18.10.05	*Battle of Trafalgar Bicent*	2574/9	2×£5 Coins	37·00
RMC47	23.2.06	*Brunel Birth Bicent*	2607/12	2×£2 Coins	24·00
RMC48	17.3.06	*Northern Ireland Definitive*	NI94/5, NI98, NI100	£1 Coin	20·00
RMC49	21.4.06	*Queen's 80th Birthday*	2620/7	£5 Coin	27·00
RMC50	6.6.06	*World Cup Football*	2628/33	Medal	22·00
RMC51	18.7.06	*National Portrait Gallery 150th Anniv*	2640/9	Medal	22·00
RMC52	21.9.06	*Victoria Cross 150th Anniv*	2657/62	2×50p Coins	23·00

Stanley GIBBONS

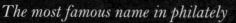

The most famous name in philately

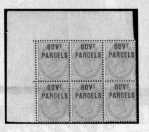

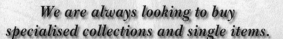

Stanley Gibbons
Roadshows

We hold regular roadshows throughout the year, covering the whole of the United Kingdom.

- Free verbal appraisals
- Put forward material for future auctions
- Excellent prices paid for selected Great Britain and Commonwealth
- Our team will be happy to examine anything remotely philatelic

So, if you were thinking of selling that single rare stamp, a part of your collection or the whole thing, then speak to our expert team first at Stanley Gibbons Ltd.

Please contact either Steve Matthews or Ryan Epps at
Stanley Gibbons Ltd. 399 Strand, London WC2R 0LX.
Telephone: +44(0)20 7836 8444   Fax: +44(0)20 7836 7342
Email: smatthews@stanleygibbons.co.uk or repps@stanleygibbons.co.uk

COLLECT BRITISH STAMPS

Priority order form
Four easy ways to order

Phone:
020 7836 8444
Overseas: +44 (0)20 7836 8444

Fax:
020 7557 4499
Overseas: +44 (0)20 7557 4499

Email:
stampsales@stanleygibbons.co.uk

Post:
Stamp Mail Order Department
Stanley Gibbons Ltd, 399 Strand
London, WC2R 0LX, England

Customer details

Account Number

Name

Address

Postcode

Email

Country

Fax no

Tel no

Payment details

I enclose my cheque/postal order for £............. in full payment. Please make cheques/postal orders payable to Stanley Gibbons Ltd. Cheques must be in £ sterling and drawn on a UK bank

Please debit my credit card for £.............. in full payment. I have completed the Credit Card section below.

Card Number

Start Date (Switch & Amex)

Expiry Date

Issue No (switch)

Signature

Date

COLLECT
BRITISH STAMPS

Condition (mint/UM/used)	Country	SG No.	Description	Price	Office use only

SUB TOTAL		
POSTAGE & PACKAGING		£3.60
GRAND TOTAL		£

Please complete payment, name and address details overleaf